NO LOVE
WITHOUT
POETRY

NO LOVE WITHOUT POETRY

The Memoirs of Marina Tsvetaeva's Daughter

ARIADNA EFRON

Edited and translated from the Russian by
DIANE NEMEC IGNASHEV

NORTHWESTERN UNIVERSITY PRESS
EVANSTON, ILLINOIS

Northwestern University Press
www.nupress.northwestern.edu

Printed in the United States of America

10 9 8 7 6 5 4 3 2 1

ISBN 978-0-8101-4504-7

The Library of Congress has cataloged the original, hardcover edition as follows:

Efron, Ariadna, 1912–1975.
    No love without poetry : the memoirs of Marina Tsvetaeva's daughter / Ariadna
Efron ; compiled, translated from the Russian, and with an introduction by Diane
Nemec Ignashev.
        p. cm.
    Includes bibliographical references and index.
    ISBN 978-0-8101-2589-6 (trade cloth : alk. paper) 1. Efron, Ariadna, 1912–1975.
2. Children of authors—Russia (Federation)—Biography. 3. Tsvetaeva, Marina, 1892–
1941—Family. 4. Authors, Russian—20th century—Biography. 5. Soviet Union—Social
life and customs—20th century. 6. Soviet Union—Intellectual life—20th century.
I. Nemec Ignashev, Diane, 1951– II. Title.
    PG3476.E43A3 2009
    891.71'42—dc22
    [B]

2009005921

I have a poor memory and lack the capacity for linear systematization that runs in the Tsvetaev clan. The occurrences, events, and faces that my memory has preserved are not anchored by dates but clipped together in an approximated string of days and years. There is so much I remember that had I the ability, I could write an enormous book, even if the pages would have to remain unbound. Had I the ability. Incidentally, there are times when even the inept are bound to take pen in hand, when love and duty are bound to compensate for deficient talent. But, is talent so imperative, if it is talent one attempts to write about? Eckermann, after all, made do without any of his own, on Goethe's alone.

Years will pass, and people will come forward who possess the wherewithal to overcome the criminal indifference of time, to insist that it restore the forgotten, articulate the silenced, and resurrect the annihilated and scorned. To aid those people I too attempt *to record what I remember* about my mother, and about the time.

—ARIADNA EFRON

Contents

Note on the Text   ix

Acknowledgments   xv

Introduction   xvii

PAGES OF MEMORIES
The Way She Was   5
The Way She Wrote   9
Her Family   10
Her Husband, His Family   15
My Earliest Years   20

PAGES FROM THE PAST
Our Last Day in Moscow   73
Berlin   79
Pasternak   103
Czechoslovakia   127

FROM *TALES TOLD IN TARUSA*
Papa's Name-Day Pie   183
Tatiana Fyodorovna Scriabina   184
Love Capital   185
Goat Soup   185
Getting Married   186
L'agent   187
Three Encounters   187
The Dream   192

FRAGMENTS

First Memories   195

Crimea, 1914   197

Crimea, 1915   198

Alya, the Finicky Eater   200

The House in Borisoglebsky Lane   201

Storytime   208

A Bad Dream   211

Caprice   212

Christmas   212

Jack the Poodle   214

Sophia Parnok's "Smart" Monkey   214

Chicken Head   215

Nannies   217

Telling Right from Left   218

Alms for the Poor   219

Napoleon's Widow   220

Irina   221

Learning to Walk Down Stairs   222

Arriving in Berlin   222

Our First Day in Berlin   224

Life in France   225

Marina's Silver Bracelet   227

Anna Akhmatova   228

From a Letter to Anna Akhmatova   234

On Loving Poetry and Poets   235

Translator's Notes   237

Biographical Glossary   269

Additional Reading   297

Index   303

Note on the Text

The formal features of this volume and of Efron's writing are significant for interpretation and merit brief explication. First, readers need to be aware that the current compilation is original: there is no comparable collection of Efron's writing that was published in Russian prior to this volume. Texts for the present edition were gathered from several sources. They include Ariadna Efron, "Stranitsy vospominanii," *Zvezda* 3 (1973): 154–80, and Ariadna Efron, "Stranitsy bylogo," *Zvezda* 6 (1975): 148–89, reprinted in Ariadna Efron, *Stranitsy vospominanii* (Paris: Lev, 1979) and, with emendations, in Ariadna Efron, *O Marine Tsvetaevoi: Vospominaniia docheri*, comp. and ed. Mariia Belkina (Moscow: Sovetskii pisatel', 1989), 33–223, and in Ariadna Efron, *Marina Tsvetaeva: Vospominaniia docheri; Pis'ma*, comp., ed., intro. Mariia Belkina (Kaliningrad: OGUP Kaliningradskoe knizhnoe izdatel'stvo and GIPP Iantarnyi skaz, 2000), 52–304. The short stories included in "From *Tales Told in Tarusa*" first appeared in Ariadna Efron, "Ustnye rasskazy," ed. E. B. Korkina, *Zvezda* 7 (1988): 41–55. As the title in Russian indicates, these stories are oral histories. They were recorded during Efron's lifetime and published by Efron's secretary, Elena Korkina, more than a decade after Efron had died. They are translated here from a second, more complete edition in Ariadna Efron and Ada Federol'f, *Miroedikha: Riadom s Alei* (Moscow: Vozvrashchenie, 1996), 95–106. The original Russian texts of the "outtakes" from Efron's "Pages," collected in the section titled "Fragments," were taken from Ariadna Efron, "Popytka zapisei o Mame," in *"A dusha ne tonet. . . ." Pis'ma 1942–1975: Vospominaniia*, comp. Ruf' Val'be (Moscow: Kul'tura, 1996), 395–418. The epigraph to this volume appears among scattered working notes in

"Iz zapisnykh knizhek," in *Miroedikha: Riadom s Alei*. Renderings of all Russian texts into English throughout the volume, unless otherwise indicated, are this translator's. For readers who want to consult the original Russian-language sources, I have provided complete bibliographic data in the endnotes to each section.

Shaping these diverse texts into a narrative, I felt it was important to maintain the distinction between memoirs Efron herself had published during her lifetime—"Pages of Memoirs" and "Pages from the Past"—and later posthumous issues that she might not have approved. Viewed over time, the posthumous publications were subjected to progressively relaxed censorship in the USSR and Russia, which made it possible for their editors to include materials Efron herself either had not wanted to or could not share. The later the publication, the more it challenges the homogeneity of the portraits Efron paints in her "Pages." To integrate these later stories and fragments into the chronological sequence of Efron's childhood and teenage years as presented in "Pages" would have undermined readers' awareness of the conflicts within the woman who put these memories to paper, even though Ariadna Efron—ostensibly writing about someone else—on the surface says little about herself as an adult.

A poet and skilled translator in her own right, Efron embellished her prose with linguistic play—from alliteration to extended metaphors and even occasional song melodies hidden in her syntax. She poses her translator an exhausting range of challenges, perhaps another reason why it has taken so long for these memoirs to be translated. The separate linguistic (stylistic) identities of Efron's two narrative voices—of the adult in the framing account and of the child in the cited diary passages—are readily discerned in the Russian originals by their distinct lexicon and syntax, as well as verb tenses. In translation the different lexical levels were relatively easy to render, but verb tenses and syntax presented special problems. To preserve distinctions between the two voices, I did not regularize disjunctures in verb tenses as energetically as I often wanted. While aiming for clarity and continuity, I also resisted the temptation to break Efron's framing adult narrator's long clauses—so easily strung together in Russian—into shorter sentences in English, although sometimes the intricacies of her logic left no choice but to replace commas with periods.

In addition, Efron includes in her account lines from a number of Tsvetaeva's poems. She also wove in passages from Tsvetaeva's correspondence with Boris Pasternak, especially from the latter's (as Efron aptly called it) "calculus period." As Efron's translator, I found myself faced with the challenge of rendering in English two of Russia's most complex poets. Translations of poetry necessarily narrow the field of possible meanings to be drawn; in my translations I aimed first at those aspects of the poets' originals that were relevant to Efron's point.

Much has changed in Russia over the thirty-odd years since Efron wrote her memoirs. Many things about her parents' lives that she could not—or would not—write about in the 1960s and 1970s are now discussed openly. Although the editor who saw Efron's "Pages" to publication claims that they were published without any changes,[1] one senses everywhere the censorship Efron imposed on herself. Like many of her contemporaries, Efron wrote between the lines, a skill she developed to perfection over sixteen years of writing letters past prison censors. In the memoirs—especially in her "Pages"—she seems everywhere to be dropping hints without, however, following ideas through to their conclusion. Efron's writing demands the participatory engagement of her readers: to ask why this or that detail, to intuit information cropped in her many ellipses, to finish incomplete sentences, and to develop unfinished ideas—which sometimes cluster in series over several pages—to their logical conclusions. So as not to complicate further already complexly punctuated texts, I have tried to observe Efron's original as rigorously as possible. All unbracketed ellipses are hers. When she introduces ellipses or interpolations into the words of others she quotes, as, for example, when citing her mother's correspondence with Pasternak, or when quoting passages from her own diary, square brackets indicate her interference, not the translator's.

Particular care was required in the final twenty pages of the section of "Pages from the Past" titled "Všenory," which consists largely of excerpts from Tsvetaeva's notebooks. All of Efron's citations from Tsvetaeva's notebooks and letters have been checked against the canonical texts in Marina Tsvetaeva, *Neizdannoe: Zapisnye knizhki v dvukh tomakh, Tom pervyi; 1913–1919*, comp. and ed. E. B. Korkina and M. G. Krutikova (Moscow: Ellis Lak, 2000); Marina Tsvetaeva, *Neizdannoe: Zapisnye knizhki v dvukh tomakh, Tom vtoroi; 1919–1939*, comp. and ed. E. B. Korkina and M. G. Krutikova (Moscow: Ellis Lak, 2001); and Marina Tsvetaeva, *Neizdannoe: Svodnye tetradi*, comp. and ed. E. B. Korkina and I. D. Shevelenko (Moscow: Ellis Lak, 1997). Efron's citations from the Pasternak-Tsvetaeva correspondence were all verified against Marina Tsvetaeva, Boris Pasternak, *Dushi nachinaiut videt': Pis'ma 1922–1936 godov,* comp. and ed. E. B. Korkina and I. D. Shevelenko (Moscow: Vagrius, 2004). The text Efron has excised from her mother's notebooks is just as interesting (and just as central to our understanding of her project) as the material she quotes. For that reason, I have restored Tsvetaeva's prose, effectively undoing Efron's ellipses. Text contained in square brackets and underlined is Tsvetaeva's original prose excised by her daughter; text enclosed by square brackets and italicized was inserted by Efron into her mother's texts. Unless otherwise indicated, emphasis added throughout is Efron's or her sources'. Particularly in this section one senses the aptness of Efron's comparison of herself to Goethe's Eckermann.

As with all Russian-to-English translations, problems arose in rendering differences between the second person formal and informal pronouns. In Efron's case it is further complicated by the unusual circumstance that Sergei and Marina, although husband and wife, used the formal address (*Vy*) with each other, and Marina insisted that Ariadna also refer to parents with the formal "you," both significant deviations from linguistic norms at the time. Where relevant to meaning, form of address has been noted; otherwise, "you" is used for both *Vy* and *ty.*

Until 1925, Tsvetaeva preferred the Julian calendar of czarist times. For consistency, differences between the Julian and Gregorian calendars have been rendered in the New Style of the Gregorian calendar; in some cases the Old Style date is given in brackets following and is indicated by the abbreviation OS.

Efron's original texts observe the Soviet standard for names: initials for first and patronymic, with only surnames provided in full. In this volume I have provided full first names and patronymics as well as surnames. The sole footnote is Efron's own, and the endnotes are mine. In endnotes I have followed the Library of Congress transliteration system for scholarly notation; in the text proper I have modified this system slightly for readability. In the main text, the Russian hard and soft signs are not rendered in transliteration. Similarly, the Russian consonant *ŭ* and so-called soft vowels have been rendered at the beginning of words as *y* plus the appropriate phoneme (e.g., Yuri, Yakovlevna) and at the end of words as either *i* (in masculine names, e.g., Yuri) or *-ya* (in feminine nouns, e.g., Alya). As is common practice, *ye* combinations have been rendered simply as *e* (e.g.,

Elena), and -*uŭ* endings in masculine names (e.g., Dostoevsky) appear as *y*. Spellings of commonly known Russian surnames (e.g., Scriabin and Koussevitsky) are used, as are Americanized spellings of other names (e.g., Sophia).

A biographical glossary has been included in the apparatus to provide background on the numerous historical figures Ariadna Efron mentions. A short list of additional readings about Tsvetaeva also has been appended.

Acknowledgments

Acknowledgment of everyone who helped bring this project to comple-tion is a story in itself. Let brevity be the measure of my gratitude. Carleton College supplied sabbaticals, technology, work-study assistants, and finan-cial support for travel and various parts of the project. Mother Antonia Kolakova (Moscow) made invaluable adjustments to the translation, and Nancy Soth (Northfield) critiqued the English text. Laura Goering patiently reviewed multiple versions of the introduction. Carleton students Robin Anderson (class of 2007), Laura Roberts (2010), and Inara Makhmudova (2011) and Carleton College Modern Language Department administra-tive assistant Mary Tatge provided technical support. Mike Levine at North-western University Press has been a supportive editor. Semyon Vilensky allowed me to do research in the archives of the Vozvrashchenie Literary-Historical Society and granted me rights to Efron's texts. Liudmila Novikova and Galina Atmashkina lent moral support in the wings at Vozvrashchenie. Our neighbors in Moscow—Vladimir Voyevoda and Irina Yakunina—threatened drastic measures when the project wandered off course. And Anna Dotlibova was there through every word, footnote, and editorial crisis.

Introduction

The story of Marina Tsvetaeva (1892–1941) and her family is one of the most tragic in Russian culture, which knows no shortage of family unhappiness and disserved genius. When the memoirs of Tsvetaeva's daughter, Ariadna Sergeevna Efron (1912–75), first appeared in the Leningrad "thick" journal *Zvezda* in March 1973 and June 1975, Russian readers understandably expected details about the poet's life. They were disappointed. Efron stated her position categorically: "everything that needed to be said and made public . . . has already been said and made public by Marina in her [p]oems." To insure the poet's privacy and as a final gesture of what she called "total Tsvetaeva control,"[1] Efron sequestered her mother's papers at the Central Archives for Literature and Art (TsGALI, now RGALI) until the year 2000.[2]

Thirty years would pass before Efron's memoirs were translated.[3] In the intervening years, deprived of archival materials, Tsvetaeva's biographers consulted Efron's memoirs, but few were satisfied, and these memoirs acquired the reputation of literary "damaged goods."[4] Only after Tsvetaeva's papers had been published could Efron's memoirs be recognized for what they are: not flawed biography but rather autobiography whose authority derives precisely from its subjectivity. Efron's situation in this regard is not unique in Russian literature. For a number of reasons, Russian autobiographers—particularly women—have often chosen the strategy of writing "about" themselves by writing "about" someone else. Like those of Nadezhda Mandelstam, Lidia Chukovskaya, and Evgenia Ginzburg, Efron's memoirs require that readers "decenter" their attention from the biography of the ostensible subject to the "submerged" autobiography of the memoir's author.[5] Read as autobiography, Efron's memoirs bear profound testimony to Marina Tsvetaeva's gift because they reveal the toll exacted by that gift on those closest to the poet.

Who was Ariadna Efron? More acutely than many give her credit, I believe, Ariadna Efron realized that the middle-aged gulag survivor who spent the last two decades of her life restoring her mother's legacy was *not* the "little Alya" of Marina's poems. In the opening sequences of "Pages of Memories," in the section titled "My Earliest Years," employing the metaphor of a child contemplating herself in the mirror, Efron disjoins these two hypostases of herself, and they remain separate and distinct—graphically, stylistically, linguistically, and psychologically—throughout the remainder of the memoirs, and Efron's life.

"Alya," the product of Marina's imagination, is the identity with which Tsvetaeva's readers are most familiar. It was to "Alya" that Tsvetaeva devoted page after page of her journal entries and dedicated twenty-two of her poems between 1913 and 1922:

> You will grow up innocent, slender,
> A charming stranger to all,
> A mistress temperamental,
> An Amazon who will enthrall.
> Those tresses of yours, I venture,
> You'll wear as a helmet of war.
> The heroine you'll be of the evening,
> The darling of youthful song.
> And many a heart, dear princess,
> Will fall at the cut of your scorn,
> And all that I can but dream of
> Will lie in wait of your call.
> And all will be as you wish it,
> And each to your whims will comply,
> Of course, it goes without question,
> You will write better verse than do I.
> But—who's to know?—will you ever
> Desperately clasp your brow

> In just the same fatal manner
> As your young mother right now.[6]

According to Efron, for Marina "Alya" would cease to exist by the time of their walk through the snowy streets of Moravská Třebová in December 1923.

A quarter century later, after sixteen years in Stalin's gulag, Ariadna Efron hardly resembled "the darling of youthful song." Olga Ivinskaya, who knew her through Boris Pasternak, recalled: "When I at last met Ariadna, I was struck by her very large and beautiful deep-blue eyes. . . . Of course her long years in extremely harsh conditions had affected her: she had begun to neglect her appearance as a woman too soon. . . ."[7] It was Ariadna Efron, not "little Alya," whom Tsvetaeva's biographers consulted during their research, and so memorable were those encounters that their biographies of Tsvetaeva all included portraits of her prematurely aged daughter. Anna Saakiants wrote: "I saw Ariadna Sergeevna Efron for the first time at Goslitizdat; that was, probably, in 1959. A stately gray-haired woman with a careless knot [of hair] at the nape of her neck had come to visit the editor Maria Yakovlevna Sergievskaya. [Her] bulging blue eyes stood out against her tanned face; her smile was peculiar and lent her face a certain ironic acerbity, perhaps because of her steel teeth."[8] Véronique Lossky, who knew Ariadna Efron in the early 1970s just before she died, recorded: "Ariadna Efron was then not yet sixty years old, but she looked worn out, seemed older, and was excessively corpulent. First a difficult life alongside her mother, then two arrests, camps, exile, and after that, nerve-wracking problems with residence permits in Moscow, obtaining housing, collecting the archive, publishing books, and all at the same time she continued working [as a translator]. I don't even mention personal psychological problems connected with a mother who was also a poet, [the nature of which] I came to surmise only later, when we were more closely acquainted. At the time she already had problems with her legs, suffered from the heart disease from which she died, smoked too much, and dreamed of ridding herself of the habit."[9] Maria Belkina, wife of critic and bibliophile Anatoly Tarasenkov, who met Efron on her return to Moscow from exile in Turukhansk and who would observe her repeatedly over the next twenty years, astutely summed up the picture of Ariadna

Efron as Moscow's literary elite[10] knew her in the 1960s and 1970s: "She was not at all like Marina Ivanovna."[11]

Efron was aware of what others saw. In 1955–56 she reflected:

> During the day I went out to look for one person, to meet with another, and to find work in between. But "the ashes of Claes rang loud in my heart," hampering my ability to speak to people in a calm and reasonable fashion. Naturally, neither my bluntness, nor my sudden attacks of slavish timidity inspired confidence, and the tears welling up in my eyes could elicit sympathy in some and just as easily indifference in others. Sympathy, though, was rare. Occasionally a spark of curiosity might flash in a bureaucrat's or secretary's eye, but it faded quickly: it was safer to keep one's distance from the "all that" which I embodied and which had not even begun to dissipate. My miserable clothing—cotton print dresses sewn in the Turukhansk "atelier" in a style that had suited me sixteen years ago, my crude shoes, my heavy orange-colored hose—also inspired little confidence. To buy shoes and clothes "like everyone else's" I needed money, which meant I needed a job, but in order to get a job one had to look the part, and look the part I most definitely did not. Were it not bad enough I possessed neither the clothes needed to make a good first impression nor the mind needed to undo the impression I did make, I lacked even a normal human skin: having rushed to molt my leathered hide in Turukhansk, I had not yet grown a new one.[12]

By all accounts, Ariadna Efron as an adult more closely resembled her father, Sergei Yakovlevich Efron (1893–1941), than her mother, and the resemblance was more than just physical. The fate of the Tsvetaeva-Efron clan from the mid-1930s through their tragic deaths was largely the result of Sergei's political intrigues. It was his misguided belief in Stalin's Soviet Union as Communist utopia that Ariadna had shared. It was following his lead and over Marina's objections that Ariadna had returned to the USSR in 1937. Once in Moscow Ariadna was hired at *Revue de Moscou* at the NKVD-controlled publishing conglomerate Zhurgaz thanks to experience writing propaganda for Soviet-sponsored periodicals in Paris,[13] for which her father had recruited her. Barely two months after Marina joined them at the NKVD safe house where Sergei hid under an assumed name, on the night of August 26–27, 1939, Ariadna was arrested, followed by her father two months later. Biographers who have examined NKVD protocols of her interrogations report that under torture, twenty-seven-year-old Efron confessed that she herself was an agent of *French* espionage and signed testimony that sent her to prison for eight years and condemned her father and his associates to the firing squad.[14] For those who knew of the "Efron" part of her past, Ariadna was, like the little girl in Alya's mirror, "not a pleasant sight": "Ariadna Sergeevna Efron? I'm afraid to talk about her," wrote a fellow resident of the Bolshevo dacha where the Efrons were sequestered.[15]

As I worked on these translations, I found myself repeatedly returning to the juxtaposition between Ariadna Efron's two lives—one in the luminous, magical fantasy world of her mother's poetry and the other in the dismal prose of Soviet reality in the mid-twentieth century. The deeper I delved into Efron's writing and her biography, the more strongly I sensed how the magic of a childhood spent alongside and inside the poetry of Marina Tsvetaeva outshone any memories of the physical hardships from which that magic was often an escape.[16] Increasingly I appreciated the burden of duty Efron had felt to restore her mother's legacy, on the one hand, and to protect it from prying outsiders, on the other. Older than Marina Tsvetaeva had been when she died, Ariadna Efron as she worked her way through her mother's papers in the 1960s and 1970s was reliving her own past as well as her parents'. Many of Efron's claims demand annotation, but fundamentally the memories that follow provide an incontestably "truthful" record of the magnitude of Tsvetaeva's daughter's loss and the pain of reliving what had been.

NO LOVE
WITHOUT
POETRY

PAGES OF
MEMORIES

THE WAY SHE WAS

My mother, Marina Ivanovna Tsvetaeva, was no giant in terms of physical stature—five feet, two inches tall—and she had the body of an Egyptian boy: broad at the shoulders, narrow at the hips, and slight at the waist. The curves of her youth yielded quickly and irrevocably to a pedigree leanness; her ankles and wrists were taut and narrow, her gait was light and quick, and her movements were light and resolute, without being abrupt. In the presence of others, when she sensed she was being observed and more so when she felt she was being scrutinized, she inhibited and slowed her movements, and her gestures became guardedly scant, though never to the point of seeming constrained.

Her bearing was at once austere and graceful: even as she hunched over her writing table she maintained "the posture of a steel beam."[1]

The golden brown hair of her girlhood, which had curved in large soft waves, later turned an early gray, intensifying the sensation of dusky-pale matte luminescence about her face. Her eyes were bright unfading green, the color of grapes, framed by brownish eyelids.

Her facial features and contours were sharp and distinct. There was nothing vague, nothing half-considered by the Master, nothing left half-chiseled or unpolished. Her aquiline nose, narrow at the top and descending over a small bump, ended not in a point but bluntly, in a small flat tip from which her lithe nostrils spread like wings to outline her seemingly soft mouth with an invisible sharp contour.

Two vertical furrows divided her light brown brows.

Seemingly consummate to the point of impenetrability or immobility, her face was continuous inner movement, covert expressiveness, ever mutable and brimming with shadows, like sky and water.

Few were those who could read that face.

Her hands were strong, nimble, those of a worker. Her wedding ring and the two silver rings that she never removed (one with a seal bearing the image of a tiny boat, the other an agate with Hermes in a smooth frame—a present from her father) neither drew attention to her hands nor adorned or encumbered them but formed, rather, an organic whole with them.

Her voice was high, like that of a young girl, ringing and supple.

Her speech was terse, her comments concise as formulas.

She knew how to listen and never dominated conversation, but in an argument she could be lethal: during a disagreement, dispute, discussion, she could cut an opponent down like a bolt of lightning, without ever exceeding the bounds of icy civility.

She was a brilliant storyteller.

She read poetry aloud in a voice not for the salon but for the concert hall.

She read with feeling and comprehension, without artistic singsong, never dropping (and never trailing off!) the ends of lines. Her interpretations made the complex instantaneously clear.

She read aloud readily, trustingly, on first request, sometimes without even waiting to be asked, offering, "Would you like me to read some poetry for you?"

All her life she had a gigantic—and unfulfilled—need for readers, for listeners, and for immediate responses to her writing.

With novice poets she could be kind and immeasurably patient, provided she sensed in them—or imagined she sensed—the "divine spark" of talent; she hoped to find in them a comrade, a successor, not to her own legacy but to that of Poetry itself! At the same time, she discerned and mercilessly unmasked mediocrities, both those still in their formative stages and those who had achieved their specious heights.

She was kind and generous in her actions, rushing to help, to rescue, to save, or at least to offer a shoulder to lean on; to share the last, the most essential things she had, for she possessed nothing superfluous.

Able to give, she also knew how to take, indiscriminately. For a long time she trusted that "one good turn deserves another," and she believed that human beings were bound by some great, indestructible sense of mutual assistance.

Never helpless, she was always defenseless.

Indulgent of strangers, of those close to her—her family, her children—she demanded no less than she did of herself: the ultimate.

She never spurned fashion, as some of her superficial contemporaries thought. Rather, lacking the financial wherewithal either to initiate or to follow fashion trends, she disdained cheap imitations, and during her years in Europe she wore with dignity clothes that had been handed down to her.

In things inanimate she most valued time-tested durability; she had no interest in the fragile, the ephemeral, the shreddable, the friable, the susceptible—in short, the "fine."

She went to bed late, reading before falling asleep. She got up early.

She was spartanly modest in her habits and moderate in her diet.

She smoked. In Russia she smoked unfiltered cigarettes that she rolled herself; abroad she smoked strong, men's cigarettes, half a cigarette at a time, in a plain, cherrywood holder.

She drank her coffee black. She roasted the light beans to a dark brown and then patiently ground them in an antique brass cylindrical Turkish grinder embellished with arabesque designs.

With the natural world she was bonded by blood ties. She loved nature—mountains, cliffs, forests—with a love at once heathenishly worshipping and vanquishing, untempered by introspection, and for this reason, the sea, insurmountable by foot or by boat, perplexed her. She was incapable of merely admiring it.

Flat, low landscapes irritated her, as did wet, swampy, reed-ridden places and those damp months of the year when the ground becomes unreliable underfoot and the horizon blurry.

For the rest of her life the Tarusa of her childhood and the Koktebel of her youth occupied special places in her memory; she sought them everywhere and found them only rarely in the undulating hills of the former "royal hunting grounds" of the Meudon woods and in the cliffs, colors, and smells of the Mediterranean coast.

She tolerated heat well and cold badly.

She was indifferent to cut flowers, bouquets, and things that bloomed in vases or pots on windowsills; to flowers grown in gardens she preferred—for their robustness and durability—ivy, heather, wild grapes, and bushes.

She appreciated human interference in the natural environment when done intelligently, when humans collaborated with nature: parks, dams, roads.

She treated dogs and cats with unfailing tenderness, fidelity, and understanding (even respect), and they rewarded her with the same.

On walks she usually had a destination: to go as far as . . . , or to climb to the top of. . . . More than store-bought items she enjoyed things hunted or gathered: mushrooms and berries, and—during our difficult Czech period when we lived in forsaken villages outside Prague—the brushwood with which we stoked our stove.

Easily orienting herself in the countryside, in cities she lost all sense of direction and could get desperately lost even in familiar places.

She feared heights, multistoried buildings, crowds (throngs), automobiles, escalators, and elevators. Of all forms of urban transportation, she rode—when alone, with no one to accompany her—only trams and the metro. If neither of these was available, she went on foot.

She had no talent for mathematics, and she was disinclined toward all things mechanical.

She despised housekeeping—for its inexorability, for the useless repetitiveness of daily cares, for the way it devoured time needed for the essential. She prevailed over it, with patience and indifference, her whole life.

Sociable and hospitable, she eagerly struck up acquaintances and less eagerly struck them down. To the company of "proper people" she preferred those generally considered eccentric. She herself had the reputation of an eccentric.

In friendship or enmity she was always passionate, and not always consistent. The commandment "make not to thy self a graven image" she violated constantly.

She made allowances for youth and deferred to old age.

She possessed a refined sense of humor, and she saw nothing funny in the blatantly or crudely comic.

Of the two spheres that dominated her childhood—the visual arts (her father's) and music (her mother's)—she chose music. Form and color—the genuinely palpable and genuinely visual—eluded her. Only the story underlying an image could engage her: she was like a child "looking at pictures." Thus, book illustrations, engravings in particular, say, by Dürer or Doré, appealed to her more than did painting.

Her early infatuation with theater, explained in part by the influence of her young husband and his and her own young friends, would remain behind in Russia—together with her youth incapable of surmounting the bounds of age or geography.

Of all the performing arts she preferred cinema, silent films to "talkies," for the greater opportunity they provide viewers to cocreate and coimagine.

Working people she—invariably—held in deep fraternal esteem; idleness, parasitism, and consumerism were innately repugnant to her, as were indolence, laziness, and empty talk.

She was a person of her word, a person of action, and a person of honor.

For all her modesty, she knew her own worth.

THE WAY SHE WROTE

Sweeping aside all affairs and urgent matters, first thing in the morning, head clear, on a taut, empty stomach.

Pouring herself a mug of boiling black coffee, she placed it on the writing table to which she sat down every day of her life, like a worker to her machine, always with the same *sense of responsibility,* inevitability, and impossibility of it being any other way.

Everything superfluous on the table at that particular moment she automatically swept to the side, freeing space for her notebook and her elbows.

Pressing her forehead against the palm of her hand, running her fingers through her hair, she focused herself instantly.

She fell deaf and blind to everything except her manuscript, boring into it with the razor-sharp edge of her mind and pen.

She never wrote on separate pieces of paper, always in notebooks, of any variety—from school notebooks to account ledgers. As long as the ink did not smear, the quality of the paper was insignificant. In the years following the revolution she bound her own notebooks.

She wrote using a simple wooden quill with a fine metal point, like those in school. She never used fountain pens, never.

From time to time she would put her cigarette to the flame of her lighter and take a sip of coffee. She would mumble to herself, testing words for their sound. She never jumped up out of her chair, never paced the room in search of the elusive; she would sit at the table as if chained to her seat.

When inspired, she wrote *the fundamentals,* moving the idea forward, often with amazing speed. When *merely* concentrating, she did the grunt work of poetry, searching for the *right* word, attribute, and rhyme, trimming the text of prolixity and approximations.

Striving for accuracy and unity of meaning and sound, she filled page after page with columns of rhymes, dozens of variations of stanzas, usually not crossing out the rejects but drawing a line beneath them, to start anew below.

Before embarking on a major piece, she shaped her ideas as concretely as possible, constructed a plan, and then never allowed herself to diverge from it, so that the piece would not pull her along in its own direction and thereby become uncontrollable.

She wrote in a very distinct, rounded, small, neat hand that in the drafts of the last third of her life became difficult to read, due to an ever-growing number of abbreviations, many words indicated by only the first letter, her manuscripts increasingly becoming *manuscripts for herself alone.*

The character of her handwriting had formed very early, when she was still a child.

In general, she considered sloppy handwriting a manifestation of a writer's insulting lack of consideration for the reader—addressee, editor, typesetter. For this reason, she wrote in a deliberately legible hand and recopied the manuscripts she sent to the typographer in large, printed letters.

She answered mail without procrastinating. If she received a letter in the morning post, she frequently drafted an answer in her notebook right then, incorporating it into her writing for the day. She composed letters with the same creativeness and meticulousness as she did her manuscripts.

Sometimes she returned to her notebooks over the course of the day. She worked on them at night only in her youth.

She was able to put her work above anything else, I repeat, *anything.*

Her capacity for work and her mental organization were equal to her poetic gift.

Closing her notebook, she would open the door of the room to all the day's cares and burdens.

HER FAMILY

Marina Ivanovna Tsvetaeva was born in a family that comprised a sort of union of lonely souls. Her father, Ivan Vladimirovich Tsvetaev—a great and selfless worker and educator and founder of the first state-owned Museum of Fine Arts in prerevolutionary Russia, which has since become a cultural center of worldwide significance—lost his passionately beloved and charming first wife, Varvara Dmitrievna Ilovaiskaya, when she died after presenting him with a son. In his second marriage Ivan Vladimirovich wed the youthful Maria Aleksandrovna Meyn, who would be stepmother to his eldest daughter Valeria and young son Andrei; he remarried while the embers of his love for his deceased wife still smoldered, attracted by Maria Aleksandrovna's physical resemblance to Varvara Dmitrievna, as well as by her noble spirit, selflessness, and seriousness beyond her years.

Maria Aleksandrovna turned out to be too much *herself* to serve as a *substitute,* and the similarities in physical appearance (high forehead, dark brown eyes, dark wavy hair, aquiline nose, and the beautiful line of her lips) merely underscored differences between the two women's personalities. Ivan Vladimirovich's second wife possessed neither the grace nor the soft charm of his first; such distinctively feminine qualities rarely coexist with the masculine strength of personality and firmness of character that distinguished Maria Aleksandrovna. She herself had grown up without a mother, and the Swiss governess who had raised her—a woman with a big heart and a tiny brain—succeeded in instilling in her only "strict rules" without nuance or halftones. Everything else Maria Aleksandrovna instilled in herself on her own.

When Maria Aleksandrovna married Ivan Vladimirovich, she was in love with another man with whom marriage was out of the question. She married in order to rule out the impossible and to acquire a purpose and reason for living in day-to-day household service to a man she boundlessly respected and his two orphaned children.

In the house that had been Varvara Dmitrievna's dowry and that still retained her presence[2] the young mistress introduced her own ways, born not from personal experience (she had none) but from her inner conviction that they must be so—ways that appealed neither to the servants nor to the first wife's relatives, and particularly not to her nine-year-old stepdaughter.

Valeria disliked Maria Aleksandrovna from childhood and forever after, and if later she was able to *comprehend* her stepmother on a rational level, in her heart she never accepted her and never forgave her, particularly the way her stepmother's nature and essence were so entirely *alien* to her own. Valeria also never forgave her stepmother her rare amalgamation of defiance and self-discipline, of obsession and reserve, of despotism and love of liberty, the unlimitedly high standards she set herself and others, and the aura of asceticism she imposed on the household, so discordant with the atmosphere of amicable conviviality that had prevailed in Varvara Dmitrievna's time. All this was too much; it went too far, exceeding acceptable norms at the time. Perhaps Valeria also could not accept the tenebrous unfeminine might of Maria Aleksandrovna's outstanding talent as pianist, which came to replace Varvara Dmitrievna's light, nightingale-like gift for song.

For one reason or the other, the incompatibility of their personalities led the family council, headed by their grandfather—historian Dmitry Ivanovich Ilovaisky—to place Valeria at the Order of Saint Catherine Institute "for young noble women" among whom she found innumerable confidantes. Andrei was schooled at home. He got along with Maria Aleksandrovna, although no real spiritual closeness ever developed between them: he had no need for such closeness, and Maria Aleksandrovna did not insist on it.

The family favorite—handsome, talented, and relatively sociable—Andrei grew and ultimately grew up to be reserved and aloof, remaining so the rest of his life, never opening up to people or to life itself, and never realizing the full potential of his abilities.

Of Ivan Vladimirovich's two daughters from his second marriage, the easier of the two for their parents turned out (or appeared) to be the younger, Anastasia. As a child she was more ingenuous, more pliant, and more affectionate than Marina, and the fact that she was younger and defenseless brought her closer to her mother, made her a comfort to her soul: Asya could *simply* be loved. In her elder daughter, Marina, Maria Aleksandrovna too early glimpsed her own qualities—her own romanticism, her own hidden passion, her own shortcomings (attendant to her talent), her own summits and abysses—as well as Marina's, and these she attempted to tame and to level. Of course, this too was motherly love, perhaps of the highest degree. At the same time, however, it was a mother's struggle with her already fully formed self within a child who had yet to shape herself, in a child who had yet to become herself; a struggle (so hopeless!) with the future for the sake of the future. . . . In her struggles with Marina, her mother struggled on her daughter's behalf, taking secret pride in the knowledge that she could not prevail.

The reasons why Maria Aleksandrovna's two daughters were not friends as children and became close only comparatively late, as teenagers, were several and had to do with Marina's childhood jealousy of Asya (to whom their mother's tenderness and indulgence came so easily!); Marina's predilection for the company of elders with whom she might match wits and the company of adults whereby to sharpen those wits; Marina's need to be a leader among equals (if not among the strongest, then at least not among those who were weaker); and, finally, the simple fact that for a child like Marina who had developed early and in her own way, Asya's infantile lack of independence held no interest. Only by outstripping herself in her own psychological development and overcoming the two-year age barrier separating them (comparable to a twenty-year difference between adults) was Asya able to become Marina's friend in their late teen and early adult years. Orphaned by their mother's early death, the girls grew even closer.

In the springtime of their lives the two sisters displayed certain similarities in appearance and character, the principal difference between them manifest in the way Marina's multifaceted talent early acquired a single, deep channel of lifelong directed purpose, while Asya's gifts and aspirations flowed in multiple directions, her spiritual thirst slaked by many springs. Later in life their paths diverged.

Sincere in her love for her father, Valeria at first treated his younger daughters, her half sisters, with equal beneficence. On vacation from the institute and later, after graduating, she tried spoiling them both as a way of "neutralizing" Maria Aleksandrovna's austerity and strictness, by which she herself remained untouched since she enjoyed total independence within the family, as did her brother Andrei. Asya responded to Valeria's treatment with total spontaneity and ardent affection. Marina sensed a trap: not to reject Valeria's indulgences and to partake of her secret patronage were as if to betray her mother, *her* lineage, *her* core, to betray herself by straying from the high road of duty to the low road of temptations such as hard candies and books from Valeria's library.

As Marina saw it, her older sister's kindness revolved on cunning and served Valeria as a weapon against her stepmother, undermining the mother's influence on her daughters. Marina's realization of the abyss that lay between treachery and fidelity, between temptation and duty, marked the beginning of the discord that came to lie between her and Valeria. The latter's short-lived and, apparently, superficial sympathy for her sister soon turned to dislike and ultimately to rejection, that is, the same inability to forgive not just shortcomings but essential traits of character which underlay her relations with her stepmother.

(Valeria was constant in her ways, and, having severed ties with Marina when she was still a teenager, she never entertained any desire to meet with her and took interest in Marina's work only when others began to talk about it, only on the eve of her own death and decades after Marina's. As for Asya, Andrei, and his family, Valeria kept in touch with them, but she always maintained her distance.)

Ivan Vladimirovich cherished all of his children equally, and he was grieved by the disputes within the family for whose happiness he attempted (and accomplished) everything he could. His relationship with Maria Aleksandrovna was filled with mutual kindness and respect. Maria Aleksandrovna, her husband's assistant in affairs concerning the museum, understood both her husband's obsession with his lifetime challenge and his distance from household affairs. For his part, Ivan Vladimirovich, though he remained a stranger to the world of music, understood the tragedy of his wife's passion for it—tragic because according to the unwritten rules of the time a woman pianist, no matter how talented, was limited to the confines of her own room or parlor. Into the concert hall, where piano music sounded for the multitudes, a woman could be admitted only as a listener. Blessed with a talent both profound and powerful, Maria Aleksandrovna was fated to remain locked inside it, to express it for herself alone.

Maria Aleksandrovna raised her children not solely on the dry crusts of duty. She opened their eyes to the eternal, never-failing wonder of the natural world; she showered them with the many joys of childhood, with the magic of family holidays and Christmas trees, and she placed in their hands the very best books in the world—their first books. At her side, their minds, hearts, and imaginations found space to roam.

As she lay dying, she grieved that she would never see her daughters as adults, but her last words, according to Marina, were "I'll miss only music and the sun."

HER HUSBAND, HIS FAMILY

On the same day as Marina, only one year later, October 8 [September 26, OS], 1893, her husband, Sergei Yakovlevich Efron, was born, sixth in a family of nine children.[3]

His mother, Elizaveta Petrovna Durnovo (1853–1910),[4] descended from a long line of nobility and was the only daughter of an officer of the Guard and Adjutant to Nicholas I who had entered early retirement. Her future husband, Yakov Konstantinovich Efron (1854–1909), was a student at the Moscow [Imperial—trans.] Technical Higher School.[5]

Both were members of the "Land and Liberty" party, and in 1879 they became affiliated with the group known as "Black Repartition."[6] They met at a political gathering in the Petrovsko-Razumovskoe region of Moscow. The black-haired girl, graced with a beauty both stern and inspiring, arrived secretly at the gathering straight from the Assembly of the Nobility, still dressed in her ball gown and velvet wrap, and she impressed Yakov Konstantinovich as "a creature from another planet." Her planet, however, turned out to be the same as his—Revolution.

Elizaveta Petrovna, who played no small role in the revolutionary democratic movement of her time, formed her political views under the influence of Pyotr Alekseevich Kropotkin.

Thanks to him, in her early youth she joined the First International and settled on her life path. Kropotkin took pride in his protégé and played a vital role in her life. The friendship between them was severed only by death.

Yakov Konstantinovich and Elizaveta Petrovna carried out all the assignments the organization entrusted to them: the most dangerous as well as the most humanly difficult. For example, Yakov Konstantinovich and two comrades were delegated to execute the sentence imposed by the Revolutionary Committee of "Land and Liberty" on Nikolai Reinshtein, a police agent and provocateur who had infiltrated the Moscow organization. Reinshtein was assassinated on February 26, 1879. The police never succeeded in identifying the perpetrators.

In July 1880, while transporting underground literature and an illegal printing press from Moscow to Petersburg, Elizaveta Petrovna was arrested and incarcerated in the Peter and Paul Fortress. His daughter's arrest dealt a terrible blow to her unsuspecting father, to his paternal bond with her as well as his monarchist beliefs. Through his extensive connections he succeeded in having his daughter released into his custody, and she went into exile abroad. Yakov Konstantinovich followed. They married and spent seven long years abroad. Their first children—Anna, Pyotr, and Elizaveta—were born in emigration.

After the Efron family returned to Russia, their life was not easy. The "People's Will" movement had been crushed, and their friends were scattered in prisons, banished to various places throughout Russia, or in exile abroad. Under police surveillance, Yakov Konstantinovich had the right to work as an insurance agent, no more. The job brought him no satisfaction and offered no promise of advancement, and his small salary barely allowed him to support—feed, dress, school, and provide medical care for—their ever-expanding family. Elizaveta Petrovna's parents, elderly and infirm, lived under a separate roof and had no clue of their loved ones' straits, and their daughter never asked them for help.

For all their day-to-day hardships, all their inconsolable grief (the three youngest children died—Alyosha and Tanya of meningitis, and seven-year-old Gleb, their father's favorite, of a congenital heart defect), the Efron family constituted an amazingly harmonic fellowship of older and younger generations. This family had no room for coercion, shouting, or punishment; each, even the tiniest member of the family, grew and developed unrestrained, submitting only to love and conscience, which is at once the most liberating and, at the same time, insofar as it is voluntary, the most exacting form of discipline.

Each member of this family was endowed with that rarest of gifts: the ability to love another (others) in precisely the way that other (those others) needed to be loved. This was the source of both children's and parents' innate selflessness without self-sacrifice, of their generosity without second thoughts, of their tact without indifference, of their commitment to— rather, self-resolve in—common efforts, to fulfilling a common duty. These qualities and abilities were hardly symptomatic of "spiritual vegetarianism." All of them—young and old—were temperamental, passionate, and, consequently, not without their biases: knowing how to love, they knew how to hate, but they also knew how to "keep a grip on themselves."[7]

At the end of the 1890s Elizaveta Petrovna returned once again to her revolutionary activities, and her older children followed in her stead. Yakov Konstantinovich, working the same job at the same insurance company, continued to serve as principal support for his "nest of revolutionaries."[8] In the frequently rotating apartments he rented,[9] the parents and their friends gathered together with the children and their friends—students at the university and in women's higher courses as well as high school (gymnasium) pupils; at their summer house in Bykovo they printed proclamations, prepared explosives, and concealed weapons.

Photographs from these and later years preserve the valiant and tender image of Elizaveta Petrovna: graying, fatigued, yet still unbent; her gaze bores deep from within; premature wrinkles trickle from the corners of her lips and furrow the high brow of her narrow face; her modest dress hangs on her emaciated frame; alongside her—her husband, his face not just open but wide-open, protected only by his small, tightly closed mouth, his eyes clear and bright, his nose upturned and boyish. The same prematurely gray hair, the same wrinkles, and the same stamp of forbearance, but hardly submissiveness, on his face.

They are surrounded by their children: Anna, who would head workers' groups and build barricades alongside Nikolai Bauman's wife [Kapitolina Medvedeva—trans.]; Pyotr, whose desperately courageous antigovernment activities and bold escapes from captivity would make it impossible for him to return from emigration until the eve of World War I, to die in his homeland; Vera, named after her mother's friend, the ardent Vera Zasulich, still a girl in braids whose path to adulthood would begin with the same prisons and exile as her namesake; Elizaveta ("the family sunshine," as Marina Ivanovna Tsvetaeva later called her), buttress and support to her seniors and mentor to her juniors; Seryozha [Sergei—trans.], who would arrive at revolution by the most difficult, circuitous route, which he then spent the rest of his life straightening, and Konstantin, who would leave this life as a teenager, taking his mother with him. . . .

Elizaveta Petrovna's political activity and that of her comrades-progeny reached its apex and its limits during the revolution of 1905. The ensuing police repressions fell upon the family, fracturing the unity of its single fate into the separate fates of separate individuals. In the fever of searches, arrests, prisons, hard labor, and then escapes and tragic fear of all for one and one for all, Yakov Konstantinovich liberated Elizaveta Petrovna from the Butyrki Prison[10] and from a sentence of hard labor by paying her devastatingly high bail—raised with the help of friends—and sent her, ill and exhausted, abroad, whence she was fated never to return. In emigration she outlived her husband by only a short while and survived her youngest son, the last hope of her wearied soul, who followed her into exile, by only one day.[11]

At the time of the first Russian Revolution Seryozha had just turned twelve years old; he was unable to participate directly, and he caught only the echoes of events, aware that any help he might lend his elders or their cause would be insignificant, which pained him. The adults pushed him back into a childhood that no longer existed, that had ended with the onset of the family's hardships, yet he strove to be an adult, a thirst for heroism and compulsion to serve seething within him, unquenched by the usual studies at a usual gymnasium. Indeed, Seryozha's studies—his whole existence—lost both their rhythm and stability after Elizaveta Petrovna's departure. Forced to live under one roof after another, he resigned himself to the troubled circumstances that replaced the ordered family life he had known since the cradle. True, [in 1909—trans.], the boy was able to spend one (for him, relatively serene) summer at his mother's side together with other members of his family, in Switzerland, in parts that reminded her of her youth and her first emigration.

As a teenager Seryozha contracted tuberculosis. Illness and grief for his mother consumed him, and his family, fearing an outburst of desperation, kept her death from him for a long while. When he learned the truth, he said nothing: his grief exceeded tears or words.

In his late teens and early adulthood he seemed, at least on the surface, to be sociable and open, but inside he remained profoundly conflicted and profoundly lonely.

His loneliness yielded only to Marina.

They met—he seventeen and she eighteen—on May 5, 1911, on the deserted, stone-covered shore of Maksimilian Voloshin's Koktebel. She was gathering pebbles, and he offered to help: a youth, almost a boy, handsome in a sad, meek way (she, by the way, thought he was cheerful, more precisely, joyful!), he had stunning, huge eyes that took up half his face. Looking into those eyes and reading the future in them, Marina made a wish: "If he finds a carnelian and gives it to me, I'll marry him!" Of course, blindly—for he was unable to take his gray eyes off her green eyes—running his fingers through the pebbles, he found a carnelian right then and there and placed it in her palm: a large, rose-colored stone that seemed illuminated from within, which she cherished for the rest of her life and which has, amazingly, survived to this day. . . .

Seryozha and Marina were married in a church service in January 1912, and the brief interval between their first meeting and the outbreak of World War I was the sole period of undisturbed happiness they would know in their entire lives together.

In 1914 Seryozha, a first-year student at Moscow University, set off for the front on a hospital train in the capacity of male nurse. His goal was active combat, but one medical commission after the next found him physically unfit. Only at long last did he succeed in entering the cadet academy, which would fatefully turn the course of his life, for, influenced by the atmosphere of the officers' loyalty to the czar that surrounded him at the academy, by the beginning of the civil war he found himself drawn into the White Guards' camp. Perverted notions of comradeship and fidelity to one's oath, combined with growing awareness of the doom awaiting the "White" movement and the impossibility of betraying the doomed, led Sergei down the most mournful, erroneous, and thorn-laden path in the world, through Gallipoli and Constantinople, to Czechoslovakia and France, into the ranks of living shadows, of people without citizenship or nationality, without present or future, with the unbearable burden of having only the past behind them.[12]

In the years of the civil war the bond between my parents was severed almost entirely; only unreliable rumors delivered by equally unreliable messengers reached them; there were almost no letters—and in those that were, the questions never coincided with the answers. If not for this—who knows!—the fate of these two people might have been entirely different. On this side of not knowing, Marina sang the praises of the "White Movement," while her husband on the other side decried it—inch by inch, step by step, day by day.

When it came to light that Sergei Yakovlevich had been evacuated to Turkey together with the remnants of the defeated White Army, Marina entrusted Ilya Ehrenburg, then on his way abroad, to track him down. Ehrenburg found Sergei in Czechoslovakia, where he had matriculated as a student at Charles University in Prague.[13] Marina decided to join her husband abroad, insofar as for him, a former White officer, all roads back were closed.

I remember a conversation between my parents shortly after my mother and I arrived abroad.

". . . But, still, it wasn't at all like that, Marinochka," said my father with great suffering in those huge eyes of his after hearing several poems from *The Demesne of the Swans*.[14]

"Then what was it like?"

"It was a fratricidal and suicidal war that we conducted without the support of the people; it was our lack of knowledge, our lack of understanding of a people in whose name, or so it seemed to us at the time, we fought. Not 'us,' but the better of us. The remainder fought only to take back from the people what the Bolsheviks had given them, and for no other reason. There were battles for 'God, Czar, and Fatherland,' and there were also firing squads, hangings, and marauding in their name."

"But there must have been heroes?"

"There were. Only the people will never recognize them as heroes. At best some of them will be acknowledged as victims. . . ."

"But what about you? You, Seryozhenka?"

"Me? Imagine a wartime train station, a large junction station, packed with soldiers, homeless people, women and children; imagine the commotion, the confusion, the crush, people clambering into train wagons, pushing and shoving each other. . . . Imagine they shove you in along with them, you hear the third whistle, and the train sets off. For a minute your sense is one of relief—thank you, O Lord!—and then suddenly you realize with deathly horror that in the fatal confusion you—along with many, many others!—have wound up on the wrong train . . . that your train is departing from another platform, and that there is no going back because the tracks have been dismantled. That the only way back, Marina, was by foot, along the railroad beds, the rest of your life. . . ."

It was after this conversation that Marina wrote her "Daybreak on the Rails."[15]

The rest of my father's life was his road back, along the railroad beds, to Russia, over innumerable obstacles, difficulties, dangers, and sacrifices. And he returned to the motherland as her son, not as her stepson.

MY EARLIEST YEARS

Early childhood comes back to me not as a dream but as my first, starkest reality, as an ongoing discovery, first of the world, then, a little later, of myself in it.

At its source that world was neither small nor large, neither good nor bad; it simply existed, beyond any doubt, and at the time still beyond comparison or evaluation. Within that world there also existed two utterly newborn, infant eyes that pored into everything and saw all, except the little girl herself to whom the eyes belonged. The little girl, who seemed at times to be hiding in the depths of her own pupils, came into being only on the day when, while staring at another little girl in the mirror, she suddenly equated her own tangible "I" with the intangible reflection. The reflection was not a pleasant sight: towheaded, scowling, dressed in a little striped velveteen dress and shod in button-top shoes, it made faces, stamped its feet, stuck out its tongue, and thoroughly deserved to have to stand in the corner. It stood there and stamped its feet and stuck out its tongue until the original, suddenly struck by a new awareness, merged in her consciousness with the copy. And then the quiet, now somewhat ingratiating "I" approached the reflection, petted it with a friendly stroke, as she might Jack the Poodle, and whispered, "My dear!"

But that all happened later. Before that there was the world and a mama who knew everything and commanded all in that world, and she was called Marina. The world depended entirely on her. If she willed it so, the child's day turned to night, toys appeared from the cabinet and disappeared again, and the measured boredom those toys evoked (I didn't know how to "play" and breaking was not permitted) would give way to the joy of a promised stroll with Marina: almost complete joy, that is, had it not been for all those despicable hoods, wraps, leggings, boots, mittens, snow pants, buckles, snaps, hook and eyes, buttons, and buttons, and more buttons!

As Marina willed, the world was delimited by the walls of the nursery or it became the street, it turned from winter to summer, it opened windows and doors or closed them shut, it came to a dead halt or—thanks to the carriage, less frequently the train—metamorphosed into movement itself, in order, after it had once again settled into place, to be called "summer house" or "Koktebel." To be called. For it was precisely as Marina willed that everything visible came to be signified by words and thereby to materialize, to achieve definition, to acquire form, color, and meaning. The unseen, the abstract, also originated with words, the three "*m*'s" of human existence—"must not," "must," and "may"—of which the first, the one repeated most often, sank in before the latter two.

Marina's influence on me when I was small was enormous, uninterrupted by anyone or anything, and always at its zenith. By the same token she did not spend that much time with me, did not take me out for walks all that often, did not indulge my whims, and did not spoil me. That was done to varying degrees by nannies, none of whom has left a single reliable trace in my memory, perhaps because they all proved incapable of adjusting to our household and, therefore, alternated frequently.

One nanny was forced to leave us because instead of taking me to the little park on Sobachya Square,[16] she invariably led me off to the Church of Saint Nicholas of the Sands to stand through endless funerals and kiss the foreheads of the dead. "And what's wrong with that, ma'am," she said to an enraged Marina as she lazily gathered her belongings. "An angel's prayer flies up to God faster, so standin' next to a coffin at least the chil's doin' some good, not like at those—ugh! it's a sin just sayin' it—dog squares!"

A second one was fired because she turned out to be as corrupt of tongue as she was of hand. Instead of "bear" and "pantaloons," for example, she (and I right after her) would say "brear" and "paltaloons."

The third and others after her, it seems, left on their own.

None of these or any other passing shadows ever obstructed my vision of Marina, whose luminosity seemed to shine unimpeded through everyone and everything, and after whom and toward whom I, like a sunflower, was perpetually drawn, and whose presence I perpetually sensed within myself, like the voice of conscience, so great was the commanding, demanding, and all-conquering power she emanated. The power of love.

In the child I was, Marina strove to develop from the cradle all the qualities she herself possessed: the ability to overcome difficulty, and independence of thought and action. She narrated and explained not in a superficial way, rather, more often at a level over the child's head, so that the little one might come to comprehend the intended on her own and, perhaps, surpass the intended. She trained me to articulate—cohesively and coherently—what I had seen, heard, experienced, or imagined. Never condescending to the level of the child, she untiringly lifted the child to meet her at the furthest point of intersection between an adult's wisdom and a child's ingenuousness, between the identity of the adult and the identity of the child.

The reward for good behavior, for having accomplished or prevailed, was not sweets or presents but a fairy tale read aloud, a walk together, or an invitation "to come visit" her room. "Dropping in" without invitation was not permitted.

That many-cornered, seemingly bezel-shaped room with its magical Elizabethan blue chandelier suspended from the ceiling, with its somewhat frightening, always tempting, wolf skin near the low-lying divan I entered with a shiver of timidity and joy in my heart. . . . How well I remember that quick motherly bend toward me, her face next to mine, the smell of her *Jasmine de Corse* perfume, the rustle of her silk dress, how she herself—out of lingering childhood habit—quickly and nimbly settled on the floor with me (less frequently, in a chair or on the divan) crossing or tucking her long legs beneath her! And our talks, and the way she read me fairy tales, and ballads by Lermontov and Zhukovsky. . . . I quickly learned them all by heart and, it seems, I understood them. True, until about age six, whenever I recited "Bend not the ship's towering mastheads, the weathercocks silent above," I envisioned otherwise restless roosters atop the ship's sails poised at silent attention in respect for the Emperor [Napoleon—trans.], but this didn't seem to lessen the ballad's mysterious charm.[17]

Marina also allowed me to sit at her desk tucked in the niche under the tiny corner window where the pigeons always cooed; to draw with her pencils, sometimes even in her notebook; to admire with respect the portraits of Sarah Bernhardt and Maria Bashkirtseva on her desk; to touch her "Iron Maiden of Nuremberg" paperweight (a frightening iron figure with thorns inside that Grandfather had brought from Germany)[18] or the other—also iron—figurine, of Czar Aleksei Mikhailovich[19] or the paper clip shaped like two hands with absolutely naturalistic fingers that held notes and bills in its firm grasp or the lacquered pencil box with a portrait of young General Tuchkov IV of War of 1812 fame[20] or the ceramic, silver-plated Sirin, bird of sorrow.

From the tummy of her escritoire came a big book in a red binding—Perrault's fairy tales with illustrations by Doré—that had once belonged to Marina's mother when "she was just as little as you are now." I would look at the pictures, turning the pages carefully with freshly washed hands, touching only the upper right-hand corner. Nothing so incensed Marina as careless, disrespectful treatment of books. Once, when I accidentally broke one of her two favorite antique porcelain cups (fortunately, not the one with the picture of Napoleon, but the other one, with Josephine) and bawled, "I smashed his wife, now he's a widower!" I was not only not scolded but comforted. However, should some *Struwwelpeter* book get ripped up because he was a nasty, wrinkled ugly little freak ("just like you, when you don't want to wash or comb your hair"), I would find myself standing in the corner, glumly picking away at the plaster. . . . I was also allowed to look at the pictures in the one-volume edition of Gogol (a supplement to the journal *Niva*) in which everything was drawn in minuscule detail still beyond my comprehension. Like a nomad extolling details of the landscape opening up before him, I would comment on the illustrations in my own little singsong: "And here's a little horsey. . . . And here a gentleman speaks with a beautiful lady. . . . And over here a young lady is asking the cook for some fried monkeys. . . ." The "young lady" was the corpse of the dead Ukrainian girl risen from the grave; the "cook" was Khoma Brut, and the "fried monkeys" were evil spirits dashing and scurrying about in all directions.[21]

Sometimes Marina wound up Grandmother's music box with its spiny brass cylinder. When you stuck a cardboard play card inside and wound the stiff little key, out came the melody of a minuet or "grandfather's dance"[22] played with the softness and distinctness of melting drops of snow in spring. There were as many melodies as there were cards. No less marvelous, but more impressive, was the gramophone with its speaker the shape of a giant morning glory, where the voices of gypsies dwelled. All her life Marina was in love with gypsies (from Pushkin's[23] to the fortune-tellers out on the street and village horse thieves) for their freedom-loving spirit, for their difference, and for their detachment from all that surrounded them. She loved them for their sorcerer-like speech and songs, for their regal carefree nature and . . . unreliability.

I remember how once after we had listened to recordings by Varya [Varvara] Panina and [Anastasia] Vialtseva—deep, sorrowful, daring voices!—Marina told me (I was not yet four years old) about the farewell concert one of them (I think it was Panina) had held.

". . . At one time she was young and beautiful, and when she sang, *everyone* went wild, every last one of them! Rich men, princes, and officers flung their hearts, their titles, and their estates at her feet; they lost their heads, fought duels. . . . But time passed (you, too, will learn that it passes), and *her* time was over! She had grown old: her beauty, her wealth, and her fame had abandoned her. . . . Only the *voice* remained. . . . And her fans? Her fans had gone their separate ways, become respectable, many of them had died. . . . But she kept on performing, although there was no one to listen to her anymore, her generation had disappeared, and as far as their grandchildren were concerned, grandchildren never inherit their grandparents' passions! And there she was, singing her final farewell concert: she comes out on stage wearing the same black shawl, but flabby, gray, and old! Not a hint remained of her former features; her face had more wrinkles than features. In the audience only a handful of the final faithful had gathered. . . . Who would have recognized in those shabby old men former playboys, hussars, and bons vivants? They were *shadows* who had come for a final rendezvous with another *shadow*. The shadow sings romantic ballad after romantic ballad, everything they had once loved, for which they had idolized her. The shadow once loved by them! The shadow who had once loved them! She bids them farewell, bids life farewell, bids love farewell. . . . The concert should have ended long ago. The accompanist has left. The ushers are extinguishing light after light and chandelier after chandelier. There is no one around. But she does not leave. She refuses to go! The songs burst and flow from her heart! She sings, sings alone in that dark, empty hall. Dark gloominess and a voice. A voice in the gloomy darkness. A voice that had overcome darkness and gloom!"

Seeing my face, Marina stopped short and asked, "Do you understand?"

"I understand," I answered and laughed. "The old girl sang and sang, and all the old geezers left and turned out the lights."

"Out!" Marina said after a brief silence. "You're still too little. Back to your nursery."

And I went back to the nursery, to my nanny, to the "brear" and the "paltaloons."

Poor Marina! How often she was the wrong age to have conversations even with adults—especially with adults!

That voice in the dark left such an impression perhaps precisely because it was not immediately heard or understood, as, for that matter, was the case with many of Marina's riddles.

Nowadays I wonder: is the image of the old gypsy singing to a deserted dark theater not the source of Tsvetaeva's tragic Sybil?

> A gray boulder of stone
> Of its epoch disowned,
> Your body is the cavern
> Of your voice.[24]

More about my laughter and about laughter in general.

When Marina first took me to the circus, I initially did not know where I was supposed to look. I kept gawking at the loges where the spotlights were, pitying and fearing for the people up there. For some reason I thought you could enter the loges only from outside, that is, by way of ladders, which was scary and dangerous. How lucky we were to be sitting *here*! With both her hands Marina turned my face toward the arena: Watch! But I was still drawn by the people working the spotlights. Only when the tigers and guardedly roaring lions came out practically right under my nose did I redirect my attention, not toward the animals, but toward the trainers, whose uniforms reminded me of student uniforms like my father's and his friends': Might that not be Seryozha playing with the animals among all those overturned silver-white barrels and cubes? Why had the students chased the animals out by cracking whips at them? Why bring them out in the first place?

Just then strangely dressed beings with painted faces—some wearing amazing blouses with glittering herringbone stripes, others dressed in undersized vests over enormous baggy trousers—came running, jumping, and somersaulting out into the arena, shouting something in their sharp, vinegary voices. With their sweeping movements, their awkward and at the same time precise jumps and twists, their explosive fights and stormy truces, they reminded me of "street kids" whose games I ("a good little girl") could share only in my imagination as I watched them through the window. Clowns! Clowns! They proved far more interesting than street kids because they were funny! Kids jumped and tussled "just because," but the clowns—with each move, each shove, each jump, each kick, each push, and each resounding slap in the face—elicited peals of laughter. And something was always happening to them: their pants fell down, or their vests split open, or their sleeves grew longer, or their hats flew away, or their stomachs and bottoms swelled up, or one pulled a chair out from another, the earth gaping between his legs.

At first, as I was gradually drawn in, I smiled, then I started to laugh, and finally I was belly-laughing along with everyone else. Everyone, except Marina.

With palms turned to steel she jerked my face away from the arena and hammered out with quiet rage, "Now you listen to me and don't you ever forget this: anyone who laughs at another's misfortune is either a fool or a scoundrel, most often both. When a person falls flat on his face, it is not funny. When a person gets covered with garbage, it is not funny. When one person trips another person, it is not funny. When a person loses his pants, it is not funny. When a person gets hit in the face, it is mean. And laughing at *that* is a sin."

It sunk in immediately and stayed with me for the rest of my life, just as would the later realization that my mother's comments did not apply to *circus clowns* as such.

. . . I began to draw the way all children do: pushing down hard on my pencil, I spun circle after circle, the circles eventually forming tornadoes. Then, once, just as happens with everyone else, I drew my first person, my first "Adam": sticks for arms, legs, and body, and a cabbage for a head. Holding my breath in delight and concentrated effort, I equipped the cabbage with eyes, then nostrils, then a mouth that extended beyond the borders of its head, and, finally, teeth. I added fingers and buttons and, thoroughly beside myself, I screamed, "Marina! Marina! Come quick!" Alarmed, Marina came running from her room next-door into the nursery.

"What happened?"

"Look! Look! I drew a *person!*"

I froze at my little desk in expectation of praise.

Marina bent over the drawing. "*What* person? That's a *person?*"

"Yes."

"Oh, come now, Alechka! People don't look like that. That's just a freak. Look! How many fingers does he have on his hand? And how many do you have? You see? And those legs like matchsticks? Look at your own! And those teeth? You ought to be ashamed! They look like a fence. And heads are never bigger than bodies. And what are all those circles?"

"Buttons," I whispered, darkening.

"Buttons wider than his stomach? Buttons by themselves, without clothes? No, Alechka, this is bad. You need to draw lots and lots and practice a long, long time. Until you get it right."

What a blow that was to the vanity and effrontery sprouting inside me! Instead of a real figure supplemented and enhanced by the artist's imagination, I now saw before me the pathetic, lopsided crookedy mercilessly deposed by Marina. . . . With a sigh as deep as disappointment itself, I took up my pencil once more to attempt to surmount the insurmountable.

Marina could tolerate nothing made easy. Thus, when acquaintances gave me coloring books as presents, she took them away, saying, "Draw your own pictures, then color them in. A person who colors, or traces, or copies someone else's work only shortchanges herself and will never learn to do anything."

When by chance it became apparent that I already knew my letters, she began to teach me to read whole words, not by breaking them down into syllables, but whole words, all at once, which I first read "to myself" and then aloud. The ink pen she placed in my hand never practiced the sticks and hooks that precede real letters, and it never knew writing samples printed in spaces between lines that mechanically organize the writing in between. I was supposed to build words from letters, and phrases from words, all by myself, and to write them straight without lined paper. This meant I constantly had to *think* about *what* I was doing and *how* I was doing it. Passive copying was proscribed from Marina's teaching method, replaced by creativity. Instead of boring examples to be copied, whole paragraphs and compositions were written right from the start; otherwise characterless epigonic notebooks metamorphosed into diaries; grammar was distilled to a minimum of the most fundamental and, as with any-thing essential, uncomplicated rules. Instead of the ability to memorize, memory itself was developed, visual memory above all, together with the skill of observation with which most children are so richly endowed and then so quickly lose. . . .

Intrepidly eliminating the middle rungs from my pedagogical ladder, Marina taught me to read fluently and with relative comprehension by age four, to write by age five, and to keep a diary that was more or less coher-ent and quite literate (by prereform orthographic standards)[25] by age six or seven.

Since the beginning of my "literacy" coincided with the beginning of the revolution, the entries I made perhaps may be of interest now, fifty years later. Here are a few of them, unedited, and abridged only where necessary.

My Mother
My mother is very strange.
   My mother is not at all like a mother. Mothers always take delight in their own children and children in general, but Marina does not like little children.

She has light brown hair, and it curls in waves along the side of her face. She has green eyes, an aquiline nose, and pink lips. She has a slender build and fingers that I like.

Her favorite day is the Annunciation. She is sad, quick, and likes Poetry and Music. She writes poetry. She is patient and tolerant to an extreme. She can be angry, and she can be loving. She is always rushing somewhere. She has a big soul. A tender voice. A quick step. Marina's hands are covered with rings. Marina reads at night. Her eyes are almost always mocking. She does not like to be bothered with stupid questions; they make her very angry.

Sometimes she walks around as if lost, then suddenly she seems to awaken, begins to speak, and then drifts off somewhere again.

DECEMBER 1918

The Four-Leaf Clover

It was a warm, tranquil day, and Marina and I were out for a walk. She was telling me the Andersen fairy tale about "The Girl Who Trod on the Loaf": in order to cross a stream, the little girl stepped on bread. About what a terrible sin this was. I said, "Marina! Probably nobody would want to commit a sin like that today!" Marina said that was because there was so little bread now, but in the past not all the bread got eaten and people threw it out. That stepping on bread was as much a sin as murdering a human being. Because bread is the source of life.

We walked uphill along a gray trail. At the top stood a large church that looked very beautiful under the blue sky and long clouds. When we approached the church, we saw that it was locked. We crossed ourselves before it and sat down on the steps. Marina said that we were like beggars sitting on church steps.

One could see far off into the distance, but not in great detail, because there was a light fog. I started talking to Marina, but she told me not to bother her and to go play. I did not want to play. I wanted to pick flowers. Suddenly I

noticed the clover growing at my feet. Old stones had been
evenly arranged there at the foot of the church steps. Each of
the stones was framed by dark clover. If you looked closely at
the stones, they revealed streaks and designs, like real paintings in green frames. I squatted down and began looking for a
four-leaf clover to bring Marina good luck. I searched so long
my ears buzzed. Just when I was ready to give up, I found one,
which made me so happy that it frightened me. I ran over
to Marina and presented her with my find. Gladdened, she
examined my four-leaf clover and asked where I had found it.
I told her. She thanked me and put it in her notebook to dry.

AUGUST 1918

What emerges from that notation written long ago today?
One of my favorite Tsvetaeva poems from August 1918:

Poems appear like stars above, like roses,
Like beauty—of no use when cleaning house.
To laurel wreaths and to apotheoses,
I've one response: How did it come about?
We sleep, and there, 'midst cobblestones of marble,
The heavenly host appears in petals four.
Oh, world, behold! In sleep the bard discovers
The laws of stars, the formulas of flowers.[26]

What emerges is the four-leaf sprout of clover itself, which really did
exist and was undoubtedly lucky and which I found long ago among other,
ordinary, three-leaf clovers at the foot of the graceful hulk of the Church
of the Intercession of the Virgin in the Moscow suburb of Fili.[27]

The clover was simply lucky, for, as Marina would repeat to me when
I was little, just as her mother had repeated to her, a four-leaf clover is a
good omen, a symbol of good luck; it adorns New Year's cards and mass-
produced lucky charms such as medallions and key chains.

The clover was doubly lucky because the humble miracle of its own
birth had led to the miracle of the birth of this poem.

As for "wreaths" and "apotheoses," perhaps they derived from the church
itself, so triumphant in its regal burgundy-red and white lace attire?

The Europeanized Naryshkin baroque[28] exemplified by the church at Fili was not to Marina's taste; its sophisticated secular pageantry, which lacked a certain ingenuity, was foreign to her. She preferred churches resembling communion bread to churches that looked like birthday cakes, which she found more hedonistic than spiritual.

Triply lucky was that "heavenly host in petals four" for having overshadowed so tall a bell tower in the mind of the poet!

Antokolsky's *Puss in Boots* at Vakhtangov's Third Studio

Marina and I set off for the theater. When we walked out of the house, it was a wonderful evening, the moon was completely round, and the cupolas of the churches shone so that they gave off rays of light. The evening was deep blue and white, the houses resembling snowdrifts with iron railings.

I was six years old, Marina was nearsighted, and it was too dark for us to make out the street signs, so Marina asked passersby. Finally she said we were there. We rang, and the door was opened by a woman in a black dress with a white apron—her name was Masha, and she helped us remove our fur coats.

We entered a large room, a bell rang, everyone rushed about, the lights went out, a curtain opened, and there on a bed lay a woman covered with a blanket. She was quite young. Suddenly there came a knock, and a crooked old woman entered and began drinking wine, while Kate (the young woman) watched her with lusterless eyes. The old woman spoke for a very long time, then she began to dance, and she danced so long that they closed the curtain, turned on the lights, and everyone began making noise and talking. Then a new scene began: I see a poor young man standing there, Puss in Boots next to him, very well dressed in fur pantaloons and a warm jacket. Puss rambles on about riches, while the young man barely listens. Then the two of them catch sight of someone outside the window. Puss says, "Let's accept him as our fate," and dives under the table.

The person, a gray-haired old man—he is the doctor—enters and walks over to the dancer Kate and calls to the young man, the miller's son, to follow. Just then Puss crawls out from under the table and says to the doctor, "My master is a very good person, so might I go instead of him?" The doctor says, "As you wish!" The miller's son removes his jacket, which the cat quickly dons, purring tenderly to his master, "So will you accept me someday?" Then waits for an answer. A kind of sorrow filled the master's eyes, but it quickly subsided, and he up and pushed both of them out the door. Then he climbed on the table and watched them leave.

Here the lights came on again, there was more noise and talking, and a few minutes later everything fell silent and the lights went out. Kate the dancer is lying on the bed again, speaking in a calm voice, "I won't let them in. No, I won't let them in!" And at that very moment they knock at the door. At which point the old woman—who had been sitting next to her, but fell off her chair and dozed off under the bed— gets up and opens the door. The doctor enters, bows, says hello, and pulls Puss out from behind the door. Without asking permission, they begin to drink wine and shout, "Viva Kate the dancer!" They all move and walk about silently and with few words, and all of this goes on for a long while. Then the doctor dons a priest's vestments, lowers Puss and Kate to their knees, and using his top hat instead of a crown, he marries them, and everyone says pleasant things. But a few minutes later the dancer says, "Oh, Lord, that isn't Pierrot, it's the cat, Puss!" And she collapses on the bed.

The doctor then scrambles up onto the table, where the wine is, kicks everything off with his feet, and disappears out the window. The cat runs up to the dancer, shouting, "Wake up, wake up!" She, however, continues to lie there, so he, too, jumps from the windowsill, making all the houses outside shake. The old woman tosses the doctor's top hat out the window after them as Kate lifts her head off her pillow. The end.

The audience started making noise again, started talking about what they'd just seen, while Marina and I went into a room where young female acquaintances, actresses, some actors, and Pavel Antokolsky, who had written the play, were. Yura Zavadsky arrived, looking young and svelte: he had curly, blondish hair, large eyes, thin legs and arms, and a round, but well-shaped face.

MARCH 15, 1919

Marina's first conscious encounter with the theater occurred—rather, almost occurred—in her early youth in Paris. At the time she was taken—no, infatuated—with Napoleon Bonaparte, ready to give her life for him, one hundred years after the fact. Like any passion that is not a vocation, this was an obsession and, like all obsessions, it soon passed.

Having read all the books there were about him in Moscow—of which there were no few—and having fallen in and out of love with all of his portraits, she set off for Paris like a crusader in search of the Lord's sepulchre to visit Napoleon's tomb and to pay her respects to Sarah Bernhardt, the acclaimed tragic actress who played Rostand's *L'Aiglon.*

The tomb horrified her with its cold polished immensity and with the deathliness of its marble, unwarmed even by the inscription: "I wish my ashes to rest on the banks of the Seine amidst the French people, whom I loved so much."[29]

No, the ashes of *Marina's* Napoleon were still on the island of Sainte-Hélène!

As for Sarah Bernhardt, she astounded Marina, not so much with her transformation into the Duke of Reichstadt as with her egocentric artistic courage. Sixty-five years old at the time, she had recently undergone a leg amputation and walked with the aid of an artificial limb, but still she performed! In an age of whalebone corsets that emphasized the female body's every curve, [Bernhardt—trans.] played a twenty-year-old youth in snug-fitting white leggings and jacket. No matter how majestic—in Marina's eyes—this display of obdurate old age, it nonetheless emanated grotesquery, and it too turned out to be a tomb—erected by Sarah to Rostand and Rostand's *L'Aiglon*—and a monument to blind artistic heroism.[30] If only the audience had been blind as well. . . .

Fortunately, there was still Paris itself, great satisfaction for the imagination and an inexhaustible history textbook set in stone for souls of all ages.

Marina's next, more enduring, contact with the theater occurred in the early years of her marriage. Both Seryozha and his sisters were students at theatrical schools and participated in studio productions. Their older brother, Pyotr, who died an early death, was a professional actor. All of them, like the young people around them, gravitated toward Tairov, were mad about Alisa Koonen, and could not imagine life without the theater. Marina contented herself with sitting in the audience, however small it might be, to partake of the general atmosphere of this passionate, joyous obsession.

The smaller the role, the greater the nerves it caused. Comical Seryozha just could not master his lines as one of the captured starving warriors in *Cyrano de Bergerac*: "If no one can supply my gastronomy with the where-withal to stir my juices, I'll retire to my tent—as-s Achilles did!" His "ass-Achilles" was the last straw for the already rehearsal-tortured troops.

On the whole, Seryozha possessed wonderful stage qualities, and viewers long remembered his performances at "Eccentrion," the satellite studio of the Chamber [Kamerny] Theater.

Among the relationships they struck up in those years, the most long-lasting turned out to be Seryozha's and Marina's friendship with the talented actor and musician Aleksei Podgaetsky-Chabrov, a restless, rhapsodic, emotionally unstable person and the unforgettable Harlequin in [Tairov's staging of Arthur Schnitzler's—trans.] *The Veil of Pierrette*. Marina dedicated her "Lanes and Alleys," written in the 1920s,[31] to Chabrov for his undying restlessness and because in an epoch bereft of gifts he once had brought her a rose.

Literally intoxicated by the stage and possessed by the vision of his own theater, independent of any school, [Chabrov—trans.] emigrated, like a sleepwalker led by his dream. His awakening brought with it loneliness, poverty, and disappointment. Having lost faith in the people and the times, he turned to God, the Catholics' God, moreover, whose elaborate spectacles of celebratory masses, stage sets of Gothic spires that peaked above the clouds, and otherworldly musical accompaniments on the organ had captured his imagination. At this point "the priests worked their dastardly magic"[32] on the unfortunate Harlequin, promising him—if he renounced Russian Orthodoxy for Roman Catholicism—not only the kingdom of heaven but a position at the Vatican library. Thus, Chabrov became a priest. They dressed him in a narrow cassock, in which he looked more like an actor than ever before; shaved the crown of his head (a landing place for the Holy Ghost); and sent him to Corsica, to the most out-of-the-way, most forsaken parish, where his flock consisted of a few furious old ladies and impenitent pirates.

He tracked us down in the 1930s, and every year or so he would visit us in Clamart and Vanves outside Paris, to spend a few days as our guest and vent his insulted and deceived soul through recollections of the bygone theatrical past and carefully expressed reproaches of the Catholic present. My parents pitied him greatly. What later became of him I don't know.

Thus, Marina's conscious interest in theater art was born of her phantasmal passion for the two Napoleons, the First and the Second, and the phantasmality of that passion conditioned the phantasmality of her interests. Her second encounter with the theater was at one and the same time secondary, illuminated not by Marina's own light but by a refracted source, and it was cut short by Seryozha's departure for the front. Her third and last [encounter—trans.] turned out to be real, for it at once solidified and concluded a whole epoch in her creative opus, her romantic period. That same romanticism, "nothing wavering,"[33] wandered the winding, snow-drifted lanes of revolutionary Moscow, leaving its unseasonably light tracks in poets' notebooks and on theater stages before dissolving in the time and space of great metamorphoses and events.

It all began with her encounter with a poet, with the very young Pavel Antokolsky and his very young and brilliant poetry, back in 1917. Pavlik turned out to be a playwright and actor as well, and he introduced Marina to his circle of friends, to the magic circle of Vakhtangov's Third Studio, which—for a time—embraced her.

Dazzled and embraced (if Marina as an artist was at all capable of being *embraced* by anything) because it was only a studio, not a theater; it was a quest, not a canon, which once achieved leaves well enough alone. But for all her absorption in the studio's members and their work, for all her romantic response to their romanticism, Marina was never abandoned by her underlying awareness of the disparity between "playacting" and the times or her own nature and "playacting." Hence the occasionally repentant, occasionally ironic tone of many of the lyric poems from her "Studio" period, the biting jest of her poem "To a Player," which opens the cycle *The Player*;[34] hence the organ-grinder singsong of several of her *Verses for Sonechka* and their parody of the form of "cruel romance,"[35] despite the (ever) intense feeling that begat these pieces. Of those channels probed by Marina in her creative work at the time, the "Studio" channel was her most festive, for it was comedic; it marked the last moments of festiveness and masquerade and the first and last comedic strains in her lyric verse.

. . . How sweet, how delightful they were in their youth, agility, inconstancy, impulsiveness, in their mettle and the seriousness—gravity, even— of their pursuit. But their pursuit was play. Play was their—adult—pursuit! I would hide quietly in a corner so as not to be sent to bed and watch them with total comprehension because I, a little girl, *also* played, *also* at fairy tales, just as did they. Initiated by circumstance to the world of adults, I quickly learned how to see through them, without them ever noticing me. Only Marina's friend Sophia Evgenievna Gollidei, the one for whom *Verses for Sonechka* were written and who was given to Marina "as a present" by Pavlik, acknowledged and accepted my sister Irina and me, especially Irina with her infantile tenderness, her curls, and her defenselessness.

Besides Sonechka and Pavlik we were repeatedly visited in those days by three Yuris—Zavadsky, Nikolsky, and Serov—and one Volodya— Alekseev, who soon after left playing behind for the civil war, where all trace of him was lost. Another person who has stuck in my mind, for her outer lack of distinctiveness and her inner kindness, was [Third—trans.] Studio actress Elena Vladimirovna (Lilya) Shik: her long nose and agreeable nature meant she always got so-called character (put bluntly, "old lady") roles.

Our visitors were constantly bringing or taking someone with them to and from our place, and our old-fashioned one-and-a-half-storied apartment with its inside staircase would be transformed into movement itself, an uninterrupted staircase that the studio players climbed up and down like biblical angels in "Jacob's Dream." In the winter we lived downstairs, in the warmest (and darkest) of the rooms, while in the summer we moved upstairs into the long, narrow cell of a room that was just under the attic with its single little window that opened out onto the flat roof of the neighboring carriage house. This room was Marina's favorite because at one time Seryozha had chosen it for himself.

> My attic-loft castle, my castlelike loft!
> Ascend! A mountain of handwritten drafts . . .
> "Your hand! Now bear to the right here!"
> That rain puddle leaked from the roof.

> Ensconced on a trunk, now feast your eyes
> On patterns of Flanders the spiders contrived.
> And heed not the idle assertion
> That women can live without lace. . . .[36]

What lace was not woven by the voices in that attic-loft castle, and what voices didn't that castlelike loft hear: what arguments, discussions, rehearsals, declamations! What quiet whispers! They were all young, and they spoke of the stage and of love, of poetry and of love, of their love for poetry, of their love for the stage, of their love offstage and without poetry. . . . It bears noting that for Marina there was no such thing as love without poetry.

She loved to listen to these voices, to the persuasiveness of their intonations and the persuasion of their words, to the truth that resounded in them . . . or the nonsense.

> And, practicing the artfulness of elders
> Self-recondite, like diamonds ebony black,
> I hear you out with tenderness and sorrow,
> Just like the ancient Sybil—and George Sand.[37]

"Ancient Sybil" was twenty-six years old.

And what firebirds of magical words and names flitted in and out of these conversations: *Princess Brambilla* and *Adrienne Lecouvreur, Famira Kifared* and *Sakuntala, Princess Turandot* and *La miracle de Saint-Antoine, Hadibuk* and *Syndafloden.* . . .[38] The names of Stanislavsky and Vakhtangov, of Tairov and Meyerhold, rang out in the present tense, pronounced with yet-to-be-tempered delight or momentary disappointment. . . .

Sometimes they took me along to the theater with them. I remember *Maître Pathelin*[39] staged in a building at the Zoological Gardens in close proximity to the predator cages; I remember, at the Moscow Art Theater, those enchanted children with their jingle-bell names, Tyltyl and Mytyl; I remember how Sugar broke his sweet fingers, how Bread, with a deep sigh, pulled himself out of the pan, how Grandmother and Grandfather appeared and disappeared in the pink-and-green candy-colored light of the footlights. . . .[40] I remember lithe—despite their angularity—figures scurrying about the stage in the manor house in Mansurovsky Lane, the striking colors of their abstract costumes, the pathetic images of marvelous, pale maidens with flowing—for some reason always black—tresses, who wrung their marvelous pale hands. . . ."[41]

What attracted Marina to the studio, besides the players themselves, that is, besides what always attracted her—her fascination for human relationships? Besides its "visual" properties, so removed from her own nature, theatrical art also contained her element, *The Word*. The difference lay in that for Marina theater *ended* with the play, with the text, that is, at that point where for all intents and purposes for actors it just began. The transformation of images imagined into images depicted was entirely their concern, not hers.

For the first time in her life she felt the desire to join her quest with that of others, to overcome the barrier between her own—fleshless—art and their art "in the flesh," to participate in the miracle of giving birth to a performance, to *see* her own work, not to keep it secret, and to make the covert overt.

Creatively she was capable of many things; she wanted to be capable of this as well.

Six plays—*The Snowstorm, Fortune, The Stone Angel, The Jack of Hearts, The Phoenix,* and *The Adventure* (later united under a single heading "Romanticism")[42]—were written by her for her friends. Two of them—*The Stone Angel* and *The Jack of Hearts*—even display (on the surface!) marked characteristics of symbolism—at the time quite to the taste of the studio players, which made it easier for them to play their roles.

All these pieces—highly effective theatrical pieces with brilliant dialogues—scored a great, polyvocalic (that is to say, booming) success when Marina read them to the studio players. However, not a single one of them was staged by them. Perhaps because the actors were not yet up to re-creating themselves, their own images, even their own appearance and personalities, on the stage. Perhaps they passed them over simply because they were incapable of comprehending that this had been given *to them,* that it was *for them,* and how important it was *for her* that her gift, her contribution, be accepted by them. She, after all, never said a word to them about this, predetermining for herself the vainness of her hopes and then, as always, drowning those hopes in her own pride and timidity.

For one reason or another, her voice never melded with the voices of the studio players, her words never sounded on their lips. What a shame!

This profound human and creative disappointment of Marina's emerged in her own hand as an epigraph to the last act of *The Phoenix,* published in 1922, Heine's "Theater is inimical to the Poet, and the Poet inimical to the Theater."[43]

Years passed (for Marina years spent in emigration, for the studio players years of self-realization), but she never forgot her "companions in that youthful time."[44] To them, two decades later, she would dedicate her major prose work, *The Story of Sonechka,* written after the death of Sophia Gollidei, in whose "reciprocal memory"[45] Marina always believed. As for the "players'" memory retentiveness, even in 1918 at the height of their friendship she considered it a "stage convention": "Starting with you, fiery Antokolsky, favorite son of passionate Muses, who remembers only that mine was the name of a Polish noblewoman; and Zavadsky, most memorable of all, who—through fault of fraternal frigidity and a network of other impediments—could remember not even that. . . ."[46]

May 1, 1919
We walked out into the street and encountered a celebration. We were walking down the boulevard. Suddenly we heard a military band. Marina said to me, "Alya, what wondrous music! That music, no matter where it's coming from, I love it." We walk over to the fence and see horses—beautiful, white horses—passing by. The riders were dressed in dark blue and light tones; their faces were simple. Some of them rocked slightly in their saddles. Some of the horses had red roses tied to their ears. Then we caught sight of the troops behind them. Ahead of them marched a drummer with a huge drum. All the troops' uniforms were dark blue. The drum's beat drifted off together with the music. Then we left the fence and set off again to wander down the boulevard. We heard the buzz of an airplane above. At first we paid no attention to it and continued chatting quietly. Suddenly it swooped overhead, scattering sheets of paper that swirled in the air like strange clouds. The pieces of paper fell everywhere, including the rooftops.

That evening we dropped in on the Balmonts, then went with them to the Palace of Arts, the former Sollogub[47] residence, where various poets were supposed to read their work. We entered the courtyard, which was like a garden. It had bushes that formed a prickly fence, and small trees along the front of the house. The Sollogub house itself was a bit yellowed, with white columns. Marina and Balmont approached the doors, we entered a small room and were helped with our coats. Balmont entered our names in a notebook. We went up the main staircase, where I saw a very tall wall clock. From the foyer we walked through a large, rather narrow room with red velvet walls and a large, wide window that looked out into the garden, and from there, up more stairs, into a wide room with a large circular table. A woman was pouring tea and offered us all some. Her name was something like "Roza," an actress. She had black hair, plaited from the front, and she wore a lilac-pink dress. Her eyebrows were blacker than any I had ever seen before. Her face was small and round. I caught sight of a gentleman with a pince-nez who looked a lot like Don Quixote, just as thin and tall. People addressed him with respect.[48]

The woman pouring the tea began in jest to read Balmont's palm, repeating the word "Apollo" over and over. When she finished, she asked, "Who wants to go with me to see the church?" Marina asked, "The Sollogubs' private chapel?" The woman answered, "Yes." We all went, and Marina said to me, "Alya. The staircase here has been worn down with the steps of real human beings."

The door of the private chapel was locked, and they opened it. We entered and stood in the choir loft. It smelled pungently of incense. I was lifted onto the railing and could see the semigloom below, a Gospel lying open on a small table, and a not-very-large chandelier up above. The walls were wooden with carved decorations. Everyone was silent except for Marina, who said, "A bit eerie in here, isn't it?"

Then we walked out and down a dark staircase into the house's public rooms. The staircase had wide steps, with bends and turns every minute. We entered a large room with a fireplace crowned with black winged lions, and from there we went into another room where a white, very beautiful, pensive sculpture stood. Marina called the sculpture Psyche.

The actress showed us her room. The room was ordinary, with a single window and a plain floor, and there was a piano. All the furniture was upholstered in red silk.

Finally, we went out into a large room with rose-colored walls. A lot of people were already sitting in their seats, and then everyone sat down. A fire burned in the fireplace.

A poetess sits down on a small sofa and recites verse in a plaintive, squeaky, barely audible voice. The poem is about how she sleeps at a cemetery gate, a cross hanging on her chest, but no one else has one, and about how she has a kind, soft heart, while the others' hearts have hardened. She reads and then walks over to the fireplace.[49]

Then a young man, almost a boy, the poet Sergei Esenin, came up. He read a poem about how the moon had jumped from the sky and turned into a pony, which he harnessed to a chariot.

Then Balmont began to recite, and he read about a worker, whom, I think, he wanted to pacify.

Then the gentleman resembling Don Quixote invited Marina to read her verse, and she got up from the window where she had been sitting with me and read a poem about how we—two pilgrims—had traveled the road of life, loved by God, and that we were not Your Majesty or Your Highness. She also read poems about Moscow and about Saint George and the Dragon.[50] Marina read in a firm voice. After the last poem people applauded, I think because it is embarrassing to be silent after a person has finished.

The actress was no longer dressed in the same dress. Now she had a little white hat on her head and wore a long white dress of heavy fabric with a black veil draped over it.

Once again, the poetess sat down on the sofa and read poems, which this time were considerably better than the first, about how she lived in a chapel that stood in the forest where no one ever went. She just kept sitting in the chapel and looking out the window.

Then another poet read a poem about how he was walking along a forest road at night when suddenly a small girl from a fairy tale whose name was Liuba appeared. At dawn she began to take her leave, and when he asked her to stay, she said, "I can't," and left.

There were still other poems which I do not remember, and there was also a soldier who gave a speech.

We left the large room for the foyer, but while we were still in the hall Esenin approached and started to talk to Mama. I was not listening and do not remember what he said.

When we came out of the Palace of Arts the sun was already setting, and Balmont's wife pointed out the moon—light, light pink—to Marina. We set off at a quick pace, almost running, through the courtyard, past small trees neatly trimmed in spherical shape. Thin new grass was sprouting everywhere.

In one of the small white annexes the windows glowed red with light, and Marina said that Countess Sollogub had been moved out of the main house, and that was where she now lived. The annex was surrounded by bushes.

We set off for the Arbat together with the Balmonts. Now we're at the Cathedral of Christ the Savior.

Suddenly a red streak flashed by overhead with a loud rumble, then sped by again, illuminating the cupola of the cathedral as if with sunlight. I was a bit afraid that a streak might fall out of the sky and kill me. Suddenly a pink cloud rose from behind the trees in the square up into the air toward the sky. People were standing wherever there was high ground, watching. There were lots of red flags. Occasionally soldiers with torches would walk past. Sometimes small red stars would appear in the sky, falling instantaneously to the ground one after the next.

Those fiery streaks were called rockets.

Marina kept saying, "Oh, we won't be able to go back in. They've probably already closed the main door!" Then she led me out into the square, and we set off for home down the boulevard, where new statues not resembling real ones had been set up, and after passing halfway down the boulevard we saw letters and numbers illuminated with tiny lights.

The letters and numbers were Bolshevik.

. . . The "former Sollogub residence," where according to legend the Rostov family from *War and Peace* had lived, became the Palace of Arts in the early spring of 1919 and to this day belongs to the arts: a small plaque reading UNION OF WRITERS OF THE USSR is fastened at its entrance. In 1918 the building had housed the People's Commissariat for National Affairs, the institution where Marina held the only job she ever held—more accurately, unsuccessfully attempted to hold—in her life.

The house is my childhood friend, the only one of my friends to have preserved its external features unchanged over the last five decades: then as now the antiquated mansion with the columned portico stood as a charming example of "Moscow" classicism, ever so lyrical in its austerity. Then as now it embraced and framed the main courtyard with the semicircular wings of its annexes. Only nowadays the driveway up to the main entrance has been paved over with asphalt, and the knotty, bushy crab apple trees alongside the main building have disappeared.

While the adults assembled, deliberated, made music, discussed, and performed in its rooms, which still resembled "private chambers" and were still covered with damask and cretonne and furnished in Empire style, we children played hide-and-seek in its cavernous basements and ran about its courtyard, which served as our first day-care center, our first summer house, and our first experience of the natural world embodied in the yard's little trees and shrubs, its flower beds gone to seed, and its clumps of burdock.

When nowadays on rare occasion I enter these gates, I involuntarily stop in my tracks: Where are we, the children? Why is it so quiet?

In those days the Palace of Arts was not just an institution, a concert hall, and a club, it was also a residence. In the summer of 1919 Lunacharsky, Rozenel, and two children—their son and a nephew—lived on the upper floor of the right annex. The two boys, no sooner had they returned home and heard our voices, slid down the stairs right into a game of "One-potato-two-potato. . . ." The boys were a bit more neatly dressed than we were and, more important, wore better shoes. So as not to stand out from the "general masses," though, they grabbed some rocks and scraps of metal and began in earnest to pull apart their shoes, then ran to jump and skip with us. In vain we waited to see if they would catch it for ruining their shoes; nothing happened to them at all.

The left annex—the very air in whose narrow cells seemed to be anise-tinted by the bushes pressing against the windows—was inhabited by "the house staff," who lived alongside the beginning writers, singers, and artists. The most amazing aspect of their rooms was the stoves, covered with ceramic tiles bearing allegorical pictures and mysterious captions, such as: "The elixir for old age is the grave," or "Better than thou have come here," or "If you love us, keep on walking," or "Foot washing is no time to drink."

Propaganda signs dried under the sun in the annex garden alongside some bizarre freshly painted plywood constructions intended for holiday and everyday Moscow street decorations, while roulades from Schubert's *Die schöne Müllerin* [*The Beautiful Mill-Girl*—trans.] poured through the open windows.

In the run-down little house that stood at the gates, the former mistress of the house lived out her last days, while her former serf—decrepit and half blind—lived out her last days in the noblewoman's former quarters: so it had been decided by Soviet power. Both old women, each leaning on her walking stick, would saunter peaceably across the courtyard to visit the other. Still other old women—some plainly dressed and bent over, wearing granny scarves, others straight-backed, with a general's attitude, rustling glass-beaded dresses and snapping folding lorgnettes—would trickle out of nearby side streets to visit them. The "serf" gropingly stoked the samovar, and while drinking carrot tea out of cobalt blue and gold teacups from a service that had not been entirely smashed to bits, they observed with detachment the comings and goings of servants and masters of the arts.

Maintenance services were located in the courtyard out back, the length of which was spanned by the furrows of a public vegetable garden, where a goat grazed, tied to a stake, and a piglet squealed in its "sty-ka." The same yard accommodated a family of Gypsies: the janitress Antonina Lazarevna, her husband (chauffeur, plumber, and master of all trades, formerly the Sollugub family's stableman), granny Elizaveta Sergeevna, and two children. All of them—young, old, and little—were kind, hardworking, and handsome, and that is how I would remember them. Naturally, Marina often looked in on them, and she even helped Antonina Lazarevna with the sewing in order to listen to her (Leskovian)[51] stories. She joked about writing a little book titled *Gypsy Fairy Tales*.

Here in this Gypsy courtyard the first director of the Palace of the Arts, futurist poet Ivan Rukavishnikov, conducted classes for Red Army soldiers, alternating literacy lessons with rifle training. He was red-haired and red-faced, dressed in something half military, half operatic, with a long silk scarf wrapped Calabrian pirate style several turns around his waist. His wife Nina headed the Moscow circuses; sometimes she would pick up her husband in a carriage drawn by horses retired from the arena. "Everything was all mixed up at the Rostov mansion," Marina used to joke. To Rukavishnikov's waltzing team of horses she would dedicate one of her short stories written in French, "A Miracle with Horses."[52]

She loved the palace, which in those years stood at what seemed to be the juncture of all arts (those on the wane and those in ascendance), and she liked the atmosphere of transitional intimacy at the concerts, discussions, readings, and literary evenings in which she so eagerly participated, together with the sparing traditionalism of the setting, which diverted one from the burdens and cares of daily life run rampant.

This same house with its columns was the meeting place for the first and last creative collective to which Marina Tsvetaeva belonged, and its polyphonic chorus included her still ringing and youthful voice soon fated to become a tragic "voice in the desert" of emigration.

The Challenge

I was writing in this notebook when suddenly I heard Marina's voice, "Alya, Alya, come quick!" I go, and there I see a wet worm on the kitchen towel. I am more afraid of worms than of anything else. She said, "Alya, if you love me, you must pick up this worm."

I say, "But I love you with all my soul."

And Marina says, "Prove it!"

I squat in front of the worm, and think: do I pick it up or not? Suddenly I see that it has a wet, herringlike tail. I say, "Marina, is it all right if I pick it up by the herring tail?"

And she answers, "Do whatever you want. If you pick it up, you will be my Heroine, and then I will tell you something."

At first I could not gather the courage, but then I took it by the tail and picked it up, and Marina said, "Good girl, good girl, now put it here on the table, that's right, just like that. Right here, just not on me." (Like me, Marina is terribly afraid of worms.)

I put it on the table and say, "So now do you believe that I love you?"

"Yes, now I know. You see, Alya, that was not a worm. It was the insides of a rations herring. That was a challenge."

Offended, I said, "Marina, I'm going to tell you the truth, too. So as not to have to pick up the worm I was prepared to tell you that I hate you."

MAY 1919

The culprits behind the "worm" were Friedrich Schiller and Vasily Zhukovsky, authors of *The Loving Cup.*

Who—noble knight or a simple soldier—
Will dive from on high into the abyss?[53]

I used to declaim as I marched back and forth across our kitchen, attempting to delay the inevitable time for my lessons. A reader's delight would overcome me, and I felt like a participant in the poem's story. More than a participant! I was the selfsame "young page" who had "already disappeared into the abyss."

"What *wonderful* lines, Marina! How *heroic*! And the princess who interceded for the page looks just like you! If the czar who threw the cup into the stormy deep had been your father. . . ."

"Then he would be your grandfather!" Marina noted.

"No, he doesn't have to be my grandfather. He need only be your father, and I would be the page, and I, too, would . . . , would . . ."

"I don't think you *could,*" Marina answered in complete seriousness as she surveyed with critical tenderness all my smallness and puniness, from the top of my head to the tips of the worn shoes which I, by now a full six-and-a-half years old, still had not mastered—which shoe went on which foot, that is.

"First of all, you are afraid of water. And not just water! What about all those creepy sea vermin and monsters! Remember?"

How could I not remember—

> Out of the fog a hundred-legged beast
> Crawls—mouth wide open—ready to eat
> A hundred slimy legs! Horrible and disgusting!

"I would still jump!" I continued to insist, the same fervor in my voice, but a chill of doubt now in my chest.

"You see, if I were that princess, or that czar, I would not allow you, or anyone else for that matter, to jump into stormy seas on just a whim. You prove love not by jumping off cliffs but with each day of your life: how you spend the day, what you accomplish, and how you accomplish it. You'll do better sitting down at the table to write your page!"

I sat down, never imagining that my "challenge" was not far in the offing, for Marina honored only declarations that were substantiated by deeds.

In the Village

Marina decided to send me to the village to spend some time with our milkwoman, Dunya. She herself would collect me later.

Dunya and I traveled by freight train. Several of our stops were very long. Then we had to walk about three miles from the station to the village of Kozlovo. Some women and girls walked ahead of us. They shouted back and forth to each other. Soon we came to an open field where we could see golden rows of rye. Everyone turned their attention to me: "Whose little girl is that?" Dunya replied, "The mistress's, from Moscow. She knows how to read and write." A little boy said to me, "Otter-puss! We'll make her do real work!" "Oh, yeah?" said Dunya. Nearby up ahead we could already make out the houses, knolls, and fences of Kozlovo.

We went inside the hut. It looked like nothing I had expected to see. A small half-dilapidated hut that leaned to one side, with thatched roof of dark straw. The windows were just as small and crooked. Inside there was only one room with a Russian stove and benches.

Dunya had five children and a husband. Her husband had a beard, he was very rude, and he spoke rudely to Dunya and the children. Once he started to beat Dunya and tried to knock her head against the stove. But I started screaming and grabbed him by his shirt. He kicked me aside and walked out. He snored terribly at night.

Dunya fed us boiled potatoes. Everyone peeled the skins with their fingers and added their own salt. When there was soup, we ate it from a large bowl, each with our own wooden spoons. The spoons were very clumsy, and at first I kept spilling soup all over myself.

Not long ago they took me to a place where they thresh grain. They sat me on a stack of hay and started beating the grain. I watched with great attention. The flails they used looked like whips tied to sticks. Small sheaves of grain lay on the ground, and everyone started to beat the ears of grain so as to eat them later. That is how you get grain and bread.

Sometimes we went into the forest to gather mushrooms and nuts, but I never found anything because I kept looking at the beauty around me.

On the evening of the last day of my lonely stay in the village a marvelous thick gray cloud with a cold golden lunar halo passed overhead. That night I woke up and saw the glow of the icon lantern. "Tomorrow is the Dormition," I thought, and fell back asleep.

I wake up early in the morning. Dunya is stoking the Russian stove. I look on my other side and see Marina's suntanned neck and curly hair. Her little suitcase and clothes lie on the bench; two cigarette butts lie nearby on the floor.

As soon as Dunya went out, Marina perked up and shook her curly mane like a ferocious lion. I kissed her gently.

Marina whispered, "Hello, Alechka. How are you doing?"

"Okay."

"So why did you rip the pages out of your diary?"

"To draw!"

"That was piggish of you," Marina answered. But after a bit she takes mercy on me and listens to my stories about Dunya's rude husband.

Our breakfast was very festive, because "the miss," as they called Marina, had arrived. They all said nice things to her and offered her sugar. Then Marina and I sat on top of the Russian stove for a while. We admired the shiny samovar and the clean, washed floor. Then we went and sat for a while in the wonderful garden among elderberry bushes and sunflowers at a table painted dark blue by the master of the house. Marina shelled nuts with her teeth and distributed them to Dunya's children—Vasya and Aniuta—and me. Then we each read to ourselves: Marina about the French Revolution and I a book called *Christian Children* that I had brought with me. The second and third days were just as monotonous, and Marina barely survived them.

Finally the time came for our departure. Dunya woke me: I was drowsy, not having slept very much. Almost everyone got up, even the husband who sleeps so soundly at night. The roosters let us know it was morning. I put on two dresses and a coat, and we headed out together with Dunya's oldest son Seryozha.

Within less than a half mile after we had set out I suddenly sank knee-deep into a puddle and started to snivel. We kept walking for a long time along a route that led through treacherous places. Puddles and ruts, still in total darkness. Seryozha walked ahead, Marina behind, with me in the middle. We wound our way through almost impassable swamps, Seryozha always managing to find a narrow path where we walked in single file. As we passed the threshing area, we saw that we were surrounded by morning fog that looked like steam rising from the earth. The sky was still brownish, but we had not long to wait for the marvelous picture ahead.

Soon we were within reach of the station. A line of fir trees stood swathed in white. Above them glowed a dark, very bright streak, thick and red. We kept walking, past someone's vegetable gardens. When we finally reached the station, I looked at the sky. A large piece of it was covered with red, blue, and gray streaks. Just then, for some reason, I started to bawl. Marina noticed. "What are you bawling about? Look at the sky instead!" I was mortified. The cold morning dawn gently hugged my face.

Freight trains kept passing by. The next-to-last train was loaded with the czar's automobiles, bearing the czar's emblems and insignia. They were very beautiful, with coats of armor on the hoods and doors.

The first passenger train pulled in soon after. We waited a long time for it to come to a stop, and while we stood waiting, most of the other passengers managed to climb on, leaving no room for us. We managed, though, to get on the next one instead.

AUGUST 1919

Our milkwoman Dunya would come to our door—canister in hand and a sack slung over her shoulder—from time immemorial until the horrible winter of 1919–20, when she just vanished. We never did learn what happened to her, whether she was alive or not.

That same winter my younger sister Irina died—the one who drank the milk: a little gray-eyed girl with a round forehead and wild blond locks who always sang "Maeena, my Maeena" (Marina, my Marina). It seemed somehow natural that the stream of milk that had nurtured her should dry up as well.

In the constancy of Dunya's visits, the humble resignation with which she accepted worthless thousand- and million-ruble notes in exchange for priceless milk she could have bartered for things (as all "the village folk" did) and the generosity with which she measured the milk into the pot, Dunya was akin to Marina herself, who was just as responsive and just as "impractical."

They had become friends each in their own way: the strange "miss" and the strange milkwoman. This friendship between two mothers barely required words. Marina had the two of us, and Dunya had three sons and two daughters. Marina frequently made Dunya gifts of objects from our chaotic household, while she—"don't take this the wrong way, don't turn your nose up"—treated us to smashed potato-wheat cakes or occasionally gave Irina a boiled egg squashed in the rush for the train.

Dunya's facial features were stern, but her expression was soft, as if she were listening to you, slightly surprised and guilty at the same time. How old could she have been? I don't know. Mothers' faces are ageless.

One time Dunya arrived at our place not by herself: Vasya, the youngest of her boys, my age, clung to her brown, tuck-waisted, puff-sleeved sweater. "I brought 'im to Moscow, ma'am, to look. He kept askin' me, 'what's it like, what's it like.' Moscow, that is."

"So, what do you think?" Marina asked. "Do you like it?"

The little boy was silent as a rock and never raised his eyes from his bast shoes until we sat down at the samovar in the kitchen, where he began to thaw, shaking and nodding his head. That was no regular samovar. Ever since Marina had tried to cook millet in it, the spigot had clogged shut, so we had to ladle the boiling water through the top.

After tea Vasya melted completely and started to doze off. Marina suggested to Dunya that she put him to bed. (The bed had a metal frame with little balls on the posts and a spring mattress.) The little boy cracked open his heavy eyelids, his eyes filled with his mother's half-amazed, half-apologetic expression. "It's the first time I ever slept on springs," he whispered.

Marina bit her lip. "Let him stay with us, Dunya," she said. "I will show him Moscow. . . ." And Vasya stayed.

Marina put my shoes on him and took him to the Kremlin and the Zoological Gardens, patiently explaining and telling him about everything.

Like me at the circus, Vasya kept looking in the wrong direction and at the wrong things. At the zoo he was more fascinated by the fence-ringed trees than by the animals. "Look at that: They even put trees in cages! Wow!" At home I took over, smothering him with books, toys, and my own superiority. After all, I could read, and I was a city girl! True, when he left, I gave him almost all my toys, even without Marina telling me to, and as for my urban superiority, it took only a few days, a few hours rather, in Kozlovo to prove that no one in the whole village was dumber than I was.

When Marina arrived to pick me up at Dunya's, she did not overstay her visit. She was incapable of "resting" when everyone else around her was working, but she also did not know how to do peasant work. Peasant, "patriarchal life" with its all-consuming Russian stove in the corner horrified and distressed her. Its backbreaking hardships could be offset neither by the wonderful outdoors, with all its sunrises and sunsets, nor by the songs sung beyond the river, nor by the embroidered towels that hung under the icons. . . .

There was one other common woman who, just like Dunya, was silently kind to Marina and dear to her heart: Efrosinya Mikhailovna Granskaya, the wife of the shoemaker Gransky, who lived in our courtyard.

The Granskys had a tiny, tidy half-basement cubbyhole of an apartment. In one of the rooms the gloomy shoemaker would tap endlessly away with his hammer. Sometimes he might be "un'er da infl'ence," and then his whole family—his wife and three children—would cringe, look over their shoulders, and keep their voices to a whisper.

No matter when you dropped in on them (the entrance was through the kitchen), the cat would be lying on the long brass waterspout over the sink, its paws tucked under its tummy, occasionally licking a drop of water that beaded at the end, while the shoemaker's wife bustled about doing housework: washing clothes, cooking, mending.

It was this little, unremarkable, ageless (like Dunya) woman who frequently came to our back door with a cloth-covered bowl of potatoes or cooked barley and pushed the food into Marina's hands, saying, "Now you eat it all up! And don't go thankin' me!" And when she sent her youngest daughter, the weak one, to the village to stay with her grandmother, she gave us the girl's ration card.

Generally, in those difficult years it was only women who helped Marina. Men simply never thought of it. Or only rarely!

A Reading by Blok

We leave the house in the evening while it is still light. Marina explains to me that Aleksandr Blok is as great a poet as Pushkin was. And her every word evokes in me the thrilling expectation of something wonderful. Marina sits in artist Vasily Miliotti's tiny "ark," looking at books. Miliotti himself is not there.

I am running around the garden. Signs announce: A READING BY ALEKSANDR BLOK, AT THE MUSEUM OF THE POLYTECHNIC INSTITUTE A READING BY PYOTR KOGAN.[54]
The atmosphere overall is one of celebration, just as on

Vorobyovy [Sparrow] Hills when the gramophone plays and flat cakes are sold under the trees in the lanes.

Finally, the artists Miliotti and Nikolai Vysheslavtsev arrive together with the poet Pavlik Antokolsky and his wife. We go to get tickets. We go in through the entranceway with the shells, where a silver idol with lance in hand beckons "To Blok."[55] We enter the pink velvet hall. All the seats are taken, but He is not there yet. Antokolsky brings us some chairs. No sooner do we take our seats than a whisper runs through the crowd: "Blok! Blok!" "Where is he?" "Blok!" "Sitting down at the table!" "'Lilac. . . .'" Everyone is delirious with joy.

His wooden face is oblong. His dark eyes are lowered, his mouth pale and dry, his face brown. He's all sort of long, the expression of his eyes, lips, his entire face is completely lifeless.

He reads the poem *Retribution*.[56] It's about a Byron—a real Byron—who charmed the younger daughter of an old noble family. And supposedly the daughter married him, and he took her away. One gloomy day she showed up by herself. Emaciated and exhausted, she held an infant in her arms. The son grew up, but instead of going off to war, he had a good time going to balls. One time at a ball, he learned that his father was dying in Warsaw on Aleja Roz. By the time he arrived there, his father was already dead in his bed. (The description of the father's appearance in his coffin coincides entirely with Blok's own appearance. The noble eyes are closed. The body is long and noble. On his finger—a wedding ring.) The son removed the ring from his father's noble finger and made the sign of the cross over his father to rest in peace.

Standing with the son at the grave is a woman in a black dress and mourning veil.

In the next section Aleksandr Aleksandrovich read about war, about soldiers, so many of whom died in combat, but they kept on coming, full of heroism, as the empress looked on.

He spoke in an even voice without modulation.

I think he also said that the son forgot about his father.

Then Blok stopped and finished. Everyone applauds. Embarrassed, he bows. The audience shouts: "Read a few poems!" "*The Twelve!*" "*The Twelve,* please!"

"I don't remember *The Twelve.*"

"*The Stranger! The Stranger!*"

"'A gray morning,'" Blok recites. "'Like a boy, she shuffled, scraped, bowed in obeisance. . . . Good-bye. A token-charm jangled on her bracelet. Some sort of remembrance!'"

(These lines have remained in my memory ever since those early years and will forever more.)

I don't remember any more lines in verse, but I can paraphrase them in prose: "Your face lies on the table in a golden frame before me. And my memories of you are sad. You left in the night, in a dark blue cape. And I remove your face in its golden frame from the table."[57]

Blok reads "*kolokol'tsy*" [bells] and "*kol'tsy*" [rings] with the stress on the final *y*. He reads stiffly, with reserve, not drawing out his words. Very severely and somberly. "'You coolly press against my lips your silver-silver rings.'"

Sometimes Blok forgot words, at which point he turned round and glanced at the woman and man sitting behind him, who, smiling a bit, prompted him.

My Marina, sitting in her humble corner, had a terrible look on her face, her lips clenched together as when she gets angry. Occasionally her hand would reach for the flowers I was holding, and her beautiful aquiline nose would inhale the scentless scent of the leaves. There was not a trace of joy in her face, but there was rapture.

It was growing dark, and Blok read with long pauses. Probably because of the gloom. Then a gentleman sitting behind us switched on the lights. All the light bulbs in the chandelier lit up, as did the huge lights, dim and fettered with thick glass, along the perimeter of the room.

A few minutes later it was all over. Marina asked Vasily Dmitrievich Miliotti to take me to Blok. When I walked into the room where he was standing, I at first pretended that I

was just strolling. Then I walked up to Blok. Carefully, lightly,
I pulled at his sleeve. He turned around. I hand him a letter.
He smiles and whispers, "Thank you." I make a deep bow.
With a slight smile he offhandedly bows back. I leave.

MAY 15, 1920

In Marina Tsvetaeva's life Blok was the only poet she revered not as
a fellow "craftsman of the lyre" but as a *deity* of poetry, before whom, as
before a deity, she bowed. All the other poets she loved she considered
comrades-in-arms, rather, she considered herself their fellow and comrade-
in-arms, and she felt that she had the right to say of each of them—from
Trediakovsky[58] to Mayakovsky—as she said of Pushkin: "How he honed
his pen quills sharp I know, With fingers never drying from the ink!"[59]

What is more, each of them—even the most incorporeal Rilke!—she
esteemed and considered brother in both flesh and blood, for she knew
that poetry was begat not by talent alone but by all the misfortunes, passions, weaknesses, and joys of live human flesh, through *its* painful experience and through its will and power, sweat and labor, hunger and thirst.
No less than her appreciation for the creative work of poets were her
sympathy for and empathy with poets' physical lives, "the confinement of
circumstances" or confinement by circumstance, through which life had
somehow to force its way to the surface.

Marina regarded only Blok's work as so heavenly lofty—not detached
from life but *purified* by life (as purified by fire)—that she in her "earthly
peccability" could not even contemplate being associated with it and could
only genuflect before it. Her poems dedicated to Blok written between 1916
and 1920–21 were forms of poetic genuflection, one uninterrupted "halle-
lujah," as was her prose about him, which she read publicly in Paris in the
early 1930s (the manuscript was never published and has not survived).

Just as readers of my generation spoke "Pasternak and Tsvetaeva," her
generation spoke the names "Blok and Akhmatova." However, for Tsvetaeva
herself any conjunction between the two was pure convention: she put no
equal signs between them, and her lyric doxologies for Akhmatova were
an expression of *sisterly* feelings at their height, and nothing more. They
were sisters in poetry but hardly twins. Akhmatova's absolute harmoni-
ousness and spiritual plasticity, which initially so captivated Tsvetaeva,
later seemed to her to be qualities that confined Akhmatova's creative

work and the development of her poetic identity. "She is perfection, and that, alas, is her limit," Tsvetaeva said of Akhmatova.

I recall how Pavlik Antokolsky brought Marina a present of Blok's *The Twelve* in a white and black ("Black evening, white snow") folio edition with Yuri Annenkov's stunning illustrations: still on the threshold to our former dining room, [Antokolsky—trans.]—his wild, coal-black eyes ablaze—began to read; he marked out the rhythm by punching the air with his fist; he moved toward us, blindly detouring around obstructions, until he ran into the edge of the table where Marina sat and from behind which she rose to her feet to meet him; when he had read to the end, Marina, in silence, without raising her eyes, took the book from his hands.[60] In moments of agitation she would lower her eyelids and clench her teeth so as not to give vent to the tempest brewing inside her, icing over on the outside.

The phenomenon of *The Twelve* not only shook her to her roots; in some fundamental way it made her feel ashamed as a creative writer, both for herself and for certain other poets. This is manifestly apparent in her prose dedicated to Blok, in particular [where she writes about how—trans.] *The Puppet Show*, which Blok had left beyond the bounds of the revolution, during the revolution in fact served as a shelter (albeit not long-lived) for a number of poets—including Marina herself, who at the time was working on a cycle of anachronistically elegant plays. . . . But

> Not the Muse, not the Muse, nor the perishable reins
> Of kinship, not your shackles,
> Oh, Friendship: Not by a hand womanly—fierce!—
> Has the knot on me been
> Drawn.
> The alliance—dreadful. In the blackness of the ditch
> I lie, while the Dawn is light.
> Oh, by whom have the weightless two
> Wings on my spine been
> Set alight?

In her poem *On a Red Steed* (1921),[61] with an encoded dedication to Anna Akhmatova that was later dropped, a complex image—dynamic in its iconographic referentiality—arises of Blok as "deified" by Tsvetaeva:

the creator of *The Twelve*, the Saint George of the revolution, the purest and most fearless Genius of poetry, and denizen of its heights, which Tsvetaeva considered beyond her own reach.

She saw and heard Blok twice over the course of several days in Moscow, on the ninth and fourteenth of May, 1920, at his readings at the Polytechnic Museum and in the Palace of Arts. She was not acquainted with him and she did not venture to make his acquaintance, which she regretted and also enjoyed, for she knew that only imagined meetings never brought her disappointment. . . .

Balmont's Anniversary Celebration

Marina and I arrived at the Palace of Arts knowing that today was an unusual holiday, the celebration of Balmont's anniversary.[62] In the garden as I lagged behind I suddenly saw Balmont, peony in hand, with [his wife—trans.] Elena and [his daughter—trans.] Mirra. Marina gets our tickets, and we go into the hall. Elena (as Balmont would say—Èlèna) has already taken her seat. Mirra signaled to me to share a soft pink hassock with her. Two chairs, blue with gold trim, were brought in, together with a third, an armchair, for Balmont. The armchair is placed in the middle.

Balmont enters, holding a notebook and the peony. His facial expression is formidable, leonine, and bored, as he sits down in the armchair, placing the notebook and the peony on one chair, while poet Viacheslav Ivanov sits down on the other. Everyone applauds. [Ivanov—trans.] bows silently, sits for several minutes, then goes over to the corner between his chair and the mirror, where, rocking the small chair, he begins his speech about Balmont, that is, the "Opening Speech."

Unfortunately, I understood nothing because there were so many foreign words. Viacheslav Ivanov's speech would be punctuated—occasionally by light applause and sometimes by the indignant whispers of those who disagreed.

I walk out of the stuffy hall for a moment and go downstairs into the garden to run it from one end to the other without cutting corners as I think about how people could live in damp, moldy basements like those in the Sollogub house. I return as Viacheslav Ivanov finishes, to emerge from his tiny shelter in the corner and firmly shake Balmont's hand.

Now I want to describe Viacheslav Ivanov. Vague, cloudy eyes, an aquiline nose, and a wrinkled yellowed face. A lost, controlled smile. He speaks with slight pauses, never jokes, knows everything, and is erudite—not so much in terms of reading and writing and such things, but educated like a scholar. He is calm, and he walks calmly and looks about calmly. He is not fiery but instead rather gray. . . .

The most touching part of the whole celebration is the Japanese woman Iname.[63]

When announced—"The Poetess Iname"—she emerged from behind Balmont's armchair, clasped her tiny hands together, and poignantly began her simple speech. She said, "Here I stand before you, and I see you. Tomorrow I must depart. We remember how you came to visit us, and we will never forget. You came to visit us then for a few days, and those few days. . . . What can I say? . . . Please come to visit us again, next time for a long time, so that we might remember for eternity that you—the great poet—had visited us."

Then Balmont said, "Iname! She did not know that I would prepare a response!" Everyone laughed. He got up, drew a small notepad from his pocket, and began to read a poem, something like: "Iname is pretty, and her name is just as pretty"—the kind any woman likes to hear.

Another woman, an English woman, got up, thereby indicating to Balmont that she wanted to say something to him. Balmont rose to his feet. The lady guest spoke in English. When she finished, Balmont took a bouquet of peonies and presented it to her. He would have done better to give the flowers to the Japanese woman who had delivered her tiny speech more simply, not as something memorized.

Someone said loudly, "The poetess Marina Tsvetaeva."

Marina approached Balmont and said: "Dear little boy Balmont! I present you with this picture signed by a number of poets and artists. It is the work of Vasily Dmitrievich Miliotti." Balmont squeezed Marina's hand, and they kissed.

Marina returned to her place, somewhat withdrawn despite the applause.

At that point, someone began to play on the grand piano: the music was so violent that the keys almost broke. The springs of the open piano sputtered and shuddered, as if in pain. Mirra covered her ears and smiled. I stood there entirely indifferent and remembered how I had seen the poet "Great as Pushkin, Blok." Not long ago.

The last to speak was Fyodor Sologub. He said, "We have no need for equality. A poet is a rare guest on this earth. A poet is Sunday and Peace Day. For a poet every day is a holiday. Not all people are poets. Only one in a million is a true poet."

When Sologub said, "we have no need for equality," the entire crowd spoke in a single voice: "We don't? Who doesn't? Not everyone! Not always!"

I was already thinking that this was the end, when suddenly Ivan Sergeevich Rukavishnikov got up. He held a poetry journal in his hands. He came out and loudly, almost shouting, recited his poem to Konstantin Balmont. When he finished, Balmont shook his hand. . . .

I go down the stairs and think, why wasn't there a nighttime celebration at the Sollogub House for Balmont, with fireworks?

Together with Balmont and his family we go home.

1920

How Marina's friendship with Balmont began I do not remember; it seemed as if they had always been friends. There are relationships between people that begin not at the beginning, but somewhere in the middle, and seem to have no end, were everything on earth not predestined to end. [These relationships—trans.] go on and on, skipping the initial, precarious period of mutual exploration as well as the final painful period of disappointment.

This linear continuum of friendship, uninterrupted and undisrupted (external disruptions are irrelevant; I'm talking about the internal), was not characteristic of Marina, who was not one to traverse beaten paths.

More often she would be passionately taken with people to such excess that she could not help but cool to them later, also to excess. (But what is "to excess" for a poet if not her natural condition!) She would raise them to heights too lofty not to succumb later to the temptation to cast them down. She adorned them with too many qualities and with virtues that they must possess without seeing those that they perhaps did possess. This characteristic of hers was not a woman's, for it was others she did up, not herself; like a man, she simply was, without ever pretending to seem, to look like, or to appear to be. This spiritual human undone-up and unmade-up quality of hers also concealed one of the causes for her misfires and separations and (the wellsprings of her poetry) the seismograms of her emotional earthquakes.

What engendered the friendship—so sustained, without rifts and ruptures—that bound these two particular poets together?

First, Marina's poetic imagination drew no sustenance from Balmont, who *already* was—just as Marina was—the *maximum* expression of himself, of his capabilities, and incapabilities. As did she, he existed only in the superlative degree, to which nothing might be added.

Second, the differences in element, scope, and depth that lay between their respective creative beings were so apparent that they excluded entirely any possibility of a confrontation: Marina demanded bigger, better, and stronger only of poets kindred to herself.

Both were poets "by the grace of God," but Marina always stood at the helm of her creativity and *controlled* the *poetry* of her poems, while Balmont was thoroughly subjugated by his.

No one before the revolution—with the possible exception of the first film actors—fueled as many legends as those engendered by Balmont, that darling of poetic fashion. For the young Tsvetaeva as well he seemed mythical and legendary. But the October revolution brought her together with a live, helpless human being—exceptionally busy but never to any avail!—whose star traveled with truly cosmic speed from apogee to perigee. This alone sufficed for Marina to lend her shoulder to his waned glory, his fated talent, and his impending old age. . . .

Balmont both resembled and did not resemble his legendary self: the refined gutturalness of his speech, the showiness of his poses, the haughtiness of his bearing, and the superciliousness of his upturned chin were hereditary, not acquired; he was always this way, regardless of the situation or the surroundings, under any circumstances, to the very end. At the same time he turned out to be unexpectedly flabby, thickset, and not muscular in build, his facial features soft and hardly as distinct as those in his portraits and set beneath a very high forehead—a strange combination of Spanish grandee with village pastor, with the grandee, moreover, prevailing.

Just as unexpected was Balmont's simplicity, his total absence of pretense, and the absence of wateriness or floweriness in his speech, which was concise, exact, and sharp. His speech was disconnected, as if he were biting the words off phrases.

Together with what was already almost an old man's vulnerability to life's hazards he had a carefree, youthful attitude toward life, come what may: easily offended, he brushed insult off like a large dog shaking off raindrops.

Balmont belonged to that rare race of beings with whom Marina as an adult was on informal terms in conversation but not in letters, as she was with, say, Pasternak, whom, at the time of their correspondence she barely knew, or Rilke, whom she never met in person. This informality, fraught as it was with the familiarity she so despised, was for her (except in addressing children) pure poetic license and convention but hardly a given of prosaic vernacular speech. Switching to the informal form of address with Balmont, Marina placed herself in an informal relationship with his hardships and difficulties; for her, helping someone else was always easier than helping herself; for others she would move mountains.

In the first years after the revolution Balmont and Marina read at the same literary evenings, met at the same houses. They often frequented Marina's great friend, Tatiana Fyodorovna Scriabina, the composer's widow, a beautiful, sad, gracious woman at whose house a small circle of people involved in the arts would gather. Of the musicians who frequented her circle I remember most Sergei Koussevitsky, who inevitably turned any conversation to the subject of Scriabin. Tatiana Fyodorovna's daughters by the composer had the same names as Marina and I. After her mother's death in 1922, Ariadna Scriabina, a teenager at the time, left Russia together with her Belgian-born grandmother and her younger sister. Twenty years later, the mother of three children, she became a celebrated heroine of the French Resistance, perishing, weapon in hand, during a skirmish with the Nazis.

The Scriabin apartment began its evolution into a museum before our very eyes. The family handed over to the government the composer's study, where everything remained just as it had been, in the same place, as when he had been alive. The museum's first occasional visitors began to show up in the large room whose windows looked out onto a courtyard garden with bushes of "bleeding hearts" that blossomed until the middle of summer.

Almost always and everywhere Balmont was accompanied by his wife Elena Tsvetkovskaya-Balmont, a small, thin, exalted creature with huge eyes of a rare violet shade ever directed at her husband. Like a vigil lamp before a miracle-working icon, she always glimmered and flickered near him. Marina would go with her to stand in lines, and she would harness herself to my children's sled to help haul frozen potatoes or rare heating fuel that turned up. When she received a two-ounce ration of rough-cut tobacco, she would measure out half for "Little Boy Balmont": he would fill his magnificent English pipe with it and smoke away in bliss; sometimes, to economize tobacco, he and Marina would smoke this pipe together, alternating drags, like Indians.[64]

The Balmonts lived two steps away from the Scriabins and not far from us, near the Arbat. Whenever you dropped in on them, Elena, covered in soot, would be puttering with the recalcitrant woodstove, and Balmont would be writing poetry. Whenever the Balmonts dropped in on us, Marina would be writing poetry, and Marina would be stoking the stove. When you dropped in on the Scriabins, it was clean, orderly, and warm, perhaps because no one there wrote poetry and the stove was stoked by the servants. . . .

When the Balmonts decided to go abroad—at the time everyone thought that it would not be for long, though it turned out to be forever—we had two send-off parties for them. The first one was at the Scriabins', where all of us were treated to potatoes with pepper and real tea served in impeccable porcelain and where everyone spoke touching words, bade them farewell, and kissed them good-bye. The next day, though, problems arose with their Estonian visas, and their departure was delayed for a short time. Their final send-off took place in a humdrum jumble of tobacco smoke and wood-burning samovar fumes at the Balmonts' apartment with all the chaos of a Gypsy camp pulling up stakes. Many people came to see them off. "Marina was the merriest of those seated at the table.

She told stories, laughed, and made others laugh, and she was very merry, as if this was her way of dulling the pain of their separation," I wrote in my diary at the time.

But heavy was Marina's heart when she made the sign of the cross over Balmont as he embarked on what turned out to be a journey of no return.

In emigration, which for Marina lasted from 1922 until 1939, the *intensity* of her friendship with Balmont remained unchanged, although their meetings occurred at considerable intervals up until the 1930s, when Konstantin Dmitrievich and Elena quit tempting fate with moves from place to place, country to country, and regretfully, like us, set down anchor in the suburbs of Paris. At that point we began to see each other more often, especially after Balmont fell ill.

It is difficult to imagine how sad his gradual decline was, how truly hopeless—intensified as it was by old age—their poverty was. Many people extended their help to him and Elena, but that help always proved unreliable and inadequate. People who were well-to-do tired of helping them, while the ranks of the poor thinned. All of this—their unrelenting poverty, their unrelenting helplessness—was encompassed by the offensive relentlessness of an alien, satiated, secure (and, moreover, well-heeled) way of life and living conditions. Shop windows that Marina walked past with true indifference drew Balmont like a child, while the ever-faithful Elena diverted him from those windows as if distracting a little boy.

Balmont's illness gradually dragged him from the surface of so-called life into the very depths of his own self, where he dwelled in his own wordless and inexpressible Oceania, unintelligible to others, in the chaotic protoworld of his own poetry.

The last time I saw him and Elena was in Paris in the winter of 1936–37 at the house of some friends. Balmont's carrottop mane had thinned and grayed, the gray lending it an unearthly pink tone. His gaze had lost its acuity, his movements—their precision. His head remained just as steadfastly unbowed as ever, despite the heavy wrinkles that pulled his face down toward the ground. He ate with businesslike detachment. Elena sat next to him, almost ethereal, straight as the staff she had always been for her pilgrim.

"Marina," Balmont said suddenly, imperiously interrupting the quiet conversation. "On our way here I saw a tall tree, round as a cloud and ringing with birds. I wanted to fly up there, to the birds, to the very top of the tree, but she [gesturing to Elena] grabbed me and wouldn't let me go."

"And right she did, not letting you go," Marina rejoined tenderly. "You're the firebird, after all, and the birds in that tree are just regular birds—robins and crows. They would have pecked you to shreds. . . ."

The Writers' Shop

"Alya! Hurry up and get dressed. We're going to the Writers' Shop to sell books."[65]

I quickly don my red velvet dress, the very best we owned, and my children's "tiger" coat. "Marina! I'm ready! I even have the blue kerchief ready!"

Marina walks out of the cold large room carrying books in a basket. The lighter ones she put aside in a kerchief for me, and we're on our way. On our way we check the time on the clock at the Nikitsky gates. "Alechka! It's twelve-thirty, and we'll get there just in time."

We approach the Writers' Shop. Marina crosses herself, although there isn't a church in sight.

"What are you doing, Marina . . . ?"

"Alya, what do you think: have I packed too many books for the writers?"

"Of course, not! The more the better."

"You think so?"

"I don't think; I'm sure."

"Alya, I'm afraid they buy them out of charity."

"Marina! They are honest people and will always tell the truth. If they're still buying them, it must mean that they are sincere."

Marina cheers up but enters with a certain trepidation nonetheless. She says hello with jauntiness and aloofness.

Someone pats me on the head. I raise my eyes in fright: in front of me stands a young man with a smiling face, Mikhail Osorgin, "the Italian," who translates books from Italian and works in the shop. "So, Alya, do you want to look at the cardboard kingdoms?" ("Cardboard kingdoms" is what he calls stiff sheets of paper with drawings to cut and paste together.)

"If we can, please."

While he extracted the "cardboard kingdoms," my gaze fell on Nikolai Berdiaev. He was a writer, too, and he had an illness that made him stick out his tongue at times. He, too, worked at the shop.

Berdiaev flipped pages and skimmed quickly through the books brought to him for purchase. "Yes, yes. [Tongue.] Yes. This one is a thousand rubles. This one—five thousand! Oh my! This play by Lunacharsky is six thousand!"

Various adults and children approach the counters, looking at the books and turning the pages. A peasant of about forty comes up to me, points to a children's book, and asks, "Excuse me, miss, dear, you can read, would this book do for Vasiutka?"

"Who is Vasiutka? Your son?"

"Yes, well no, my nephew."

"I think so. It's about two ancient Russian warriors, Eremei and Ivan."

"How much is it? Probably a thousand, huh?"

"No, it's only a hundred rubles!"

Smiling, the peasant heads off with the book for Vasiutka.

Swarthy Aleksei Dzhivelegov suddenly appears from nowhere. He goes to stand behind the counter and affably asks everyone who approaches what he or she needs. Those who come to sell their books and get sent to Dzhivelegov have a hard time. He did not pay much and terrified people with his appearance. Whenever she goes to the shop Marina always says, "If only I can avoid that Dzhivelegov!"

Today he is wearing a tall yellow fur hat and a short, woman's coat.

Marina is looking at books and has already made her way to the last shelf, when suddenly Osorgin asks her, "Marina Ivanovna, would you like to see some other books?"

"What other books? Do you have more besides these?"

"Of course, we do. Let's go, I'll show you."

He leads an astounded Marina by the hand. The building where we go was once a hotel. The entrance was on the street side. The staircase is wide and made of granite. Osorgin merrily tells Marina about the shop's warehouse and everything else about books.

At long last we enter a narrow labyrinth, a corridor, and I am amazed that Osorgin does not lose his way. He knocks on a door, and two men let us in. They were sorting and categorizing books, talking as they worked. I started helping them, putting books that have fallen on the floor back on the shelves and collecting boards in a box. Marina searches frenziedly for German and French books that she needs, handing them to me to put aside. Suddenly, under a mountain of dusty gray books I see one that appears to be decorated like a Russian embroidered towel. I tell Marina, and we both try to pull the beautiful object out from under the pile. The mountainous pile collapses, covering us with dust. Marina holds a beautiful calendar with depictions of young boys and old men, depending on the season. Setting aside several books and the calendar, we go into another room. It contains yet another mass of books large and small, albums, papers, book jackets, drawings, journals, sheet music, primers, enormous Latin tomes, books of French verse, and scraps from all corners of the earth.

Not finding anything there, we go down the corridor to the other end. Osorgin unlocks a hidden passageway and lets us in. It is a small room with a huge window filled with sunlight that falls directly onto a small desk with a large armchair piled over with books. Osorgin says with delight, "Starting this spring this will be my summer office."

Having surveyed the three rooms, we go back down. I race Marina down the stairs.

Now we are back out on the street. We return briefly to the Writers' Shop to pay for the books. Osorgin gave me the calendar free. We walk out into the springtime street still piled with snow.

That is how Marina does book business: she sells a few
and buys a lot.

MARCH 1921

In 1918, shortly after the August proclamation on the liquidation of
privately owned periodicals, Moscow's first and only Writers' Shop came
into being. A cooperative bookselling enterprise, according to founders
Boris Griftsov, Aleksei Dzhivelegov, Pavel Muratov, Mikhail Osorgin,
Vladislav Khodasevich, Boris Zaitsev, Nikolai Berdiaev, and others, it was
supposed to evolve over time into a cooperative press.

Initially the Writers' Shop occupied a small "facility" at 16 Leontievsky
Lane, badly damaged by shooting during the recent October revolution;
it had once housed a library, and the shop inherited shelves and books
from its predecessor. Toward the beginning of 1921, the shop moved to 24
Bolshaya Nikitskaya Street.

The only person working there who had no connection with literature
was, I think, the courier; the writers themselves managed everything else.
They sold books on commission as well as for cash. They searched for
books that had lost their old owners and sold them to new ones. They
selected rare books for placement in the Rumyantsev Museum, whose
collection laid the foundation for the Lenin Library. They sweated over
financial accounts. They lectured and spoke at the Studio Italiano, which
they had created as part of the shop. They worked as sorters, loaders,
appraisers, and what else DIDN'T they do!

Besides the printed word, at the shop one could also obtain handwrit-
ten manuscripts of writers and poets, handmade editions that came in all
sorts of paper, from vellum weave to wrapping paper, sometimes illustrated and bound by the writers themselves. Over the lifetime of the shop
over two hundred such editions were sold, including several of Marina's,
unembellished but sturdily bound with waxed thread and neatly written
out in block letters in red ink.

In the little store itself, with its unreliable and mysterious lighting, its
all too antiquated smell of upended books, and, mainly, the appearance
of the people who stood behind the counters (their clothing and their
speech) there was, as I now recall, something of the Russian *lubok*,[66] and
from the Western Renaissance, something at once strange and timeless.

However, Marina, who herself lacked nothing in terms of strangeness and timelessness, was not in the least attracted—rather, she was repulsed—by these qualities of the "shopkeepers." *Her* timelessness was a *dynamic* inability to march in step with time—either lagging behind (". . . Time: I never have enough!") or stridently rushing ahead (". . . for the only gift I stole from the gods was the chase!"), while the spirit (of classicism? of the academy?) that reigned in the shop between the second and fifth years after the revolution *resisted* the march of time, at very least through its unwavering *stasis,* and this, stasis, was thoroughly foreign to Marina.

She came to the shop only on rare occasions, principally for the sake of the meager earnings she made selling books or autographed editions she sold on commission. She never just "dropped in." She never visited the Studio Italiano, a sort of club that competed with the Palace of the Arts. The Palace—open to all literary movements, influences, and trends of the time, with it discordant evenings and discussions, in which she was an active and equal participant—was closer to her heart.

The "shopkeepers," for the most part, tolerated Marina, and she them; with the exception, that is, of Griftsov and Osorgin, they did not like her, and she, with the same exceptions, did not like them.

Her longest and most equivocal relations were with the writer Boris Konstantinovich Zaitsev: amicably hostile in Russia, they lost even the semblance of amicability abroad. At the high point of their relations, Marina was immeasurably annoyed by Zaitsev's virtues and he—by Tsvetaeva's vices, among which, by the way, he included all her creative work. He never forgave her her extremes, and she—him his golden-meanness.

Their relations were further complicated by the fact that Boris Konstantinovich and his wife Vera did much to assist Marina in the 1920s. But if Vera, whom Marina sincerely considered her friend, lent her assistance in total simplicity and generosity of spirit, Boris Konstantinovich's actions smacked of a benefaction that secretly censured another's (for him foreign!) misfortune and publicly condescended to it.

Benefaction—in all its (humiliating) nuances—never elicited from Marina the slightest sense of gratitude, perhaps because she all too often was forced to seek help from others when that help *should have* come of its own.

In addition, in emigration Zaitsev never forgave Marina her husband's "Bolshevism," which he interpreted as her own. For their part, Vera Zaitseva and her daughter Natasha, my friend, remained unprejudiced, and we continued to communicate across the fence-tops of intraémigré infighting.

I remember how once when Marina was reading one of Zaitsev's newspaper columns she said, "Sugarcoated sour grapes." Of Boris Konstantinovich's appearance she used to say, "He's got Dante's profile and Oblomov's[67] gut," although Zaitsev was relatively thin.

I do not remember a single meeting between Marina and the other founder of the Writers' Shop, Vladislav Felitsianovich Khodasevich, and she never mentioned any. In emigration they—the stoic classicist and precipitous neoromantic (both "Pushkinists" in their own mutually exclusive ways)—were at daggers drawn; however, toward the middle of the 1930s they closed ranks, each having come to recognize the poet in the other. They were brought together by the same law that lends poetry itself, for all its dissonance, a single direction. And they were both pleased that, as Khodasevich wrote to Marina, "they had met while still alive and not in some posthumous anthology," as happens all too often with poets who were contemporaries only on paper.

Their late friendship was most amazing, however, in that once having arisen and come to replace their former enmity, it was cemented at a time of great isolation for Marina, a period of great opposition from the émigré community where Khodasevich had set down roots, and yet he, at least in this instance, was able to rise above it all to his full human and poetic heights.

Khodasevich died in June 1939, shortly after Tsvetaeva returned to the USSR. She did not know and never learned of his death, and talked about him with me as if he were alive and showed me a poem of his she had copied into her notebook: "There was a house like a cave." Underneath it she had added the comment, "These verses could be *mine*. M. Ts."

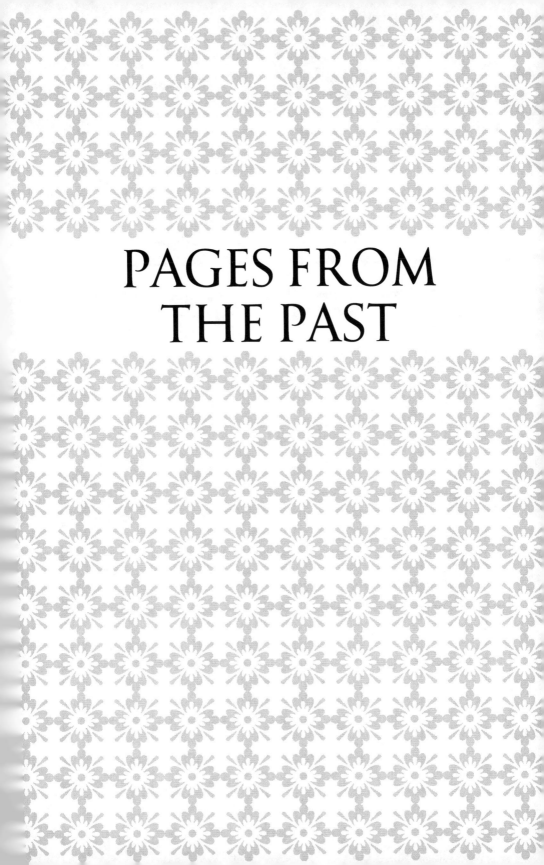

PAGES FROM
THE PAST

OUR LAST DAY IN MOSCOW

It was a typical overcast day of a Moscow spring long overdue. The spring of 1922. A gray, routine weekday[1] that seeped through gray windows last washed how many winters ago.

We got up early, Marina stoked the little woodstove and warmed up some kasha for me and a pot of coffee for herself. We gulped down our breakfast, and Marina set out for the People's Commissariat of Foreign Affairs, leaving me to care for a pot of boiling soup and the woodstove.

I slouched about the rooms, of which by that time only three were still ours: the walk-through dining room, half cast in shadows and lit only by a dim skylight in the ceiling; the little room with its one window out into the courtyard—Marina's; and the big room, the lightest, airiest, and least remarkable of the three, long uninhabited—the nursery. The upper half story of our apartment was occupied by new tenants whom I cannot recollect now because they were not part of my consciousness back then. In the fourth of our downstairs rooms—the living room—a hunchbacked corset maker, who was nasty and hypocritically saccharine with her clients, had taken up residence with her hourglass mannequin on its tall post.

In our half of the apartment there reigned depressing predeparture chaos, which had nothing in common with the vital, inexhaustibly mutable, at times merry disorder in which we—deprived of servants and bereft of their skills—had "kept" the apartment, or it us.

Now our things, until recently possessed of the attributes and drawbacks of weight, form, volume, and color—necessity-things and whimsy-things, habit-things and burden-things; things inherited, things purchased, and things received as gifts; sturdy things, flimsy things, chance things, comfortable things, ridiculous things, cozy things, and essential things, all of which had surrounded us and which we were now abandoning—seemed suddenly to have lost both their substantiality and the broken-in warmth imparted them through live contact with and service to human beings.

As for those things you would not call things insofar as they are more soul than things, there were: all our favorite books; Seryozha's portrait, painted by the Koktebel artist Magda Nakhman; Grandmother's music box; the bust of a wounded Amazon (precursor to Tsvetaeva's forthcoming tragedies on classical themes); my parents' wedding icon (known as "Grandfather's blessing"); a stereoscope with hundreds of Moscow and

Crimean slides—"Linger on, thou art so fair!"[2]—depicting my parents in their youth and their friends at different ages and all the pretempest care-freeness of years now faded from memory! There were Marina's childhood notebooks with her first poems, including—

> Fly afar, my stallion prancing,
> Over field and over dale,
> Flourishing your mane fantastic,
> Take me to that other place![3]

—Marina's infant Pegasus (then still but a pony) that I so loved when I was little; with her sweeping, angular drawings (a little girl falling down stairs with a treacherous bucket of slops at the bottom!), and with album-sticker vignettes on embossed and glossy paper. . . . All of this and much more—or at least part of it, whatever she would choose to take—was supposed to be picked up by Mama's sister Asya, who was out of town at the time.

Our baggage (a small trunk of manuscripts, a suitcase, and a plaid traveling bag) except for the woven oval basket with our "travel household" was packed, strapped, and standing at the doors to the dining room.

What did we take with us? Here is a list that survived in one of my mother's notebooks:[4]

> List (of valuables to take abroad)
> Pencil holder with portrait of Tuchkov IV
> Chabrov's porcelain inkwell with drummer boy
> Lion plate
> Seryozha's tea-glass holder
> Alya's portrait
> Sewing box
> Amber necklace

(in Alya's hand)

> My Felt Boots
> Marina's leather boots
> Red coffeepot
> Blue mug (new)

> Primus stove, needles for Primus
> Velvet lion

The velvet lion as a victim of fire singed by the candles at my first Christmas tree lighting was my absolute favorite stuffed animal. The lacquered pencil holder with the portrait of the young general of 1812, the heavy earthenware plate with its golden brown full-maned "king of the jungle with the face of Max Voloshin" slinking through a ring of floral ornament, the silver tea-glass holder with Seryozha's initials (Marina's wedding present to him), and the amber necklace (crudely honed archaic "wheels" the color of dark beer, strung on a coarse waxed string) acquired, instead of bread, in a barter she made somewhere near Ryazan during a year of famine, were inseparable from Marina and traveled with her everywhere—to Germany, Czechoslovakia, France—and in 1939 returned with her to Russia, where they perished during the war. At some point along the way the porcelain inkwell with the drummer was given to someone as a gift.

Also traveling with us were: Marina's favorite plush blanket (the last present she had received from her father), some handmade wooden toys (a present for Ehrenburg), and the first Soviet children's books, among them a wonderful illustrated primer. The rhyme for the letter *I* was

> With his broom of steel Ilyich
> Sweeps the filth into the ditch . . .

and the illustration showed Lenin in janitor's apron, giant stick broom in hand, sweeping little uprooted, somersaulting figures—czars, generals, and capitalists—into the gutter.

Of our clothing and shoes almost nothing remained: everything was either worn out or sold or given away, so that we now took very little with us: just my new (for spring! for the trip abroad!) felt boots (listed in capital letters among our "valuables") and Marina's multicolored ornate Tatar leather boots.

I kept adding wood to the little stove and water to the boiled-down soup, poking the meat with a fork: the horsemeat was tough and refused to soften.

To brighten Marina's spirits a bit—she was so care-laden and tired of late—I decided to prepare a "surprise" for her: I put my rubber squeak doll (the same color red as the horsemeat) into the soup pot and imagined how Mama would fish it out with the ladle and how funny it would be. . . .

A knock came at the door. No, it wasn't Marina. It was Maya Kudashova and Marusya Grinyova. Maya was one of Voloshin's recent (but perpetual!) pupils and Marina's not-very-long-lived friend, who soon left for France and later became the wife of writer Romain Rolland. Marusya Grinyova (the second wife of Asya's husband Boris Trukhachov) had arrived with her small daughter Irina, who was Asya's son's half sister, yet—to my unceasing astonishment—of no relation to me.

In an attempt to distract our visitors I told them stories and showed them our books, but Maya soon grew bored and left without waiting for Marina. Finally, Marina rapped at the door with her sharp, impatient knock, and I ran to open up. Marina entered with a determined stride, all concentration and tension. "Oh, Alya, I couldn't care less about Mayas!" she responded to my "report." "The train leaves at 5:30. Hello, Marusya! Let's eat, quick."

We spooned up our soup cooled with the morning's leftover kasha. Marusya spoke touching, heartfelt words that shattered into pieces upon contact with Marina's concentration, and asked us to pass on to Seryozhenka that she loved him and thought of him often. Marina answered in monosyllables. When, as she ladled out the meat and found my "surprise," she looked at it without a smile, then tossed it off to the side, commenting, "How stupid!" The only one to laugh at my joke was Marusya; her daughter, who felt sorry for the doll, first pushed her plate away and then started bawling at the top of her lungs, in earnest and without letup.

Marina sent me off to the Scriabins' to get Aleksei Chabrov (who lived at their place) to bring him back right away. I set off down streets I knew by heart—Borisoglebsky Lane, Nikolopeskovskaya Street—across Sobachya Square and past the fountain with its quietly gurgling streams shot from flat-muzzled lion faces, past sleepy houses, and round, still budless trees, and all of this, though I took it in with my own eyes, no longer belonged to me.

At the Scriabins' I pecked Mara on the cheek: only yesterday she had been a girlfriend; today in some strange way she was no longer mine. Chabrov, who had been waiting for Marina's call, was ready. The two of us set off.

Marusya Grinyova and Irina had already left. Marina, who was pack-ing our "travel household" into the basket, flashed a smile at the sight of Chabrov with his demonstrated readiness to be of assistance.

In a letter written not long before, in March, Marina described him to Ehrenburg:

> . . . Chabrov is my friend: smart, sharp, with an appreciation for the comical side of things . . . , with a wonderful under-standing of poetry; very quirky, always in love with the most unexpected things and always with a passion! A friend of the deceased Scriabin.
>
> I drop in on him once . . . , he's stoking the stove, and we have coffee and needle each other over our respective depar-tures—
>
> "So, how is yours?"
>
> "And how is yours?"
>
> —our talk never serious. But he is a gentleman, capable, when necessary, of living the pampered life, and I—what am I?—not even a bohemian.
>
> He has a remarkable face with eyes like hungry holes that burn with a fire that is (not male, but, perhaps?) satanic, a shiny forehead, and the snarl of an Englishman. . . . [5]

Having poured our last guest the last of our soup, I for some reason decided to wash the dishes we were leaving behind. Gulping down his soup, Chabrov went to hail a cab. He returned soon after, announcing, "That's it." We rushed about, putting on coats and checking for the umpteenth time that we hadn't forgotten something really important. Then, to focus our-selves before the trip, we sat down—whoever wherever—and in keeping with tradition observed a moment of motionless silence. "God be with us!" Marina said, and grabbing our things, we hauled them down the stairs.

The cab was waiting in the courtyard. (The horse was dappled and looked very merry, which made me happy.) We set our bags on the floor-boards and squeezed in. Chabrov had to follow us in a second cab, because the open carriage seated only two.

"Giddyap!"

As we passed the white walls of the Church of Saints Boris and Gleb, Marina said, "Cross yourself, Alya!" and then crossed herself. She kept crossing herself the rest of the way every time we passed a church, bidding farewell to Moscow.

At Kudrinskaya Square we checked the time: four o'clock. "Alya! We're not late, are we?"

"No, Marina!"

We ride in silence, looking this way and that at familiar but now unrecognizable streets, lanes, and alleys, which slip away as if in a dream, dimly and evenly illuminated by the monotonous overcast afternoon light, at the rare pedestrians, at oncoming carriages, and at everything that—there it is, right over there!—then quickly falls behind.

Third Meshchanskaya Street: "Alya, we're late!"

"Come now, Marina!"

Finally, Windau (now Riga) Station—an elongated structure with a multitude of festive windows—which, I thought, could be a Moscow country estate, if you took away the passengers. A porter grabs our humble baggage, and we approach the commandant, who checks Marina's documents and issues us a pass.

Our platform is not very crowded and not very talkative: no shouting or pushing, although the train has already pulled in.

Alongside one of the train cars among a handful of well-wishers (not ours) I see the familiar face of a pleasant young woman, a secretary at the People's Commissariat of Foreign Affairs who had helped Marina with predeparture formalities and complications. She smiles at us, squeezes her way along with us behind the porter into our compartment, which is very cramped and very polished and where two other women are already seated. Next to one of them—modestly dressed, hair pulled back—leans a pair of crutches; I can see that her leg has been amputated. . . . We walk back out onto the platform. "Who is that lady with the crutches?" I ask the secretary. "That lady? That lady works for the Cheka.[6] She lost her leg during the civil war and now she is going abroad for treatment: they will make an artificial leg for her, just like a real one. For a man losing a leg is difficult, but for a woman it is simply impossible. . . ."

Chabrov reappears at that moment, beaming and carrying a longish, beautifully wrapped package in his arms, which he hands to me: "This is for your trip: unwrap it when the train pulls out."

The adults talk, as I climb in and out of the car, wracked with fear of leaving without Mama or, if I dawdle, of being left behind on the platform, again without Mama. . . .

The first bell. They only call it a bell, when in fact it is really a person I cannot see striking the fateful bell whose sound wrenches people departing from people seeing off, taking us all aback momentarily, like a huge gulp of ice-cold water, and forcing us to awaken from the protractedness and prolongedness of parting by declaring it separation.

Final kisses, hugs, instructions, a last momentary scurry at the train car's steps, and now only those seeing us off are left on the platform, while we crowd in the narrow corridor, pulling collectively at the window sashes in order to look out one more time and say something, hear something, to be *in time* to do something.

Standing on his tiptoes, Chabrov hands us a note: "I just heard that Isadora Duncan is traveling in your car."

The third bell. The train pulls out.

I unwrap Chabrov's package: a box of candy with a brunette flapper on the cover. "How touching," Marina says, grabbing the box before I manage to stick my nose inside. "We'll save those for Papa."

That was how we left Moscow: quickly, without fanfare, as if we were suddenly disappearing into thin air. . . .

BERLIN

The trip from Moscow to Berlin lasted more than four days, including a day spent in Riga waiting for the train to Berlin. Inside the train car we quickly found out that the Isadora Duncan Chabrov had promised was not Isadora but only her companion accompanying her baggage out of Russia. As for the acclaimed dancer's baggage, it consisted of eight hefty trunks whose contents never ceased to perplex customs inspectors at every border: implements from a vanishing Russia, not colorfully painted or antique or museum quality, just a lot of broken junk: cracked ax-hollowed troughs, dried-out wooden buckets, oven forks missing their prongs, hole-ridden baskets, chipped mugs, metal pots, and more of the like unlike anything else. Perhaps this was her way of remembering Esenin's peasant origins. . . .

In Riga one of our fellow passengers, a rather short, very modest young man who turned out to be [People's Commissar for Foreign Affairs—trans.] Georgy Chicherin's private secretary, [Boris Korotkin—trans.], accompanied us to the Soviet legation, where we and other "transit" passengers were promptly offered shelter between trains. He also took us for a tour around the first non-Russian city I had ever seen. I was struck by the stark, gaunt silhouettes of the antiquated houses capped with smoked tiles; by the intense Gothic style of the cathedrals whose spirituality was almost inhuman; by the blunt elegance and ingenuous cacophony of the signs—all those wrought-iron keys, pretzels, spurred boots, gloves, beer mugs, and hats—suspended vertically because of the narrowness and close quarters of shops and stores, one abutting the next. No less amazing, albeit in a different way, was the massiveness and ostentation of modern structures in the business districts, whose matter-of-factness and complete practicality overwhelmed and nullified the mannerism, even playfulness, of the art nouveau style in which they had been built.

The gardens, squares, and parks were green with well-organized, picturesque, manicured greenery. . . .

Marina had a hard time taking it all in. Her controlled anxiety, her nervous fever, had not abandoned her. Holding on tight to my hand, she passed as if in a dream through the array of houses, shop windows, and people. Nothing we saw held her attention, although ever since childhood she had loved the multilayered Gothic landscapes of Western cities, and she generally enjoyed revisiting what she had seen no less than encounters with the new.

We ate dinner—which hinted barely of meat and strongly of split peas—in a pathetic half-basement greasy spoon. Marina drank a cup of coffee. . . .

In the evening, when it was already near dark, we set off for the station, claimed our things at baggage storage, and got on the train for Berlin—not in sleeping compartments but in second-class coaches—and only here, for the first time during the trip, did Marina finally close her eyes. Until then, no matter what time I woke up, I saw her sleepless profile set against the background of the black windows, a large white moon rolling along outside.

The morning brought views of Germany that flew past our windows like flipping pages, as shiny and quaintly tidy as the illustrations in

Grandmother Maria Aleksandrovna's children's books, a whole cabinet of which remained in my room back in Moscow. Just as strangely and anachronistically quaint and tidy were the costumes of the country people (one wanted to call them "yeomen") who worked in their compartmentalized fields, gardens, and orchards—and the fields, farms, villages, and towns themselves that floated past only to reappear around the bend.

Tidiness and more tidiness is what staggered our imagination in the towns of Germany after familiar Moscow with its then immense unkemptness, its territorial sprawl and urban whimsicality, the inexplicable harmony of its architectural incongruities.

(Fifteen years later, in 1937, on the trip back home I would revisit all this in reverse order: these very same, yet quite different, passing landscapes and cities of Germany. Having already shed their snow but still not bedecked by spring, they stood in flat relief under the low-hanging, murky sky, and they no longer reminded me of the illustrations in Grandmother's book. Everything animate, varicolored, living or alive was encased in iron and tin; the doll-like figures of the "countrymen" had disappeared, replaced by "toy soldiers" that were hardly tin, dressed in the funereal uniforms of undertakers. Town halls and individual buildings, small depots as well as large train stations, were draped with quarantine signs warning of some epidemic and with flags bearing black swastikas against a white background. As for "tidiness," by that time it was on the verge of becoming pathological.)

Finally, the train reached Berlin, making stops at three stations: Alexanderburg [*sic*], Zoo, and Friedricherburg [*sic*].[7] We got off at the fourth stop, Charlottenburg. A porter dressed in green agilely carted our effects to a cab.

The day—May 15, 1922—was sunny; the large, dignified, austerely elegant city rolled out before us in broad streets and massive houses in massive ivy finery that crept up walls and along balconies. Pragerplatz with the pension[8] where the Ehrenburgs lived (rather, slept at night) and the café Pragerdiele (where they spent their days) turned out to be a cozy little square, or minisquare, like our Sobachya Square in Moscow, foreign style.

By coincidence, just as we were hesitantly scrutinizing the doors of the pension, they swung open, and there on the threshold—in a wide-brimmed skimmer and with his invariable pipe—stood Ehrenburg himself. Almost colliding, he and Marina looked at each other in astonishment, burst into laughter, and embraced.

"So, hello, Ilya Grigorievich! Here we are . . . !"

"How was the trip? Is everything all right? No, questions later. Let's take your things!"

Going up in the elevator, we quickly found ourselves in Ehrenburg's large, dark, book-strewn room, which he immediately placed at our complete disposal and which we occupied up until his departure for the seaside town of Binz on Ruegen Island. Marina's friendship with Ehrenburg—like most of her friendships of the personal, not epistolary variety—was not long-lived, but it was more reciprocal than many of the others. Attracted by strength, Marina nonetheless not rarely inclined to weakness as a sort of temporary channel for her floods and excesses. Drowning feeble souls in her bounties, she discovered in them her own treasures, relished them and praised them, but the river bottom was always close, always too close, and these relationships dried up, leaving only the poems, which by then had forgotten the source that had spawned them.

For fairness' sake it should be said that some of these souls were feeble only by comparison with Marina's might, that in *their own* (generally recognized) dimensions they turned out to be not that shallow, but this mattered little to Marina with her "immensurability by means of measures"![9]

Marina's friendship with Ehrenburg was the friendship of two mutually (almost) impenetrable forces. Marina was impervious to Ehrenburg's rationalism (present even in his fantasy writing) as well as to the journalistic breadth that his creative work had acquired already in the 1920s, just as he was immune to the cosmic chamber quality of her lyric poems, to the simple ethnic (simply ethnic!) qualities of her *Czar-Maiden,* and to the greater Russian, legendary, national-heroic strain that runs through her poetry, including the Russianness of her language, to which he remained respectfully deaf all his life.

Later their mutual inconsequentiality (not to mention circumstances in general)[10] led them apart, but initially *it* was precisely what helped their friendship become a friendship. The relationship between the Ehrenburg of long ago and the Tsvetaeva of long ago was truly comradely and productive—each demanding nothing of the other—and filled with true concern and amazing tenderness. I am not contradicting myself: there was a time in Ehrenburg's evolution as a writer and as a human being when his mounting intransigence could not help expressing itself in softness, his irony in tenderness, albeit at the same time his pen was acquiring the edge of a scalpel, his voice—the intonations of the dais, and his thought (having rejected individuality) was attempting to embrace the breadth of humankind in general. . . .

In his memoirs *People, Years, and Life*, in the part that concerns Marina[11] not a hint remains of Ehrenburg's former tenderness: probably, the memory of such "tonalities" in relationships simply dissipates with time.

I cannot recall Ehrenburg's first appearance in our house in Borisoglebsky Lane (1917–18, to judge by what he wrote); I know only that at age five, I, naturally, was still not familiar with Blok's love poems, and our large, sprawling, but comfortable apartment had yet to acquire the shipwrecklike disorder that shocked everyone who entered it at the beginning of the 1920s.

It was precisely at that time that Ilya Grigorievich arrived from the Crimea and came to Marina with news of Max Voloshin and his mother, my godmother; through Ehrenburg's strident goodwill toward us shone glimmers of Voloshin's memory of and concern for the entire Tsvetaeva-Efron family, which he loved so much (and for so long) and which responded to him in kind.

Leaving to go abroad in 1921, Ehrenburg promised Marina that he would seek out her husband—who at that time was already in emigration—and deliver our letters and photographs and her most recent poems to him.

My childhood notebooks contain notations from February through March 1921. Here are some excerpts:

Ehrenburg's Heart of Gold

I am ill and sitting in bed, and Marina is preparing food. A short, sharp rap at the door. Someone enters. "Hello, Marina Ivanovna!" Marina says hello and offers him a chair. "Yes. . . . You live here now? The other room was better!" I understand that it is Ehrenburg. "A strange place you've got here! So many useless things!"

Marina sits at the table and laughs. "Ilya Grigorievich, you'll forgive me, but I have copying to do. I just happen to be copying some poems for you. . . ."

Ehrenburg offers to read his "portrait of Marina."

She listened very meekly: "A small, narrow lane, two large trees opposite the entranceway, a small staircase with wobbly banisters. A mass of unnecessary things, like you'd see at your old aunt's or an antique dealer's. She resembles a schoolgirl," and so on. Then he reads his portrait of Valery Briusov: "A wide low-ceilinged room with numerous images of Sukharevskaya Square.[12] The master of the house himself is an inhospitable 'Russian American' . . . who spends his time taking apart the gramophone and various other machines. . . ." Then I showed Ehrenburg my drawings. He praised them and for some strange reason asked for explanations. . . . Soon after, he left. . . .

We set off [for the Ehrenburgs'—trans.] through the slush and the mush and genuine puddles. Intricately intersecting side streets led us to the "Kniazhy dvor," a hotel-dormitory where the Ehrenburgs settled upon returning from the Crimea. . . .[13] We go up the granite stairs to room 49. We knock. "Come in." My God, Ilya Grigorievich and all those people here! Eight of them! Ehrenburg is in a very jolly mood and gives me a whole stack of sketches he has done. I kneel at the table and admire them. *Heaven and Hell.* On the border between heaven and hell stands a large golden throne. On the throne sits God. Men, women, children, and dogs stand before him. In hell the sinners sit in tubs of boiling tar and weep. Devils with red whiskers and green eyes run about brandishing smoldering pieces of firewood. Next is a picture with a different God standing with his hands at his side. . . . A woman with huge feet and a rose at her neckline stands just above his head. . . . The third picture is *The Cabman and His Horse.* They are surrounded by a ring of imagist visions: flying houses and standing birds, everything in reverse. In the middle stands an old cabman with his horse. . . . There is one more picture, a large one: the Virgin Mary, in a charming yellow dress with black stars. . . . Alongside her stands a crane, its beak raised toward the moon as a snake wraps itself around its legs. . . .

Having looked at the pictures, I began watching the people. There is this one woman with a mean little face, in a white sweater, looking over Ehrenburg's shoulder and running her fingernail along a picture and saying that if he just added a bit of red and blue paint, it would be just wonderful. There on the sofa sits a woman with curly locks, diligently drinking her tea. Ehrenburg's wife is wearing a "stylish women's dress." She has short black hair and thin, well-spaced fingers with shimmering, glasslike nails. . . .

Ehrenburg sits down next to me and asks, "So, Alya, do you like my pictures?" "Oh, yes, Ilya Grigorievich!" Thinking for a moment, he pulls out the Madonna in the golden dress . . . , grabs a pencil, and begins to write: "To Alya. *The Madonna with the Golden Heart*. Ilya Ehrenburg. . . . Hail, Mary, our hope! Hail, Mary, who has lost her heart!"[14] I thank him and put the sketch in my book, Aksakov's *The Childhood Years of Grandson Bagrov*. . . .[15] Finishing her conversation with the others, Marina said that it was time for us to leave, but Ehrenburg stopped us. He stood there for a minute, then returned with a small notebook and read several poems. . . . Climbing up in his lap, I said, "Dear Ilya Grigorievich, if you see my papa, tell him that we live only with thoughts of him, and pass on to him, please, all our greetings and all the words of praise you know. . . ." He looked at me with smiling eyes and said, "Oh, I absolutely will . . . !" And with a sad radiance he bid us farewell.

. . . When he arrived abroad, Ehrenburg found Seryozha. On July 14 (July 1, OS), 1921, at 10:00 P.M. Marina received her first letter from him.[16]

My dear friend, Marinochka,
Today I received a letter from Ilya Grigorievich stating that you are alive and well. After reading the letter, I spent the whole day wandering around the city, mad with joy. [. . .]
What should I write? Where should I start? So much needs to be said, but I have forgotten not only how to write,

but how to speak. I am kept alive by my faith that we shall meet. Without you there is no life for me: please live! I will demand nothing of you; I need nothing except that you be alive. [...]

It was the greatest of miracles that you and I should come together, and the reunion that lies ahead for us will be an even greater miracle. Whenever I think about it, my heart skips a beat—I am terrified—for there can be no greater joy than that awaiting us. However, I am superstitious, so I won't go on about that. All of our years apart—every day and every hour—you were with me, inside me. You, of course, must know that. [...]

It is difficult for me to write about myself. All the years I lived without you have passed as if in a dream. My life is divided into "before" and "after," and "after" is a nightmare from which I would gladly waken, but cannot. [...]

I have kept a diary for you (the larger, more valuable part of it was stolen along with my things): you will know *every-thing*. [...]

Your letter awaits me: Ilya Grigorievich did not want to forward it without my exact address. I await it with trepidation. The last letter I had from you was two years ago. Since then—nothing.

[...] Right now the room where I live is full of people. They are talking and making lots of noise. [...] As soon as I receive Ilya Grigorievich's response with your letter, I will write in more detail; I want to send this letter off right away so that you receive it as soon as possible. Ilya Grigorievich writes that you still live at the same place. Being able to imagine your surroundings makes me feel good.

What can I say about my own life? I live from day to day. Each day is a struggle, and each day brings our meeting closer. That gives me energy and strength. Otherwise, everything around here is very bad and hopeless. But about all that when we meet.

The people around me get in my way. I have absolutely no one near or dear to me here. [...]

I hope that Ilya Grigorievich will send me your new poems. He writes that you are working a lot. [. . .]

Forgive me, my joy, that this letter is such a confused jumble. [. . .]

Take care of yourself, I beg you. You and Alya are the very last and the most precious persons I have.

God keep you.

Your S[17]

A postscript to me:

My dear little girl! I received a letter from I.G., and he wrote about how he saw you and he passed on the words you asked him to say to me on your behalf. Thank you, my joy. All my love and all my thoughts are with you and with Mama. I trust that we will see each other soon to begin our life together so as never again to part. [. . .]

I bless you and kiss you.

Your Papa

"Beginning today—life. I live for the first time," Marina wrote in her notebook, adding immediately,

A Letter to S

My Seryozhenka!

If happiness does not kill people, then it at very least petrifies them. I just received your letter. And turned to stone. The last news I had of you was your letter to Max. And then nothing. I have no idea where to begin. No, I know where to begin—the same place I will end, with my love for you. [. . .][18]

A bit later—a letter to Akhmatova:

My Joy!

Life is complex. I am torn by the knowledge that he is alive. On July 1 I received a letter, the first after two years of silence. I am torn, and I spend the whole day waiting on others. I cannot live without hardship—I have no right. This

sense of mutual assistance: I help others here, while someone else takes care of him there. [. . .] Strangers' lives that
need fixing, for other people are even more helpless (I, at
least, have something to be happy about!); the day long spent
fixing some stranger's life where I, perhaps, am not even that
needed. [. . .]

I write in spurts, as a reward. Poetry is a luxury. Always
the sense that I am not within my rights. Despite it all, thanks
to it all, a certain happiness, only not as simple as it seems.
[. . .][19]

Who were those "strangers"? More often than not, truly "strangers,"
here-today-gone-tomorrow people who accidentally arrived at Marina's
doorstep, took shelter at our place as if it were a train station, warmed
their hands at our stove, and had a bite to eat (never enough to be full!)
of our bread and our kasha. Some of them—helpless to the point of saint-
liness—were "forwarded" to Marina by her sister Asya, then living in
the Crimea. Some came on their own. Some Marina with her infallible
sensitivity to (even the most deeply hidden) physical need and spiritual
homelessness would pick up on her own, propping them up with her own
shoulder. . . . Having caught their breath, these "strangers" left for docks
at more reliable shores; some (exceptions few and far between) went away
but remained (no longer strangers) with us, even if in memory alone.

As for the poems, the poems were written despite it all and thanks to
it all, for they were neither "luxury" nor even "necessity" but *inevitability.*
They got written despite all the obstacles and distractions, which Marina
knew how to put aside and part the same way she moved aside superfluous objects cluttering her worktable in order to free up space for her
elbows and notebook.

From the day she received Seryozha's letter—the letter that determined her decision to join her husband—up until the day of our departure, Marina created more than a hundred poems, the cycle "Lanes and
Alleys,"[20] the outline and first chapter of the long poem *The Swain,*[21] can-
tos of the first redaction of the long poem *Egorushka,*[22] a whole act (lost,
unfortunately) of a play tentatively titled *David* (which would remain
unfinished), and a multitude of journal entries, not to mention her work
on the archive she was preparing to take with her, the manuscripts she

submitted for publication in Moscow, and dozens and dozens of letters, the majority veritable anthology pieces of Tsvetaeva's prose.

By fatal coincidence Marina left Russia just as Russia—together with the revolution—had burst into her work, taken root in her with all its multi- and polyvocalism, with all the national character of its dialects, sayings, and vernacular, with all its songs of glory, all its funeral laments, potions for the evil eye, and other sorcery.

Raised in the traditions of the fin de siècle, having grown up under the care of governesses and studied at Swiss boarding schools, and having acquired French and German on a par with her native language, Marina, naturally, had total mastery of the Russian *literary* language, the language of the intelligentsia, and in her youth this was the language she wrote in, honing it à la Rostand or lending it Goethean solemnity. That, though, was but the icing, not the cake; the cake—the speech of the people itself—remained hidden until its time arrived, again by way of *literature*, to be heard, reflected, and delivered to her by others, both the classics and contemporaries.

A "city girl" and a "summer vacationer" in her childhood and youth, Marina had no contact with the people's lives or with their speech—neither in the village, which she never knew, nor in the city's industrial outskirts, where she never set foot. The "simple folk"—servants, caretakers, janitors, washerwomen, and drop-in seamstresses—were people of few words, reticent and deferential. It seemed like all of prerevolutionary Moscow was reticent and deferential.

All that changed in a single moment, that very moment when "the music of the revolution"[23] thundered forth, when what Marina had never heard or apprehended before suddenly acquired a voice whose strength she took up and made her own from that time forward for the rest of her life. (Time would pass and in a letter to Mayakovsky she herself—that same and yet far from the same Tsvetaeva—would proclaim not only the *strength* but the *truth* of revolutionary Russia.)

Precisely then, when the streets and squares of Moscow filled with heretofore silent and unthinkable new masters who burst forth with heretofore unheard words, Marina began to fill her notebooks with records of conversations, stories, and comments she caught on the fly—here, there, and everywhere: in children's soup kitchens and at theaters, at train stations, in trolley cars and at flea markets, in offices and on church steps, on the boulevards and in lines. Precisely then—enthralled and excited by what were new voices for her—Marina pressed her ear to the folkloric sources of her poems as sources for these voices, unearthing for herself in Afanasiev's collections[24] not children's fairy tales but a chronicle of bygone fates and bygone events, of eternal passions and human feats, a chronicle of tragedies and of hope for miracles of deliverance encoded in the form of children's fairy tales. . . .

Precisely then—having blossomed for the last time in the cycle of plays she herself would later call "romanticism"—the graceful "Chopinian" quality of Tsvetaeva's creativity was supplanted and gradually disappeared altogether. Taking leave of her muse as she did of her youth, Marina entrusted her fate as poet to her inexorable, merciless, lonely genius:

> Not the Muse, not the Muse, nor the perishable reins
> Of kinship, not your shackles,
> Oh, Friendship: Not by a hand womanly—fierce!—
> Has the knot on me been
> Drawn.

In the pension at Pragerplatz lived writers, publishers, and paraliterary figures of all varieties—some with families, some alone—recently arrived from Russia. The café Pragerdiele—where they all came together—was a sort of small-scale dress rehearsal for Russian émigré Montparnasses to come. At its tables, as if there were nothing particularly extraordinary about it all, the "fates" of world and Russian art—indeed, of the fatherland and of the whole world—were "decided."[25] Publishing contracts were negotiated. Business and personal relationships were struck up and struck down. Arguments arose and truces ensued—all over cups of post–World War I ersatz coffee or mugs of beer. Ehrenburg drank beer, and I along with him, until my father arrived: horrified, with a firm hand, he switched me to lemonade.

Marina quickly got to know everyone, but befriended, as always, only a few and none for long: the artist Lyubov Kozintseva, Ehrenburg's wife; another woman artist, a student of Ivan Bilibin, Lyudmila Chirikova (daughter of a writer famous in his own time), and the young publisher Helicon. (At Pragerplatz publishers were called by the name of their presses, not vice versa!) Back then I wrote the following about

Helicon and His "Office"

For him his office is his entire world. A table that stands near a window with thick glass where Helicon [Abram Vishniak— trans.] has spread all his editions (he doesn't allow anyone else's editions to stand on his desk). Three bookcases with a Chinese deity on top. In a small room on the other side of the wall his translucent girl-secretary types away, occasionally joined by a young cutthroat type, that is, by Ehrenburg himself doing his own typing.

The most sundry characters come to visit Helicon: an old gentleman with his watch on a piece of dog chain (his gold chain had been sold); thin, dismal writers' widows who hope Helicon will offer them some sort of financial wherewithal in the name of their departed husbands; writers who whirl convulsively in their chairs hoping to pay Helicon the immense favor of a translation of their own book into Spanish. . . . Everything that could be of no use to anyone arrives (on two legs) at or is delivered (in briefcases) to Helicon. He tries not to offend anyone, but everyone curses him for paying so little.

Helicon is always split between two poles—day-to-day matters and affairs of the soul. Day-to-day matter is the weight that keeps him on the ground and without which (it seems to him) he would immediately float off into the heavens, like Andrei Bely. In fact, he need not bother being split: he has very little soul, because what he needs is peace and quiet, rest, sleep, and comfort, precisely what the soul does not provide.

When Marina drops in at his office, she is like that soul that unsettles and deprives a person of peace, raising him to her own level without condescending to his. In friendship with Marina there are no lullabies or cradles. She pushes even babies she talks to out of their cradles, divinely certain, what is more, that she is lulling the child—who's lucky to survive. Marina talks to Helicon like a Titan; she is as incomprehensible to him as the North Pole is to someone in the Far East— and just as enticing. Her words make him feel as if there is light and something not so run-of-the-mill at the end of the tunnel of his onerous day-to-day affairs. I could see how he with his fractured stem was drawn to Marina, as if to the sun. However, that sun was far off in the distance because the entirety of Marina's being is restraint and clenched teeth, while he is willowy and soft, like a pea sprout.

I must point out that this—and several other descriptions of "adults" in my diary—gave Marina pause: she found them unduly perspicacious for a little girl not yet ten years old and, what is more, unceremonious and lacking requisite distance between younger and older generations. Giving the matter some thought, she swiftly returned me to childhood by plac-ing me in the care of the quite uncharming governess who shepherded Helicon's four-year-old son, Zhenya. Zhenya and I took to grazing whole days on end in the squares and parks of Berlin, and my notebooks dute-ously acquired the little-boy colors of Helicon Jr.'s sketches.

Only kind Ehrenburg would on occasion pull me back into the world of adults, rather, into his own world, by reading me passages from his *Thirteen Pipes*,[26] and he even made me a "present" of one of them: the one where the hippopotamus eats the missionary. (I had grown and put on weight, and Ehrenburg called me "Hippopotamus.") Sometimes the two of us would wander the streets, admiring the dogs, particularly those pulling milk delivery carts. "A dog's life in human terms," Ehrenburg explained to me, "is when you cannot afford to own a dog. . . ."

Post–World War I Berlin—pungently fragrant with oranges, chocolate, and good tobacco—had a sated, comfortable, and self-satisfied look about it but in fact suffered from inflation and followed a strict diet of suffocat-ing frugality. Prices swelled by the day. The meals they fed us at our pen-sion consisted of ever-smaller portions of radishes, kasha, and noodles, albeit impeccably served. As for Helicon's honoraria, they were downright minuscule, as were, for that matter, his print runs and the format of the elegant little books he published, and it was a wonder we managed to come up with enough money for Seryozha's trip (he was living on a tiny student stipend in Prague at the time) and for our subsequent departure for Czechoslovakia.

When Liubov Mikhailovna took Marina and me to KDW [Kaufhaus des Westens—trans.], then the largest department store in the capital, she directed our attention to the gigantic ashtray on a special table in the lobby. It held unfinished cigars identified with the smokers' last names printed on the store's own special labels. . . . Shoppers entering the store with cigars in their mouths would leave their cigars in the ashtray in order to relight them on their way out. . . . Little—business-card-size—blank cards and a pencil on a string lay nearby on the table, and there was a gas burner to light up at, to save oneself the match. . . .

Marina purchased her first presents for Seryozha since their unbearable separation: warm underwear, socks, a scarf, and—to lift his spirits—a cigarette case: "He probably smokes now. . . ." For me, shaking her head at the price, [she bought—trans.] a striped dress with a sailor collar, and, at Liubov Mikhailovna's categorical insistence, she bought herself a thoroughly plain *Bauerkleid* dress. She loved this chintz dress with its laced midriff and gathered skirt and wore it the rest of her life, every summer.

She also bought herself some crude, sturdy shoes: mountaineer walking shoes with thick soles and tasseled leather lace-covers. . . .

That was in the days when women wore high-heeled pumps, azure hose, muslin, batiste, and veils. After October 1917 Marina never again paid heed to fashion: it was too expensive and impractical . . . and always going out of style.

. . . Occasionally Andrei Bely—devastated by the breakup with his wife, Asya Turgeneva, lost, strange, and profoundly unhappy, with mad, fanatic eyes—would make the trip to Berlin from nearby Zossen. Marina immediately took the brunt of his blow upon herself, into herself, donning this harness innately, as if by second nature. While those surrounding him cared sincerely and solicitously (although not without a grain of deferential terror) for him, only Marina would become a harbor for his storm-rocked soul. . . . "My dear, dear, dear, dear Marina Ivanovna," he wrote to her in a letter that June 1922, ". . . in these last, especially difficult days of drudgery you have *once again* rung out to me with an ever so tender, amazing note of trust. . . . Miracles, after all, do happen! And it is a miracle that certain people waft such joyous grace on others, and not because of . . . Do you know what yesterday was like for me? I crossed Asya out of my life for once and for all. . . . And it seemed to me that along with Asya I had ripped out a piece of my own heart, and together with my heart—my whole self, and from my head to my chest there was nothing but emptiness inside me. . . . I went down to the square and sat, totally numb, on the bench, then dropped into cafés and beer halls, where I sat some more, totally numb, with no sense of space and time. And it went on that way until evening. When I came back in the evening, I suddenly, unexpectedly, once again sensed your gentle currents: the chirping of swallows and dear, dear, dear words about how I have a motherland and that nothing has been lost forever. . . .''

Twelve years later, in 1934, having read in the newspapers of the death of Andrei Bely, who had returned to Russia in 1923, Marina wrote her requiem-cum-memoir of him, which she titled *A Captive Spirit*.[27] There she said all there was to be said about their meetings, the meetings of two captive spirits.

One more vision—fleeting and my last while he was alive—of Esenin sauntering like an exalted pasha *past* tables at the Pragerdiele set out on the sidewalk to take advantage of the warm May weather and swarming with Russian émigrés.

Esenin is dressed to the nines, like a mannequin in a store window, every piece of clothing on him brand, spanking new, starched stiff and unwrinkled, a cane in his hand and a derby—the ridiculous "crowning glory" of businessman and bourgeois—on his head; his eyes—the most heavenly blue color on earth—look out haughtily. Met by a chorus of merry greetings, he answers on the fly—as he parades slowly and ceremoniously by—with a caustic, insolent phrase that makes everyone at first uncomfortable and then indignant.

By that time he's already gone, turned around the corner, vanished.

My memory has not preserved the exact date of my father's arrival in Berlin.[28] Something happened that day: either the telegram announcing his arrival came late or Marina was not around when it was delivered. All I remember is that the long-awaited news took Marina by surprise, and she and I did not just set off, we rushed at breakneck speed to meet Seryozha's train, hurrying, losing our way, and confusing directions. Someone offered to go and scurry along with us, but Marina declined all escorts: she had to meet Seryozha alone without any onlookers.

When we rushed into the station, our veins bursting from excitement and running, it was deserted and echoed with the futility of a cathedral after mass. Seryozha's train had already pulled out, pulled out a long time ago, and not a scent remained of its passengers or those who had come to meet them. Cooling down from our run and chilled with horror, we frantically and futilely searched the platforms and waiting rooms, the baggage check and the restaurant—Marina in her new dark blue frock and I in my new sailor dress, all decked out and as sad, lost, and clueless as one can be only in dreams. . . . Neither the polite service people nor the explicit train schedules hanging on the glossy walls nor the no-less-precise hands on the faces of the station clocks offered any explanation or hope.

We ran out into the sun-bleached deserted square, and the sunlight—reflected by all the square's multiple planes—struck our eyes painfully. We felt the burning city heat, the weakness in our knees, and the enormous emptiness left by our nonmeeting. Marina began to riffle blindly and distractedly through her purse for cigarettes and to rattle her matches. Her face was drained. And just then we heard Seryozha's voice: "Marina! Marinochka!" From somewhere at the other end of the square, hands waving, a tall, thin man came running toward us, while I, already realizing that this was Papa, still did not recognize him because I had been quite small when we had been separated and I remembered him differently, rather, as someone different, and before the image from my childhood memories could blend with the image of the person running toward us Seryozha had made his way to us—his face contorted with happiness—and was embracing Marina, who slowly extended her seemingly frozen arms out to meet him.

For a long, long, long time they stood locked in a deathly still embrace and only later began slowly to wipe the tears from each other's cheeks.

I saw little of my father, who spent only a short time in Berlin.[29] He spent all his time with Marina; with me he was silently tender, pensively—as he drifted off far away in his thoughts—stroking my head first "with the grain," then "against the grain."

The Ehrenburgs welcomed Seryozha like a member of the family and celebrated Marina's reunion with him like a tree lighting for Christmas, decorating the tree with the tinsel of goodwill and the rainbow-colored ornaments of various projects. Everything would be all right, work itself out—and not just "sort-of-kind-of," but well, even exceptionally well.

The main thing was that they were alive and had found each other!

On the evening of Seryozha's arrival we drank champagne: it helped all the incongruous bread-breakers gathered at the pension's pushed-together tables if not to find a "common language," then to set a common tone, at least for that one evening. Seryozha, who that fall would turn twenty-nine, still looked like a boy recovering from a serious illness—he was so thin and his eyes so large, still very much the orphan, despite Marina sitting next to him. She, for her part, seemed to have grown up—instantaneously and forever, down to the strands of early gray already shimmering in her hair.

The Ehrenburgs soon left for their spa at Binz on Ruegen Island, both to create: he his *Thirteen Pipes* and she her sketches. We moved to a small hotel on Trautenauerstrasse, where instead of one large room we occupied two tiny ones, but with a balcony. On the occasion of our "housewarming" Seryozha presented me with potted pink begonias, which I watered liberally in the morning, trying hard not to drip on pedestrians: you don't want to mess with the Germans!

Of this slice of life in "Trautenauer Haus" what stands out most is a mere trifle: my daily morning looks down and around at the clean, faceless, sunny street with its early unrushed pedestrians and the accompanying sensation of the transitoriness of the world around me and of not belonging to those surroundings, which allowed me to take it all in abstractly and independently, without pangs of either pleasure or rejection.

This sensation could only have been reinforced by my parents' plans for the immediate future—incubated and hatched in the two little rooms behind me—and by their conversations, which drifted in my direction. Stay in Berlin? In Germany, which has just been through a war and is going through economic crisis, where there is no and will be no chance for Russians to attend university or to work or to send their children to school? True, life here is more equable and better organized than in Czechoslovakia, but for whom? How long will those precarious Russian publishing houses, the publishers themselves, be able to hold out? Who will buy the books and newspapers they print? How will we get by? And what will we get by on? Does this mean we move to Czechoslovakia? That option has at least one financial invariable in its favor: Seryozha's student stipend. They say that Tomáš Masaryk's government will be offering (in fact, is already offering) aid for refugees in the sciences and in the spheres of art and culture. A benevolent government? Not quite. Mere kopecks from the Russian gold reserves brought back by Czech legionnaires who fought on the side of the entente during the civil war.[30]

Prague has Charles University (the oldest in Europe!), which has already witnessed an influx of former professors and students from pre-revolutionary Russia. Czechoslovakia already has a boarding school for Russian émigré children (so many of them orphans). True, there still are no (and will there ever be?) émigré publishing houses, but there is a thick monthly journal with a large literary section. Old Prague is beautiful beyond words with its Gothic and baroque, fantastic! The city is stupendous! True, living there is beyond our means. We cannot afford it. Single students are crammed into the "Svobodárna," a dormitory with closet-size booths, each with a bed, a makeshift table, and a stool. There is not even room to pace back and forth while you study. Students who have families have settled in the suburbs, more precisely, in outlying villages. Yes, real villages—no, not quite like the ones we have in Russia—with tile-covered roofs, but with otherwise rural living conditions: water from wells, kerosene lamps, no sidewalks (that goes without saying), and no paved streets. Although, if one can find a place not too far from the train station, getting into Prague is simple and easy, since suburban trains run frequently. The Czechs are favorably disposed toward Russians, and on the whole everything is different there: no snobbism, no tables of ranks. They are more—how should I put it?—ingenuous: Slavs, after all, their language is close to ours, and besides, they are incredibly musical! Musical, like Italians. . . . The landscape? There are hilly (mountainous, even) areas, forests (like ours, and pine forests as well), a wonderful little river called the Berounka (a tributary of the Vltava [Moldau—trans.]), and fields, and meadows, and wide open spaces that have not been fenced in or built up, and you can see far and wide. . . .

Then Marina's spirited: "Mountains? Hills? Music? We're off to Czechoslovakia!"

Following Seryozha's departure—he had to prepare intensively for the beginning of the academic year: he had lost any skill for memorization, his heart and mind were preoccupied with other things, and his initial suspicions had by now evolved into full recognition of the irreparableness of the mistake he had made in 1917—which turned out to be only the first in a string of innumerable exigencies and hopeless situations that arose one after the other as a result of that original mistake. Following Seryozha's departure, Marina and I began to pack our things and to say farewell to Berlin, to which we had never really said hello. The time had come for Marina to put dampers on relationships that otherwise might have sparked at this juncture: our departure in and of itself marked their end.

In the two-and-a-half months we spent in Berlin Marina never went to the theater, to concerts, or to museums. She visited only the Zoological Gardens and the Luna Park—the first for obvious reasons since everyone in our family worshipped animals. But the Luna Park? With Marina's distaste for "public" entertainment and for fairgrounds in general? Perhaps it had to do with the fact that besides the usual attractions at parks of this sort, Luna Park also offered the unusual: a full-scale model of an entire neighborhood of a medieval German town, executed with typical German attention to detail. Given Marina's eternal fascination for the past as the *source,* foundation, and explication of the present and the future, this had to appeal to her. Perhaps, though, she just wanted to make me happy. For whatever reason, one day in the middle of that sweltering July, under the guidance of Lyudmila Evgenievna Chirikova, we set off for Luna Park with the most serious of intentions: to look at everything that did not move and to ride on everything that did.

We began with the carousel (pink, white, and raspberry-colored, like a giant's wedding cake), which revolved to the sweetest music. We rode in the chariots, then switched to the horses, first trotting evenly, then breaking into a dancelike gallop. My stern mother sat proudly and gracefully in her golden saddle (her faced closed and stony because there were people around), giving not the slightest indication that she was having fun, as if she were fulfilling some sort of ceremonial rite. Getting off the carousel, she told me quietly that I was not yet ready to be an Amazon because I rode like a lump of sourdough, with my mouth gaping open, to boot. I took due note but no doubt continued to gape, mouth wide open, in all directions.

Nor did Marina give any indication that she was having a good time in the fun house, where with a certain disdainful fascination she scrutinized the three of us as reshaped by the crooked mirrors first into Don Quixotes, then Sancho Panzas, and finally upside-down samovars with buttons.

The shooting range appealed to her, however, for she liked anything that required skill and accuracy—not only intellectual but physical—just as she liked movements and actions that excluded approximation. There were several shooting ranges, where men shot from bows, pistols, air rifles, and even from some sort of crossbow, to strike down flying, sliding, and somersaulting targets and win cute prizes that I eyed with burning envy.

There were jugglers in tents and magicians in wagons, wrestlers, and gymnasts, and acrobats who stepped with catlike springiness along a wire that cut across the sky the way a diamond cuts glass. There were super-swings that shone with nickel plating, on which we sailed through the air (Marina had loved swings since her childhood in Tarusa!) and pug-nosed rowboats that zigzagged along in an unevenly undulating circle. At a café under the trees there were waffles and lemonade and scoops of ice cream in cups ringed with condensation.

The medieval town—brand new, from stairsteps to crossbeams, and consisting entirely of facades—turned out to be a lifeless imitation, despite (or, perhaps, owing to) the excessive verisimilitude of whetstones, beer barrels, tethering posts, and pottery wheels (with halberds propped up alongside them) positioned with painterly deliberateness along a street that led from modernity back in time, to return full circle.

When the adults tired of the attractions and I was only beginning to get my fill, we wandered into a corner of the park where there was nothing on display, nothing being hawked, and nothing being played, and sat down on the rough grass under pine trees alongside a shimmering little lake. Looking around, Marina said to Lyudmila Evgenievna, "Not even nature gets to rest. I wonder: when I lie dying, will I have the same feeling I have here by this lake? A feeling of sadness? Of celebration? When all the noise, all the wheel spinning will be behind me—isn't that what rest is . . . ?"

Our visit to Luna Park turned out to be the "final chord" in Marina's Berlin, her last swoop over the city from the height of the swings. Less than a week later, on an early, barely awakened morning, we left Berlin, and on August 1, we alit from our train in Prague.

For Marina Berlin never happened. It never happened because she did not fall in love with it. And she had not fallen in love with it because after Russia, the Prussian—and after revolutionary Moscow, the bourgeois—satisfied neither her eye nor her soul: they were inadmissible. In the massiveness of its buildings, the traditional comfort of its cafés, and the rationalism of its layout—in the establishment and amenity the city exuded—Marina sensed only one thing: *barracks*.

Rain sings a lullaby to pain.
Beneath a torrent of cascading shutters
I sleep. Through shuddering asphalt lanes
Horses' hooves—like thunderous applause.
The rain ran its course, then streamed away.
And in the rainbowed emptiness remaining
You condescended to take pity
On the most enchanted of orphanhoods, you *barracks*!

Did they, in fact, take pity? Yes, perhaps so. Hats off to those barracks and caserns: not condescending to notice us, they thereby allowed us the possibility of ignoring them. A city always means reciprocity.

Tsvetaeva's first line of verse written in Berlin was: "Under the cobblestones, under the wheels. . . ."[31]

Her last quatrain written in Berlin was:

So suasively, so
Murderously artless:
Two birds have woven me a nest:
Veracity and—Orphanedness.[32]

From the middle of May until the end of July Marina prepared for publication her collections *Psyche*[33] and *Craft*[34] and the second redaction of her poem *Czar-Maiden*,[35] which all came out in Berlin in 1922–23. She wrote over thirty poems, an epistolary short story titled "Florentine Nights,"[36] and an article on the work of Boris Pasternak, "A Downpour of Light,"[37] which came out in 1922. The collections *Separation*[38] and *Poems to Blok,*[39] which she had prepared in Moscow, were published under Ehrenburg's supervision in early spring 1922, in Berlin, before Tsvetaeva arrived there.

Besides this, Marina translated into German a poem by Mayakovsky for the almanac *Thing,* published by Ehrenburg in three languages.[40] She translated it while still hot on Mayakovsky's trail—which for her never cooled—after her last meeting with him in Russia.

That meeting, judging by an entry in her notebook, took place on one of the days on the eve of Marina's departure, in the early morning, on a still empty Moscow street. Mayakovsky called out to Marina and asked her how things were going. She said that she was leaving to join her husband and asked what message she might deliver abroad for him. "That the truth is here," he answered with a smirk, pressed Marina's hand, and marched on.

She watched him walk off and thought to herself that if he turned around and shouted, "Come on, Tsvetaeva, enough, you're not going anywhere!" that she would have stayed and marched after him, with him, like a person enchanted.

Marina's thought about following Mayakovsky may be "poetic license," a romantic surge and complete impossibility, but it is also the deep-down truth. For in leaving she was vanquishing that half of herself that would always remain in Russia, with Russia: "My Russia! Oh, my Russia, why do you burn so bright?"[41]

"That the truth is here." Those words of Mayakovsky found their way into the well-known text of Tsvetaeva's address to him written after his reading at the Café Voltaire in Paris in 1928 and published in the leftist émigré newspaper *Eurasia* (my father was one of the editors). That address made it possible for Marina to experience feelings of lofty and profound celebration—the joy of an open handshake. It also caused her no little unpleasantness—if you can call mere unpleasantness her "excommunication" for "Bolshevism" from the editorial board of Pavel Miliukov's *Latest News* (which sometimes published her),[42] leaving her for a long time without the earnings that served as principal source of survival for our entire family.*

In the early spring of 1929 Marina met with Mayakovsky for the last time. In response to a request by Communists in one of the outlying regions of Paris, he agreed to read for an audience of French workers in the small ("wedding and banquet"!) ill-lighted space of a workers' café.

The reading was arranged helter-skelter, without advance preparation. One of its organizers (my father's comrade) invited my parents. Encouraged by the small attendance and the absence of acquaintances (curious eyes), Marina approached Mayakovsky and introduced him to her husband.

"Listen, Tsvetaeva," Mayakovsky said. "There's no one here but French people. You gonna translate? Otherwise they won't understand squat."

---

* The address she wrote to Mayakovsky in this connection was exhibited by him at his show "Twenty Years of Work" (restored and updated last year [1973—trans.] for the eightieth anniversary of the poet's birth) and was reproduced in the volume *Maiakovskii delaet vystavku* [*Mayakovsky Mounts an Exhibit*] (Moscow: Kniga, 1973).

Marina agreed, but she did not sit down on the chair offered to her: she was accustomed to performing standing. Mayakovsky would provide the name of the poem and summarize it in a word or two, and she would translate. Then he would recite.

Afterward there was a question-and-answer session with the audience. They were not so much interested in poetry as they were in the life and affairs of the working class in Soviet Russia. In those days they did not often get the chance to talk to people from there. Some of the questions were provocative, and Mayakovsky answered them with his usual straight-from-the-shoulder trenchancy, giving Marina a real workout insofar as certain Russian turns of phrase have no comparable equivalents in French.

These general remarks are all my memory has preserved of my parents' stories forty-five years (!) since that reading, which I myself did not attend because I was at home watching my little brother. Any notations Marina might have made immediately after the reading have not survived: they perished during the war together with the part of her archive that she left for safekeeping with friends in France.[43]

To say that Marina loved and understood Mayakovsky's work sounds limp, trite, today, now that he has come to stand for what he was—poet, person, and personality—as well as become a part of our landscape: city square, metro station, steamship, and monument to himself. Now that he is loved and understood by every schoolchild.

But she understood him and came to love him and acclaimed him at a time when he was still incomprehensible and inadmissible for many hearts and minds; at a time when he was still so immeasurably far from being a proven talent of long-standing reputation; when he was just one of the youngsters, one of the first whose shouts made it hard to hear and to recognize the *poetry,* which until that time had presented itself in an altogether different, time-honored, tone of voice; when it was still not apparent whose creative ceiling and limits were imminent and boundless, who would go forward and upward, and who would go round in circles; who would swerve neither from his voice nor his path; when everything that we now know about the past was just barely looming in the distance, clearing its way in a direction that was still just one among many possibilities.

She understood him and came to love him in all his then self-contradiction, him, the annihilator of legendary truths she herself had so romantically extolled and about which she herself would soon—already in 1922—say, "Of old truths this house knows only stench and rubbish. . . ."[44]

All her life Mayakovsky remained for her an immutable truth; all her life she preserved her great fidelity to him as brother. She understood that his attitude toward her—and her work—was determined by the extent of her affiliation with émigré society, and, for all her volatility, for all her conviction that such an evaluation was unwarranted, she never took offense at him, she, who could be whipped into a storm by eminently lesser vexations. . . .

To Mayakovsky she dedicated a large cycle of poems in 1930,[45] and in 1932 she wrote about his work in her article "Epos and Lyric of Contemporary Russia."[46]

Her first poem dedicated to Mayakovsky—"High above crosses and chimneys . . . ,"[47]—was written in 1921; she read it to him in Moscow and later recalled that he had liked it.

PASTERNAK

Of the many circumstances and situations that constantly got in Marina's way and caused her indignation, disappointment, and downright suffering—particularly while in emigration—the foremost hindrance was the *language* barrier, the *linguistic* barricade that isolated her from the people around her—close or distant, writer or just reader.

The power of her gift, magnified by her insatiable thirst to express and to give of herself—in friendship, love, or social intercourse—with fatal invariance ran head-on into the apathy (parsimony, paucity) of those with whom she spoke and corresponded, into their *otherness* and the *otherness* of their ability (desire) to communicate on the heights of Mount Everest.

"Bearers" of ordinary feelings and thoughts quickly wearied of having to lumber on stilts or stretch on tiptoe; they tired of the unconventional intensity Marina imposed on them, of the *effort* she demanded of their minds and spiritual musculature, if they had any, that is.

Those of a creative bent were often irritated or intimidated by the persistence with which Marina chiseled away at their very core, reshaping and remaking them to fit her own special, powerful, and unconventional mold, which she accomplished by way of her special, powerful, and unconventional language, talent, character, her very essence.

For Marina new relationships with new people frequently began with her noticing (if not imagining) some spark of possible commonality, which she then began to fan with such hurricane force that the spark either died out without ever breaking into a flame or, at best, smoldered secretly for decades only to glow later with the timid light of a candle for the dead.

Certainly, Marina was also capable of "just being" friends, or good neighbors, or at times even neutral, and she did not seek or attempt to find a spark of possible—or, in those emigrant times and circumstances, rather, *impossible*—commonality in just anyone.

However, the discrepancy she encountered back then between response and beck and answer and call forced her—like a musician playing (with rare exceptions) for the deaf or hard of hearing or distracted—to write "for herself" or to address herself to a reader yet to be born, which tormented her and propelled her constant search for a soul both alive and close to her own.

And the miracle happened: on June 27, 1922, the postman delivered to 9 Trautenauerstrasse yet another letter from Ehrenburg in Binz-am-Ruegen. ("Yet another" because Ilya Grigorievich and Marina wrote to each other frequently, two or three times a week, as he continued to fulfill from afar his obligations of "trustee" and she "reported" her affairs and ideas.)

This time the envelope was much heavier than usual. Carefully, as always, Marina opened it with her favorite letter opener—a miniature sword given to her as a present by Seryozha many years ago—and extracted several sheets of grayish paper inscribed in an unfamiliar, slanting, flying hand and with an accompanying note from Ehrenburg:

> Dear Marina,
>
> I am sending you a letter from Pasternak. At his request I have read his letter and am very happy for him. And happy for you, too: you, after all, know how I feel about Pasternak.
>
> I await your poems and letters.
>
> Tenderly yours,
>
> Ehrenburg

"Feel about!" Marina said with a smirk. "Him we love, while us he 'feels about.'" And she set to reading Pasternak's letter.

June 27 [June 14, OS], 1922, Moscow
Dear Marina Ivanovna,

Just now, my voice trembling, I began reading to my brother your "I know I shall die at sunset or sunrise! But which of the two . . . ," and I was overwhelmed by the wave of another person's sobs welling up in my throat and finally gushing forth as if my own. When I transferred my efforts from that poem to "I shall tell you a tale of enormous deceit," I was taken aback by you in the same way, and when I moved on to "Milestones, milestones, milestones, and dry hard bread!" the very same thing occurred.

You are no child, my dear, my golden, my incomparable poet, and I hope you understand what this means in our times with the current *abundance* of poets and poetesses (and not only those whose names appear in trade union rosters), the current *abundance* of nonimagists[48] alone, and the current *abundance* of such unsullied talents as [*Mayakovsky and Akhmatova*].[49]

Forgive me, forgive me, forgive me!

How could it happen that trudging alongside you behind Tatiana Fyodorovna Scriabina's coffin, I had no idea who I was walking next to?

How could it happen that having listened to and heard you on more than one occasion, I blundered and missed your milestone Swinburneana?[50] (Even if you do not know him— my idol, he has entered you by way of tangential influences, and he moves *freely* within you, my Marina Ivanovna, just as Byron once moved freely within Lermontov, and as [Russia moves] within Rilke.)[51]

How strangely and stupidly life cuts its pattern! A month ago you were within a hundred steps of my reach, and your *Mileposts* already existed, as did the bookstore at street level, with no threshold, where a lazy wave of warm crimped

asphalt deposited me! I take no shame in admitting my vil-
est of consumer transgressions: not buying a book because it
was there to be bought!!! And so, forgive me, forgive me!

The letter was long, symmetrical in its disconnectedness, written at a
single sitting, in a single ecstatic breath—the same breath that was also
Marina's, written not by one of the brethren but by a brother writer. A
brother she had not gotten to know and had left behind in that place
where she had just come from; abandoned by her and now reaching out
to her; a brother who "a month ago" had been "within one hundred steps"
of her reach and from whom she was now separated by a gaping abyss and
barricaded borders.

Marina answered not immediately—allowing Pasternak's news time to
"cool" (this given the usual lightning speed of her epistolary ripostes!)—
and not as in depth as she was wont. In her response she recalled the circumstances of their chance meetings in Moscow, the meetings themselves,
even the words the two of them had exchanged (Marina's memory—tena-
cious, observant, and lasting—was one facet of her gift). She admitted that
she had only "once heard you perform, you kept forgetting," that she had
not seen his books and had read only five or six of his poems, no more. She
accepted Pasternak's news that he might soon arrive in Berlin with cordial
restraint: "Let me know how things stand with your departure. Are you
really—in the real world of visas, applications, and billions—coming? [...]
I press your hand. I await you and your book. M. Ts."[52]

Marina's restraint derived from her bewilderment at this voice that was
almost her own; from her inability to conceive how this voice might ring
out among the others around her; from her urgent need to ascertain its
genuineness and her vulnerability (or invulnerability) to it; from her need
to give it time to dissipate if it were a delusion ("Amen, away!")[53] or to nest
and take root in her soul if it were a reality.

Her departure from Berlin on the eve of Pasternak's arrival there had
something in common with the nymph's flight from Apollo, something
mythological and otherworldly—even if the decision and act itself made
doubtless sense given her need to reach Czechoslovakia before autumn
in order to settle in and adjust to impending rural life before the onset of
winter, always a difficult time for new arrivals, even in urban conditions.

But perhaps it was a (no less mythological) escape with an already acknowledged, an already proven treasure in hand—an appropriation, an abduction, an unwillingness to share [that treasure—trans.] with everyone else in the vacuum surrounding the little tables of the Pragerdiele, her fear of prying eyes, her need to get out of sight, so typical of Marina in her quest for and attachment to the *secret* of possessing any treasure, be it a book, a piece of the natural world, a letter or a human soul. . . . In the realm of immaterial values Marina was a grand claim staker who tolerated neither co-owners nor collaborators.

For one reason or another, her "I await you" turned out to be absolute poetic license in 1922 and the absolute human truth over the long years that ensued.

The relationship that formed between both poets never knew and would never know anything comparable: it was unique.

Two human beings—equals in age, in the strength of their innate as well as chosen poetic vocation (as opposed to the music inculcated in them or the figurativeness of the arts that surrounded them!), and in language—who had lived side by side at one and the same time, in one and the same city where they episodically encountered each other, he and she, would come to possess each other only in irreparable separation, only through letters and poems, yet as if in the strongest of earthly embraces.

This was true friendship, authentic communion and true love, and the letters that contained it provide not just a detailed and revealing chronicle of the relationships, affairs, and days of those who wrote them but self-portraits, without either embellishment or distortion.

I do not know if Marina brought all of Pasternak's letters back with her to the Soviet Union in 1939 (she saved them all, everything, including wrappers from the parcels he sent her), but those she brought back have survived, without loss or disclosure, because for three-and-a-half decades no outsider's hands, no one's curiosity, carelessness, or self-interest has come into contact with them.

In his memoirs Pasternak tells the story of how he lost part of Tsvetaeva's letters during the war. However, at some point copies of some of them had been made by Pasternak's and Aseev's onetime friend, in his early years a poet, Aleksei Kruchonykh, who, without Boris Leonidovich's knowledge, liberally supplied motley collectors with typewritten knockoffs. Littered with typographical errors and abundant lacunae, those cop-ies circulate to this day.

Besides these, drafts and outlines for many of the letters have been preserved in [Tsvetaeva's—trans.] notebooks, in her archive.[54]

Marina Tsvetaeva's correspondence with Boris Pasternak lasted from 1922 until 1935–36, climaxing in the 1920s, then gradually tapering off. Of the meetings they at various times planned, not a single one took place; they met—unexpectedly and inauspiciously—in June 1935, when Boris Leonido-vich arrived in Paris for the First International Congress of Writers for the Defense of Culture.[55] He arrived only after the congress had opened, ill, in a deep depression brought on by events and changes in his personal life, and up to his ears in those affairs, which, as Marina sensed, left no room for her.[56] His aloofness and enchantment with someone *other than her* stunned and wounded her profoundly, all the more so because her *long-distance* [*zaochnoe*] *relationship* with Pasternak had been her only stronghold and shelter from the *real* failures and insults of her last years in emigration.

Later, upon returning to the USSR, Marina saw Boris Leonidovich rather often, and he helped her considerably and eagerly, and he sup-ported her, but the otherworldliness of their friendship was over: once you descend from such heights, there is no returning to them a second time, just as there is no stepping into the same river twice.[57]

The impact of their correspondence on Tsvetaeva's work was as signifi-cant as it was singular, for it expressed itself not in degrees to which one personality had appropriated or devoured the other, not in some mea-sure of "assimilation." No, it made itself apparent in the newly found focus in Marina's creative self-dedication—self-dedication that had acquired a concrete addressee.

Besides two essays—"A Downpour of Light" and "The Epos and Lyric of Contemporary Russia," of which the latter concerns Mayakovsky in equal measure—the quantity of Marina's work dedicated to Pasternak or directly inspired by him is not that large. She dedicated no fewer to Akhmatova, Blok, X, and Y, and always with no assurance that her voice might reach them. By the same token, however, in the 1920s and in the beginning of the 1930s (the period of her creative maturity and prolifi-cacy) everything she wrote, regardless of who or what actually inspired its creation, was directed toward, aimed—from one heart to the other—at Pasternak, focused on him and addressed to him, like a prayer.

In him she acquired the only *auditory abyss*[58] that could ever accommodate her with the same artistic space as that with which she herself created, lived, and felt.

Pasternak loved her and understood her, never judged her, praised her, and the brick wall of his praise shielded her from her incompatibility with her surroundings, from her dislocation within her surroundings. . . . Marina, after all, required praise, otherwise she might wither from a deficiency of love and attention or explode from her own enormous disproportion to the yardstick by which émigré readers and critics measured her. (With the exception of a few close and faithful friends, of course.)

The then intensifying complexity of her poetic language—intelligible, nowadays, in the 1970s, to a "mass" readership but difficult of comprehension for the "select" reader of the 1920s—is also in part explained by Marina's orientation toward Pasternak: this was speech comprehensible to two and encoded for all others! After all, those who have just acquired the basics of arithmetic cannot immediately expect to be able to decipher calculus. . . .

Here is what Pasternak writes to Marina in one of his letters from 1922, the "calculus" period of his own opus:

> I know you love—what we call, for short—poetry with no less passion than do I.
>
> What I mean is this:
>
> More than anything else on earth I love (and this, perhaps, is my only love) the truth of life in the form it *naturally* assumes for a single moment at the very aperture of artistic form only to disappear within it at the very next moment. This movement of life is not imposed from without. Birnam wood crawls into the furnace of its own accord. We should not delude ourselves. Likely, we know only one side. It is quite possible that life branches out in various directions, its flow forming a delta. We with our thoroughly painful knowledge of but one of its stretches are able to imagine its mouth only at the bend in that stretch. And from any one of its upper reaches and knowing nothing of the sea, eyes closed and through extreme superhuman concentration on the tone of

the current and the shape of the waves, we can imagine what
might eventually become of it [. . .] and deduce the nature of
its essence at the present moment. . . .[59]

Then, shifting from the deltas, currents, and upper reaches of poetry to
its specific manifestations in Berlin—the branches and shoals that lay just
around the bend of emigration—he adds:

> I was very distressed and discouraged not to have found you
> in Berlin. Bidding farewell to Mayakovsky, Aseev, Kuzmin,
> and several others, I in the same way, the same order, had
> counted on meeting with you and with Bely.
>
> My disappointment in your case, though, was true happi-
> ness as opposed to my disappointment with Bely. Everyone
> here has quarreled with everyone else, having located at the
> juncture of arbitrary polemics and theatrically enhanced
> facsimiles a fiction that substitutes for the absent object. You
> would think that all members of this artel should respect
> each other, contenting themselves with their mutual discon-
> tent, without which there would be no fiction.
>
> Not even Bely has that logical consistency. . . .[60]

Marina was already in Czechoslovakia, and she had no hope of meeting up anytime soon with Boris Leonidovich—of simply picking up and
packing off with just a few things and for just a short time—because she
had no one who could "push official buttons" for a visa, because the price
of such a trip was beyond her means, and, most of all, because it would
have been an abrogation of her responsibility to her family for the contents of that pocketbook! (Everything in Czechoslovakia turned out to
be beyond her means, except for the truly delightful countryside in the
suburbs surrounding Prague. . . .)

But that was the superficial—the nuts-and-bolts, so to speak—side of
the impossibility. With her energy and will for challenges, Marina, perhaps, might have overcome this impossibility, were she convinced of the
necessity of this meeting and of her own inner readiness for it. Were she
not, deep down, terrified of it.

And so, with anxious trust, with anxious delight, Marina accepts Pasternak's proposal (romantic and unfeasible) that they meet in Weimar in the shadow of Goethe—whom they both adored—in May 1925:

> . . . And now about Weimar: Pasternak, do not joke with me! I will live with this for the next two years straight. And if I die in these two years (I won't!), this will be my next-to-last thought. Only do not play with me. I know myself. Pasternak, just now I was on my way home by way of a dark country road—groping my way through mud and ditches and past dark lampposts. Pasternak, I thought about you with such intensity—no, not about you, about myself without you, about those streetlamps and roads without you—ah, Pasternak, my feet will trek *billions* of miles before we meet!
>
> . . . Two years of growth lie ahead, before Weimar. (Suddenly—out of madness!—I am beginning to believe!) I want to make you a promise, to make it silently: All my verse and everything that happens in my life I will send to you. . . .[61]

Of the two appointed years one passes: an enormous year of "life as it is" in all its deliquescent banality and predictability, with all its cares, disappointments, joys, rainstorms, rainbows, insomnia, misunderstandings, new acquaintances, old disputes, noisy primus stoves—an enormous year of creativity in (and upstream against) the stream of life, a year of letters to and from Pasternak, a year of mounting titanic, poetic passion, passion "beyond the barriers. . . ."[62]

> June 14, 1924
>
> Marina, my golden friend, my marvelous, supernaturally fated destiny, my morning mist-on-the-rise soul, Marina. [. . .] Why do I hate [letters—trans.]! Ah, Marina, they are inattentive to the details. They simply do not convey the *fatigue,* the fatiguing *length* of time one spends in admiration. That is what is most stunning.
>
> Everyday existence is run through by an electric current that passes as if through water. It polarizes everything. [. . .]

And when the heart wrenches—oh, that *wrenching* of the heart, Marina! [. . .] It is so us, that wrenching, for it is so thoroughly *stylistic!*

[. . .] This electricity—the *fundamental style* of the universe, the style of creativity—passes momentarily before the human soul, ready to take it up into its own wave, [. . .] to assimilate it, to make it one with itself.

And then [the soul—trans.]—charged from birth but almost always neutralized in youth and only in rare instances of great gift (talent) preserved into maturity (and even then functioning in spurts and often by inertia, interrupted by the rhetorical sputtering of extraneous rotational movements— unfatiguing thoughts, impulses, "loving" letters, derivative poses)—and then [the soul—trans.] recharges itself anew, afresh, and once again the world becomes a polarized tank: one pole feeds the current of times and places, of rising and setting suns, of reminiscences and intentions, while the other [emits—trans.] the wrenching delight, infinitely minuscule like the press of a finger on the heart when it aches, of a spark disappearing into the water. [. . .]

[. . .] What amazing poems you write! How it pains me that you are now larger than I! And, in general, you are a disgustingly immense poet. In terms of that wrenchingly minuscule and elusively electrifying delight, of the spark, of love—what I talked about. I know this *for certain*. But there's no expressing this in one word, and to express it with the aid of many [words—trans.] is an abomination.

Here is a wretched poem from 1915 from *Barriers:*

> I love you all blackened by ashes
> From passages burned, in the soot
> Of expired andantes, adagios,
> And a ballad's white dust on your brow,
> The scabby dry crust left by music
> On your *workaday* soul, there amidst
> The skill-less: a coal miner woman
> Who spends all her days in the pit.

Oh, letter, letter, blather thyself done already! You are about to be sent off. But a few more words from me myself.

Loving you as you should be loved is something I shall never be allowed, above all by you. Oh, how I love you, Marina! So freely, so innately, with such enriching clarity. It is so natural to my soul, and nothing is easier! [. . .]

You see how often I cross out my words? That's because I'm trying to write as I really think. Oh, how I long for the *real!* How I want to experience life with you! Above all, that part of life known as work, growth, inspiration, and discovery. It is time, the time is long overdue to start. I have not written anything for devil knows how long; I have probably forgotten how to write verse.

By the way, I recited your poems here. "Tsvetaeva, Tsvetaeva!" the auditorium shouted, demanding more. [. . .]

[. . .] And then the summer of our meeting will arrive. I look forward to it as an encounter with a *knowing* force, that is, with what is closest to me and what I have encountered only in music, but never encountered in *life,* ever. [. . .] Once again, a letter says nothing. Or perhaps even it speaks your poems in its own words. How superb they are! [. . .][63]

". . . I will be patient," Marina writes, "and await our meeting as I would death. [This is the source of my:

With the patience of crushing gravel,
With the patience of lingering death,
With the patience of imminent tidings,
With the patience of cherished revenge—
I will wait (as with hands tightly bound
The consort his Empress awaits)
With the patience of rhymes to be found,
With the patience of fingers clenched,
I will wait for you . . .]

[. . .] One needs to be patient, magnanimous—if you wish, older than one's years. Only an old person (one who needs

nothing) knows how to take, to accept, that is, to allow someone else the possibility of being by accepting what remains.
[...]

Your acknowledgment of me as a poet touches me—I do
not deny it. You are a poet; you see—*the future.* Your praise
for today's (work) I attribute to tomorrow's. If you see it, then
it *is,* therefore, it *will be.*

I need no one's praise and no one's recognition, except
yours. [...] Oh, don't be frightened by my unmeasured words:
their fault lies in that they are just words, that is, that they
cannot yet be *only* feelings.

[...] I am very calm. No fever. I pass my days in bliss.
For the first time in my life there is knowledge, not *enchant-
ments.* [*You exist in the world as a fact without me.*]

[*Oh, no*] exceeding one's rights or taking comfort in oneself! Besides Elysian Fields of the spirit there is also the Czech
forest with its branches and brushwood, with its bits of bird
feathers and rabbit fur: forehead facing Elysium, feet planted
in the Czech soil. Consequently, only my head is calm. While
my feet—in order to go to you—need a hand extended out-
ward.... I want your letters [, *your extended hand...*].[64]

As for "life with you...":

An innate and complete inability to "live with a person"
while living through him: to live through him while living
with him. How can one live with a *soul* in an *apartment?*
In the forest—perhaps. In a train car—perhaps (but doubt-
ful, for there is first class, second class, third class, with third
class in no way better than first, just as first class is in no way
better than third, and second class is worst of all. Categories
are awful.).

Living (coexisting) "with him," while living "through him"
is something I can do only in my dreams. And—it's wonderful. Exactly as in my notebooks.

... I think that out of stubbornness I will never say *that
word* to you. Out of stubbornness. Out of superstition. (The

emptiest of words—for it encompasses all, and the most frightening, after which everything begins, that is, ends.) It can be spoken about trivialities, when obviously a hyperbole. But by me to you—never.

. . . A juniper grows on my mountain. Each time after I have come down [from the mountain—trans.], I forget about it, and each time I go up, it takes me by surprise: who is that? Then I smile to myself: it's just a bush! I lose myself in thoughts about you, and when I return to my senses, [the juniper—trans.] is gone, behind me, I've passed it by. I have yet to see it up close. I think it is you. . . .[65]

In 1924 Pasternak informs Marina of the birth of his son, and she congratulates him on his firstborn! "The firstborn is always *the one and only,* no matter how many brothers he might have!" And she takes joy in his name, an extension of his mother's: Evgenia, Evgeny, despite the fact that she *actively* disliked names ending with y, finding them insufficiently masculine or manly. With the exception, that is, of the name Georgy—manly because he was "the Vanquisher"—which she gave to her own son, born in 1925.[66]

Boris, my dear!
I have no idea whether my letter—from [*long, long ago*]—has reached you. The length of the silences between us equals only the length of a letter's reverberation; rather, the intervals are filled with reverberations. Each of your last letters (always the *last!*) suffices just long enough for the next one to arrive. A more frequent correspondence would be like one continuous heartbeat. The strength of a heartbeat is equal to the duration of its resonance. Is there such a law of physics? If there is not, there is.
Boris, in case [my letter—trans.] has not yet flown home to you, I will recount briefly: in February I am expecting a son. . . . I am dedicating him to you, as the ancients dedicated their children to the deity. . . .[67]

She did not, however, name her son for the "deity."

"To name my boy Boris would be to fold Boris Pasternak into our family, to make him something we share in common, to domesticate him—and lose him as my very own. . . . A subtle, but stinging thought." What is more, "the name Boris will not make him a poet or Pasternak!" she penned in the same notebook where *The Ratcatcher* was taking shape, soon after the child's birth.[68] To Pasternak himself, in a letter dated February 14, 1925, she wrote:

> Dear Boris!
>
> On February 1, Sunday, at noon, my son Georgy was born. For nine months inside me and for his first ten days in this world he was Boris, but it was Seryozha's desire (*not* his demand!) that we name him Georgy, and I relented. Since then—relief. Do you know what feelings were at work inside me? A murky confusion, a certain awkwardness: Introduce you (love!) into our family. Domesticate a wild animal (love!)? Render the panther harmless?
>
> Take *him* from his own and to give you to them. Make you common property . . . ?
>
> Something *wild* (tamed)—like nephew and uncle . . . ?
>
> [. . .] This is not insanity, but the most deliberate of calculations (NB: That's what all madmen say!). . . .[69]

To illustrate how the subject of children wove itself into the celestial symphony of this correspondence—a subject that to some degree determined the infeasibility of their meeting (meetings, for one nonmeeting led to the next, and all of Pasternak's schemes—including a joint translation of *Faust,* again in Weimar, but many years later—never materialized)—I cite a fragment from a letter by Boris Leonidovich about his (two-year-old!) son. The letter is written using the familiar form of address (the year is 1926), which (being so *long-distance*) Marina resisted out of fear of reducing their relationship to the banal. . . .

> [. . .] For God's sake, do not send anything to our son. I am touched to the bottom of my heart by the way you write about this. [. . .] You once asked why I don't write about him. Because the whole house [. . .] has him in their arms; because

he doesn't have the kind of nanny that I'd like him to have[, and all this] can wreak havoc on his language. Because his mother (an artist) spends whole days on end, from morning to night, at VKhuTEMAS.[70] Because I can say nothing to her for I know that I too would go to VKhuTEMAS, and no family would stop me. Because love from all corners of the house is turning the child into an egotist and a spoiled brat, and it diminishes his tenderness and originality in my eyes, which sometimes perceive him otherwise. Because my love for him is riddled with footnotes. Because this composition of mine is being written in someone else's hand and I am powerless to counteract that, because the longer this nonsense persists, the more I am forced to earn money and the less I can devote myself to it. [. . .] That is why I do not like to talk about him. He so resembles me in my baby pictures that when one happened to surface in the process of sorting my father's archive, it was taken for his. Perhaps he will not be as ugly as I am, or perhaps only in a different way. But all of this, all of this at some point will have to be redone. . . .[71]

However, it is possible that Pasternak's misgivings about the purity of a two-year-old infant's speech and about his appearance, and his fear of the destructive influence that love from all sides would have on the child's character, were prompted in no small degree by the coincidence that this letter was written . . .

with an impossible toothache. The third one I have had [*of late*]. At the height of my work, when my nerves are already stretched taut, the right half of my lower jaw starts to ache. The abscess I had not long ago was something different, on the left side. This time the symptoms are all the same. The pain more aristocratic than that of a plain toothache, and more intolerable. What kind of punishment is this? [. . .] What am I to do? . . .[72]

Oh, how Marina responded—with all her pagan-maternal instincts— to these particularly *earthly* signs from Pasternak, to his *simple* toothache, to his *simple* physical exhaustion and the aggravation with household muddles that rent the poetic fabric of his letters! She loved mythology, for the same reason, for the ways deities and heroes slipped, fell, and hurt themselves in earthly ways while performing superhuman feats and deeds. Not just loved it, but drew constantly on its allusions and collisions in her own work. . . .

But in his letters Boris Leonidovich had an amazing talent for glossing over everyday tribulations that might elicit pity or sympathy, so as not to burden his reader with them—and so as not to invite the same in return. With Marina he liked to speak differently and about different things. He wrote the following to her after reading *The Poem of the End:*

> March 2[5—trans.], 1926
> [. . .] For the past four months I have been carrying around in the pocket of my overcoat a piece of murky-slushy, smoggy-foggy nighttime Prague with its bridge now in the distance, now right before my eyes. I wheel it out to whoever turns up next to me in line or to whoever my memory conjures up and with cracking voice initiate them to the abyss of this wounding lyric of Michelangelan sprawl and Tolstoyan density called *Poem of the End*. It came into my possession by chance, in typescript, without punctuation marks. . . .
> With what excitement I read it! Exactly as if I were playing in a tragedy. Every sigh, every nuance has been cued. "Hyperbolically—that is." "And when the train pulls up . . . , entrusting." "Smells of trade secrets and ballroom powder." "It means, you shouldn't, It means, you shouldn't. . . ."
> Alive within—and spoken by—me all these days: "my happiness fallen from heaven," "my darling," "astonishing," "Marina," and all the other involuntary sounds you, sleeves rolled up, are capable of extracting from my depths. . . .
> What an immense, damn immense artist you are, Marina! But not another word about *The Poem*, or else I will have to abandon you, abandon my work, abandon my family, and sit down, back turned to you all, and write without end about art . . . , about the revelation—never thoroughly discussed by anyone—of objectivity, about your gift for approximating the

world, because your bead, like any true creation, aims at the very mark of these heights.

Just a small remark about one expression. I am afraid that our lexicons do not entirely coincide. . . . You could leave the words "artist" and "objectivity" behind, while I take them with me. . . .[73]

[March 27, 1926—trans.]

[. . .] You are objective, you are, most of all, talent, *genius.* Cross out that last word, please. In common usage it is a peanut-gallery, barbershop-hairdresser word. Whenever I encounter it, it makes me queasy, as it probably does you too. Someday it will be said about you, or not said. Regardless, it is not the negative occult conjecture but the positive mysteriousness of the word that looms above you like an aerial roof, under which, year after year, you display your element.

What is important is what you are doing. What is important is that you are building a world *crowned with the mystery of genius.*

In your daytime, in your own presence, that aerial roof dissolves into the sky, into the blue expanse above the town where you live or that you imagine as you unleash your element. In times ahead people will tread this surface, and the earth of other times will come to lie upon it. Cities rise from the soil of the demystified genius of other centuries.[74]

[August 7, 1927—trans.]

[. . .] You write about not being understood on first reading, about the silence all around that reigns afterward. My experience in this respect suffers if not from the same, then from a very similar truth. Only my very earliest and rawest pieces—from fifteen years ago or so (that is, literally, my first and very beginning pieces)—were understood (by a total of one-and-a-half persons) immediately.

Soon I came to regard the two-year delay between a piece's debut and its being understood as a single moment,

an indivisible unit, because only in rare cases did that delay
last two years. More often three or more. . . .[75]

Two-three, even, let's say, three-four years between the creation of a
difficult piece and its being understood by readers! That is almost parallel,
almost synchronic evolution of writer and reader! No, Marina could not
even dream of such time frames. She could not dream of any time frame
for being understood within her own lifetime there, in foreign parts,
because *her* reader (not the reader exception, but the reader as a natural
mass phenomenon) was not to be found in emigration. He just did not
exist. And given the times and the conditions, there was nowhere for him
to come from. Having brought with him his own cohort of writers and
poets, together with his own cohort of critics, [the émigré reader—trans.]
had no inclination toward the new, had no notion of it—whatsoever, how-
soever, by soever—and at his best and most charitable could be as indifferent and deaf to it as a post.

Marina, who had written to Pasternak, "I need no one's praise and no
one's recognition, except yours," made this claim with her eyes squeezed
shut. Who knew better than she that poets write not for other poets and
not even for "the Poet" with a capital *P* that Pasternak was for her? That
sculptors sculpt not for other sculptors? That musicians create not for
musicians? That anything authentic is created for the masses, to quell *their*
hunger for the daily bread of creativity?

Who, if not she, knew how short-lived a *single* reader could be, even if
he were a poet, especially if he were a poet . . . ? She herself, after all, could
be most inconstant in her lofty fidelities.

In the meantime, the two of them pursued each other, longed for
their meeting that would never happen, exchanged manuscripts of just-
completed writing, books, and journal publications. Spilling over the
banks of their letters, the two of them became the property of many.
Pasternak—of whose "communalization" Marina's imagination lived in
terror—soon became a corresponding member of our family, that very
same "wild (tamed) nephew and uncle," the friend of Marina's and Seryozha's close friends, the poet read and loved by that handful of people
whose heads and hearts were already turning back in the direction of the
new Russia. The first publication of poems by *Soviet* writers (Pasternak, it
goes without saying, included) to come out in the beginning of the 1920s

abroad appeared in the Prague Russian-language student journal *By Our Own Paths,* edited by my father. . . .[76]

In 1924 Pasternak placed several of Tsvetaeva's poems from her "Czech period" in the almanacs *The Russian Contemporary*[77] and *Moscow Poets.*[78] The remainder of her work that made its way—through Pasternak and Ehrenburg, for the most part—to Soviet poets was accorded by many both the recognition and the understanding she neither encountered nor expected from her émigré "brethren." Here, for example, is a fragment from a letter written in August 1926 by Semyon Kirsanov to his friend Emili Furmanov:

> . . . Remember we read Marina Tsvetaeva? Guest what! Pasternak received two pieces from her from Prague: *Poem of the End* and *The Ratcatcher.* In my opinion, as well as that of others—including Aseev and Pasternak—this is the best thing written in the past five years. *Poem of the End* is complete genius (excuse my excitement). *The Ratcatcher* is the pinnacle of mastery. If I manage to copy them, I'll send you excerpts. . . .[79]

In 1927, in response to Pasternak's question was Marina not suffering from her obscurity in emigration, from the unfairness of this obscurity and lack of recognition, she wrote:

> . . . You are worried about *fame*? [*That*] I am deprived of my "hour in the limelight"? Whether that makes me bitter? Disappointed, yes. Here is why: when I write, I think about nothing except the piece itself. Then, when it's written, I think about you. When it's published—about everyone else. [. . .]
>
> And it is my profound conviction that were I to publish in Russia, *everyone* would understand me. [. . .] Yes, yes, everyone—because of my *basic* simplicity, because each would find his *own*, because I am *many*, a plurality. And I would be transported by this love. [. . .] Simply put, there is a vacancy in Russia, which is by right mine. . . .[80]

Explaining why she considers herself more "understandable" for readers in Russia than Pasternak, Marina wrote:

You lead readers in [. . .]. I lead them *out,* thereby liberating them. In the life of a reader I am one second, a jolt. What follows is his business, his doing. You transform the visible into the invisible (you turn the obvious into a mysterious), while I make the invisible visible (the mystery revealed). [. . .]

But, returning to the subject of fame, my books do not exist in Russia, hence the poet also does not exist.[81]

[. . .] My estrangement from life is becoming all the more irreversible. I have "transmigrated"—taking with me all the passions, everything yet unexpended. Not as a shadow debilitated by life, but as a living person departing the *living. . . .*[82]

This misfortune, this estrangement from "the living" Pasternak could do nothing to about. And who—or what—could? Torn from Russia but not integrated into émigré society, Marina was gradually becoming an island separated from its mainland by the flow of History and her own fate. She was becoming solitary, like an island, with all its (her!) unexplored treasures. . . .

Pasternak sensed sharply and painfully Marina's estrangement and the unrelenting persistence with which the threads of live human relationships connecting her to Russia were fraying, one by one. Therefore, when he learned that Anastasia Ivanovna Tsvetaeva (whom he knew well) was traveling abroad on invitation from Maksim Gorky, he delighted at the news of the two sisters' meeting.

Of course, you have already been in touch with Asya and are more amazed than I by this impossibility made possible. [. . .] My brother delivered the news. He himself did not speak to her over the phone; his neighbors passed on the message. [. . .] The fact that she did not inform me of her trip earlier—what with the inevitable confusion of last-minute packing—is not worth mentioning. [. . .] I might have asked her to take something for you. All the same, she has things to tell you about and to pass on to you, provided the details that deluge your meeting with her do not sweep all us Merzliakovskys and Volkhonkas from her memory.[83]

(At the time Anastasia Ivanovna lived in Merzliakovsky Lane, and Boris Leonidovich—on Volkhonka Street.)[84]

He waited impatiently for Asya's return, went to meet her at the train station, and listened hungrily to her stories, with sadness and hope at the same time. . . .

Dear Marina,

The snow is piling up, I have a cold, and the morning is overcast-overcast. A good time, probably, to fly over Moscow in an airplane to intermingle with this horde of snowflakes and see with their eyes what it is they're doing to the city, to the morning, and to this person at the window. [. . .]

Such are the main neural pathways of my attraction to you, which are capable of superseding more direct routes: I need to "seduce" you into a fate with more light and less abnegation than your present one. I feel this as intensely as if precisely this were the stuff of my breast and shoulder. [. . .]

In Asya's words, she was trying to describe me in the worst terms possible (in order to protect you from inevitable disappointment?). She is either knocking herself or did precisely what she should have, or . . . , it's all the same to me. What is remarkable is that she talked about you in such a way that I could barely hold back my tears: obviously, she has no misgivings on my account. [. . .]

She gave me her own copies of your "From the Sea"[85] and "A New Year's Poem";[86] Ekaterina Pavlovna Peshkova will deliver mine soon.

What can I say, Marina? Indescribably good! I used to read Blok that way. I used to write the very best of my own work the way I read yours now. Terribly sincere and sad and transparent. Expressiveness that grows and develops (as yours does always) thrives on the coincidence of meaning with passion, of knowledge with emotion. [. . .]

Above and more than anything else I, of course, love you, which should be obvious to a child. But I would not be my present self, if I were to remain at this insane source and not follow it downstream along all the consequences time sculpts.

Time, your magnitude, and my desire.

Plans, and more plans. Your situation seems natural to you but not to me.

To set right this blunder of fate—these days—remains a herculean task. But it is the only way; I know no other. [. . .]

In my letter to Gorky, by the way, I expressed this intention in the following way: "If you were to ask me what I was planning to *write* these days, I would answer, *anything I have to* in order to wrench this immense talent (you, that is) from the grip of a wrong and unbearable fate and return it to Russia."[87]

But the years passed, and plans not turned into actions faded and dissipated, while the fate remained wrong and unbearable, and the children grew, and the cares mounted, and the letters, beginning in 1931, started arriving more and more infrequently.

"The poems are tired," I once said as a small child to Marina when she could not write.

The time came when Pasternak's letters "got tired."[88] Sensing this in an at first subtle shift in tone, Marina stopped eliciting them; she endured exceptionally long "control" pauses between receiving and answering them; in her answers she did not suppress her mounting bitterness.

In 1935, exactly ten years since their "nonmeeting in Weimar," they had a fleeting, flawed encounter in Paris behind the scenes at the First International Congress of Writers for the Defense of Culture. In October 1935 Pasternak wrote in response to a letter that has not survived in Tsvetaeva's archive:[89]

Dear Marina,

I am still alive, I live, I want to live, and I must. You cannot imagine how awful I felt, then and for a long time after. "It" lasted for nearly five months. "It" means: not having seen my parents for twelve years and riding the train past [Berlin—trans.] without stopping to see them; refusing on return to Moscow to visit Gorky, with whom Rolland and Maya were staying, despite their insistence; having your proofs with me and not reading them; some force like none that had ever hit me before [. . .] robbing me of my sleep with the regularity of a curse as I awaited a good night's sleep after which I might renew my familiar and usual life following that unrecognizable, pitch-dark nonexistence.

Only then could come my parents, you, Rolland, Paris, and everything else omitted, conceded, and passed by. [. . .]

Perhaps it stretched on through my own fault. More than the intervention of doctors, this required time. I made matters worse with my own impatience. [. . .] It was like a bundle filled with things that keep falling out when you're in a rush: you pick up one and out falls another.

It ended only just recently, when everyone moved back to the city (from the dacha), and I returned to my usual routine. I started to sleep and set to putting my health in order. [. . .]

Now I have read your prose. It is all very you: you always get to the root of things and define things in complete, easy-to-remember terms, everything right on the mark. Still, more marvelous [than the rest] are "Art in the Light of Conscience," "[The House—trans.] at Old Pimen," and, to a degree, [your essay—trans.] on Voloshin. In these, especially the first two, the analysis—the very insatiability of the analysis—so to speak, is evoked by the nature of the subject, and the fire and energy you devote to them are natural and contagious.

In "Mother and Music"[90] there seems, at first glance, to be less necessity, or, as you yourself note, the terms of analysis (sharps and flats) miss the point. But even here there's a veritable ton of your images and dashes.

Over the summer your letter was forwarded to me. [. . .] I could not answer you right away because I was ill. Do you remember your phrase about absolutes? Everything in it is blown out of proportion. While my condition—to which you were witness—is minimized. But I encountered similar misunderstanding—it is only natural—from my parents as well: they were stunned that I did not visit and stopped writing to me.

I want to live, and I am afraid of bringing something down upon myself. Let us think of this as just an intermission in my life. [. . .]

But assume that I suddenly recover, and everything comes back. And once again I desire to look ahead. Whom will I see with the power and originality that was Rilke's besides you? [...]

When are you coming? [...]

Tell me, am I not imposing myself on you—after your summer letter?

Your B

The downward pitch of this letter—its descent into tepidness by comparison with the fire and surge of the past years—stunned and wounded Marina no less than individual phrases that referred to her, such as "you ... and everything else ... passed by," no less than his indifference to the last things she had written (which Pasternak had read—for the first time ever—only after some delay), and no less than his offhand mention of not visiting his parents.

Recognizing only *expression,* Marina did not understand *depression:* she did not consider it (unlike toothaches!) an illness, and it seemed to her to be no more than nasty personality traits allowed to come to the surface: laxity, lack of willpower, and egoism—weaknesses a person (a man!) had no right to. What ensued was not an answer but a rebuke, which Pasternak—given his state at the time—probably needed less than anything else.[91] This rebuke is one of Tsvetaeva's fiercest and most furious epistolary self-portraits, a bitter and ardent confession of her life-asserting and driving spirit, her fundamental of fundamentals.

... If both poets were not destined to meet in life as they had in their letters and manuscripts, they did have the chance to say good-bye to each other.

Boris Leonidovich together with the then young poet Viktor Bokov saw Marina off at the Northern River Station in Moscow in July 1941 when she was leaving to be evacuated—something he attempted in vain to dissuade her from doing.

Here is what Pasternak wrote to me a decade later, in October 1951, about the years of his lofty friendship with Marina: "Over the course of several years I was kept constantly in cheerful high spirits by everything your mama wrote at the time, by the sonorous, glorious resonance of her headlong, impetuous spirit. I wrote *1905* for you and *Lieutenant Schmidt* for your mama. That never happened in my life again. . . ."[92]

CZECHOSLOVAKIA

I remember neither our departure from Berlin nor our arrival in Prague, neither our reunion with Seryozha at the Prague station nor our shelter those very first days. (Probably, it was one of the "booths" at Seryozha's dormitory, "Svobodárna.")[93] Not the slenderest of "Ariadne's threads" back to those events remains in my memory, as if Marina and I, eyes shut, jumped from the swings in Berlin straight into that Czech village with its clumsy, canine name "Mokropsy," which—were "Mokropsy" by itself not bad enough—had to be "Dolní Mokropsy"![94]

[Nový Dvůr–Dolní and Horní Mokropsy—trans.]

In fact, it all started in [Nový Dvůr—trans.], where we spent a day under the uncertain roof of two sweet young lady-students, Seryozha's acquaintances, Marusya and Valya, while Seryozha and Marina looked for appropriate accommodations in the environs.[95] The roof was "uncertain" because the hut—all done up inside in curtains, embroidery, bedcovers, and bed skirts—belonged to a witch of a landlady. When she was around, the students were not to put the teapot on to boil, not to get up, not to sit down, and not to breathe—and we outsiders all the more so.

True, the hut's guardhouse atmosphere was mitigated by the loveliness of the two lovely young lady students, but it was also probably elicited by the powerful attraction the two girls held for the male half of the student population in [Nový Dvůr—trans.]. Out on the street potential husbands-to-be and indubitable "suitors" strolled with suspicious nonchalance back and forth along the fence, while the old lady muttered to herself. It was like something out of Gogol.

All around, wherever you looked, an amazing summer unfolded across green expanses framed by lilac-colored hills of spruce and dissected by a small river. All the surrounding little villages—each and every house—

peeked out of bushy bands of leafy fruit gardens. Dahlias blossomed in the flower gardens, and each gate boasted a little sign that read POZOR NA PSA! which meant not, as it sounds in Russian, "shame on the mutt," but "beware of the dog."

In my naïveté I initially delighted at the immense quantity of geese— a mandatory decorative element in the Czech rural landscape in those days. But alas! They turned out to be a bellicose tribe, quick to attack and prone to bite, and I often caught it from them if I was not quick enough with a switch. . . . They were particularly nasty when they walked around "naked," their feathers plucked for comforters. (The down on their chests grew back before winter.) Despite it all, though, they were amusing, those nipping clouds of snow-white feathers that ferreted the ground with snakelike necks as they waddled along the shoulders of country roads lined with tall, smooth-barked plum trees.

We settled on the other side of the Berounka River, which we had to cross near the high railroad bridge by a raft under whose boards the seemingly quiet, peaceful water of the river roared ominously. Here the hills receded to the sides, and the village rested as if in the palm of a green hand, which is why the area was called Dolní "lower" Mokropsy. For groceries we had to walk to other villages, but I loved carrying sacks to help Mama.

"Protocol entries" in my diary describe our home life during those first months after arriving in Czechoslovakia:

The House Where We Live

The house where we live lies in a valley. It has three rooms, one of which we occupy. The yard is small, the garden medium, and there is a dog named Löwe and some chickens. The house is painted yellow and white, and the roof is pink tile. Seven people live here, four of them children. Not far from here is a large village called Všenory. It has two stores, three-storey houses, and a railroad station. Our day passes as follows: we get up around eight, Marina makes breakfast, I put away all the bedding and clean the two tables and the two window-sills and sweep the floor using the landlady's broom. Then I go for milk, take out the trash, and bring water from the nearest well. After breakfast I wash the dishes, while Marina puts on dinner and sits down to write. I also sit down to write my four pages. After dinner I go out for a walk; sometimes Marina takes me with her. In the evening I read and draw and go to bed early. Sometimes we have guests, and sometimes Marina goes out.

Seryozha usually spends four days a week in Prague at "Svobodárna." He studies a lot. The rest of the time he lives here. In the morning he refuses to eat and gets angry when Mama gives him cocoa instead of tea or makes him butter his bread or boils one egg for him alone, even though it is absolutely essential that he eat because he is so thin and exhausted. After breakfast he sits down on his gray bed and surrounds himself with books or paces back and forth about the room, memorizing the contents of his notebooks. After dinner he refuses to go for walks, and Marina's invitations are in vain:

"Come on, Seryozhenka, let's go to the woods or to Všenory or to the cliffs!"

"Let's go, Papa! Please!"

"Marinochka, I can't. I still have a lot of studying to do. Fall exams are starting, and I don't want to fail."

"You really can't go?"

"No, Marinochka!"

"Then at least lie down and rest for a bit."

"Okay, okay, I'll lie down."

Marina and I leave for Všenory or for the store or for one of our five or six favorite cliffs.

The day arrives for Seryozha to return to Prague, and then we all get up at six, Marina makes cocoa and fries French toast for Seryozha, while Seryozha shaves and gets dressed, and I set the table, hurrying so much that my hands tremble. I put out the sugar and salt and everything else. Finally, we eat breakfast, very quickly if Papa is to make the 7:20 train. That's it! We give Seryozha his little borrowed suitcase. I have packed his razor, his soap, his toothpaste, his toothbrush, his towel, his handkerchiefs, and his notebooks. I bring his waterproof coat.

We go to see our Papa off. Marina has forgotten some-thing at home and goes back, while Seryozha and I hide in a ravine filled with fallen plums. We hear the sound of heels—Mama's footsteps. We start roaring and meowing. Marina exclaims: "Bah! You look like two creepy hobos or beggars!" We quicken our pace to a jog and take a shortcut. There's the bridge, and there's the station. Seryozha buys a ticket, and we all sit down on the bench. Suddenly, shoo-oosh! The four-car *rychlík* from Paris to Prague speeds past. (*Rychlík* in Czech means "express train.")[96] Boom! The train is crossing the bridge.

Then: ding-ding-ding . . . Seryozha's train. This is it!

"Goodbye, Marinochka! See you on Friday!"

"Goodbye, Papa! Come back soon!"

"Goodbye, Alya! Goodbye, Marinochka!"

And the train sets off.

I think that of all the train stations from which Marina ever departed or at which she ever arrived (or met or saw someone else off) the one at Všenory occupied a special place in her heart: a well-kept, empty suburban train station with beds of nasturtiums under the awnings, two streetlamps along the edge of the platform, a signal light, and the rails.

Marina often went to Prague. Waiting for her train under the streetlamps, she carried on imaginary conversations with Pasternak. Her thoughts whisked her away on the *rychlík* to Rilke's sick bed or to Weimar—so near and yet so hopelessly far away.

Along this platform she paced out her poems. Along these rails the distance rolled in on her from afar—Russia.

While day has yet to rouse
Its petty poisoned passions,
From dew and mist and rails
I resurrect my Russia . . .
. . . From dew and mist and flocks . . .
And, crowing frantic tidings,
The raven rails prevaricate:
There's Moscow down the line![97]

And

> . . . As if my life were stolen
> Down a steely row—
> In loamly gloom—two distant worlds
> (To Moscow bow down low!)[98]

My childhood notebooks record the earthly signs of Marina's days in the first of those Czech villages: in just over three years, right up until our departure for France, we lived in Dolní and Horní Mokropsy, Nové Zámky, Jíloviště, Všenory, and one winter (1923–24) Marina and Seryozha lived in Prague, while I attended boarding school in Moravská Třebová.

The otherworldly signs were Marina's first "Czech" notebook, begun August 6, 1922, and the first poem in it—

> The Sibyl has burned; the sibyl a tree trunk.
> The birds have died, but God has come . . .[99]

—dated August 5. That is, it was conceived still outside the notebook, before the notebook, in the heat of our move, the search for a new place to live, settling in, and getting acquainted with new people, new circumstances, and new conditions—that is, in the day in, day out hurly-burly and hustle-bustle of which poems are not born. This notebook's epigraph, which also prefaced the last collection of poems published during her lifetime—*After Russia* (Paris, 1928)[100]—bears the words of Vasily Trediakovsky: "That the poet is a creator does not mean that he is a teller of untruths: untruth is a word that violates common sense and conscience, whereas poetic imagination is often—in terms of common sense—what *could* and *should* be."

And so, the notebook began with "Sibyl," and Sibyl—like all of Tsvetaeva's images—descended from time immemorial and rushed far ahead, metamorphosing and acquiring concrete shape along the way: from the semiadolescent, inquiring "O, for what have I grown to be big? Salvation comes not!" and "A phrase so strange—old woman! Its meaning unclear, its utterance—morose . . ." to the prophetess's thematic crystallization as "departed from the living" and "having severed ties with her time," as the petrified repository of a divine, immortal gift and spirit.

Over the course of her life Marina never abandoned her central themes, and they—evolving from one hypostasis to another—seemed to cluster in such a way as to generate ever-newer offshoots of their trunk and roots.

For example, according to the original plan, the cycle *Sibyl*—three poems—was to consist of nine poems. The intended content of the fifth and sixth poems—"Sibyl having lost sense of herself" and "Sibyl having lost sense of others"—naturally flowed from mythological Greece into fairy-tale Russia, that is, into the second part of the poem *The Swain,* where it metamorphosed into the enchanted amnesia of Marusya, the poem's heroine. (Work on *The Swain,* which continued the line of Tsvetaeva's "Russian" poems, was begun in Moscow on the eve of our departure and completed in Horní Mokropsy over the course of the two last months of 1922 uninterrupted by any other poems.)[101]

Along the way, the theme of the Sibyl gave birth to (or engendered within itself) related themes of passing youth and gray hair—"it means that God is at my door if the house has burned down!"—where God is that same Phoebus, god of immortal inspiration and vocation, who lay waste to his mortal abode, the flesh of the prophetess. Sibyl's "fire under the tripod" also was reflected—in that very same notebook—in the cycle *Trees*[102] as well as in many other poems.[103]

As for the Swain himself, decked out in his red calico shirt and surrounded by the bewitching horrors of the Russian fairy-tale world: is he not an alternative reading, another interpretation, of the invisible but principal hero of *Sibyl*? Is he not the hero of the poem *On a Red Steed* who dismounts his horse and takes from his loving beloved all she has that is dear to her, but mortal—including life!—in the name of the undying and eternal? Even the endings of both poems, which carry—lift—the heroine into the blazing blue firmament of poetry, are related:

> . . . Until I am borne
> Off into the blue
> On a red steed by
> My genius! (from *On a Red Steed*)

> . . . Fire—to fire,
> Lash—to lash!
> Ho-me-ward,
> Into the blue inferno. (from *The Swain*)

A quality of Marina's lyric notebooks—among them this first Czech one bound in striped calico with Seryozha's inscription—which never ceased to amaze me was the art with which she transformed calendar pages of years long past with their otherwise unremarkable banalities, that is, her way of dissolving existence (everyday life) into nonexistence, the way the everyday so often served as the impetus for works far removed from the here and now.

Certain notations in my childhood notebooks might be likened to the pages of a calendar of our everyday activities that survived; they make it easy to track the immediate stimuli underlying some of Tsvetaeva's poems, rather, how the haphazardness of those stimuli brought Marina's thought—incessantly at work under the surface—to the surface of the page. Here, for example,

An Ordinary Description of an Ordinary Stroll
Marina and I are at the river. On the surface, half waves and half ripples float who knows where. We approach foamy small rapids and walk under the bridge with its thundering echo. The damp path between the willows is like a corridor. . . . Slowly and carefully, we make our way from rock to rock toward a certain tree that Marina has already—in advance—fallen in love with. There it is, coming close, and two minutes later we are sitting on the hump beneath it, on its intertwisted dried gray roots. I want to talk with Marina, but she says, "Be quiet! Let me listen to the water!" While she listened, Mama smoked two cigarettes, feasted her eyes on the river, jotted down some fragments of verse in her little notebook, and on the way back we gathered blackberries and saw a molted snakeskin. . . .

The poem sung to Marina that day by the "half waves and half ripples" of the tiny, cozy Berounka River was "Two is too many even for a morning's joy," with its spellbinding refrain:

At the fountainhead,
Adam, listen . . . , listen:
Lotic waters—
To their shores:
"Take heed! . . ."[104]

Next is a note of mine about our "entertaining" trip to Prague to see Seryozha, which included a visit to the theater (we attended Dickens's *The Cricket on the Hearth*).[105] Before *The Cricket* we strolled around the dismal industrial region surrounding "Svobodárna"—no Gothic and no baroque here!—then drank coffee with salted hard rolls and "beer" cheese in a worker's *kavarna* (café), talked, joked, laughed, and then walked around the stores trying to buy the frying pan we needed for our household (not knowing what it was called in Czech). After *The Cricket* we spent the night in an unoccupied booth in Seryozha's dormitory, leaving early the next morning so that Seryozha could finish preparing for exams, which were just beginning. All of it simple and sweet, sweet and simple, with only *The Cricket* to add a festive high point to the flatness of the day and a half. . . . And what did Marina's notebook absorb of this sweetness and simplicity?

All the gathered momentum of the cycle *Trees* grinds to a sudden halt, interrupted by the theme of *Factory Testaments*—essentially the antithesis of *The Trees:* "Smoke-cured edifices stand in unskilled-labor desolation . . ."[106] and "At the last, very last of urban outposts. . . ."[107]

Yes, this was the "Golden Prague" that tugged at Marina's heartstrings: its working-class outskirts, its factory smokestacks and plants, the nerve-rending complaint of its factory whistles, and the fates of "young and old, iniquitous and righteous in iniquity," which she inferred as if she had witnessed it all with her own eyes and borne its brunt on her own shoulders. All that it had taken was for her to walk—without a care in the world, so it seemed—down those desolate streets. . . .

[In Prague—trans.] the *industrial essence* of the outskirts of capitalist cities appeared to Marina in a new light: old Moscow had no wealth of factories and was not renowned for them. Only the West exposed Marina to the incongruity of cityscapes, and not just the view. . . . For at the time she was working on her "In praise of the wealthy"—an equivocal madrigal dedicated from the height of all the wealth of her own poverty to the great poverty and vanity of wealth: ". . . and because I can never be bought by inventories, tedium, gold plate, yawns, and packing wool—I affirm: I love the rich! . . ."

In yet another piece that appeared in the same stream of "urban outskirts" poems—"God save—the smoke"—one can sense the reality of our moves from one village and hut to the next along with the recollection of

Prague "outposts," where, in just the same way, the urban poor made their way from apartment to apartment, rather, from slum to slum. How many of our future address changes in the Parisian suburbs were foreshadowed by that poem!

As for our moves between various Czech villages, let those same excerpts from my childhood diary tell the story. . . .

Our Move to the Attic

Our landlady comes to us, her husband and a line of children trailing behind her. Their magnificent red dog, Pan Greko, lies on top of our things, his paws outspread. Our landlady is horrified: "Who let that dog into the house?" I know who, and I lead the dog back out. We pack all our things into a cart and are very happy that the landlord will haul it and that we do not have to carry it all. I put on my coat, put handfuls of junk in my pockets so that it won't be left for our landlords, and we say good-bye to all and leave. The landlord pulls the cart as we walk ceremoniously alongside: Marina carries her lamp ("With that same lamp! The lamp of poverty, student life, and life on the outskirts . . .")[108] and oil for the Primus stove, while I carry the kerosene and the coffeepot. We walk and walk until finally we turn into a filthy little street. We make our way to a shop, the owner's name printed over the door: MARIANNA SASKOVA. We turn into the back entrance and while Marina goes to break large bills to pay for the move, our new landlord helps our old landlord haul our things upstairs. The room is wonderful. A crooked window and relative darkness. Two tables, two beds, three chairs. There is even a trash can.

. . . We live here now. Marina admits the sun and the moon through our crooked window. When not standing next to the Primus, cooking or boiling something, she will invariably be sitting at this window and writing. Through the window you can see the most color-variegated trees: dark green, reddish, and brown. They grow on the mountainside. Our landlord's two cats (one gray, the other black) also live on the mountainside. They're impossible to catch. . . .[109]

That was the end of September. In the beginning of November we moved again.

The other day when Marina and I were on our way to the forest we passed a cozy little yellow house with a green gate. I said to Mama, "Oh, how I would love to be little (I'm ten years old!) and live with Grandmother and Grandfather in that little house!" The next day, in the evening, Papa arrived and took Marina to see a room. When they returned, I listened to my heart's content to stories of our new place: low ceilings, three windows, a ceramic tiled stove, etc.

The next day, November 2, [1922—trans.], we began moving our belongings. Papa and I went first. Papa draped a belt across his shoulder and hooked to it our plaid travel bag and a huge suitcase filled with our things. I carried a basket with all Mama's, Papa's, and my shoes. We walked for a long time, and when we finally arrived I saw that it was that same little yellow house with the green gate. There is a dog house in the yard, and a small, white, very fine dog runs out, barking madly and turning somersaults in frustration at not being able to reach us. The old landlady turns out to be deaf, which is why she took so long to open the door. When we walked into the room, I saw that it indeed had very low ceilings and that to the right of the entrance door there was a tiled stove with an oven and many little dampers; to the left were two small windows with green frames, with a third very small one next to the stove. There was a table, a long bench, and two beds, one with its headboard backed to the window. How nice that the little house is right next to the forest! I won't have far to go for tinder. In vain Seryozha attempts to bargain with the landlady for hay or straw stuffing for our mattresses. She either does not hear or chooses not to understand and offers to sell us potatoes and onions instead. We unpack our things and go back [to the old place—trans.]. Marina sits Seryozha down to rest and to read *War and Peace,* while she and I stuff the travel bag and the basket and set out again. It's raining, and rivulets of dirty, clayey water flow along the roads. At one point we wade through water up to our ankles. We finally reach our new dwelling, unpack another load of things, and head back by way of the same mucky road, sinking repeatedly into the mud. We return to our now almost desolate attic. Seryozha has warmed up the soup and fried potatoes. We eat together, very quickly, because Seryozha has to catch a train to his lectures. The next time we meet will be at our new place.

After saying good-bye to Papa, Marina and I make two more trips to move the rest of our things, using a backpack and the basket, then one more trip with a basket and a bucket into which Marina puts the coffeepot and coffee, a tin can of grain, a bottle of kerosene, and a wad of rags to keep it all from capsizing and spilling. Mama carries the bucket in her right hand and a lamp in her left, while I carry the basket with the dishes, first in one hand, then in the other. We try very hard not to slip, so as not to break anything, especially the lamp.

Finally, we arrive with the last load. The landlord's little dog, called Rumyga, recognizes us by now: she still barks but doesn't jump at us anymore. We unpack our things, arrange all the dishes on the shelf above the stove, and hang the pots and mugs on special hooks along a shelf decorated with scalloped paper.

It is getting dark. Because of the move Marina allows me not to do arithmetic and to read Gogol's *Inspector General* instead. She sits down with her notebook, and we both eat apples, as many as we want. . . . [110]

Thus we spent the winter in that room with its green window frames and low, unpainted ceiling in the house of that old deaf woman with her dog Rumyga. We had a good winter—all of us together, close to each other—even if times were hard. The hardships became apparent to me later; as a little girl I simply did not realize what they were, perhaps because I had never known an easy life. That a part of the housework fell to me I considered not only natural but a pleasure. That I had only two dresses did not cause me to dream of having a third, although I really could have used an extra one, if only because I was always catching my clothes on fences or snagging them on branches, and then, tears streaming down my cheeks, I would have to carefully darn the holes. That treats and presents were rare only enhanced their magical value in my eyes.

The main thing was that Marina's and Seryozha's valiant poverty—the dignity, patience, and particularly the humor with which they struggled against all the day-in, day-out hardships, supporting and encouraging each other—evoked in me a *burning* love for them and *camaraderie* with them, which in and of itself was a kind of joy. Other moments of happiness were those evenings we occasionally spent together at the table after it had been cleared of food and dishes and gaily wiped down with a damp cloth, and a cozy, solemn kerosene lamp—its glass and round tin reflector gleaming—placed at its head. Seryozha would read to us aloud from books he had brought from Prague. Marina and I would sit and listen as we darned, patched, and mended. Since that day I still hear Gogol, Dickens's *Dombey and Son* and *Little Dorrit* in my father's voice, and they still give off the slightest scent of kerosene and of a stove fired with brushwood.

Books were few and far between, and each one was an event.

Once Seryozha brought home Gorky's *Childhood.* It was very unusual, unlike anything we had read before or anything I had known in my own childhood experience. Marina—who on occasion might doze off with needle in hand to the sounds of Gogolian devilry or Dickensian sweetness she knew by heart—listened to this book in a special way, occasionally interrupting Seryozha's reading with short exclamations of approval.

Sometimes Seryozha read small fragments and short stories in French (one of his requirements at the university), which he translated on the fly into Russian. Like a village bonesetter setting dislocated joints, Marina firmly corrected his pronunciation and told him the meaning of words he did not understand.

Once, though, even Marina was stymied by the word *défroque* (rubbish, tatters), which came up unexpectedly and somewhat beside the point in an otherwise flat, almost saccharine text. She had to look it up in a dictionary, an old edition with many verbs but of little help. "De—ded—des—def," Papa mumbled as he ran his finger down the columns of small print. "Def . . . , there it is! '*Défroque:* the possessions of a dead monk.' Hmm . . . How strange! What have monks got to do with it? The story is about a young girl, a young boy, spring. . . . How strange!"[III]

"And expressive!" Mama chimed. "What sadness, dejection, and poverty. . . . Who could be more impoverished than a dead monk? By the way, what *possessions* could a monk (not to mention a dead monk) have? He slept on bare boards, drank his soup from a monastery bowl, and was buried in his own cassock . . . in a hair-shirt."

"Well, maybe he had a *spoon* of his own?" Papa proposed hesitantly, a smile already in his eyes. "Of cypress, with a cross on it."

"A spoon! A spoon is not a possession. Possessions are clutter, junk, like what we have. But you're right, what's a monk got to do with it?"

"A *dead* one! A dead monk!" I interjected in earnest. "Probably, that is the whole point. Everything else is just camouflage. Maybe he was a vampire and a werewolf, and now he is pretending to be a young man? Just as in Zhukovsky's poem *The Loving Cup*! Or in your *Swain*, Marina!"

Marina at this point started to laugh, and "in its leaves that day we read no more"[112]—at least not in French.

. . . Another source of happiness was our family fairy tale, which Marina and Seryozha would tell me before I went to sleep—if I had behaved myself, which happened not every day. It was a long animal story with adventures and to-be-continueds, whose beginnings were lost somewhere back in my parents' youth and my very early childhood, if not infancy. Seryozha was a wonderful Lion and Monkey, while Marina played Cat and Lynx.

The original cast of animals had multiplied into secondary characters. Their travels, high jinks, escapes from captivity, chases, and rescues always began on the central square, Wenceslas Square, in Prague. From there they scattered to kingdoms far, far away in never-never land. Lion was noble; Lynx was crafty and unpredictable, and the other characters possessed other qualities. All of them landed in amazing predicaments, from which they then rescued each other. They had to: otherwise I would not fall asleep.

For as long as I can remember they had a tender ritual: Marina called Seryozha Lion, Löwe, and he called her Lynx or Mrs. Bobcat. These fairy-tale names entered our daily family routine, replacing their real names, and so it continued until the end of their lives. Marina's notebooks are scribbled with Seryozha's "leonine" drawings. On his way (usually running) out the door—"tramping with his paws," as Lion in the fairy tale says—to catch the train to classes at the university or to run some umpteenth odd errand, Seryozha would sketch the silhouette of a lion—grateful, well fed, with a full tummy (or sometimes, what was more familiar, skinny)—jumping onto the platform of the last car of a departing train.

Or a lion crying giant tears. Or a lion laughing with gaping jaws. Opening her notebook, Marina would smile after him as she took up her work. . . .

Marina often signed her letters to Seryozha and me with a capital *L*, the flourish forming a long-tailed wildcat or just its ear, with a tassel: the keen ear of the lynx.

Here is one of Marina's "Lynx" autographs from my notebook entered alongside "A Character Study of Nozdrev"[113] written in my lazy, careless hand: "A drunkard, but hardly stupid, who drove his wife into an early grave and whose next victim will be the wet nurse, and then another woman . . .":

> Today, October 8 [September 26, OS], on the day of my thirtieth birthday, at 7:30 P.M., you—deceitfully having no desire to write and angered by my perspicacity—responded to my offer to draw you a lynx with "Pooh! on your lynx" (you repeated it twice).

There is a slight leap in logic between my laziness, Mama's perspicacity, and her offer to draw me a lynx (the highest, so to speak, reward for diligence). Apparently, I caught it from perspicacity for being lazy, got my feelings hurt (it was, after all, a day for celebration!), and then Marina had had second thoughts and decided to console me, but I was angry and dug in my heels. . . . One way or another we must have made our peace because there she is in my notebook: Lynx, as depicted by Mama, Lynx in the role of the Dove of Peace, although with the tassel on her ear is a bit threatening and her pose suggests a certain readiness to lunge. . . . Farther down the page, alongside that same Nozdrev essay, follows my self-placating grousing:

> Dear Lynx,
>
> Since today is your birthday, I wish you a happy birthday and will ignore all your insults. Though you are now an aged, thirty-year-old Lynx, you still sit tall in your chair. . . . I gave you as presents a box of matches, my drawing of a lion in the desert, a pear, three notebooks, and three cigarettes, and You said that I wrote badly. I am sorry that on Your birthday the Lynx in You has been awakened with a terror. . . .

With Lynx one could use the informal second-person singular form of address—you; with Marina only the formal second-person plural—You.

. . . There was yet another source of happiness, one so familiar to us all that it would not be worth mentioning were it not for that special combination of its "component parts" which we seem now to have lost: the joy of children's holidays! That sense of having earned them, for they were more than just numbers on a calendar.

The happiness of a tree, which you began to decorate in moments bought with angelic behavior and herculean performance of your chores, although—alas!—not without lapses that threatened to topple your entire creation!

The happiness of ornaments made with your own hands out of prescription bottles and candy wrappers, cutouts and pictures, eggshells and matchboxes, pinecones collected in the woods and tiny bouquets of dried rowanberries, all carefully collected in a cardboard box stored underneath your bed. For what is an ornament if not an invention, an idea materialized . . . ? Colored paper Papa brought, scissors, flour glue boiled in a tin can, a cardboard paint palette with dull buttons of watercolor paints, thread, bobbins. . . . In order to get one's hands on these riches—the raw materials of future tree treasures, in order to have the right to invent, cut, glue, and paint to your heart's content, you had to do a good, conscientious (and fast!) job of daytime chores and duties. And then—here!—your well-earned corner of the table, your well-earned (on a par with the adults) recreation, the well-earned miracle of a holiday you yourself were creating and bringing closer to happening.

They were probably just awful, those pigeon-toed cardboard tigers of mine in their prison stripes, those rag-doll Father Frosts, lopsided stars, matchstick angels, eggshell clowns, and windmills and sleds made of matchboxes. The snowflakes were no doubt gaudy, and the paper chains worthy of Bonivard,[114] but what factory-made ornaments with their impeccable shapes and mass-produced luster could compete with a child's homemade creations and all the *soul* invested in them, all the effort, and creative delight? Only the stars in heaven can match them!

And how those ornaments came alive in the warm flickering of candles! Acquired a life of their own, no longer dependent on us! How proudly though humbly they reigned among strong, jutting, green branches awakened from their icy constraints!

. . . There was also the magic of "their" holidays, the Czech villagers' holidays! For Saint Mikuláš [Nicholas—trans.] Day Pan Baloun's store in Všenory[115] and Pani Saskova's store in Mokropsy sold gingerbread figures of the saint, which ranged from little cheap ones to those so big only the storekeepers themselves could afford them. Each gingerbread cookie was generously iced with colored glaze that outlined against a rust-brown background the folds of his coat, his stole with its crosses on each side, and his bishop's staff. A saintly wrinkled paper face stuck on with sugar gazed out at the consumer with an expression that forgave all, which was most apropos, for once they tired of admiring him, underage pagans and heretics would gobble him up to the last crumb, with their only gesture of respect that they nibbled from the feet up. . . .

On Christmas Eve the wretched windows of the village shops displayed nativity scenes with crudely hewn, angular wooden Virgins, Josephs, and infants in mangers with real straw, Magi, oxen and asses, all topped by huge stars with long silver-thread tails. The children came running from afar to marvel at these primitive wonders, and even the adults would stop and look with tenderness. The village breathed with the multilayered, spiced, saturated aroma of a rural holiday, of roasted geese, onion, saffron, vanilla, and of *vanočki* (from the word *Vanoce,* "Christmas")—long, braided buns with almond and raisins fresh out of the oven.

From somewhere beyond the blue mountains puppeteers would appear to give shows in the little hall of the office of the "mayor." The puppet theater fit on a single table; the show was hosted by Kašparek, the Czech Petrushka,[116] a long-nosed little man with an intractable half-moon smile who wore a striped, tasseled hat. The show began with a riddle Kašparek put to the children about a little star stolen by a terrible black eagle and kept in captivity for a good three hundred years. "And then came the hunters and—bang! bang!—all that remained of the eagle were his feathers! His prisoner, released from his talons, once again shone in the sky. Now, my dear little boys and girls, what star was that?" "Československo! Czechoslovakia!" the little viewers shouted and clapped. (At the time, Czechoslovakia's 1918 independence from the Hapsburgs was all of four or five years old.) "Correct, my dears. Entirely right, ladies and gentlemen! And now we're going to show you the ancient legend of the famous Doctor Faust, which has been performed by our actors on this stage for hundreds of years!"

The legend turns out indeed to predate Goethe, and the puppets are real brocade and velvet antiques set into supple action (down to their tiny fingers) by hundreds of invisible threads. The craft—rather, the high art—of itinerant puppeteers has been handed down from generation to generation together with the marvelous, gothic-style elongated figures of the marionettes, their costumes, set decorations, and props. Together with a demanding love for their trade and gentle respect for their viewers. Together with their traditional—for the most part, folk—repertoire. Together with kerosene- and candlelit illumination.

I allow myself to resurrect these moments of happiness—while suppressing many others, for they are not to the point—only because they were, without doubt, islands of happiness for my parents as well, rest stops on a road of pressing hardship and mounting alarm. But a child's happiness resides on the surface of events. Taking joy in others' Christmas Eves, others' space to roam, and others' hospitality, the children of emigrants—for a while, at least—do not realize their own *national* exclusion from all this and many other things. They do not realize that they are national orphans and have no right to such things. Living in the here and now, they do not yet know what it means to worry about the future or to bear responsibility for it. They believe in miracles that happen on their own, without being earned or in any way suffered for. And so, while Seryozha was trying to decide how he could straighten out and repair a life broken in two, and while Marina closed herself off in her work as if in a monastery cell, I dreamed only of how I would find "a wallet with two million." One million I would give to my parents and the other to the "poor Russian students," Mama's sister Asya, and Max Voloshin . . . , "and 500 koruny will go to Lyudmila Chirikova for books. We will be rich, travel wherever we want third class (!); our floors will be scrubbed more often and our linens washed regularly. And one day, while sweeping the floors, I will find a cage next to my bed with two pink-eyed rabbits inside." Ah, the dreams of a millionaire!

[Moravská Třebová—trans.]

At the end of August 1923 my parents took me to Moravská Třebová, a small town on the German border where there was a boarding school for the children of Russian refugees. Seryozha had tutored me in arithmetic, at which I was idiotically inept, and Marina attempted to add some grammatical foundation to my already fluent writing and voracious reading. Having learned the short prayers long ago, I also memorized the Russian Orthodox Creed and the Latin alphabet.

Marina did not want to let me go. She was of the old school that believed formal schooling for girls was pointless, and she also feared our separation. It was my father who insisted both on my schooling and on our separation.[117] What's more, the directors of the school were recent comrades-in-arms of his, the Bogengardts. Vsevolod Aleksandrovich Bogengardt was tall with red hair and a dandy's bearing, a former officer in the czar's army. Olga Nikolaevna, a former army nurse and an officer's wife, was broad and stocky, with black whiskers visible above her upper lip and hair piled in a tight bun at the nape of her neck.

At the front, he had been critically wounded and she had nursed him back to health, cured him of vodka, dissuaded him from committing suicide, and become his wife. To lend their life some semblance of rhyme and reason they dedicated themselves to raising orphan children. (Many years later, in the mid-1930s, in a car at a Parisian cabstand, I saw that red beard that so reminded me of my childhood. It was Bogengardt! We renewed our almost forgotten friendship. My parents and I visited them in their apartment far from where we lived, in a little house where little foster children—the umpteenth generation of them!—rolled and scampered around an aged, even stouter, but no less energetic Olga Nikolaevna. It was almost impossible to support the children on the unpredictable earnings of a cabdriver, but love for children in misfortune can work many miracles. These were people with big hearts!)

Marina and Seryozha stayed with them for the short period of my entrance examinations and then left, not to return until Christmas.

On September 2, 1923, my parents moved from Mokropsy to Prague.[118]

The only "science" I acquired in Moravská Třebová was that of dormitory life. I kept up in my other subjects, thanks to my homeschooled preparations. Before long, I was first in Russian and last among forty in arithmetic.

The fates of the children "interned" in the school's long, white barracks fenced off from the surrounding world by a solid brick wall were uniformly fantastic and infinitely sad.[119] After lights-out in the dormitory the girls would talk about themselves and about their loved ones, many of whom had been lost forever. The glow of the night-light gave rise to shadows of Russian towns and villages I had never heard of; of houses, apartments, estates, and families; of bumpy escape routes; of hellish ghettos in fairy-tale Constantinople, and of the haunts where Mama or an older sister "danced" or "sang.". . .

After reveille, the children were like children everywhere: attending lessons, playing, crying, misbehaving, fighting, and making up. When a correspondent from some French newspaper once arrived at our Třebová backwater in search of our "sensational" autobiographies, many of the younger children were unable to put them to paper because for them what they had been through seemed so "uninteresting." Others merely made things up. For example, one of my little comrades began the story of his life with the words: "When I was born I was five years old." He ended with "and that's where I was eaten by a lion and they laid me to rest."

The principal's name was Adrian Petrovich. His name day was celebrated with pomp and circumstance. Our awful priest—a former army chaplain in thundering boots who was rude and misanthropic—subdued himself to lead the prayer service. Then, one class at a time, the children approached the principal and presented him with letters of congratulations beautifully written out on Whatman drawing paper with headings and borders in the Russian style. I too drew some fioriture (they came out just terrible I was so afraid of ruining the paper) and composed a congratulatory message in verse. Although written on behalf of the entire first grade, it opened with a certain "personal" ring to it: "How wondrous to my ears the sound: you—Adrian, I—Ariadna." I forget what followed that nonsense, which is a pity: it must have been pretty funny. . . . The principal wiped away a tear and lifted me straight up—so that I counted the buttons on his waistcoat with my nose, pressed me to his chest, and exclaimed, "I don't know about the mother, but the daughter is a regular Pushkin!"

For a long time after I was teased undeservedly for that "Pushkin."

Arriving in Moravská Třebová for the Christmas holidays,[120] my parents rented a room in a quiet apartment made dark by the clutter of Gothic-topped varnished furniture and the folds of plush pompon curtains and tablecloths.

"Do you like it?" asked Marina, who had just taken me beyond the school grounds.

"Very much!" I answered with all my heart.

"Too bad. It's enough to make me gag. All imitation something, all of it be-like-the-neighbors. Clichéd respectability. German bourgeois taste. Let's go for a walk while your father is with the Bogengardts!"

We went outside.[121] It was snowy and clear. An ornate baroque fountain stood silent in the center of the square. Not far behind it, snow-dusted houses with sculpted facades leaned into the imposing town hall as if supporting it respectfully from both sides. After four months of uninterrupted boarding school, the little town seemed like heaven to me. I craned my neck this way and that, trying to take it all in at once, together with Marina, whom I chatted up with stories about the other girls, about my lessons, about how we were fed so well that there was even bread left over. All the while I held Marina firmly by the hand, as if I were a little girl. She listened without interrupting, sort of melancholy and far, far away. Occasionally she would ask short questions: Did I comb my hair with a fine-tooth comb? Did I understand the math problems they gave us about merchants, trains, and swimming pools? Who were my friends? Why them? Was I reading Charskaia? ("Of course not, you didn't give me permission!")

Yes, she was scrutinizing me from the side, taking mental note of the words and phrases I had picked up from other voices, of my new behaviors, of all the foreign contaminants, undue familiarity, vulgarity, carelessness, and trivialness that had stuck like barnacles to my tiny boat sent out on its maiden voyage. Yes, I, the child of her soul, the pillar of her soul; I, whose immediate presence had replaced Seryozha's all those years of his absence; I, who was gifted with the rarest of talents—the ability to love her the way *she* needed to be loved; I, who from birth had understood what was not to be known and had known what I had never been taught, who could hear the grass grow and the stars ripening in the skies, who could sense a mother's pain at its very source; I, who had filled my notebooks with her, and I, with whom she had covered her notebooks—

> We were—remember in future,
> In sorrowful times to come:
> I was your very first poet,
> And you—my very best poem. . . .[122]

—I was becoming an *ordinary little girl.*

*

There was more, during a walk, this time together with Seryozha:

"Yes, of course. If Goethe had been born here. Or if he had lived here, as he had in Weimar. Or if he had at least stopped here on his way somewhere else. Then the city would have acquired some meaning—soul!—for time eternal, along with this city hall, and that fountain."

"What is Goethe without Weimar? Everything! That is, Goethe in his entirety: *Wilhelm Meister, Faust,* even *Hermann und Dorothea.* And Weimar without Goethe? A little German town for . . . well, for its inhabitants, for a bunch of philistines. . . ."

"A city of unsung heroes, that is?" Seryozha conjectures.

"A philistine is not a hero!" Marina cuts him short. "Weimar without Goethe is the city of Hamelin. Remember? From the legend of the Pied Piper.[123] A city waiting for its Pied Piper, to its own undoing. That deserved him, for all its practicality and lack of soul, for proclaiming philistinism the only possible, only logical form of existence. . . ."

Thus, by imperceptible degrees, Marina's *Ratcatcher* was conceived and came to be.

Marina's draft notebook (the second Czech one): "Begun May 10, 1923, on the Day of the Ascension, in Czechoslovakia, in Horní Mokropsy, at exactly noon. (The bell tower is sounding.)"

Its first line is "Time: I never have enough." The second: "Space: I'm too large to fit."

There are variations of "In Praise of Time":

> Cobblestones in downtown Bezhensk!
> Snap!—All hell breaks loose
> Into a headlong spin of wheels.
> Time: I never have enough.[124]

Then, developing the theme of time, follow variations on the poem "Steal Away":

> Perhaps, the best diversion ever
> Is to hide and at the same time be?
> That the fingers of J. S. Bach
> Never touch the organ's echo?[125]

And, once again—Sibyl—arrested in time, she simultaneously prophesies times to come—the future! Greece, Sparta:

> Here no one gives up, surrenders,
> Here no one ever sings or laments
> Or complains of ill luck. Instead
> Of pastorals and pastel idylls—
> Grass, birds, sheep, and amaryllis—
> Sparta's valiant bas-relief.[126]

And

> Sparta scorches: cruel and dry!
> Sparta stifles: in equine strides,
> The law here rides the steps of souls.
> Each nurturing his own fox cub
> Under his cloak. . . .[127]

And more and more Greek, Italic, and mythological flashes and flares, and reflections of that distant classical fire scattered throughout her poems:

> High above a smitten Phaedra
> Soars the curtain like a vulture . . .[128]

> Through soporose eyes Ariadnas—
> Beguiled and deceived . . .[129]

> . . . Like Lot's wife
> Posts stiff in the cinder track bed.[130]

> The [graying] Roman she-wolf's
> Gaze glimpses in her fosterling—
> Rome . . .[131]

> Hour of the Soul—like the hour of David's string
> Amid the dreams of Saul . . .[132]

> Thus, Polyxena, spying Achilles
> There on the rampart wall . . .[133]

Again and again, the theme of time—of eternity and time—of the "minute missed,"[134] bursts of Russian longing, biblical variations, and—running through and tying it all together—Sibyl, the sibylline theme of Fate . . .

All of this—mounting, growing more complicated, and surging forth—demands an outlet, the realization and purport only a major work can provide; it demands the backbone of a large-scale piece with its own rules to both contain and at the same time liberate and organize.

In her draft notebook, Tragedy—for the time still only a suggestion—begins to interject itself among her poems as large horizontal planes of prose that intersect the nervous columns of her verse: preliminary plans for the play *Ariadna;* "biographical" sketches of her heroes; their character traits. The bed of ancient tragedy is being prepared for a contemporary and timeless stream of passions and human calamities.

Verse—in Marina's case always monologues and always unanswered!—once endowed with the flesh of her heroes, will finally acquire the right to *dialogue.* . . .

[Prague—trans.]

Following her move from the village, the city—precisely that city, the inimical—glimmers through poems and individual lines and stanzas written already in autumnal Prague:

> Acrid though your chimneys' smoke be,
> Yet every gulp—is ecstasy! . . .
> For at night the city is
> The sky turned upside down . . .[135]

> The lane's last scarlet light . . .[136]

> Along embankments, where trees are gray . . .[137]

Streetlamps lit by a flaming gas
That chills . . .[138]

The streets bear no blame for the horrors
Of our soul . . .[139]

Prague, a poem writ in stone . . .[140]

And it rises to its full nighttime height as "The Prague Knight":

Pallid, gray, pale,
Guarding the wash of time—
A knight, the knight
Keeps the river under watch.[141]

And from the Knight, from that bridge over that Vltava, by way of rough drafts through the already live fabric of the first scene of *Ariadna*—[the city—trans.] gropes its way *past* and along the thread leading from the labyrinth into the light of day back toward the labyrinth and the great despair of *The Poem of the End* and *The Poem of the Mountain* which at the time mounts ineluctably in the distant reaches of her soul and in the depths of her notebook.

Soon they, those poems, would burst the floodgates of her other creative designs, just as the feeling that gave birth to them (the *Poems*) would surge over the strongholds of plans, propriety, and the acceptable.

"There are feelings," Marina wrote in those days, "so serious, authentic, and large that they fear neither shame nor distortion. They *know* that they are but shadows of authenticities to come."

The *Poem of the End* and *The Poem of the Mountain* were to become such authenticities.

The rift between their heroes occurred, judging by Marina's notation, on December 12, 1923.[142] This was not a "total" rupture of their "relationship," which had been commenced long before the Prague autumn of 1923 and lasted until Marina's departure for the Soviet Union—and, for the hero of the *Poems*,[143] to this very day, for over the entire course of his hardship-laden and courageous life he has preserved the lofty, loyal, and self-abnegating memory of the brief and sorrowful happiness once visited upon him.

I would not have undertaken to speak about the hero of the *Poems*—this is none of my business (or anyone else's) and everything that needed to be said and made public about him and about the heroine has already been said and made public by Marina in the *Poems*—were it not for "distortions" of precisely the kind that "feelings never fear" but which hurt people as well as the truth.

Far from all with whom Marina spoke and exchanged letters, fleeting "friends," and just acquaintances would subsequently prove equal to her trust in them or, at the very least, practice the basic good manners they had been taught as children, when, in "memoirs" published abroad, they touched on circumstances and turns of fate in the lives of Tsvetaeva and her loved ones. I am not talking about "memoirists" whose memory failed them in old age (whom hasn't it failed!) or of those who lack both heart and depth (what can't be cured must be endured!). I am talking about not disinterested sensation-mongers and boorish ill-wishers who—from a safe distance beyond the arm of the law—were out to settle accounts, be those accounts of the living or posthumous, personal or political. [I am talking—trans.] about speculators in paraliterature who in their so-called studies of the life and work breed conjecture and falsehoods and maim the facts.[144]

The hero of the *Poems* was endowed with a rare gift of charm that combined courage with spiritual grace, gentleness with irony, responsiveness with carelessness, passion (the ability to be passionate about something) with frivolity, youthful egoism with selflessness, and softness with volatility. "Amid the crudely unceremonious and idle-prattling crowd of Russian Prague"[145]—the qualifiers here belong to Valentin Fyodorovich Bulgakov, Lev Tolstoy's last secretary, a wonderful human being and a true friend of our family—that charm seemed an anachronism, something out of the eighteenth century (which not long before had so captivated Marina's imagination): idle, carefree, and devilish, and at the same time, and above all else, chivalrous. . . .

There was a certain charm to his appearance, to his bearing, to his quick-wittedness, to the ease with which he spoke, and to the speed with which he made decisions. There was charm in his very youth at the time— his boyishness. . . .

That charm lay on the surface—within arm's reach!—but it came from within, where everything was so much more substantial, sad, mature, and even tragic, for this person's life, like that of my parents, was unwilling and unable to graft itself to the alienation of emigration.

And did not.

The hero of Marina's poems—a Communist and courageous member of the French Resistance—smoothed out the initial and woeful messes in his life by devoting his mature years to the struggle for the *right* cause, to the struggle for peace against Fascism.

What else is there to say? Through wars and German extermination camps he kept Marina's letters and the manuscripts of the *Poems* safe, and later he sent them to Russia for inclusion in the Tsvetaeva archive by way of someone he considered *loyal,* that is, incapable of violating the secrets of such a profoundly personal correspondence, who would honor the memory of the woman who had written them and the will of the addressee.

He awaited that loyal courier for a long time. . . .[146]

I have his photographs here before me: the face of a young man, the face of a Spanish civil war freedom fighter, and last year's (1973) snapshot: how many years have passed! How many epochs! "But those eyes—those eyes of yours I see: those same . . ."[147]

No, the years are powerless against charm, just as they are powerless against the heart's noble memory, or against courage.

I will also say that Seryozha loved him like a brother.

I just referred above to Lev Tolstoy's last secretary and biographer, Valentin Fyodorovich Bulgakov. In those days he was one of the founders and presiding secretary of the Union of Russian Writers in Czechoslovakia, and together with Marina and Professor Sergei Vladislavovich Zavadsky (chair of the Committee for the Welfare of Russian Writers in Czechoslovakia) he was elected to the editorial board of *The Ark,* an almanac conceived in Prague and its environs.[148]

The [almanac's—trans.] title had been Marina's suggestion: "seven pairs of pure and seven sevens of pairs of impure"[149]—all of them writers whose frail frigate had come to rest on the banks of the Vltava!

The almanac was a long time (literally years) in the making and pulled itself together with difficulty, and this gave Valentin Fyodorovich more than enough time to become close—first through their collaborative work and later by right of their friendship—with Marina and with Seryozha.

(The author of a small book of short stories titled *Childhood*,[150] Seryozha had published in Moscow before the revolution and became a member of the governing board of the Union of Russian Writers.)

Valentin Fyodorovich was in dissonance with the milieu around him no less than Marina herself, but in a different way, one diametrically *opposite* hers: in the émigré ark she was the indubitable *serpent* and he—the indubitable dove who professed "chastity, meekness, and patience, and love" as preached by Saint Ephrem of Syria[151] and, to a degree, by Lev Tolstoy. Even in appearance he was "dovelike" and beauteous, and he lived with his small family in beauteousness apparent even to the untrained eye—in purity, in vegetarianism, and in what seemed to be spiritual prosperity, all of which combined elicited ironic smirks (as well as unquestionable respect) among those around them who had seen (and still saw) their share of war and hardship: "Tolstoyism! Vegetarianism! Nonresistance to evil!" "I should have your problems!" And they readily burdened him with their problems.

The "pastelness" of Valentin Fyodorovich's visage, however, masked a soul that was hardly vegetarian and a mind that was sharp, penetrating, wide-ranging, and far from dogmatic, and precisely this allowed him to become close with my parents, to understand them, and to come to love them.

Particularly noteworthy was his receptiveness—exceptional for those (half-century-ago) times—to Marina's creative work of her "difficult period," which was incomprehensible to the vast majority of her contemporaries abroad. Recalling their collaboration on *The Ark,* Bulgakov writes that

> Marina Ivanovna contributed her large *Poem of the End* to the collection. Publishing it anonymously would not have helped. Marina Tsvetaeva's unusually dense, idiosyncratically precise, image-laden, and ringing—if not to say, snapping—verse was recognizable a thousand miles off, without any captions to indicate "This be a lion, not a dog! . . ."[152]
> We, the editors of the collection, *were severely criticized* later for having published *Poem of the End,* but I maintained and still now [in 1960] maintain that this poem—like everything written by the inspired Marina—was remarkable. Only in this particular case one needs ears to hear.

Valentin Fyodorovich also had eyes to see. He sketched a portrait of Marina that is both dynamic and precise:

> [...] Her eyes were [gray], large, sharp, and bold: "falconine."
> [...] Not a drop of color or blush to her face. So strange,
> and ... pitiable! ... Her small head sat proudly on her neck
> and turned just as proudly, quickly, and energetically—now
> to the right, now to the left. Marina Ivanovna's gait and all
> her movements were generally quick and decisive. [...] I
> never saw her crying or even despondent. At times she could
> be sad, complain of her fate—for example, of her separa-
> tion from Russia, of being overburdened with housework
> and household affairs that distracted her from her literary
> work—but those (on the whole, rare) complaints and dis-
> contents of hers never sounded regretful or pitiful; on the
> contrary, they were always proud, I would even say defiant:
> defiant of fate and of people. In the not just poor but literally
> destitute setting of her apartment Marina Ivanovna—with
> her pale face and her head held proud—moved like a queen:
> calm and with confidence. ...[153]

In the years that followed when the majority of émigrés relocated to other countries—principally to France, Valentin Fyodorovich with his wife and two children remained in Czechoslovakia. There he invested con-siderable energy and labor into creating the Russian Historical-Cultural Museum, for which he collected "goodwill offerings": objects, manu-scripts, works of art brought from Russia or created by Russians abroad. No one provided any funding for the acquisition of these valuables, for at the time they were not yet considered valuable. ...

From Marina, Valentin Fyodorovich received imprints and handwrit-ten copies of many of her works, as well as the light bamboo pen with which she wrote for nearly ten years. She also gave him—right off her finger—the beloved silver signet ring (at one time embellished with a car-avel engraved in the stone) which Marina always had with her and which was so familiar to those who knew her. By then, 1936–37, when Bulgakov came to Paris in search of materials for his museum and met with my parents for the last time, the antique ring was aged beyond repair. The elegant etched caravel and the caption TO YOU MY SYMPATHIA framing it had been diminished to obliteration and the band had thinned almost to the point of transparency. The hand that had worn that ring had done a lot of work!

Bulgakov's museum did not last long. Soon Hitler's invasion of Czechoslovakia altered the "peaceful course of events" as well as the fates of the members of Bulgakov's family, who participated in the heroic Czech Resistance. The lives of Valentin Fyodorovich and his family had run the course from nonresistance to resistance in the face of evil. He later told me:

> Soviet troops liberated us from the Fascists' concentration camp and I made my way to the museum, where soldiers were loading into trucks the remnants of what had been ransacked by the Germans: folders ripped in half, heaps of tattered books, and sheaves of spilled papers. The fact that this was all being shipped to Russia and would at least survive comforted me somewhat, but everything else, obviously, was lost, never to be found . . . ! What is more vulnerable and more fragile than the work of human minds and hands! The sight of gutted rooms, emptied cabinets, and broken display cases was so unbearably sad that for the first time through all my trials and tribulations I was unable to hold back my tears.
>
> I began sorting through the stuff on the floor, the rubbish and the trash, the bits and the pieces. And suddenly, there in the dust, in the corner behind the door lay Marina Ivanovna's pen! And her ring!
>
> It was a miracle!

After the war the Bulgakovs returned to the USSR, to Yasnaya Polyana, where Valentin Fyodorovich lived and labored to the end of his days. He brought Marina's pen and her ring with him and kept them safe, as mementos of her, of the museum, and of that miracle. . . . Later, burdened by years and cares and realizing that his days on this earth were not infinite, Bulgakov—with the help of Ehrenburg—tracked me down and passed these relics on to me.

Now the same burden weighs on my shoulders, and so I in my turn have transferred the pen with which *Poem of the End* and *Poem of the Mountain, The Ratcatcher, Ariadna,* and *Phaedra* were written and the ring from the hand that wrote not only them but much, much more, on to TsGALI,[154] and there at long last they have acquired safe haven together with the remnants of manuscripts at one time kept in Bulgakov's museum and then returned to Russia.

Objects—like books and like people—have their own fates.

Marina's Prague autumn of 1923 and winter of 1923–24 were replete with work, encounters, acquaintances—both friendships and enmities, which so often exchanged places later on! There were strolls through evening and nighttime (in the mornings she wrote) Prague, and gradually she immersed herself in the life of the city that so (among all others) appealed to her. She was fascinated by Prague's legend of the golem[155] and enchanted by the statue of the knight on the bridge with its secret resemblance to her in profile, hair, and bearing, like an encounter with a monument to yourself raised long before you were born, a prophecy materialized, the anticipation of yourself as you walk by. . . .[156]

"Immersed herself in the life of the city," I just wrote and immediately stopped myself: not true! There was none of that. It was more like "trying on" a city and it—you, in the sense of here is where *I would like to live, could live,* if . . .

If . . . what?

Through cities and suburbs—I speak not of the Russia she left behind— Marina passed *incognito,* like Twain's pauper prince, unrecognized and unacknowledged by Berlin, Prague, Paris (where she is in fashion these days . . .).

If she *had been* (and had not just passed for!) an émigré, then—someway or somehow—she would have found her niche abroad, among "her kind."

If she had been simply her husband's wife and her children's mother, would it not have been all the same in the end where she lived, as long as they were together?

If she had been a "poet transplant," like some others, the bohemian cafés of bohemian quarters would have provided her shelter. . . .

If she had not been herself!

But she was herself, always.

*

The integrality of her character, the integrality of her identity, was a sum of juxtapositions. Intrinsic to her was a *duality*—but hardly duplicity!—of perception and of expression; of feelings, which sprang from the burning depths of her soul, and of perspective (on those feelings, people, events) so externalized that it seemed as if from another planet.

Her amazing mental retentiveness was equaled by her forgetfulness; her childlike inconstancy equaled her great fidelity; her insularity—her trust and openness. In the joy of every meeting she herself sowed the seeds of separation, just as from the ashes of every separation she was prepared to fan the coals of a new flame. Such selflessness in love—and such jealous protectiveness of the ashes. . . . Such a "dissonant" balance of abysses and heights, such reciprocal gravitation of worlds and antiworlds within her inner universe. . . .

Also: her ability to make sense of the present principally by way of and through the past (day, century, millennium), to test the enigmatic future against the painful experience of the past. . . .

In Prague Marina made the acquaintance of and was passionate (although not fast) friends with the writer Aleksei Remizov and his paleontologist wife Serafima Pavlovna. Serafima Pavlovna was, as they say, an imposing woman—tall and even then afflicted by excessive portliness, whereas he was tiny and thin and wore large glasses with bulging lenses that magnified the alarm in his nearsighted gaze: from a distance you might take him for her timid teenage son.

They loved each other very much and were inseparable: up until her death they were always and everywhere together in everything. She was his fortress, his guide, and the constant in his life, and he more closely identified with her life before they had met than with his own life, never dedicating a single work to his own childhood and youth.

Remizov was a great authority on and advocate for premodern Russian literature and history, and for him Old Church Slavic was a language so vital and his own that he wrote letters to friends in medieval *Ustav* and *Half-Ustav* script,[157] embellishing them like a professional calligrapher with drop letters, capitals, and flourishes. He seasoned his speech with Church Slavicisms, jested and played the buffoon, and filled his writing with so many parables, ancient documents, and hoary antiquities that the squiggly notation made you see spots.

After a while Marina's eyes also saw spots and her ears rang: Remizov's fanciful, devilish minuscule, she intuited, not only did not lead out to the great expanses, it did just the opposite, locking you in a circle of head-spinning antiquities that led you away from the great expanses that lay beyond.

This intuition, however, came to her only later, in France, where, while Serafima Pavlovna taught paleontology to her students and kept house, Remizov slowly metamorphosed into a half-fairy-tale hero of his own—a hybrid holy fool cenobite chronicler–cum–forest swamp goblin who surrounded himself with devil-kin toys of his own design fashioned from twigs, corks, bobbins, fish bones, and other rubbish. What was affectation in all this, what—play, what—truth, what—whimsical shell under which he could hide from real life, and what was a real life that hardly merited being called one?

. . . As long as she could, Marina took pleasure in his peculiarity and the fact that he never spoke about politics, just as Serafima Pavlovna [never spoke—trans.] about paleontology.

Marina also became close with several people—dear to her for various reasons—at the editorial offices of *Russia's Will*,[158] the journal where many of her works were published: lyric poems, long poems, and prose, including both "the difficult" and "the complex." The editorial board was not scared off by Marina's lack of interest in politics, and the political orientation of the journal was of no interest to Marina, while the breadth of its literary dispositions sustained and encouraged her. Over all her years in emigration this was the sole periodical that for the entirety of its existence offered its pages to Marina's creative work out of an appreciation of it and not just "out of pity," and (almost) without condition. As I recall, only Tsvetaeva's article-apologia in defense of Soviet children's literature ("On the New Russian Children's Book") was placed in the journal with the editorial "proviso" that it serve as the subject for debate.

One of the journal's editors—thickset, nimble, boisterous, bright-black-eyed Vladimir Ivanovich Lebedev, whose curly beard could (depending on the occasion) spew forth an exploding collision of irate phrases, peals of laughter, questions straight to the jugular, answers that never beat around the bush, and frequently downright mischievous maladdresses—introduced our family to his. His wife, Margarita Nikolaevna, in her quietness and harmony was the polar opposite of her husband, whom she calmed and counterbalanced with her inner essence as well as with her physical presence. The regular, hard features of her face were softened by the elusive velvet of a feminineness best transmitted visually by masters of the Italian Renaissance in the countenances of their at once stern and meek Madonnas. But *this* Madonna from a Russified [German—trans.] baronial family in her youth had been a fearless revolutionary who participated in the Kronstadt, Sveaborg, and Sevastopol uprisings and was subjected to police repression. . . . In 1908 she emigrated to Switzerland, where she graduated with a degree in medicine. In emigration she married Vladimir Ivanovich, her comrade-in-arms; in Geneva their first daughter was born and died in early childhood, to be followed by their second, Irina, who became my friend at first (childhood!) sight and for the rest of my life.

In the beginning, both Vladimir Ivanovich's peremptory loudness and Margarita Nikolaevna's inexhaustible quietness made Marina wary, and she jumped to the conclusion that they were polar manifestations of that *self-contentedness* she so despised; that the steady, tempered structure and organization of the Lebedev household—contrasted with the disorganization of most émigré households, her own included—was the "wealth" she found so unbearable, "In Praise of the Rich"[159] not withstanding.

[The Lebedevs'—trans.] wealth, however, lay hardly in material well-being, and as far as "self-contentedness" was concerned, they were as far from it as Marina herself. Of which she soon became convinced, never again having cause to doubt these friends' *human qualities*.

Marina had many friendships, but all of them—at least those that I remember—came with flaws, drawbacks, reservations, missed signals, disappointments (both mutual and unilateral), and insults and injuries (either surmountable or irreversible).

Except for her friendship with the Lebedevs, which was unique for its dignity, its profundity, its simplicity, loyalty, and longevity.

At their house no one ever tired of Marina's calamities, needs, and messes; no one ever distanced him- or herself from the weight of her talent or the weightiness of her personality, and they were *always* happy to see her. This was the only house to which Marina was entrusted with a key—not in the allegorical sense, but the real, metal kind with which in the owners' absence you could open the door, walk in, make yourself at home—even better than at home, for it was quieter there, with more room—and take a rest, from yourself.

This friendship not only lasted with never a downward turn, its trajectory was ever on the ascendant and achieved its pinnacle precisely in the most difficult, most emigration-poisoned years that immediately preceded Marina's return to the motherland.[160]

"We came by and you weren't home. We'll drop by around 7:30 P.M. The meeting with František Kubka (the poet) is all arranged." A note to Khodasevich, who had arrived in Prague with Gorky and with whom—because of his (Gorky's!) "Bolshevism"—the Russians refused to associate.[161]

Behind these lines in the notebook of 1938—into which Marina, in preparation for her departure for the USSR, recopied and amended excerpts from that part of her archive that she would leave abroad (and which was lost during the war)—lies the story of her fleeting Prague encounter with poet Khodasevich and her nonencounter with Gorky.

On his way to Marienbad for treatment, Gorky arrived in Prague at the end of November 1923, and among the small group of family and friends accompanying him was Khodasevich, with whom Marina had been acquainted before the revolution. To the address given him by Pasternak (who, like Marina, held Khodasevich's work in esteem) Vladislav Felitsianovich sent a letter requesting a meeting [with Tsvetaeva—trans.] and her help in making the acquaintance of certain Czech writers and poets.

Contemplating the possibility of settling in Prague (though hardly as an "average," that is, struggling, émigré), Khodasevich was in search of contacts who might help him secure a stable and independent position among the country's local intelligentsia, about whom he knew very little. . . .

Marina responded to his call with characteristic alacrity, although her own contacts with the Czechs could hardly be deemed secure. She turned for help to a woman she considered kind and whose Petersburg upbringing and education many years ago had bonded her to Russia: Anna Tesková, a community activist with progressive views and chair of the cultural-philanthropic society Česko-ruská Jednota. The Russian—to wit, *White*-émigré faction—of Jednota opposed the idea of organizing an evening for Khodasevich to read his poems. The hardnoses took a hard line: "If he came with Gorky, then he's a Bolshevik as well."

The majority, Czech, contingent hemmed and hawed, understanding that its primary order should be an evening for Gorky himself to read, or in his honor, but what was to be done with the émigrés? Gorky would soon be gone, but contention within the ranks would remain.

As the haggling, confusion, and war of words in two languages dragged on, Marina and Sergei set up a meeting for Khodasevich with the Czech poet and critic František Kubka. This meeting turned out to be unproductive: Khodasevich failed to make a positive impression on Kubka, to "show his best side. . . ."

He impressed Marina, though, perhaps owing to her spirit of contradiction, perhaps owing to the lofty confraternity they shared that evening over cups of coffee at the café Hotel Beránek.

Later, in France, they did not get along; worse, they were enemies, and only in the final years of Marina's stay in the West did they find a common language, the one native to them both—poetry.

Marina used to tell the story of how back then in Prague Khodasevich had not merely offered to introduce her to Gorky, whom he loved very much, but was eager to do so, particularly since Gorky was staying in the same hotel and was literally within arm's reach. Marina, however, refused, out of that same complex sense of inner taboo that had once led her to melt into the crowd around Blok at his last performance in Moscow, the taboo that kept her from *simply* approaching, *simply* introducing herself. ("Pride and timidity—sisters of one blood . . . ," she wrote in a poem of 1921.)[162]

And then there was the boundary of *her* emigration, which lay between her and Gorky. How could she impose herself with *that*?

After a few days Gorky and his traveling companions left for Marienbad, while Marina "inscribed on the tablets"[163] yet one more, Gorky-bitter,[164] nonencounter.

Two letters Tsvetaeva wrote to Gorky—in gratitude to him for inviting her sister Anastasia Ivanovna to spend time with him in Sorrento—are extant; they were published based on 1927 drafts in the April 1969 issue of the journal *New World*.[165]

What follows is the story of yet another of Marina's letters and Gorky's answer to it. (The letters themselves have not survived.)

At the very end of the 1920s or in the beginning of the 1930s, in France, something incredible happened to one of our acquaintances, [Pyotr Petrovich Suvchinsky—trans.]. That acquaintance, a musicologist by training and profession, was an erudite specialist, enthusiast, and consumer of art in all its permutations (". . . if only you had seen the 'mug'—broad, intelligent, shaved, and aristocratic, the face of Sunday from Chesterton's *The Man Who Was Thursday*[166]—[Suvchinsky—trans.] pulled when he asked me for your address!" Marina wrote to Pasternak in 1927).[167] He also possessed a pleasant voice, the strength, beauty, and range of which came to light entirely by chance.

One day our acquaintance was strolling—rather, as was his wont, idling—in an abandoned, overgrown corner of the park at Versailles, admiring the "regular" part of the grounds that spread out before him and belting out his favorite arias from his favorite operas—the way you sing when you are out in the middle of nowhere, bothering no one and no one bothering you.

Just as in fairy tales of old (or musicals of new) a certain someone—who (as dictated by the rules of the genre) just happened to be either a then-famous impresario or the director of the Milan opera—overheard his voice, popped out of the bushes, approached, introduced himself, and was astounded to learn that the voice that had lured him—that miracle of a voice, that treasure of a voice—belonged to someone who was hardly a professional. After several meetings, several exacting auditions—mind you, there was nothing to be exacting about: this God-given, nature-trained voice needed only a bit of polishing—the Italian proposed to the émigré that he go to Milan to study with a coach "to put the finishing touches" on his voice, after which he was guaranteed a debut at La Scala and a career of transcontinental dimensions.

All the ingredients for a miracle were there, except for the money needed to cover predebut expenses: the trip to Milan, living expenses, and the cost of voice lessons.

[Suvchinsky's—trans.] relatives and few friends scurried to raise the needed funds, but they scurried in vain: economic crisis and unemployment had cancelled out wages and were draining pocketbooks and pockets. There was not enough money to buy bread, and this was a whim, some voice. . . .

At that point Marina wrote to Gorky.

Aleksei Maksimovich replied immediately—quickly, to the point, with a sense of humor. He sent a check for five thousand francs (no small amount) for the future singer, with a request that the donor's name remain anonymous. He expressed his hope that the voice would sound forth and reach as far as Russia. He thanked Marina for the trust she had shown him: he was happy to assist talent, for talent was excellent, for talent was the stuff of life. The letter was written in Gorky's very legible, reader-friendly hand in black ink on a small, neat sheet of thick white paper. . . .

. . . Alas, our acquaintance never did become a singer. An incurable nervous spasm that attacked his vocal chords during public performances (but never evidenced itself at lessons, rehearsals, or auditions) foiled his sensational debut at the Milan opera house, as well as all future engagements around the globe.

The only voice that in fact rang forth in this fairy tale–not-come-true turned out to be the quiet, muffled, very sincere voice of Aleksei Maksimovich himself.[168]

[Všenory—trans.]

I arrived from Moravská Třebová for the summer holidays of 1924 on my own, having been put on the train by the Bogengardts and met by my father at the Prague station. I brought with me my toothbrush, a thin and dumbed-down diary, a retake of the final examination in arithmetic, and a (hereditary) shadow on my lung. The last convinced Marina beyond doubt that middle school was of absolutely no good for little girls, and that for certain select types it was even harmful.

Once again our family packed itself off to the outlying villages, and our nomadic trail began anew: Jíloviště, Dolní and Horní Mokropsy, Všenory.[169]

As always, Marina worked a great deal, but, in contrast with Prague, she now tired more than usual, and day-to-day household life annoyed her with its eternal disarrays and absurdities.[170] She longed for firm ground beneath her feet: after the asphalt of not long ago, the mud to which rain turned rural roads and paths was especially difficult to bear. Acquaintances of ours referred to one of the distant corners of a village where we were temporarily settled as the "Efron Mudflats."

Attempting in my own way "to help my parents out," I decided to economize on my shoes: when heading out to the woods for berries and mushrooms, I would hide my sandals under the bridge at the edge of town and put them on again on my way back. Like many of my bright ideas, this attempt to save money did more harm than good: one day a thunderstorm hit, and the dusty ravine under the little bridge unexpectedly turned into a torrent that swept my poor sandals into the Berounka River, perhaps even into the Vltava. No matter how long I whimpered alongside the stream, the sandals were never to return. We had to buy new ones. And I caught it from my parents.

Looking back on it now, rural émigré life [in Czechoslovakia—trans.] preserved features of prerevolutionary summer house life [in Russia— trans.], which for many at that time had been not so long ago. We visited each other's houses, both by invitation and without warning; we were constantly arranging birthday parties and organizing leisurely group walks and picnics, amateur theater performances, evenings, children's parties, and literary readings.

In Všenory kitty-corner from Pan Baloun's little store stood the beautiful Villa Boženka, a large, capacious summer house that was rented (one half) by Evgeny Nikolaevich Chirikov and his large family (all of his children were already grown with children of their own) and (the other half) by the widow of writer Leonid Nikolaevich Andreev, Anna Ilinichna, with her beautiful young daughter from her first marriage, Nina, and her three teenage children from her marriage with Andreev—Vera, Savva, and Valentin.

She was a bizarre woman, oppressive sort of, despite her nimbleness, despite the quickness and spontaneity of her reactions, movements, decisions, and judgments, despite her striking appearance, her burning dark eyes, and her seeming simplicity. She had loved her deceased husband to distraction and continued to love him as if it were part of a challenge, as if seeking to defend him, to argue on his behalf, and to vindicate him. . . . Before whom?

She took with her abroad not only his manuscript archives but crates full of his concurrent hobbies: photographs he had taken, pictures he had painted, some very complicated tools, instruments, and gadgets, and she kept all of this—guarded it—jealously and zealously.

Marina was equally drawn to her and put off by her. One might admire her, but actually to love her was, well, impossible: there was something *not human* about her. Or so it seemed.

Her children had a difficult time with her.

In Anna Ilinichna's large—immense—room with its immense windows looking out into the garden, people sometimes gathered for literary "socials": some read, others listened. For one of Andreev's anniversaries she organized an artistic reading of her husband's then unknown, unpublished play, *Samson in Chains.*[171]

The elocutionist, actor Aleksandr Aleksandrovich Brei—whom she had scouted with her keen eye and carefully auditioned—was a talented man with a sharp mind, fox-red hair, and a Byronic limp. The manuscript of the play was delivered to him well in advance so that he would have enough time to give it serious preparation. . . .

I can see it as if it were today: the single spot of light—a classic green-shaded lamp on the table; next to the table—an armchair for the elocutionist; the audience, like those at Peter the Great's "assemblies," lines the walls and stands in precious, tense poses. In the semidarkness Anna Ilinichna's magnificent eyes burn with an ominous dark light.

But no Brei. Is he running late? Did he forget? Is there going to be a reading or not? Finally, when everyone's patience has been stretched to the limit, when everyone is all itchy and antsy, in flies the elocutionist, bowing elegantly, with affected ease, and apologizing as he makes his way through the room. There is a collective sigh of relief.

Brei sits down in the armchair, clears his throat, pours some water from a carafe, takes a drink, clears his throat again, carefully removes the manuscript from its well-worn folder, smooths the pages, makes himself more comfortable—Anna Ilinichna following his every move with the intent gaze of a tiger—and in a crescendoing, velvety-loud, *theatrical* voice declaims: "Leonid Andreev. *Samson in the Trenches.*"[172]

In the Chirikovs' half [of the villa—trans.] life went on in good-humored, natural fashion, without any oppressiveness, although, as in every large and very friendly family, they had their tensions, and troubles, and suffering. And homesickness.

The homesickness resided in the little room of Evgeny Nikolaevich and was embodied and (continued to be embodied) by him not in his manuscripts but in the wooden models of Volga steamboats that he fashioned at his workbench near the little window looking out into the thicket of the garden. His room was populated with little steamships and, a bit larger, barges of all varieties from various regions along the Volga: with hoppers and without, covered and uncovered, with sails or oars and without. This child of the Volga felt cramped in Všenory, and the Berounka River ran too shallow for him!

Marina did not have the wherewithal to be friends with all the Chirikovs: the family was too large and disparate in age! One at a time, first Lyudmila (who would soon leave), then Valentina, and then the parents would show up at our place. In Evgeny Nikolaevich's honor Marina even baked pies—which was very out of character: Chirikov, chuckling, called them "fortune-teller pies" and ate them with great relish, while his wife, Valentina Georgievna, asked politely, "So how do you make these?" as she hesitatingly broke off a tiny piece. . . .

. . . The benevolent memory of childhood preserves only the good: the child's eyes select from her surroundings only the beautiful, and the child's ears are attuned only to the "interesting," the amusing, and the unusual. *My* Czechoslovakia was the time of my childhood, the one time—in my entire life—of true freedom, and it comes back to me as a happy time.

But what was it like for the adults? How did they fare?

In the early spring of 1924 my father wrote to his sister in Moscow:[173]

> . . . I am not doing well in Prague. I live here as if in a bell jar. I know many of the Russians here but am drawn to few. Although by nature I like being with *people.* And I am terribly drawn to Russia. [I never thought the Russian in me was so strong.] How soon, do you think, will it be possible for me to return? Not in terms of safety, but in terms of moral wherewithal? I am prepared to wait another two years. I fear I won't hold up much longer after that.[174]

In the fall of that same year [he wrote—trans.] to her again:

> The most difficult thing about my letters to you is that I have to write about my life. I am so disgusted by it that each time I get to "that very same place" my hand stops. [I am hauling a cart laden with stones and I have neither the strength nor the cruelty to discard the stones and set out on my own with a

lighter load.] If only the wall that divides you and me would come crumbling down! Lord!

But not to write about myself means not to write anything at all. [For what can I write to you about if not about myself?!]

This winter I am not moving to the city. I live in a shallow ravine surrounded by mountains and forest. My window looks out onto the most marvelous hill and a southern-blue sky. It is Indian summer. Frost at night and hot during the day. Every day I commute to the city, about fifteen miles from here.

I await winter's arrival with horror.

Nineteen twenty-five promises to bring me hardships. I am torn between the university and the need to start earning a living immediately. It is possible that for the sake of an income I may be forced to relocate to Paris [*where there is at least some chance of finding work, while here there is none. There are too many of us Russians* / and abandon my doctoral examination]. This does not really distress me, for isn't it all the same [whether I'm a doctor or a nondoctor]? Had I known earlier, I would have structured my life differently. [The hell with them, my affairs, that is!]

[. . .] I am now busy editing a small journal of literary-critical orientation. [The student journal *By Our Own Paths.*] I would very much like to receive something from Russia about the theater, about the latest prose writers and poets, about goings-on in the academy and science. If the powers that be do not object, ask people who might be able to supply me with materials in these areas to send them to my address. [Everything will be well remunerated.] I would really like to have articles—or at least notices—about the [Vakhtangov] Studio [and Meyerhold]. The editorial board would be happy to accept both poetry and prose. Talk to Max [Voloshin], with Antokolsky: perhaps they will submit something? [Maybe you might write something about the theater or about the late Vakhtangov? Submissions should not exceed 20,000 characters or twelve pages of print.] Let me know immediately if I should expect anything. [The journal is strictly lit-erary. Send me Vera and Max's addresses. For a year now,] no one has written to me. [I've already written to you that I have] the feeling that all of Moscow has forgotten me. I know that the years that stand between us separate us more than thousands and thousands of miles. [*I know that I myself am to blame.*] But it still hurts. [And on top of that your many months of silence.]

    . . . Write, Lilenka! Your letters are my only real connec-tion both with Russia and with the past, and, perhaps, with the future. . . .[175]

Jottings about our moves occur throughout Marina's notebooks, amid the rough of her drafts and the polish of her clean copy.

    July 1924, in Jíloviště—where *Poem of the End* wends toward comple-tion along a trail gone cold: "But the *end* is inside me—*how could it come earlier!* Having begun it as a breath, I finish it as a duty!"[176]

    July, Dolní Mokropsy:
    . . . moved from Jíloviště to Dolní Mokropsy into a ruin of a little house with an enormous Russian stove, crooked ceil-ings, crooked walls, and a crooked floor—in the courtyard of a (formerly) enormous family farm. There is an enormous barn, which the landlady dreams of renting to some Russian "Studenten," a garden with a stone fence just above the rail-road tracks. Trains.

    I am beginning the third scene of *Ariadna* this July 21, 1924. God—and gods—help me![177]

    August, another dwelling in the same Mokropsy: ". . . by ferry across the river. A tiny stone house, with walls a foot thick. I diligently work away at *Theseus* [*Ariadna*]. Lots of disconnected lines set aside for the time being. . . ."[178]

    September (and to the very end of our stay in Czechoslovakia), Všenory: "The move to Všenory: the village idiot hauls our stuff, and along the way we lacquer him with beer and drug him with cigarettes—he doesn't smoke! Three days ago—knitting that came to naught . . . [God keep us!][179]

Individual lines:

Everything is more important, more necessary, more immutable than I am [. . .][180]

To know how to die, before it is too late.[181]

This life's closeness and closedness.[182]

A torn shawl on a thin shoulder.[183]

[Not having the right to give presents (marriage)]; not having the right to lose anything (indigence). [In both cases] nothing is yours, [in the former not even a smile, in the latter] not a kopeck.[184]

The soul cannot be *filled* by anyone or anything, for it is not a vessel, but its contents. . . .[185]

Phantoms are evoked by longing. Otherwise, they would not dare. Allow yourself to long to the point of despair, and they will become total masters of your days. . . .[186]

Tears not shed don't count.[187]

> I writhed in captivity
> From torsion and from contortion. . . .
> To the end of my name—
> To "Marina"—add "martyr."[188]

On rare occasions, covertly, another strain surfaces: ascendant, it fears the evil eye; it is barely noticeable, except, perhaps, for the knitting, mentioned in passing above.

Marina knits a shawl, although she is not showing her pregnancy yet: with her slim figure it is still not noticeable. She knits, stubbornly prevailing over her indisposition for handicrafts. She knits—and will finish—more than one [shawl—trans.], succumbing to the age-old, tried-and-true creative and calming magic of women's hands busy at work, which allows the mind *time to rest* and the possibility of carrying on a secret deaf-mute dialogue with what still cannot be seen but already exists.

The notebooks are something else entirely. The notebooks are unrelenting *no-time-to-rest,* unrelenting work and obligation, unrelenting thought uttered,[189] inspiration squeezed into immutable form, and feelings named. The notebook is a way of voicing—if not for now, then for the future. The secret revealed.

The notebooks for these months contain poems, letters, ideas—and *Theseus. Theseus [Ariadna]* with all its digressions, its flashes of Phaedra and the unrealized Helen, with all its variations on the theme of *Fate.* The notebook contains everything, as always, only

> Woman, what have you under that shawl there?
> "The future!"[190]

A poem in four unfinished stanzas, begun but put aside out of superstition:

> . . . Over your cradle-bed so needy
> Myriad myriads from God we'll plead. . . .[191]

What was growing and coming into existence was what Marina had written in that letter to Seryozha sent from Moscow through Ehrenburg— "Don't grieve for our Irina. You did not know her at all. Just imagine that *you dreamed it all* and don't accuse me of heartlessness: I just don't want to hurt you—so I am taking it all on myself! We shall have a son: I know that this will come to be. . . ."[192]

Only later, when "the secret becomes apparent," does she begin to talk about it aloud, to prepare for it in visible ways, to consult with doctors, and with the help of friends to put together "a dowry" of hand-me-downs outgrown by other children. In the notebooks, *overt* notations begin to appear. Here is one of them, both characteristic and full of character:

> Alya has the delightful delicacy to refer to my future son as "your son," and not as "my brother," thereby indicating his

affiliation (his place in life) and by anticipating and averting it, disarming my maternal jealousy, [the only kind where suffering is neither surpassed nor extinguished by contempt].[193]

Finally come triumphant lines—whole pages—of pure joy, radiant gratitude, and simple happiness:

> My son Georgy was born February 1, 1925, on a Sunday, at noon, during a snowstorm. At the very moment of his birth the alcohol on the floor around my bed combusted, and he came forth in an explosion of blue flame. [Sonntags, Mittags und Flammenkind.]
>
> [He was born unconscious, and it took twenty minutes to revive him.] His life and mine were saved by Grigory Isaakovich Altschuler who, today, [February] 12, is taking his last examination.[194]

Doctor Grigory Isaakovich Altschuler, then a medical student at Prague University, was the son of the doctor who had treated Lev Nikolaevich Tolstoy.

> On the evening before, January 31, Alya and I were at the dentist's in Řevnic. The reception area was full of people and we didn't feel like waiting, and so we went for a stroll and walked almost as far as Karlov Týn. Then we went back to Řevnic, and then, not waiting for the train, walked along the river and through the meadows back to Všenory.
>
> In the evening Seryozha and I were at A[nna] I[linichna] Andreeva's and looked at some antique icons [and] color photographs, and returning home at around two in the morning. I read in bed for a bit—Dickens's *David Copperfield*: ["I am born."]
>
> The boy made himself known at 8:30 A.M. At first I did not understand—could not believe it—but soon I had no doubt, and I rejected all admonitions that "we do everything we can to get to Prague." [I knew that because of the frequency of

the pain I would not make it as far as the station, despite all my Spartanism.] Seryozha then began his mad chase all over Všenory and Mokropsy. Soon my room was overflowing with women and entirely unrecognizable. The Chirikovs' nanny washed the floor, everything unessential (i.e., the room's entire contents!) was taken out, I was wrapped in Andreeva's nightshirt, the bed was pulled out into the middle of the room, and the floor around it was doused with alcohol. (Which is what combusted—at the *required* moment!) All the commotion partly distracted me. At 10:30 A.M. Grigory Isaakovich Altschuler arrived, and at twelve noon Georgy was born. [His silence did not register with me at first: I was watching the alcohol burn out. (Altschuler's desperate shout: "Just don't move!! Let it burn!!")]

[Finally, seeing the same methodical—as if in a dream—movement: down, up, upside down, I asked, "Why isn't he screaming?" But for some reason I wasn't frightened.]

Yes, that it was a boy—I learned from Valentina Georgievna Chirikova, who was present at his birth. "A boy—and very handsome!" [And in my head the sound suddenly resounded: "Boris!"]

[Finally, he cleared his lungs. They bathed him. At 1:00 P.M. the "midwife" came. If Altschuler hadn't been there, we would have perished: I maybe not, but the boy for certain.

I will never forget his kind, sincere voice: "He's going to be born soon, Marina Ivanovna. . . ."]

They say I held up well. In any case, not a single scream. (All the women kept saying, "Go ahead and scream!" "Why?" Only one of them—"So, how are you?"—in response to my quiet "It hurts!" said, "It's supposed to hurt!" Those single wise words, uttered [by the one who loved me most of all] Anna Ilinichna Andreeva.) People sitting in the next room contend that if they had not known what was happening, they never would have guessed.

[Sonntagskind—he will understand the language of animals and plants. Mittagskind—but Mittag already contains Sonntag: at its height. Flammenkind—

Flamm' wird alles was ich fasse
Kohle—alles was ich lasse—
Flamme bin ich sicherlich![195]

And (a mother's pride)—a particular flame: blue.]

Georgy had seven nannies: the she-wolf coal woman who kept looking into the woods [*hired to help Marina, she left a week later!*], Anna Ilinichna Andreeva; Valentina Georgievna Chirikova; Muna Bulgakova; Katya and Yulia (!!!) Reitlinger, [*and "that boy's" mother, Anna Zakharovna Turzhanskaya . . .*].[196] [A Czech woman, a Gypsy, a Russian woman from the Volga region, a Tatar, and two Germans. (The town of Reutlingen is either on the Neckar or on the Rhine.) One of the Germans] [*Yulia*] [—a (fierce) Russian Orthodox nun], in a black [habit/*dress*] and a wide belt, austere to the point of severity [and severe to the point of austerity, an icon], a painter—sat under the window and for three hours straight silently sanded a board for an icon[, driving me thoroughly out of my wits in the process]. The embodiment of pure *duty* entirely unpainted, unlacquered, and cheerless. [She sat there like a Protestant—better, a soldier of the Salvation Army—fulfilling her duty.]

Muna B[ulgakova, the Tatar] was like a shadow and [was probably thinking about her unborn son by Rodzevich, about whom I thought as well with a slightly condescending—toward myself, him, and everyone else—smile (mustn't forget to record that savage fit of jealousy, in the café, when he found out that I would have a son. At first—joy, and then, when he figured it out—jealousy. But all that was washed away by the stream of birth blood.)]

[Muna B., when she was with the child,] reminded me of a hostage Tatar princess—perhaps that very same one held captive by Razin[197]—the black beads of her eyes *forming* a veil . . . [An exotic silence over the secret. . . .]

Valentina Georgievna Chirikova (an actress, from the Volga region) [flirted constantly with everyone], an old actress . . . merely acting the part: of young mother [I say this without malice: being a young mother, she had continued to act until the very last moment], of young motherhood— it was all the same whose, hers or mine. . . . "But he's so c-u-u-te! [His nose is almost aquiline!] And those nostrils! What nostrils! A regular Chaliapin!"—filling the room and my head with the gesticulations of bracelet-laden arms and the swishing of synthetic silk skirts that were *particularly* rustling.

[. . .]

[The Gypsy,] Anna Ilinichna Andreeva, in caring for the child was the embodiment of [bestial] motherhood, . . . a mother-beast, even she-beast [Having at first paid tribute to his singularity—

"That forehead!!! It's obvious now that he's the son of intellectual parents!"—and to his exceptional dowry—

"Look how many 'jackies' you got as presents, all the vests! Just the pants alone!

"You're not feeding him right! Hold him higher! You call those breasts? How can there be any milk in those breasts?? What could possibly fit inside those things? No wonder he's not happy; if I were him. . . . If I were you, I would feed him whole cow's milk. Doctors? He's a strapping giant!

". . . What? That's all? And you think he can be full? It's nothing that there's nothing there, you can at least leave him with the illusion. But if I were you, I'd simply soak him up some oats—etc., etc."] [*with her*] autocratic, jealous, intolerant and intolerable [*speeches and advice*] bringing me to silent tears, which I, of course, tried to chase back into my eyes or brush from the sides of my temples—I even remember their quiet tapping sound on the pillow—for I knew that all of this was out of love (for me, for him, *the living*) and out of burning—perhaps unacknowledged—pain that all of this was not happening to her and never again would. [(She had been madly in love with Leonid Andreev for forty, perhaps more, years.)]

"Anna Ilinichna has a grandmother's natural feelings for him," *my* doctor said, smiling.

Not a grandmother's, I thought. Grandmothers are more detached. Not a grandmother's, but a mother's, for the impossible, the unrealizable, the last. Now—or never. And she knows that it's never. . . .

[. . . And still more nannies. There's Katya Reitlinger, the sister of the Quaker with the sandpaper.] Katya R.—tall, blond, and zany. Always on bended knee [—first before one, then before another. Falling to her knees with a thud.] Katya R. with a whole [eternal] sack of friendship and adoration on her back—over the mountains and hills of Prague—that khaki sack, that khaki raincoat—in enormous strides over the mountains and hills of Prague, and from Prague to Všenory, if need be—carrying other people's affairs and obligations and worries in her pack—carrying her love on her back, the way a Gypsy [carries—trans.] her children. . . .

Katya R., so infatuated with my verses [—and so in love with S.]. . . .

. . . She also carried Alya on her back, at a gallop, through the no-laughing-matter mountains of Všenory: huge, fat, ten-year-old Alya, to make her happy and to prove—one more time—something to herself. [The same Alya who on that Mokropsy (juniper: Boris) hill had fed her sugarcoated goat . . . , saying they were chocolate candies.]

This tempest waited on me quietly, this lyrical waterfall quietly gurgled against the sides of little pots and little bottles, as our food cooked on the flames of passions. [In the person of Katya R. Georgy was served by vanquished demons.]

"That boy's mother." [Aleksandra Zakharovna Turzhanskaya—trans.] [Who also was in love with Sergei.] The mother of little Lelik, a single mother abandoned by the father. [I had rushed to her back then with my horrible sorrow (R[odzevich]), and she had embraced me like a calm lake.]

Her white room with its floor washed daily with a passion and with particularly inhuman passion during malaria season. You open the door and in the garden—that is, in the window in which there is a crabapple tree—stands a crabapple tree. I remember it as always in blossom. Simply paradise. A little bed. A stove cleaner than a mirror. Others went to her for her pies; I—for the secret of her total, incomprehensibly and implausibly simple being. And with my own secret—of myself. "There are things on this earth, my friend Horatio, that wise men haven't dreamed of."[198] Here Shakespeare, of course, speaks of *simple* things. "That little boy's mother" was precisely such a "thing," of *that* simplicity a thing. Which no one understood except me. (And she?)

[A little nun. Russian Orthodox.] Perhaps [*the face of*] Flyonushka from "in the forests and the mountains."[199] . . . A wilted Flyonushka who's run her course. A bloodless complexion with translucent blue (for seconds at a time impenetrably black–navy blue) eyes, and exactly enough lips for a smile, that is, for a smile *without* lips.

Straight-nosed, with the face of a *young* icon. [In days of old, women with eyes like hers were burned at the stake. Nowadays, the ones with those same eyes "do" the restaurants. And get good "tips" for those eyes. (Mine did, too, in Constantinople.)]

[By some quirk of fate she adored my juvenile Magic Lantern,[200] and of all her books it was the only one she took with her when she emigrated. It and The Gospel. (Perhaps because it resembled a prayer book.) In Constantinople it was stolen (as the Russian expression would have it, "overread," that is, read until there was nothing left for the owner. The same thing as "overlying" a child.) We became acquainted through Alya who played with "that boy's mother's" son. Not right away. She did not seek me out just because of my name. She waited for an occasion to arise.][201]

[I can honestly say that her ensuing love for S[ergei Efron—trans.] in no way impeded her love for me. She knew him, and she knew what I was for him.] Trust those who knit you sweaters and nanny your children! For you—they will walk through flames.

[Her daily apparition on my threshold.]

["Hello, M. I.! Hi, little Boris!" without—like my jealous Gypsy—asking "Why Boris? They're all Boris these days."]

[To which I, "?"]

["In honor of Pasternak? Pasternak ought to be renamed, and not that. . . . There are other ways to honor Pasternak. Write a book for him. . . ."]

She was the embodiment of quiet, of propriety, and of physical ability. Just as those pies of hers at home would rise of their own—without a hand or at most with the help of her hands, and not even of her hands, but of a few movements (conjuring, concessionary, and *at the behest of the thing itself*)—so it was here: reswaddle [Boris,] remake my bed, without touching me—hands by themselves, things by themselves, a magical dream, quiet.

[(Katerina from "A Terrible Revenge,"[202] Katerina from *The Thunderstorm.*[203] And

> Katerina-Katya
> Pretty as a picture.
> Embroidering her carpet,
> Waiting for her corporal.
> "Little corporal, soldier-boy,
> Won't you see me home today?
> There's my house—on the mount,
> With two windows looking front."]

[Two—like eyes. And, not like, but—eyes. Two dark blue eyes.)]

["I never loved my own the way I love this one. I didn't love mine when he was little. I was afraid to. I wouldn't pick him up for anything," [she says], never realizing the extent to which this admission is all her—all her virginity and first-womanhood, and everything womanly that follows, to what extent it all lies in this admission. To what extent this admission is law.]

[Those, Mur,[204] were your nannies.]

[Mustn't forget the visit—no, visitation, not visit—from the Catholic priest, Father [Vladimir Vladimirovich—trans.] Abrikosov. His silk cassock, his silken words, his congratulations, his best wishes. Of all male visitors him alone I . . . Only with him, in front of him, was I aware of myself as a woman, not as myself and not as a mother. As a woman in a nightshirt. Before a man in a silk cassock. An elegant conversation. Repartee. No human warmth. No holiness. I parry as best I can. (Lying on one's back makes this physically difficult.)]

[Actually, I was more embarrassed for him than I was for myself. Rome in Všenory!]

Mustn't forget—no, not a nanny, but a benevolent genie, the good fairy of these parts, Anna Antonovna Tesková. Who arrived with a huge, prewar, at one time traditional, box of chocolate candies—TWO LAYERS, no cardboard, no tricks. Gray-haired, magnificent [Catherine without sensual desire, no, better than Catherine!], regal from the inside out. An aquiline nose like a mountain ridge between blue lakes of truly calm eyes, a gray crown of hair [(glaciers, eternity)], a long neck, high chest, *everything*—tall. A gray silk dress, *of course* her only one but not too good for the Všenory mud, for this was—the first son!

["I can watch little ones like that forever. Their faces still have all that written on them. What do they see? What do they remember?" with such open adoration in. . . . (I write poorly. All of this is draft. Otherwise I will never get it down. It will be lost. 1933.)]

And finally, returning to the first night, the night of the February 1–2:

The Czech coal woman. The first. I will never forget the fire howling in the stove stoked to a glow. (The place had to be kept incubator-hot because the boy, like all my children, had jumped his due day by two weeks, although, like all of my children, he was neither smaller, nor weaker, just the opposite, larger and stronger, than other children.) It is hot. I can't sleep. It seems that for the first time in my life I am in bliss. It is unusually white all around. Even my *hands* are white! I am asleep. *My son.*

"O-o-o-o," howls the fire threateningly, triumphantly, exactly as if it were not in the stove, but within me myself, [exactly as if it were running me through myself,] carrying me off out of my very self by way of the chimney of my esophagus through the pipe of my neck, [trailing along my temple and curling to the back of my head, pulling the back of my head lower than the pillows and sinking me lower than possible, and once again, starting at my feet. . . .]

And the old woman's hurried, sleepy, incomprehensible mumbling—all "ts" and "zzh" sounds—a Czech woman from *that* Bohemia: of Jan Žižka, George Sand,[205] and "bohemian crystal."

[. . .][206]

If I were to have to die now, I would wildly pity the little boy, whom I love with a certain yearning, tender, grateful love. Alya I would pity for another reason and in another way. [That most of all I would have pitied the children means, in human terms, that I am most of all a mother.]

Alya would never forget me; the little boy would never remember me.

[About his name: my name was Boris. If Boris had been here, from day one he would have been Boris: Boriushka, Barsik. Georgy is Seryozha's name, my bow to Seryozha and blow to myself, which is why—must be—it doesn't sound right.]

[When will I begin?]

I will love him—however he turns out: not for his good looks, not for his talent, not for his resemblance, but for fact that he *is*. [Perhaps this is the greatest love of my life? Perhaps a happy love? (I've never known that kind of love. For me love is calamity.)][207]

And, a bit later,[208] the notation: "Boys *need* to be spoiled: they, perhaps, may have to go to war."[209]

FROM *TALES TOLD IN TARUSA*

PAPA'S NAME-DAY PIE

The night before Papa's name day we had a visit from Aunt Vera, the youngest of Papa's older sisters, whom Mama didn't like very much, because insofar as she was, if the truth be known, smarter than Aunt Lilya, she more fully appreciated (in practical, not just emotional terms) the true toll of Mama's kidnapping Papa from them. In addition, in Mama's opinion, Aunt Vera, with those large, kind, sad eyes of hers (so inconsonant with the rest of her face) resembled Princess Maria from Tolstoy's *War and Peace*, a character Mama absolutely despised.

So, Aunt Vera arrived and said, "I've baked a pie for Seryozha's name day tomorrow." It was an enormous apple pie with a crust of interwoven latticed strips quite artistically pinched and tucked around the rim of the pan: in a word, an amazing pie. And standing in the center of the pie was a tiny Thumbelina doll. "For Alya," Aunt Vera said.

In anticipation of the next day's celebration, the pie was placed in the hutch that stood in my bedroom. I went to bed, clutching Thumbelina in my fist, chatting with her and thinking about her until gradually my thoughts turned to the pie where she used to live. I got up and in my bare feet walked over to the hutch, stood on my tiptoes, broke off a small piece of the lattice crust, climbed back into my bed, and with Thumbelina still clutched in my fist I ate a tiny piece of her house. Then I got up again, broke off another piece of pie, went back to bed, and ate it. I made the trip several times before finally wearing myself out and falling asleep.

The next morning the sun shone so bright, there was so much light, and it was Papa's name day! They dressed me, and I forgot all about my nocturnal scouting expeditions. Suddenly someone remembered the pie and went to bring it into the dining room. They went over to the hutch, looked . . .

"Marinochka, look, we've got mice!" said gullible Papa.

"That's not mice, that's Alya!" Mama gave me a piercing look.

"It can't be."

"I'm telling you, she did it!"

"But that's so strange, Marinochka. She never eats anything; it's impossible just getting her to swallow. Why in the world would she . . . ?"

Mama looks at me and asks, "Did you do it?"

I move closer to Papa, look Mama straight in the eye, and say, "Me? Why of course not! I never eat anything! Why in the world would I . . . ?"

"And what is this?" Mama says, squinting shortsightedly at the trail of crumbs leading from the buffet to my bed.

"Just like Tom Thumb!" I thought to myself, mortified.

TATIANA FYODOROVNA SCRIABINA

Tatiana Fyodorovna was Mama's friend, and I would go to the Scriabin house to play with her youngest daughter, Marina. The whole house was a cult of Scriabin.

Tatiana Fyodorovna's mother was Belgian, and Tatiana Fyodorovna was planning to move back to her mother's home. Then, just before her departure, after all the visas had been obtained, Tatiana Fyodorovna fell ill: she developed headaches and couldn't sleep. So at night she would wake her youngest daughter and have her read to her aloud. Her daughter read, while her mother just stared out into the distance. Everyone took this to be quite abnormal: not letting an eight-year-old child get her sleep! But it turned out that Tatiana Fyodorovna had a brain tumor, from which she would soon die.

As she lay on her deathbed, Tatiana Fyodorovna fell into delirium, and her delirium obsessed my mother. Tatiana Fyodorovna kept saying, "All I want are slippers, so that I can run across the street!" On the other side of the street was a church. That was where they held her funeral.

But there were no slippers. Instead, people wore handmade shoes with hemp soles. The dead, though, are supposed to be placed in the coffin wearing brand-new slippers, and there weren't any, and so there was nothing to bury Tatiana Fyodorovna in. This troubled my mother terribly, and she made an appointment at the Palace of Arts with [Anatoly] Lunacharsky himself to ask him personally to help her get slippers for Scriabin's dead widow. Which he did.

And Tatiana Fyodorovna was buried in her "cross-the-street slippers"! You see?

Besides me, there probably isn't another soul left who remembers this.

LOVE CAPITAL

My mother once asked me, "Have you ever heard of Lyubov Stolitsa,[1] 'Love Capital'?"

Any other child would have answered that "Love" is love, and "Capital" is a capital. I said it meant that love capped it all.

GOAT SOUP

At the market once, Mama bought some young goat meat, which was cheap, and made soup with it. The menu at our house was always the same: meat and potatoes boiled together, that is, soup and main dish in one pot.

We sat down to dinner. Mama ladled out the soup. Papa was the first to lift a spoonful to his mouth and . . . for all his reverential respect for Marina, he said, "You know, Marinochka, somehow I just don't really feel like soup today."

Mama arched her back. "Why not?"

"I just don't, for some reason. . . ."

"Well, if you don't, don't."

Then my brother Mur swallowed a spoonful and said that he, too, like Papa, somehow. . . . He was Mama's favorite and, besides, he was still little, so. . . .

Then I put the first spoonful in my mouth, and my eyeballs nearly popped out! It wasn't a question of tasty or not; the taste was extraterrestrial, like something from the planet Neptune. But I had no choice. There was no way I too could refuse to eat it, after everyone else had said no. As for Mama, she never ate soup: she didn't like soup and was always watching her weight.

Since everyone was waiting for the main dish, I rushed to gulp down that dreadful soup. It was so inedible that I burst out in tears, although I was about fifteen years old at the time.

When I finished, Mama dipped the ladle into the pot in search of the meat and pulled out something that made her put on her glasses. The rest of us got up and looked. She pulled out a small, well-poached celluloid duck, the one Mur floated in his bath.

"I did it!" Mur proudly announced his contribution to our common pot.

"You see what you made me eat!" I said.

"Never mind," Mama said, unruffled.

"Never mind?! What about the paint?"

"What about it?" said Mama, who always loved to be right.

GETTING MARRIED

I remember how once I came home, and Mama was sitting at the table, cigarette holder with half a cigarette in her right hand, her left hand propping up her forehead, and thoroughly immersed in her notebook: her ability to turn herself off from the rest of the world and to focus only on her work was phenomenal.

"Mom!" I say.

No reaction.

"Mom!" I say again.

Tearing herself from her notebook, she raises her head.

"What?"

"Mom, among other things, I'm getting married."

"Among other things? Congratulations!" And she goes back to her notebook. Then, having thought a moment, she raises her head. "So do you love him?"

"Very much!"

"That means you really don't. If you really did, then you would just say that you love him. 'Very much' is not the real thing."

I paced around the apartment, sat a bit in the kitchen, thought about it, and decided that "very much" really was not the real thing. I went back.

"Mom!"

"What?"

"Among other things, I'm not getting married."

"Among other things? Congratulations!"

L'AGENT

In Paris it is almost impossible to walk down the street if you're wearing a skirt. Age is irrelevant; what's important is your sex. They're always making passes. . . . For a while after I came back to Moscow I couldn't get enough of walking up and down the street or sitting on the boulevard by myself.

Once when I was walking around Paris, this character starts to follow me, bobbing and bowing this way and that: "Mademoiselle, oh, mademoiselle, may I walk with you, please, mademoiselle? I can tell you're a foreigner." And so on. I don't say a word, since that's the only way to get rid of them: God forbid you start to argue. So I hold my tongue and lead him right up to an *agent* post.

This hulk of an *agent* is standing there, in his high cap and regulation mustache. I go up to him (the character has dropped back and is waiting on the sidewalk) and say, "I can't go anywhere, because that character over there is following me and won't leave me alone. Can't you get him to go away?"

"I can," the police officer says and looks at me, "but, mademoiselle, if I weren't on duty, I'd do the same thing."

THREE ENCOUNTERS

When we lived in Paris—or, rather, as always, in the suburbs of Paris—I took classes at the art school at the Louvre. I was studying book illustration. My parents could afford to pay for only one trimester, so I used that trimester to show the French what real Russian brilliance was, and they granted me a stipend to continue.

At the time I was addicted to cinema, overdosing to the point that later on I would never again feel any desire to go to the movies. I stuffed myself with all sorts of trivia about film actors. In fact, the only things I have ever really known well in my life have been mythology and movie trivia.

Once, Douglas Fairbanks and Mary Pickford, then movie superstars, came to Paris. At the time, Fairbanks was the ideal man, and quite the acrobat, leaping from rooftops, et cetera, in his films. And Pickford was the ideal woman, the type that is so completely out of fashion these days: a petite blonde with big, dark brown eyes and a teeny-tiny mouth.

They were staying at the American embassy, and everyone was under the impression that they never came out of there. The embassy was surrounded by a dense ring of journalists. The first press notices were favorable, but after a while they grew progressively angrier because, by not coming out, the actors were essentially depriving the reporters of their bread and butter. . . .

One day I'm walking down the Boulevard Montparnasse, which is not really a boulevard, just a regular street lined with cafés and stores, stores and cafés, not a tree in sight, with Ehrenburg sitting in this café, then Ehrenburg sitting in that café, and Modigliani look-alikes simply everywhere. You see, there was one building on that street that back in those days seemed absolutely spectacular, and people would come especially just to see it, although nowadays it's just a regular building. It had eight or nine stories, and the entire facade was glass. The building belonged to a florist company of some sort, with a store on the ground floor and the company's offices on all the rest. They took orders from all over the world and sent flowers direct or filled orders through other companies for exactly the same flowers. The store on the ground floor had a huge display window that changed every day. One day there would be lilacs, in massive quantities of every possible sort and color; the next day there would be violets from Parma potted in green moss in woven baskets. And a fine spray of water streamed constantly down the glass window, creating the humidity needed by the plants. It was such an adorable sight that every day on my way back from school to the Gare de Montparnasse to catch my train I would detour to go stare at the window.

So, there I am, standing and looking at the flowers, the inside of the store cast in shadows, with only a few people in the store. Just by chance I look closer and see Mary Pickford picking out roses, with Douglas Fairbanks standing next to her! Without waiting to catch my breath, I go running inside. Knowing perfectly well that she didn't speak a word of French but that he could make himself understood just barely, I walked right up to him and boldly demanded his autograph on one of my sketches, saying how ever so nice it was to see them both in Paris. He thanked me in very poor French, she purred something in English, and suddenly he hands me a bouquet of roses! Just like hers!!! Magnificent roses, black as shoe polish, on long, long stems!!!

Swept off my feet, I take off for home. I fly into the apartment, and there's Mama sitting at the table, bent over her notebook, holding her head with her left hand just so (she always sat that way), a lock of already gray hair hanging over her forehead. . . . I burst into the kitchen.

"Mama," I shout in that naive way she couldn't bear, "Mama, guess whom I just saw!"

"Whom?" Mama asks, raising her head.

"Douglas Fairbanks and Mary Pickford!"

"And so?"

"What do you mean: 'and so'? Look at the roses he gave me!"

Mama cast an apathetic eye at the roses. "He'd have done better to buy you a pair of shoes," she said, going back to her notebook.

I sat down and right then and there shot off a letter to one of the movie magazines—so what do you think of this? You guys can't get a thing, but I saw them and talked to them and even got roses as a present from them! And you know what? They printed it, because there really wasn't anything else to print. A short time later a letter arrived from the magazine: "Dear Mademoiselle: Why haven't you come to pick up your honorarium?"

Mademoiselle, naturally, made a beeline for the honorarium. The editor said to me, "Mademoiselle, you have a marvelous style, you could become a journalist, but in order to do so you need to have more than style: you need luck."

"Oh," I said cockily, "I'm always lucky."

"Well, then let's make a deal. If you manage to have two more encounters of this kind, for a total of three, you can come to work for us. There is only one condition, mademoiselle: they have to be chance encounters; you can't go looking for them to happen."

He gave me a whole stack of magazines with my "work" printed alongside photographs of Douglas Fairbanks and Mary Pickford, and I left.

I'm walking down the street with the honorarium in my pocket and a stack of magazines under my arm, crowds all around, and suddenly, head towering over the crowd, there he is: Chaliapin! Out walking with his wife. Blond, taller than everyone else, with sharp creases outlining his mouth. I dash toward him and, knowing that he couldn't stand Russians and refused to talk to them, I say in impeccable French, "Monsieur, how happy we are to see you in Paris! Is it true that you're currently filming *Don Quixote*? Will we really get to see you in the lead role?"

He melted into a smile, "Yes, I was just shooting *Don Quixote*." He told me about the shoots, about how his daughter also had a part, about how the filming was already over, and how he had just returned from Nice.

I pulled out my notepad and demanded an autograph. He wrote, "To a dear French girl in memory of our meeting." Then he said, "Mademoiselle, I'm not only going to give you my autograph, I would like to present you with a copy of my record, which just came out." He stretched out his hand (he was walking empty-handed while his wife carried a bag of records), pulled out a record, signed it simply "Chaliapin" in Latin letters, and handed it to me. I thanked him and flew back to the editorial offices.

They weren't expecting me back so soon and greeted me this time less cordially than before. "And so, mademoiselle, whom have we seen this time?" "Chaliapin." "Mademoiselle," the editor said softly, "you and I agreed to real encounters. You couldn't have seen Chaliapin, because right now he is down in Nice on the Côte d'Azur shooting *Don Quixote*."

I heard him out, and then spread the two autographs in front of him. As he examined them, not believing his eyes, I remarked nonchalantly, "I think I'll take a seat and write it up right here."

I walked out of that office convinced that I would score my third encounter just as easily, even though they had given me a month's deadline.

I walked, and I walked, and I walked all over Paris, looking into store windows and all the cafés, but there was no one, absolutely no one! My month was coming to its end, I hadn't run into anyone, and I was even beginning to forget about the whole thing. At about the same time a letter came from one of Mama's acquaintances, Elena Aleksandrovna Izvolskaya. She was vacationing at Fontainebleau and invited Mother to come visit, adding, "If you can't come, then at least send Alya." And I went. Fontainebleau is a delightful place Napoleon used to frequent, but since then, I think, life had quieted down considerably and never really did pick up again.

As soon as I arrived, Elena Aleksandrovna asked me, "Alya, would you like to go boating?"

"Yes, I would."

"Do you have a bathing suit?"

"No."

"Well, then why don't you put on our hostess's husband's suit?"

The Seine in those parts was marvelous, and there was a small dock with a rowboat tied to it. I clambered into the boat, not knowing how to swim or to row, and started swinging the oars. The shoreline slipped by quickly, or so it seemed to me, though in fact I was plugging very slowly against the current. Then I let loose the oars, threw my head back, and stared into the sky.

Suddenly, my rowboat ran into something. I looked up, and there was this huge yacht! A millionaire's yacht, all decked in white, was standing at anchor. I try to push away from the side with my oar, when just at that moment someone leaned over the side and dumped what looked like coffee grounds out of a silver urn, almost hitting me on the head. I looked up at the man with the urn: it was Alfonso XIII, the king of Spain, just deposed from his throne! He had the jaundiced complexion of a Spanish degenerate.

"Monsieur, monsieur!" I shouted.

He glanced in disgust over the side.

"Monsieur, could you tell me what time it is, please?"

He grumbled something in response, like, half past two, and disappeared.

I set off back to the dock at full speed.

I walked into the house. "Do you know who I met on the Seine just now?" I asked.

Elena Aleksandrovna says, "Alfonso XIII, probably."

"Yes. . . . How did you know?"

"Everyone has seen him. His yacht has been standing here for a long time now, and everybody keeps rowing over to ask the time."

Which is exactly what I wrote to my movie magazine, not concealing the fact that I had been far from the first to ask Alfonso XIII the time. This convinced them that I had not only style, but luck, and after that they very kindly tossed occasional assignments my way: I got sent to a few receptions and to some film shoots and wrote articles about what I had seen, and I went to the train station to meet various stars as they came into town.

And that was when I fell beyond redemption in my mother's eyes!

THE DREAM

I had this dream just before I left for Russia in 1937.

I dreamed that I was walking through a graveyard late at night, and since in real life I'm not afraid of cemeteries—never have been—I didn't experience any fear in my dream: I'm just walking. It's an autumn night, dark, not a star in the sky, but quiet and warm. I get this feeling that there's someone walking alongside right next to me. I keep walking, not turning my head to see who it is, because you don't do that in a dream, because dreams have their own logic. We get to a dark downward passage, like the entrances to the Paris metro, where you're walking along and suddenly there's a staircase down with a doorway at the bottom. Well, there was the same kind of underground entrance in the middle of this cemetery. We go down the stairs. At the bottom there's a long, long dimly lit tunnel with tiny cells separated by partitions (or maybe they were just niches in the wall) along both sides of the corridor. Each of the cells has a person sitting inside. We keep walking farther and farther down the corridor, me and whoever it is next to me, in lockstep, shoulder to shoulder. I can see that all these people are not just sitting there; they're all doing something. Every one of them is thoroughly absorbed in some task or another, but the tasks are all horribly senseless. Each person has some sort of funereal object: a cross, a wreath, artificial flowers, etc., and in the dim light they're unraveling the wreaths, separating the wire from the artificial flowers; sorting the dusty, faded, half-disintegrated flower petals; unstringing the beads from various grave decorations; and performing other similarly bizarre tasks.

The corridor finally terminates at the other edge of the cemetery with an exit again just like those in the Paris metro. We come out into the same dark, quiet night.

"What are they all doing down there?" I ask.

"Don't you know: *not all* people will rise from the dead?" my invisible guide answered.

End of dream.

FRAGMENTS

Ariadna Efron tells us that her mother recorded her life in notebooks; when necessary, Marina Tsvetaeva would bind those notebooks herself. In the gulag her daughter, trained by her mother to keep a diary in a notebook, for many years was denied even scraps of paper on which to write letters home. In fact, during Stalin's reign of terror and for many years after, a diary could be a liability, typewriters were registered with the police, and even carbon paper could be difficult to obtain. Not surprisingly, Ariadna Efron cultivated alternative methods for preserving the past. She wrote thousands of letters. She treated her trusted acquaintances to stories she told aloud—only a handful of which were set to paper by her literary secretary Elena Korkina. And sometimes she wrote things down, but when she did, the sheets of paper more often than not were not bound. Some she collected in folders, but far from all. Seven years after the Tsvetaeva papers at the Russian State Archive for Literature and Art (fund 1190) were made available to researchers, the curators of Efron's portion of the archive have yet to publish any collections of her writings.

Since Efron's death in 1975 several publications have emerged, which, in addition to the "authorized" memoirs, have brought to light fragments of Efron's autobiographical writing. These fragments are of uneven quality. However, in overall style, tone, and spirit, they provide valuable glimpses into their author's life that complement—and in no way contradict—the larger picture drawn in her published writings. For that reason, they are included in this volume.

Unless otherwise indicated, titles for these fragments were devised by the compiler of this volume and are intended principally as an indexing mechanism. Fragments have been arranged in chronological order of the events described and not following the provenance of their writing.—Trans.

FIRST MEMORIES

My first memories of Mama, of what she looked like, resemble surrealist drawings.[1] There is no cohesiveness to the image, for my eyes are not yet capable of taking it all in, and my mind—of gathering all the component parts into a single whole.

Everything surrounding me and everyone around me is unwieldy, immense, incomprehensible, and disproportionate to me. People have huge shoes, legs that trail off high above, and enormous all-powerful hands.

I cannot see faces: they are somewhere up above, and I am able to glimpse them only when they bend toward me or when someone picks me up in their arms. Only then can I see—and touch with my finger—a big ear, a big eyebrow, a big eye that blinks as my finger draws near, and a big mouth that now kisses me or now says "aahm," while attempting to snap at my hand, which is funny, and thrilling.

The concepts of age, sex, beauty, and degrees of kinship do not exist for me, and my own "self" has yet to coalesce: my "self" is utter dependence on all these eyes, lips, and, most important, hands. Everything else is a fog. Most often it is Mama's hands that break that fog: pat me on the head, feed me with a spoon, spank me, calm me, fasten me, and put me to sleep, doing what they wish with me. They are the first reality and the first active, moving force in my life. Narrow at the wrist, tanned, restive, they are better than all others, because they abound with the luster of silver rings and bracelets, a luster that comes and goes together with her and is inseparable from her.

Lustrous hands, sparkling eyes, a resonant brilliant voice—this is the Mama of my earliest years. I saw her and perceived her as a whole for the first time only when she, having disappeared from my life for several days, returned from the hospital after an operation. The hospital and operation I came to understand many years later; at this point the door into my nursery opened, Mama walked in, and suddenly, with lightning speed, all the separate pieces she had been for me until this moment melded together as a whole. I saw her in her entirety, from head to toe, and rushed toward her, breathless with joy.

Mama was of middle—rather, short—stature, with correct facial features distinctly sculpted, without being sharp. Her nose was aquiline, with a small bump and with beautiful expressive nostrils, truly expressive, especially good at expressing both wrath and scorn. In fact, everything about her face was expressive, and wily: her lips as well as her smile and the arch of her brow, and even her tiny ears, almost without lobes, were keen and ever alert, like those of a faun. Her eyes were of the most rare, light bright green color known as fairy green, which never altered, never dulled or paled, even to her death. For a long time the oval of her face preserved something childlike, a certain very youthful roundness. Her light golden brown hair waved softly and carelessly: everything about her was unembellished and required no embellishment. Mama was broad at the shoulders, with narrow hips and waist. Trim, over the course of her life she preserved her figure and the nimbleness of a teenager. Her hands were not feminine but like a boy's, small, though hardly miniature, strong and firm when giving a handshake, with well-developed fingers some-what squared at the tips, but with beautifully formed nails. Her rings and bracelets comprised an integral component of those hands and grew to be part of them in the same way peasant women wore earrings: having once put them in their ears, they never removed them. The same—once and forever—was true of her two antique cast-silver bracelets, both con-vex, one speckled with turquoise, the other smooth and with an amaz-ing flying bird engraved into it, its wings spanning from one edge to the other to embrace her entire wrist. Three rings—her wedding ring, which "had survived on the tablets," an agate in a smooth frame engraved with Hermes in his winged helmet, and a heavy signet ring, also silver, with a tiny caravel engraved on it and encircled by a caption that read TO YOU MY SYMPATHIA—obviously a present from some long-gone sailor to his long-gone bride. Over the course of my memory the caption almost entirely wore off, and the caravel grew barely visible. There were still other rings, many of them, which came and went, but these three never left her fingers and disappeared only when she herself did.

On that evening when Mama came together for me as a single whole she wore a wide, rustling brown silk dress with a narrow bodice, and her arm, bandaged after the operation, was in a sling, and I remember even the sling: a dark cashmere scarf with an Eastern design.

CRIMEA, 1914

My very first memory of her—and of myself—involves some stairs (I am standing at the top) that lead down into a large, unfamiliar room.[2] Every-thing seems out of place to me because it is a half basement. The lightbulb hangs high from the ceiling, but the ceiling itself seems low, since I am standing on the stairs. I cannot figure out what's closer: floor or ceiling.

Mama is there, down below, just beneath the lightbulb: she first stands, then turns slowly, spreading her arms slightly, and she is looking not at me, but at herself. Alongside her, on her knees, is a woman who is touching something on Mama, smoothing it out, tugging at it, while the air fills with unfamiliar words—"flared skirt, flared skirt"—repeated over and over again. In the corner there is yet another woman, but she has no head, and no arms either, with a lacquered black stand instead of legs, however, the dress she is wearing is alive and real. I am given orders to stand still, and I stand still, but I will soon start bawling because no one pays any attention to me and I am still small and can fall down the stairs. That, Mama said, was in the Crimea, and I was turning two.

Of that summer neither people, nor things, nor the rooms where we lived have survived in my memory. It was then for the first time that Papa became part of my consciousness: because he was so tall he remained beyond my field of vision longer than did Mama, and my first memory of him is of how I did not recognize him. Mama is carrying me in her arms, and a man in white is walking toward us, and Mama asks me who it is, and I don't recognize him. Only when he bends over me do I recognize him and shout: "Seryozha! Seryozha!" (In early childhood I referred to my parents as they referred to each other: Seryozha and Marina, more often, Seryozhenka and Marinochka!)

Mama's slippers also come to mind: I once threw my new shoe off a high cliff into the sea. The slippers I remember, but not the sea: it was so huge that I paid no attention to it.

CRIMEA, 1915

The next summer in the Crimea already abounds with people, events, shades, sounds, and smells.[3] Etched into my memory are the unbearably sun-whitened wall of the house and the red roses with their pungent, almost tangible smell and their thorns. I already distinguish the sea and make out the horizon, but I still have no sense of space: when I stand on the shore, the sea for me is a high, grayish blue wall. I stand beneath it. In my opinion, the sea is good only from the shore. Bathing in it is horrible. When, grasped firmly under my arms, I am dipped into a hissing wave, I burst into tears and shriek without pause to catch my breath. Then Mama dries me with a terry cloth towel and scolds me, but I don't care: the main thing is that I am on dry land. To accustom me to the water, my godmother Pra [Elena Ottobaldovna Voloshina—trans.], Max Voloshin's mother, dives into the sea and swims around, still fully dressed. When she comes out onto the shore, water streams from her silver-embroidered white Tatar robe, her balloon-leg trousers, and her colored leather boots. I, however, find watching her neither funny nor interesting. I remember Pra as very large, very gray-haired, and noisy, that is, loud.

At times, my cousin, Andriusha [Andrei Borisovich Trukhachov—trans.], shows up alongside me. He is a good boy: he is not afraid of water; his pants are dry more often than mine are; he does a good job eating his cream of wheat and even swallows it, and he "listens to mama." Despite the fact that he is such a good boy, I love him in my own way. I like the striped, tasseled, bell-shaped cap on his head, and I like riding the teeter-totter with him. So what if we often fight because we are unable to share something. I am still drawn to him because I sense in him someone of my own breed: he is just as small and just as dependent as I am. Like me, he gets carried off at the best part of playtime, and just as unexpectedly as me, he gets put down to sleep or fed or spanked or stood in the corner. He is my fellow tribesman and the only real human being in the assemblage of celestials surrounding us.

True, our first acquaintance evoked in me a sense of real hatred. Apparently, that took place the preceding winter in Moscow. A little fair-haired boy in a long shirt and red high shoes showed up in my nursery. "This," Mama says, "is your cousin Andriusha." "My cousin Andriusha" apprehensively extends his hand toward me, but I hide both of my hands behind my back and proceed to stomp painfully on his red baby shoes with my little black baby shoes. I stomp with all my might, silently, sniffling with envy and wrath. He, he, "my cousin Andriusha"—and not I—has such beautiful red shoes! If they cannot be mine, then I must destroy them, crush them. Andriusha withdraws, and I advance, aiming once again for his feet. Andriusha grabs me by the hair, and I—with relish—poke him in the face. Our mamas—his and mine—pull us apart and spank us on the hands, and I howl in vexation and at my inability to express the passions engulfing me: I still have no words, and I cannot explain that the red shoes either must be mine or cannot exist at all!

That same summer in the Crimea it becomes clear, first of all, that I am a coward. Pra gives me a hedgehog as a present, but my fear and disgust at its prickly needles overpower my delight that it—unlike me—knows how to drink milk from a saucer. Everyone pets the hedgehog—Mama, and Pra, and even Andriusha rushes forward to touch, but I am incapable of forcing myself to extend my hand toward this bundle of needles, the very air around which, it seems to me, stings!

Second, it becomes clear that I do not know how to eat. I am capable only of chewing, chewing for an eternity, but incapable of swallowing, and so I conscientiously spit it all out. Mama's struggle with these first two faults of mine marks the commencement of my upbringing, which will continue for many long years. She combats my cowardliness with admonitions and punishments, my fear of water simply by bathing me, but both of us hold our own, neither yielding her position.

"You were afraid of petting the hedgehog? So God has punished you: now the hedgehog's croaked, you understand? Dead, gone to sleep for a long time never to wake up. No, there's no way to wake it up. Now even if you wanted to pet it, it's too late. Poor, poor hedgehog! All because you're such a little coward!"

I cry bitter tears, and for a long, long time I remember—to this day I have not forgotten—how the hedgehog Pra gave me croaked, died, went to sleep forever, all because I was afraid to pet it. But I am still not certain that I could have forced myself to touch it, even if the God who punished me were moved to pity by my sorrow and brought it back to life.

ALYA, THE FINICKY EATER

As far as eating went, I was quite horrible as a child.[4] I would chew, absent-mindedly gawking to the right and the left or peering fearfully at Mama, who was already fuming, and kept on chewing, increasingly terrified by the realization that I had to swallow all of this, and then refused to swallow. I chewed until I could chew no more, and then I spat it out. I spat, knowing that retribution was inevitable, and I resigned myself to it with mulish stubbornness and Christian meekness.

My spitting got to the point that Mama would strip me bare, bib me with a napkin embroidered in red thread with a cat's head and the words

"Bon appétit" (a present from Mama's sister, Asya), put on an apron, and sit down opposite my high chair, with spoon and a bowl of cream of wheat in hand. My feedings involved hosts of people, each of whom remarked that they had never seen anything like it and then proceeded to offer advice. Pra, whom Mama respected and obeyed, advised her not to feed me at all until I got hungry and asked for something to eat. Mama agreed. The summer was hot, and I kept drinking milk (for three days I drank only milk), which kept me from growing hungry, and so I never asked for anything to eat. On the fourth day Mama said that she refused to be witness to her own child's demise, and once again I found myself naked as a jaybird, napkin under my chin, unable to gulp down anything except my tears.

(Many, many years later, having returned to the Soviet Union as a twenty-three-year-old,[5] I was working at Zhurgaz in the editorial offices of *Revue de Moscou*,[6] when the phone rang.

"Ariadna Sergeevna, please!"

"Speaking."

"This is Elena Usievich. Do you remember me?"

"No."

"Right, you were still just a baby then. . . . How are you? Have you settled in?"

"Fine, thank you."

"Are you eating all right?"

"Actually, I'm making enough money to be able to feed myself just fine," I answer, perplexed by this display of concern.

"Oh, that's not what I mean," Usievich interrupts me. "How are you eating? Do you swallow? As a child, you know, you never swallowed. . . . To this day I cannot forget you sitting naked as a jaybird, smeared from head to toe with the cream of wheat Marina Ivanovna tried to feed you! I just found out that you were in Moscow, and decided to call you to find out. . . ."[7]

THE HOUSE IN BORISOGLEBSKY LANE

The house where mother spent her early adulthood and I my childhood remains standing to this day.[8] House 6 in Borisoglebsky Lane,[9] not far from the Arbat, Povarskaya Street, and Sobachya Square: two-storied on the street side and three-storied on the courtyard side. Back then two trees grew opposite our house, and Mama dedicated to them her poem "Two trees yearn for each other,"[10] but today only one, orphaned, remains. We moved to apartment number five of that house from our place in the Zamoskvorechie district of Moscow, where I was born. It was a real, old-fashioned, uncomfortable, illogical, inelegant one-and-a-half-story Moscow apartment, and very cozy. There were two doors from the entranceway: the one on the left led into a room that belonged to no one and with which I draw no early associations, and the one on the right led into a large, dark, walk-through dining room. In the daytime the dining room was dimly and strangely illuminated by a large skylight in the ceiling. In the winter, the skylight gradually would be covered over with snow, and the janitor would climb onto the roof and dig it out. In the dining room there was a large round table—directly under the skylight—and a fireplace, bearing two stuffed foxes (of which we will speak later), a clock in the shape of a bronze camel, and a bust of Pushkin. Along one of the walls stood a long, high-backed, uncomfortable black—either oilcloth or leather—sofa and a large dark sideboard with dishes inside.

The dining room's second door led by way of a narrow, dark corridor into Mama's small room and my large nursery. In the nursery, the sunniest room in the apartment, there were three windows. I remember these windows as enormous, from floor to ceiling, sparkling clean and with the light of the snow flitting outside them! Not long ago I walked into the courtyard of our former house and discovered that in fact those three windows were tiny, dim, and dingy: so small and so unsightly they cannot displace or overshadow those other windows created in my memory by my childhood perception and enhanced by my childhood imagination!

To the left of the nursery door stood a black iron coal-fired stove-heater, and behind it a large, ceiling-high bookcase that held children's books once belonging to my grandmother M[aria] A[leksandrovna] Meyn, my mother's, and my own. In the very bottom section of the bookcase lived my toys, which I could take out on my own, while Mama always took the books out and gave them to me herself. Adjoining the bookcase was my bed with its netting, and my headboard jutted up against the latest nanny's trunk. I do not recollect there being any big tables or chairs for adults in this room, although there must have been. I remember the soft sofa between the last window and the door. I remember the pictures in their round frames, copies after Greuze, one of them *Girl with a Bird.*[11] Above my bed hung a sad little boy in a velvet frame. Some of these pictures—perhaps all of them—were the work of my grandmother, Maria Aleksandrovna. The nursery was spacious and uncluttered.

Exiting the nursery back into the same dark, narrow little corridor, running your hand along the left wall, you could grope your way to the door of Mama's room. To my recollection it was the only real room Mama ever had: not some corner imposed by fate, not some short-term shelter for which there soon would be no money to pay and which would have to be abandoned for another, more or less the same, except a notch worse and a flight of stairs higher. . . .

The room was not large, somewhat long, irregularly shaped in the form of an upside-down L, and somewhat dark, since the window had been cut in the far corner of the shorter wall and was partly obstructed by the adjoining wall of the nursery. Almost all the light from this window was consumed by the large writing table. On the right-hand side of the desk along the shorter wall of the niche that housed it stood books stacked in a short row, with papers and notebooks lying nearby. Among the knick-knacks . . . ("Knickknacks," by the way, is the most inappropriate word possible for Mama's desk! Those weren't knickknacks. They were objects with souls and histories, hardly chance objects and not always pleasing to the eye.) Among the things that I as a little one keenly and futilely stretched to reach was a tall, circular, black lacquer box for quills and pencils, known as "Tuchkov IV" owing to its lovely miniature portrait of the twenty-two-year-old general, hero of the War of 1812, crimson and gray cape draped across his shoulder.[12] Particularly tempting was Grandmother Maria Aleksandrovna's paperweight: two little metal hands peeking out of lace cuffs that hid a spring mechanism—two dark hands that secured a bundle of letters. My fear and curiosity were aroused by a strange black figurine of the Madonna brought back from Italy at some point by Grandfather Ivan Vladimirovich Tsvetaev. It was a medieval Madonna with a high forehead and wide-open unseeing eyes, palm-sized and very heavy, made of cast iron or steel. The figurine's stomach had a double-hinged door—the iron maiden turned out to be hollow inside—studded with sharp thorns.[13] "In the Middle Ages," Mama told me, "there was a larger-than-life statue just like that in Italy. Heretics were locked inside: when they closed the door, the thorns would pierce them through." The Middle Ages, Italy, and heretics were altogether foggy concepts for me, but looking at those thorns and touching them with my finger I objected with all my soul against medieval Italy and *that* Madonna in favor of heretics.

Between the desk and the door was a recess, like a niche, that could be closed off with a dark blue curtain. On one of its shelves, wrapped in a silk scarf, was the white plaster death mask of Papa's brother Petya [Pyotr Yakovlevich Efron—trans.], who had died of tuberculosis. That marvelous sleeping face, so tormented and so calm, resembled Papa's and always evoked in me feelings of tenderness and pity. I often asked Mama to "show me Petya" and would kiss the closed sad, cool lips and the big-big, cool, shut eyes. "He knew you," Mama would say, "but you don't remember him. He loved you: he had a little daughter who died. And he had a wife, a dancer, who didn't love him. . . ."

A little daughter who died? A dancer who didn't love him? How incomprehensible it all was! How could someone die? How could someone not love?

The shelves held all sorts of interesting things: starfish, seashells, a turtle shell, and a stereoscope with a plethora of disks with double slides to go with it—of the Crimea, Mama, Papa, Max, Pra, Andriusha and me, various acquaintances, and views of the landscape. The stereoscope made everything seem real and completely alive, although motionless.

The wall to the right from the door was unoccupied, with nothing alongside it except an old armchair, so you could walk right up to it and run your finger along the roses on the light-colored wallpaper. You could stroke the beautiful grayish blue pelt fastened to a background of red broadcloth with pinked edges. The pelt was that of Mama's favorite cat, Kusaka [Nipper—trans.], which she had brought back from the Crimea when it was still a tiny kitten by hiding it under her sailor shirt for three days. Kusaka had been very smart and understood everything, like a dog, even better. He was so smart that he even understood the purpose of my chamber pot, which he used more successfully than I did, with great difficulty and effort grasping the slippery enamel edges with all four paws. Our thieving cook, whom Mama fired, poisoned Kusaka in revenge. The dying Kusaka, foaming at the mouth, his fur matted and dull, dragged himself across the entire apartment over to Mama to say good-bye to her and died in her arms. Mama sobbed uncontrollably, and I wailed, too, and then we got in a carriage and took the dead Kusaka to a taxidermist. The latter proposed that we immortalize the cat "as if it were alive," slinking after a bird on a branch of a supposedly real tree! Although the taxidermist offered the bird for no extra charge, as a bonus, Mama refused to agree to make an abomination of our Kusaka, and so he came to be that pelt on the wall.

(I remember how once, without any help from the cook, Kusaka had taken sick, and the veterinarian had written out a prescription that Mama kept for a long time as an example of amateur verse. The prescription for cat syrup ran as follows:

> Every hour and a half
> Feed a teaspoon to the cat
> Of Madam Efron.)

On that same wall were some small color reproductions of paintings by Mikhail Vrubel that I really liked: I remember *Pan* and *The Princess Swan.*[14]

On the opposite wall was a large portrait of Papa painted by my parents' friend, the artist Magda (have to ask Lilya her last name) [Nakhman—trans.] at the time of Papa's illness. He is reclining in a chair, book in hand, his legs wrapped in a small travel blanket. The background was bright orange—either a curtain or a hypothetical sunset. . . .[15]

The portrait hung over a wide, low daybed covered with a piece of violet and green wavy-striped silk, the very same kind from Uzbekistan that they still use to make robes. A beautiful dark blue crystal antique chandelier with long tinkling pendants of cut glass was suspended from the ceiling. On the floor, directly under the chandelier, was a wolf skin which, given its proportions and mine, seemed like a bearskin to me. It was pleasant knowing that I could stick my little fist into the wolf's gaping mouth and it would not bite me, even though the fangs were real!

The entire space running from the edge of the daybed to the wall with Kusaka's hide was occupied by a huge antique escritoire from which Mama occasionally extracted a rather heavy music box of dark wood with incrustations. It played several sad, slow songs, crisply punctuating the notes of the melodies. Its brass cylinders turned with pins that struck the teeth of a metal comb: the mechanism that extracted music from cylinders and holed cards was exposed, but the music box remained mysterious and magical nonetheless. Besides the music box, Mama also had a genuine antique hand organ bought from a genuine antique organ grinder. Mama and Papa and their young guests would crank away at the organ's handle as it wheezed with unexpected syncopation [Mikhail Glinka's nocturne—trans.] *La Séparation.*

To get to the second floor of the apartment you had to go all the way back down the dark corridor into the dining room and from there back to the entranceway, where, by way of another corridor, you ascended a rather steep, high staircase. The staircase led to a landing illuminated by a window and with doors leading off to the large kitchen (where I as a small child was forbidden to go), to the bathroom, to a storage room, and the toilet. One more small corridor led past a small room (where all that fit was a bed with a bare mattress, a table, a chair, and a linen cabinet) to Papa's room, which was large and not very well lit because, like Mama's, it ended in a niche. I don't remember Papa's room in much detail because I rarely went there: from the nursery it was easy to get to Mama's room or the dining room, but here you had to climb the staircase and pass the forbidden kitchen, which was, all told, an entire journey, on which I braved to venture only upon special invitation.

To the left of the door in Papa's room stood a daybed. To the right, near the window, was a desk, and directly ahead was a round table and a buffet that housed such delights as "Albert" and "Maria" cookies as well as cocoa in a tin can with a little Dutch girl on it, the cocoa itself inextricably linked in my memory with Osip Mandelstam. But more about that later!

On my visits to Papa's room I would be seated at the round table and "treated" to cookies, and the fact that these cookies—all too familiar and not so very tasty in the nursery—were a "treat" meant that I ate them with pleasure and even a sense of celebration. It was here that I was once given as a present for Easter a real scale model of the Trinity Lavra of Saint Sergius:[16] an entire box of little pink houses and churches (some with a single dome, others with multiple domes). Until then I had had only toy blocks, and I still remember how thoroughly astounded I was by this toy city that one could lay out any way one wished. I kept that toy monastery until we went abroad, at which point Mama talked me into giving it to little Sasha Kogan because she had decided that Sasha was Blok's son (Blok, they said, had been infatuated with [Nadezhda Aleksandrovna Nolle-Kogan—trans.] the wife of Pyotr Semyonovich [Kogan—trans.]). . . .

Although I was hardly possessive, had no difficulty giving away my toys, and passed on this toy with similar ease, I came to regret parting with the monastery and thought about it for a long time after. In fact, Sasha turned out to be no more than the son of his legal father. . . .

My memory will long continue to roam our apartment in Borisoglebsky Lane, catching, just like pins on a music-box cylinder, on the many things that occurred in those rooms, but the little room next to Papa's is tied only to three early reminiscences, which I'd like to relate now so as not to have to return to that room again.

Aunt Vera, Papa's sister, and I are sitting on the striped mattress of the unoccupied bed in that room, talking. Vera asks, "Do you love me?" "I love you terribly," I reply. "'Love terribly' is not a good way to put it," Vera corrects me. "'Terribly' means 'very badly,' and you can't love very badly. You should say 'very much'!" "I love you terribly," I repeat stubbornly. "Very much!" says Vera. "Ter-rib-ly," I repeat in anger this time. In walks Mama. I run to her. "Marinochka! Vera said it's not all right to love terribly, that that's not a good way to put it, that the way to say it is 'love very much.'" Mama picks me up. "You can love terribly, Alechka. To love terribly is to love more and better than just to love or to love very much!" says Mama, distending her nostrils, which means that she is angry with Vera.

Why does that striped mattress stick in my memory? Because once I found a real piece of candy on it! No one besides the mattress and me was in the room at that moment, which meant that the mattress must have been responsible for this miracle, which meant that candy could be found on all mattresses. And more than once afterward, to my nanny's astonishment, I would rummage through my bedding in the nursery and get angry when I did not find anything. The candy I found was my secret; I didn't even tell Mama, and perhaps that's why I never found candy after that.

My third memory is of a young, ruddy-cheeked, friendly woman known as "the drop-in seamstress," who sits in the room at the table, hemming sheets on her portable sewing machine as she tells Mama a story about how once when she was a little girl she fell asleep and could not wake up, and how she heard the doctor come and say that she had died, and felt them putting her in the coffin, and she heard her mother's weeping and the service for the dead, but still she couldn't wake up. "Lethargic syndrome," Mama says. "They could have buried you alive!" I freeze in horror: bury means to put in the ground! Put a live sleeping drop-in seamstress in the ground!

"What happened next?" I ask with trepidation.

Mama remembers that I am there: "This fairy tale isn't for you!" she says as she leads me out of the room.

"Marinochka, did they bury her alive?"

"Of course not! She woke up and, see, she's sitting there, sewing. . . ."

"Marinochka, what did they do with the coffin?"

"I don't know," says Mama. "Probably they gave it to someone as a present."

I calm down. I know well what a coffin and funeral are from one of my short-lived nannies, the one whose "son is at the front," which for some reason often makes her cry, and who frequently takes me on secret walks to church, to funerals, where she makes me press my lips to the foreheads of other people's dead. Generally, this is more interesting than just a walk, because Sobachya Square is always the same, while corpses are always different. What's more, for me they are sort of like church implements, a most incomprehensible but, obviously, essential church attribute! I always mean to tell Mama about it, to share my pleasure with her, but a child's memory is short, and on the way back home I always forget the whole thing. The one time I did not forget turned out to be fatal for the nanny: Mama fired her immediately. . . .

STORYTIME

There were as many worlds in our apartment as there were rooms, and only grown-ups were allowed to move among them with ease or of one's own accord.[17] For me those worlds were barricaded off by multiple "don'ts," principal among which was the prohibition against intruding on the lives of my elders. But even when I was allowed into those lives, the "don'ts" continued to pursue me, and me alone. There were days when I would be seated at the table with everyone else; the adults—no small number of them gathered around our round table—chatted, argued, laughed, and their movements were free and their voices loud, and their plates held some other, special kind of food. They clinked beautiful stemmed glasses of red wine. While I had to eat despicable spinach or buckwheat colored blue by the added milk, to be eaten, moreover, with the assistance of a crust of bread, not with my fingers. I must not "interrupt elders" and interfere with their conversation, dangle my legs or put my hands under the table to pet Jack the Poodle, who kept vigil down below, and my participation in conversation at the table was usually limited to "thank you" and "please." I didn't mind this arrangement, and whereas in the nursery I would have had free rein to be rude to Nanny, to run about, yell, and be naughty, that freedom held little appeal for me: the adults' life was too captivating, and for the chance just to be present I was entirely and thoroughly prepared to squeeze myself head and all into the foot bindings of "good behavior."

"Good behavior" was adjudicated by Mama, and it was impossible even to contemplate that any little girl who had misbehaved would dare to enter her room.

Mama's room was the treat of my childhood, and this treat had to be earned. It began the moment I crossed the threshold: the music box would be wound up for me; I was allowed to crank the handle of the hand organ; I was permitted to play with the turtle shell, to roll on the wolf skin, and to peek into the stereoscope. Papa would take me on his knees and tell me fairy tales no one else knew. I particularly liked the tale of the robber-bandits, but for some reason Papa never told it in Mama's presence. It went as follows: "One time little Alechka was left home all alone. . . . Papa had left, and Mama had left, and Nanny had left, and Jack had left. . . . The robber-bandits found out about this. And they came into the house. They made their way up the stairs. They opened the door and looked inside. Where is little Alya? Then they went into the hallway. First they went into the kitchen, and from the kitchen—into the washroom, their knives in their hands. . . ." "Damask steel?" I ask, trembling. "Damask steel," Papa confirms in a momentous voice. . . . "They're looking for little Alya. . . . Now they've gone into Papa's room . . . , they look under the couch, still no little Alya. They look in the cupboard: no little Alya! They look in the armoire: no little Alya! Then they come out of Papa's room. . . ." ("No, no!" I shout in horror, for I absolutely must, at whatever cost, detain the robber-bandits on the second floor a bit longer. "They can't come out yet! They still haven't looked under the piano! . . .") "They look under the piano: no little Alya there either! Then they go down to the dining room. . . ." "No, no! Not the dining room. They still haven't been in the toilet!" "Right," Papa continues, unruffled. "They look in the toilet: no little Alya there either. . . ."

The robber-bandits' torturous journey went on for a long time. With each step they made their inevitable way toward the nursery, where little Alya was hiding. The tension and terror continued to mount, but this hardly bothered Papa. He was not afraid; he, after all, was not at home, and the bandits were not looking for him! . . . "Now they're coming down the hallway . . . , closer . . . and closer, then one of the bandits takes hold of the doorknob. . . . Then . . . he . . . opens . . . the door. . . ." Unable to endure any more, I shriek, while Papa, who for some reason keeps looking at the door, in soothing, cheerful patter brings the tale to its happy, albeit bloody conclusion: "But just at that moment Papa returned home. . . ." "And killed all the robber-bandits!" I conclude with glee. "And slew all the robber-bandits!" he confirmed. What joy! What relief! I am saved!

With the exception of this one, Papa's fairy tales were all sweet and comforting. And Papa himself was so sweet and so much "better than everyone else" that I decided I would marry him when I grew up.

On one of the shelves alongside Mama's treasures stood three of Grandmother's children's books, apparently, Mama's most favorite or—by some measure or other—her most treasured books, for she kept them in her own room, apart from those in the bookcase that stood in the nursery. These were Perrault's *Fairy Tales* and *The Holy Bible,* both with illustrations by Gustave Doré, and a one-volume edition of Gogol—three large-format tomes in heavy bindings. Still not having learned how to read, I had already been instructed—for the rest of my life!—on how to treat books, for in Mama's school of pedagogy "don't" related first and foremost to books. One must not touch them without first washing one's hands; one must not turn the pages by lifting them by the lower corner—only by the upper right-hand corner!—and, of course, one must not dampen one's fingers with saliva or dog-ear the corners or, most difficult for me, under any circumstances add to the illustrations!

Perrault's fairy tales were told to me by Mama, who simplified them as she went along, while Doré illustrated them for me. To this day I can still picture Tom Thumb in the dark forest surrounded by trees with enormous trunks and bushy boughs, the Ogre's daughters asleep in their crowns, the banquet at the castle of Prince Ricky of the Tuft, and beautiful Donkey Skin riding off into the distance by the light of a crescent moon.

In fact, these fairy tales were not just told to me, I had to tell them myself, that is, to retell in my own words the fairy tale I had just heard or to explain what was depicted in the pictures. I was quite drawn to the illustrations of Gogol's works with several small, highly detailed pictures set on a single page. As for what was depicted in them and what they meant, that I had to figure out on my own, because no one read Gogol to me: he was still beyond my three or four years of age. "And what is that? And who is that? And what's he doing?" Mama would ask me, while I, searching for resemblances to things I already knew, provided answers. Thus, I lent the following prosaic interpretation to an illustration depicting Khoma Brut reading over a [dead] girl, the girl herself, the devils, and the coffin lid flying above their heads: "Here the young miss is asking cook for some fried monkeys." ("Miss" was the dead girl, "cook" was Khoma Brut, the coffin lid was a stove top, and the devils were "fried monkeys.")[18]

A BAD DREAM

I am ill.[19] I'm lying in my bed in the middle of the day and not allowed to get up. Mama has brought Doctor Yarkho into the nursery, his red hair streaked with gray, the same doctor who had treated her when she was little. This in no way keeps me from screeching like a maniac as he listens to my heart and lungs and taps his cold fingers along my spine. I have pneumonia. This is very good: Papa and Mama play with me all the time, take my temperature, and tell me fairy tales.

In the evening, when they think I have fallen asleep, they go out. But I am not asleep; it's Nanny who's asleep. I have just shut my eyes for a minute.

A bear crawls out from the shadows behind the stove. That's where he lives. He crawls up to my bed and begins to roll me this way and that with his paws, like a cook rolling dough. I shout, but to no avail. Nanny is asleep, and everything in the nursery is as it was, everything is in its place, the lamp burns in the corner, Nanny sleeps . . . , and the bear keeps rolling me back and forth. Just then the door squeaks, and the bear immediately hides behind the stove. "What's the matter with you? What's happened?" Mama asks. "Did you have a bad dream?"

Dream! I'm drenched in sweat, and a long time passes before I can unroll myself out of the bolster the bear had rolled me into back into the shape of a little girl.

CAPRICE

For the most part I am a quiet and well-behaved child.[20] But sometimes— relatively rarely, it seems—I am overcome by anger and rebelliousness. I demand things. Argue. And stamp my feet.

"Oh-ho," Papa says. "Caprice has got into you. We're going to chase him out right now."

From my howling mouth he extracts Caprice, who is so tiny that I cannot even see him. Then Papa unclenches his fist and blows on his palm, and Caprice flies up to the ceiling or out the open window. I calm down and am happy to be rid of him. But Mama does not always remember that it's Caprice who is to blame. And sometimes instead of him, for some reason, she punishes me, puts me in the corner, which keeps Caprice raging within me until I manage somehow to chase him out of mind by myself.

CHRISTMAS

One year we set our Christmas tree in Mama's room, and it was precisely then that I sensed for the first time the fine line that separates joy from sorrow.[21] How can something be so good that it is almost sad? The Christmas tree was not that large: though it reached the ceiling, it stood not on the floor but on a low table draped with a blue coverlet studded with silver stars onto which the candles dripped their multicolored wax. A golden heart of flame flickered above each spiraled candle. In its radiance the tree itself seemed to be the enlarged tongue of flame of an invisible candle. There was the smell of spruce and tangerine peel, the warmth and the light multiplied and reflected in the grown-ups' eyes. There were many eyes that Christmas Eve, many guests, but of all those eyes the ones I remembered were those most beloved, bright green eyes of Mama's, and Papa's large gray eyes. As for the guests, I remember only Pra, and of all the presents—only the little handmade shell box that she brought me from the Crimea.

That was not the first Christmas tree my memory retained. The first one was . . . the first one did not yet border on sorrow! The door to the nursery, where I had not been allowed to go all day, suddenly opened, and there before me stood an enormous pyramid of luster, light, and glittering trinkets bound together as a single whole by the iridescent silver of garlands and tinsel. "What is it?" I asked. "A Christmas tree!" Marina said. "Where's the tree?" I asked, not seeing the tree behind all the glitter. Mama led me by the hand over to the tree, removed a chocolate ball in a foil wrapper, and gave it to me, but this brought me no closer to the tree, and I did not feel like having any chocolate. I was spellbound, even a bit overwhelmed. "Go say hello to our guests," Mama said, and only then, when I looked around, did I see the many guests—all of them adults and all of them people I knew—sitting in chairs along the walls. I obediently went to greet and shake hands with each one of them, treating each to my chocolate, and for some reason all of them laughed as they watched me.

All of this was *incomprehensible,* and I could not shake the spell brought on by the *unusualness* of it all. Then suddenly everything changed, and the wondrous became a reality and acquired meaning, when it was affirmed by yet another miracle. The door opened, and with the words, "I'm late! I'm late!" a jolly, exceptionally kind old man with a long gray beard entered the room. Papa and Mama ran over to greet him, and I, too, suddenly released from my spell, rushed over to him. The old man took me into his arms and kissed me merrily, his soft beard still emitting the cold from outside.

"Hello, hello," he said to me. "Do you remember me?"

"I remember," I said confidently. "You're Father Frost!"

And everyone began to laugh again, "Father Frost" loudest of all.

Our visitor was an old friend of the family, a friend of my grandmother Elizaveta Petrovna Durnovo, Pyotr Alekseevich Kropotkin.

What happened the next day? What happens on any day after a holiday? I do not remember: a lone Christmas tree stands in my memory, with no yesterday and no tomorrow, and merry Father Frost holds me in his arms, and alongside us stand Papa and Mama, Seryozha and Marina, merry and happy, laughing. . . . And that's all.

JACK THE POODLE

We're sitting in the dining room, eating dinner at our big round table; rather, we've just started dinner, the soup having just been served.[22] Suddenly something snaps, followed by a short crash, followed by a thump: the sky opens, and our black poodle, Jack, falls onto the table, right in the center. As if by command, all of us jump to our feet, while Jack, in the din of broken dishes and napkin rings rolling along the floor, scatters cutlery and pieces of bread with his paws as he jumps from the table and, tail between his legs, runs off into the nursery. A trail of noodles and soup follows in his wake. There is a moment of total silence, then chatter, laughter, confusion. . . .

Somewhere up in the attic Jack found a crawl space, through which he slipped out onto the roof, where, while running around, he landed on the skylight over our dining room. The frame gave way under his weight, and Jack came crashing down onto the table, without, fortunately, injuring himself and with comparatively little damage to the dishes.

As Mama told the story, I learned to walk by hanging onto Jack's tail as he patiently led me around the nursery. Jack was coal black, trimmed poodle style, of course. He was smart as a whip and gentle. He was done in by that very same roof: once, after he again somehow crawled out onto the roof, some little boys noticed him and began to tease him. Jack lunged at them right off the roof to his death.

SOPHIA PARNOK'S "SMART" MONKEY

Mama has a girlfriend, Sonya Parnok: she also writes poetry, and Mama and I sometimes go to visit her.[23] Mama reads her poems to Sonya, and Sonya reads hers to Mama, while I sit in a chair, waiting for them to show me the monkey. Because Sonya Parnok has a real live monkey on a chain in the other room. The monkey is dark brown, almost black, and it has four arms with real palms. Its little face is very expressive, almost human, the "almost" being what is so fascinating and terrifying. Sonya says that the monkey is very smart: one time they forgot to hide the key to the lock on its chain, and the monkey grabbed it, opened the lock, removed the chain, got loose, caught the cat, which it hated because it wasn't chained up, trimmed all its claws with manicure scissors, then tossed it into the slops bucket. With those same scissors the monkey also gouged out the eyes of all the portraits hanging in the room, maybe so that they would not witness its revenge on the cat. But what does this have to do with it being "a smart monkey"?

CHICKEN HEAD

"Alya, eat your chicken!"[24]

"I can't, Marinochka!"

"Alya, eat your chicken!"

"Marinochka, it's nasty!"

"It's you, not the chicken, that's nasty! You keep chewing and chewing. . . . Swallow, right this instant!"

"I can't, Marinochka!"

"You can't? Listen to what I tell you. If you don't swallow right now, this very minute, you'll grow a chicken head! Do you hear me?"

"I hear you, Marinochka!"

But someone distracts Mama, and I quickly spit the chicken mush into my fist and give it to the cat, who's been circling my chair for a long time now, knocking its head against the wood. Marina returns:

"So, did you swallow?"

"I swallowed, Marinochka! Honest!"

"Watch out, or you might grow a chicken head. . . ."

I return glumly to the nursery and grope at my head. I think it's beginning to happen. For certain: the nape of my neck is already different. I wonder what kind will grow, a boiled chicken head or a raw one? Having a chicken head won't be so bad if I sit at home. After all, everyone at home will know that it's me. They might even still love me. Suddenly a thought burns me to the quick with shame: but what if I go for a ride in a carriage?

A large mirror had been placed in my room for several days. "Let it stand in Alya's room for the time being," said Marina. From inside the mirror another little girl stares at me, and that other little girl is me. But that can't be! When my Marina appears in the mirror next to her, that other little girl, there is nothing surprising. I always see Marina from the side, from the outside. But I am I, and I sense myself from the inside. To sense oneself from the inside and see oneself from the outside is not possible. In short, I used to be one, but now there are two of "me," and that is vexing. Where does the other me live? You cannot live in a mirror, because it is flat, and in order to live you need space, depth. There is no one behind the mirror. Maybe between the mirror and its rough, unpolished back? No, I am too big to fit there. What is this? What is this, and why? My second "I" gives me no peace, keeps beckoning me. She guesses all my intentions and anticipates my actions. I am still just planning to stick out my tongue, and she has already stuck hers out. I am still thinking about how I will amaze her with a funny face, and she has already made a face I could not even imagine.

The mystery, though, is solved, with Marina's help. The fact is, she and Seryozha can always unfailingly discern when I am telling the truth and when not. No sooner do I tell a lie than Marina looks me in the eye and says, "You know, it's written all over your forehead that you told a fib." Seryozha, too, can read what's written on my forehead, which leaves me no choice but to tell them what really happened. It was precisely this attribute of my forehead that helped me unmask the little girl in the mirror. The very next time the writing on my forehead led to my having been pronounced guilty of yet another fib, I ran over to the mirror. My second "I" was already there. Staring and screwing up my eyes, the way Marina does, I began to examine the little girl's face. Her forehead was absolutely blank: not a letter, not a scribble on it, just amazingly blank. Which meant that the girl in the mirror was not me, but someone else! I, after all, had a label on my forehead (Marina and Seryozha had just read it), and she had nothing. It's not me, not me, not me! Only the dress is the same! Having convinced myself of this and celebrated my discovery at the mirror, I calmed down. There are lots of other little girls in the world: what's it to me! Besides, the mirror was soon removed from the nursery, along with the little trickster with the blank forehead.

NANNIES

The whole difficulty with pants is the nannies' and only the nannies' fault.[25] Marina always knows when it is time to undo them for me. Even if she is talking to grown-ups and has completely forgotten about me playing quietly in the corner, Marina suddenly springs from her seat, with lightening speed unfastens the three back buttons from their loops on my top, and whispers crisply in my ear: "Right this minute . . . march . . . to your pot!"

With nannies it is not like that. Nannies never know when I need to go, and I am the last to know, since I get caught up with my play and forget. Sometimes I just do not have time to remember about my pants. Especially when out on a walk. More often than not, it happens on Sobachya Square, when my nanny sticks a pail and shovel in my hands and runs off to sit with the other nannies and nursemaids. Sometimes I play by myself, sometimes with other little girls, but no matter, I always get caught up in my play. Sometimes I remember that I need to find a spot out of view only after the need has already passed. But it also happens that I manage to run over to my nanny just in time, then dance from one side to the next as I wait for her to untangle and unbutton me. Nanny is in no hurry, of course. She is distracted by the story being told by a magnificent nursemaid in an ostentatious outfit and beads that make every "little girl from a respectable family"—and I am precisely one of those—want to grow up as quickly as possible in order to become a nursemaid just like her. The nursemaid is talking to my nanny about something terribly interesting, about adult things, and phrases like "then the master" and "then the mistress" keep popping up. My nanny's fingers absentmindedly grope under my little coat, then under my dress, searching for the buttons and loops, but it is already too late. I return home disconsolate at the inevitable denunciations and punishment ahead. "Nanny, don't tell Marina," I ask, sensing my own ignobility. "Why should I say anything," the nanny answers with indifference as she husks the pine nuts the nursemaid gave her. "She'll find out for herself."

When, at long last, the door to our apartment opens, I yell in des-peration from the threshold, "I'm dwy, I'm dwy!" "Dwy, huh?" Marina responds from afar, her voice boding no good. Here she comes, swooping down over me, paying no attention to the letters burning on my forehead, always knowing everything in advance, and doles out the appropriate number of spanks. But that's not the end of it. After that I sit in the din-ing room near the fireplace, in winter or summer, no matter, holding my pants just rinsed and wrung out by the nanny. And everyone who walks by asks with hypocritical sympathy, "Is that you, Alechka? What are you doing here?" "Dwying my pants," I snivel.

Not too long after, at that same Sobachya Square, for the same reason noted above, the fact that I am indeed "a child from a respectable family" was acknowledged by a certain man who, to judge by his appearance, also was from a respectable family. He was sitting on a bench all by himself, far from the nannies and the children, reading the newspaper *The Russian Chronicles.*[26] A pince-nez gleamed on his nose, and his gray beard hung in a sharp triangle. On his feet he wore equally shiny high lacing boots: black boots with elastic straps and fasteners. I got a good look at them because while looking for a place out of view, I found myself at this very gentleman's feet, whence I watched intently as my little stream made its way toward his boots. The gentleman also noticed my little stream. He jumped up, snapped his newspaper shut, and walked off, hissing "and that child's from a respectable family." His spine was erect and for some reason indignant.

TELLING RIGHT FROM LEFT

I just can't get the hang of, first of all, how to go down stairs the way grown-ups do—I have to place both feet on each step—and, second, of how to tell my right hand from my left and to distinguish right from left.[27] "Right" and "left" have nothing fixed about them, nothing set and final that one might get accustomed to.

Things otherwise sturdy and stable—such as, let's say, churches and houses—for reasons entirely incomprehensible to me show up first on the right, then on the left, without having budged an inch. I, a little girl, need only turn around, and the whole world—buildings and trees, dogs and people—change places: while my back is turned, they all run from one side of street to the other. Marina says that it is all very simple, that the right side is always where my right hand is. But which of my hands is right? The one I cross myself with. But I cross myself with both. When I cross myself with one hand, I get whacked, and with the other, I don't, but I can never remember which is which. Both of my hands are identical, both know how to hold a spoon and a pencil. Both of my feet are the same, too, but the shoes for them are different. When I put my shoes on myself, I am told, "They're on the wrong feet." I take them off and put them on again, and once again, "They're on the wrong feet." Which foot is the right one? Which hand is the right one? Which side is which?

Before I knew nothing of left and right, everything was fine and clear. Now everything is all confused and complicated, and in all the confusion there is nothing I can rely on so as not to make a mistake. Say a guest just arrived—more often than not, it's Volodya Alekseev, who always brings me presents. Greeting me, he extends his hand. Aha! That means his right hand is on that side! Which means my right hand is also on that side. I extend my hand, and, of course, it turns out to be my left hand. But why? Why? Marina, having lost all hope of being able to explain it to me, says to Papa, "You'll see, Seryozhenka, she'll be just like me, with *absolutely* no talent for the exact sciences!"

ALMS FOR THE POOR

When Marina and I go for walks, we always give alms to the poor.[28] There are lots of beggars: old, bent-over, poor, sick people. Some chant "Alms for the sake of Christ!" Others are silent. We give money to them all. Usually beggars sit on a bench or right on the ground and hold a cap out in front of them, where you put your kopecks. Some beggars have an awful lot of kopecks in their hats; these, apparently, are the rich beggars. But there are also those whose hats are entirely empty. Marina is very nearsighted, which means I am always pointing the beggars out to her: "Marinochka, there's a beggar sitting over there!" Marina gives me a coin, and I run to drop it into the beggar's hat. This time Marina still has yet to see anything, while I have spotted another beggar sitting on a bench, a visored hat in his hands. I run over to him with a kopeck clenched in my fist and drop it into his hat. This beggar is really poor: he hasn't a single coin on the bottom of his hat. He is, though, very handsomely dressed: his trousers have stripes down the side and his visored hat has a broad band around it. And his beard is beautiful, parted in two halves. But he is also most ungrateful and impolite: instead of saying "God bless you, my child," he jumps up and starts shouting at me and at the approaching Marina, so that we both take fright. Marina pulls out her lorgnette and looks at the beggar as he stamps his feet—shod in shining high-laced boots—and screams silly words at us: "This is an insult! An outrage!" Marina folds up her lorgnette, grabs me by the hand, and we run off around the corner.

"Is he crazy, Marinochka?" I ask in fright.

"You're the one who's crazy!" Marina answers, laughing and angry at the same time. "You gave a kopeck to a general! A general sitting on his own bench outside his own house! How could you have taken him for a beggar?"

"But he's an *old man,* Marinochka!" Old people are beggars. Doesn't that make sense?

NAPOLEON'S WIDOW

Marina gave me as a present a cup with Napoleon's picture on it as a way of making it more interesting for me to drink my milk, which goes down very poorly from an ordinary cup.[29] This cup is all gold inside, and the more milk you drink, the more gold shows. On the outside it is striking dark blue, with Napoleon painted in a white circle: he has a straight nose, black hair, and he looks out into the distance. He is a hero. He is a general. He is an emperor. And to play tricks when drinking from a cup like that is simply shameful.

Nanny would place Napoleon on the stove in order to warm up the milk a bit. She did that every day, and the milk and the cup were usually barely warm. But this time Napoleon got overheated, and I burned myself and dropped the cup, and it broke into tiny shards.

In horror and grief, bursting into tears, I ran to Marina: "Marina, Marinochka, I smashed Napoleon! Marinochka, I smashed Napoleon!"

Marina did not get angry, but picked me up, comforted me, and said that it was not my fault. "It was my fault!" I shouted, not letting up. "It was my fault. I smashed Napoleon!"

Then Marina took from the cupboard another striking cup dark blue on the outside, gold on the inside. Framed in a white circle was a portrait of a beautiful woman with curls of dark hair cascading onto her bare arms and shoulders. "You see, this is Empress Josephine, Napoleon's wife. He loved her very much. And when you grow up a bit I will give you this cup as a present to replace that one!" But I feel only more pity for the smashed Napoleon. It turns out that he had a wife! A wife who was an empress! Whose husband I smashed. . . ."[30]

IRINA

But here's what's important: my sister Irina was hardly hopelessly ill.[31] She simply was born and grew up in horrible, hungry times. She was a small, undernourished child who, because she was undernourished, was slightly underdeveloped, that is, when she was three she spoke like a two-year-old, not in phrases, but using single words. On the other hand, she knew some poems and little songs. Her legs were slightly rachitic, and Mama would always put her up on the windowsill in the sun, thinking that would help. Irina was a delightful, very pretty little girl with ash blond curls, a large forehead, a pug nose, and father's large eyes and a charming little mouth. Of all the people who came to our house she loved Sonechka Gollidei the most and called her "Galid" and "Galida." Sonechka loved her terribly, always hugged her and took care of her. I can see the two of them, both of them so tiny, so delightful, my God! (I have managed to preserve two photographs of Irina.)

And then practical people—good practical people—convinced Mother to place us temporarily in a model children's shelter in Kuntsevo: "If you keep the girls they'll perish, but there they'll be fed rations from the American Regional Association." Mama resisted for a long time and then gave in. Alas, the director of the model children's shelter was a scoundrel who speculated on the black market in American children's food. When Mama came to visit us a month later, she found me almost hopelessly ill (with typhus, and typhoid, and "influenza," and something else). She wrapped me in her coat and carried me out of there in her arms, all the way to the highway, and found someone to give us a ride home (there was no "public transportation" in those days). Irina was still "holding on." She was walking, not flat on her back, and she kept asking for "a little tea." While Mama was fighting for me, nursing me, trying to save me, Irina died in the shelter (she died of starvation) and was buried in a common pit. It later emerged that several children each day died [at that shelter—trans.].

They simply didn't feed us. As Mother wrote in her poem: "While extracting the older one from darkness, I didn't protect the other."

LEARNING TO WALK DOWN STAIRS

My walks with Marina to the Cathedral of Christ the Savior[32] are always spoiled by the staircase.[33] Going upstairs is easy and fun, but I already know that I am going to have to come down these same steps, and I don't know how to go down stairs the way everyone else does, the way all the other children do, and Marina once again will to try to teach me and once again will lose her temper with me. Which is exactly what happens. The enormous, resounding, solemn, gilded depths and heights of the cathedral—a cathedral so large that a chapel the size of a whole church stands inside it—are already behind us. The red-velvet-covered armchairs near the altar set off from the congregation by a golden cord—the czars' chairs; the czar himself sits on whichever one he pleases, during services—are already behind us.

Everything pleasant and beautiful is behind us. What lies ahead is an interminable gray descending staircase that I have to learn to walk down the way everyone else does.

ARRIVING IN BERLIN

... Suddenly cities began to appear again.[34] "Well, this is Berlin," says Mama, gathering our things. We ride through all three stations: Aleksanderburg [*sic*], Zoo, Friedricherburg [*sic*], finally getting off at Charlottenburg. We hire a green-colored porter, and he hauls our things down the stairs, and there we are in Berlin. The tile roofs, the light, the flowers, the squares. . . . There's our cab. We get in, put our things inside, and say farewell to our attendant. Mama says something to the driver, and he drives. I look about the city. The houses are tall and very wide. There are lots of tiny shops, newspaper stands, women in hats selling flowers, society women, cafés, and fashionable stores. There are not many people. Here is Pragerplatz. I search for Ehrenburg's pension. There it is. With a café next door. We take our things out of the cab, when suddenly out of the door walks Ehrenburg himself.

"Ah! Marina Ivanovna!"

"Hello, Ilya Grigorievich! Well, here we are!"

"How was your trip? No, questions later. Let's take your things!"

Ehrenburg took our things in both hands, the doors of the elevator opened before him, and we all rode up. A minute later we were upstairs. We went by way of innumerable corridors and finally found ourselves at a dead end. Ilya Grigorievich opened the door, let us into a large room, and added, "You can wash up." Mama immediately started washing her hair, after which Ehrenburg returned. I sensed a great happiness, and sitting down next to Ehrenburg, I start to snuggle up to him, and some pleasantries were conferred in my direction, among them the nickname "Hippopotamus." Later Liubov Mikhailovna came in. She resembled a tall young sapling. It was the first time I was able to study her features in detail. She had short black hair and dark brown eyes. She sat down next to Mama and started asking her how our trip had been, whether our things had been searched, if there had been a lot of people with us, how long we were in transit, and so on. Mama quickly made friends with her. Then Ilya Grigorievich came back and invited Mama to dinner. Mama declined because we had just had lunch in the dining car. Our hosts went out, and we were left on our own. Mama examined the books, while I stood at the window and admired the little garden below, silver poplars high as the rooftops, and the houses, and sky, and everything on earth. Then Ehrenburg came back with Liubov Mikhailovna, and all of us went downstairs together to the café Diele. Mama drank coffee with Ehrenburg, Liubov Mikhailovna had spiced rum, and I—hot cocoa. Finishing my drink, I went over to the café railing and started looking at the houses and the people. Horses drove by, farmers, women went in and came out of the stores and nail salons. There are dogs in muzzles pulling carts with milk. (It was the first time I had seen dogs used to haul cargo.) Suddenly Mama asks whether I need to go upstairs, and I answer in the affirmative. Liubov Mikhailovna graciously leads me upstairs, then goes back down to the café. Left alone, I read Ehrenburg's *Tarzan of the Apes* book. Soon Mama arrives. The joy of seeing the Ehrenburgs and the new city set me jumping, but Mama forbade me to be rowdy.

After a bit Ehrenburg summoned us to supper. I set off gladly, for I was very hungry because the portions served abroad are very tiny. At supper we were given two radishes with a piece of fish. For the main dish there were noodles (a very small quantity), and for dessert three whole tea-spoons of ice cream. I went to sleep.

OUR FIRST DAY IN BERLIN

. . . After breakfast I went to the Ehrenburgs to find out what time it is and to ask if I[lya] G[rigorievich] could lend Mama some tobacco and tell us where the post office is located.[35] They told me the time, gave me some tobacco, and promised to take us to the post office. I planted a kiss on Ehrenburg's face. He smelled of pipe smoke. Returning [to our room], I immediately wrote a letter to Papa. Liubov Mikhailovna came for us, and we set off together for the post office. My God, how much greenery there is! Every house has a long garden in front, and often the house is com-pletely covered with ivy, and the overpowering ivy makes the windows and balconies resemble powerless hollows. There are flowers on the bal-conies and flowers on the windowsills, and a large square on every street. There's the post office. Along the sides of the courtyard there are square hedges fenced in by gratings. We enter the murky, chilly sanctuary of let-ters. Ladies speak in soft voices on the telephone. Women, girls, fräuleins, and the like, stand in not very long lines. And what quiet! What must it be like in the churches? While I gave myself over to such reflections, Mama and Liubov Mikhailovna finished their business. We headed back home. Soon the dinner bell rang. I arrived before anyone else and was already drinking my bouillon from a teacup. The publishers Helicon—husband

[Abram Vishniak—trans.] and wife [Vera Arkina—trans.]—lunched with us. Ehrenburg said, *"Bitte, Bier,"* to the passing waitress. A minute later three bottles of beer stood on our table. I was not mistaken: they poured some for me as well. After lunch our baggage was delivered. We immediately started unloading our suitcases. From the depths we extracted an Easter cake [*kulich*] and Easter sweet cheese [*paskha*], along with a dancer and little boy on a sled for Ehrenburg. All made of wood. Mama gave him a gift of something else besides.

Ehrenburg resembles a hedgehog. His upper and lower pockets each hold one of his favorite smooth black pipes. Liubov Mikhailovna is just the opposite. Clean, slender, with skin completely white in color, in a white dress with a gauze scarf. Her whiteness makes her resemble the moon. Ilya Grigorievich, on the other hand, is like a gray, cloudy day. But with eyes like a dog's. Ehrenburg puffs like a czar from his two favorite pipes. Mama and Liubov Mikhailovna smoke cigarettes.

Liubov Mikhailovna wants to take Mama and me to KDW to buy clothes there. We take the U-Bahn. We enter an enormous building. There is an ashtray with cigars. Liubov Mikhailovna tells me that men going into the store leave their cigars here, then smoke them again on their way out. . . .

I really regretted that I went to the zoo not with Mama or with Ilya Grigorievich. That evening at our table we had a guest: Boris Nikolaevich Bely [Bugaev—trans.]. He was not very tall, with a bald spot, quick, with crazy eyes, like those of a cat. I liked him a lot, and I kissed him sweet dreams. . . .

LIFE IN FRANCE

What can I tell you about our day-to-day existence?[36] In Czechoslovakia you yourself probably remember the huts at the edge of the village and poverty made merry by our youth. We lived on Seryozha's stipend, on rare, irregular honoraria and relief aid. In France the first two years, while [Marina—trans.] was publishing widely and at the height of her ephemeral popularity, our lives were not that bad, but as time went on, everything got worse and worse (materially, that is).

Propping up the external chaos of our household was Mama's iron discipline and organization. Everyone was fed, dressed, and shod, which cost Mama great effort, given our almost total lack of funds. Rent was expensive, and the lion's share of our means (earned, "contributed," or borrowed) went toward rent. Of meat products we ate only horsemeat. We bought the smallest potatoes and the cheapest remnants of greens, etc. Eggs were for Easter; butter only for father (who had TB) and for Mur (who was little); sweets did not exist. Our clothes always had belonged to someone else first, the same for shoes. For all the time I lived in France, over all those years, I had only two new dresses. The first was sewn for me by Natasha and Olya Chernova the year we arrived (at the beginning we lived at their place at 8 rue Rouvet, XVIII), the second was sewn by my girlfriend in 1937, the year I returned to the USSR, when I was twenty-four. True, Mama had things altered or made for her, but she had to appear at readings and had to "look decent."

Mama would rise early, and in the morning hours—no matter what was going on, no matter what was happening in our lives—she would sit down at the table and work, sitting down to her table daily, every morning, as a worker goes to his machine. She ate nothing in the morning, drinking only a cup of black coffee. I would prepare a simple breakfast, and something was always cooking on the side for little Mur. Usually I would do the grocery shopping, and that would be part of Mur's stroll. Then Mur and I would "finish our stroll" while Mama put on soup (in which she boiled potatoes for the main dish), and there were usually horsemeat patties: a lot of bread, a little bit of meat, but everyone would be full.

And she would continue working. We would eat dinner together. Mama ate very little. She would try to prepare food for two or three days, sometimes in the evening. In the late afternoon Mama liked to stroll with us children. We would go to the woods in Meudon, to Bellevue, take long walks around the *banlieue* [suburb—trans.], going as far as Sèvres and the Seine. Sometimes we would take the electric train somewhere and wander around there. On rare occasions we would spend the whole day at Versailles. Walking and nature were essential to Mama. She always sought to overcome space, and she loved mountains, hills, and uneven landscapes most of all. Communion with nature never left her disappointed. Nature always renewed itself and had no "ceiling," unlike us people. She preferred the south to the north and land to the sea; she loved rocks, heather, pine,

and dry land. She loved to walk by herself and with others. Every summer we would try to get away out into the open. In the early years we
went to the sea (the ocean) with Papa, in the later years—without him,
since he was always deep in his work. When he was ill we made separate
arrangements so that he would be cared for. We lived "out in the wide
open spaces" in the most pathetic (living) conditions, and frequently our
basic diet consisted of mushrooms, berries, bread, and oatmeal for us children. That was because we paid for our tickets out of our food budget. We
lived in the middle of nowhere, but at least it was unbounded nature and
unbeaten paths. At the time, Favier was an uncivilized settlement, and we
would walk several miles to the closest town and return with backpacks of
bread, grain, sugar, and coffee for the week. In "the wide open spaces," too,
Mama worked in the mornings. In a small village three miles away from
the farm they made and sold bread once a week, and cheese, and nothing else. The nearest town was five or seven miles away and there was no
public transportation. The mushrooms and berries really helped us out.
But we also had all that beauty, wild animals, and freedom.

Mama did not like housework because it was greedy and ate up time,
leaving nothing in exchange, nothing essential or timeless. Food would get
eaten and more food had to be made; clean dishes once again demanded
washing, linen—laundering, hose—darning, and so on. But Mama knew
how to do everything that was essential, and the unessential she would
do always resisting this waste of time. She would stoke our *poêle Godin*
[iron stove—trans.], prepare our meals (the Primus stove was our eternal
companion on these trips), and do the laundry. I would help her with
everything, but as I realize now, I was no good at housework and took
no interest in it, which was entirely unjustified, for I was not the one
who was talented. But I was at that age: children and teenagers don't like
housework!

MARINA'S SILVER BRACELET

Last year, in 1956, in the winter, I believe, I dropped in at the Ehrenburgs'
for a minute on business and looked in on Liubov Mikhailovna, who had
called for me.[37] She said, "I don't believe in such premonitions and omens.

But such things do happen in life. Long, long ago, before she left Russia, Marina presented me with a bracelet, and I wore it all my life," immediately adding, ingenuously, "not because Marina gave it to me, but simply because it suited my wrist and I liked it. The bracelet was cast silver and heavy, the kind that is impossible to break. But one day, as I was walking into a store, something fell with a ringing sound to the floor. I looked, and there at my feet lay half of the bracelet, the other half still on my wrist. I picked it up, looked at it, and there was a crack running through the whole bracelet. It had cracked right on my wrist! I suddenly had this eerie feeling, and, nolens volens, the date stuck in my head: August 31, 1941. Then, a while later, Ehrenburg learned that on precisely that day, that very date, Marina had died. Now I want to give that bracelet to you (I never repaired it, left it the way it was). Leave it as it is, if you want, or, if you want, have it repaired and wear it yourself. . . ."

Liubov Mikhailovna handed me the heavy, cast-silver bracelet—familiar to me from my childhood—rather, not the bracelet, but its two broken pieces, with the fracture line angled across it, its edges jagged as lightning. . . .

ANNA AKHMATOVA

I met [Anna—trans.] Akhmatova for the first time at Pasternak's in Peredelkino in January 1957.[38] It was a clear, very sunny, very cold day, and with my habit (genetic trait!) inherited from my mother of losing my way and not remembering locations, I wound up wandering for a long time along the edge of the settlement.

Zinaida Nikolaevna [Eremeeva—trans.], as a rule indifferently rude and inattentive to me (Boris insists she is not really, and I am talking about my purely superficial impressions), greeted me with unusual affection. She was animated, which suits her well and rarely happens, and the atmosphere overall was festive: the bright blue sky outside, a giant Christmas tree in the dining room.

Zinaida Nikolaevna was talking about Boris and about *Doctor Zhivago*, about how she was worried about him and it and that this book was going to bring him a lot of grief and disappointment, and how he was bewildered by friends who flattered him to his face but would dump on the book behind his back.

Boris himself appeared after his stroll with certain friends, *en question* [in question—trans.], including Boris Nikolaevich Livanov. Livanov as usual was boisterous and drunk. His wife, Evgenia Kazimirovna, was more fashionably dressed than censorship and good taste allow: her hair dyed a pale pink; plastic earrings the size of good-sized saucers hung from her ears; narrow trousers on legs the girth of Don Quixote's horse, and oversize military boots. Her hair was so bizarrely cut it seemed moths had gotten into it. Well, who cares about her anyway! There was someone else with them, but I don't remember who. Boris looked wonderful: kind, with his dark complexion, gray hair, and golden eyes. He and I kissed each other on the cheek. (He loves to kiss and smooches friend and foe alike loudly on both cheeks with what the French call *des baisers de nourrice* [the kisses of a wet nurse—trans.].) His face was a delight. At one time he had been a young red-skinned islander; now he had become a real "last of the Mohicans," the bronze-faced chieftain of a vanishing tribe. (I'm not speaking figuratively. He really does resemble a Native American!) The combination of pride and shyness on his face when he speaks about something or someone particularly dear to him is charming.

We sat together for a bit, talking about nothing really, when we noticed a taxi drive into the yard, and a minute later into the room walked a very large—corpulent, tall—woman already well in her years with a calm—majestic? (wrong word)—benevolent demeanor that lacked the feverishness, the fire, we remember from Annenkov's portraits. Akhmatova. Boris introduced us, and we went into another room not as sunny or festive as the dining room and sat down somewhat formally and stiffly on chairs set at a small distance from the walls—exactly the thing that always creates a certain stiffness.

What was the conversation about? We tried to get Anna Andreevna to read selections of her prose work on Pushkin that was supposed to appear in *Literary Archive,* I think (I'm not sure it actually came out):[39] she declined, without coyness, rather, with a kind of habit-ingrained indifference. We spoke of poetry: Boris praised Anna Andreevna, Anna Andreevna praised Boris, and we in attendance praised them both. Akhmatova sat with her back to the door—stately and massive in her black dress—and played with the beads that hung on her breast. Livanov told a funny story about an evening of Georgian poetry that had taken place long ago: Boris laughed an awful lot and A.A. smiled with condescending detachment. A perfunctory child named Andriusha (I don't remember his last name)[40] hung on every word and smiled as if he had a hanger in his mouth. His poetry imitates Pasternak's, but Pasternak, who sees neither the borrowings nor the influences and senses only their congeniality, praises him.

Z.N. invited us to the table, which was huge, the length of the dining room. Who was at the table? Z.N., Boris, Genrikh Neygauz Sr., Stanislav Neygauz Jr. and his wife, A.A., Konstantin Fedin, the Livanovs, Andriusha, and someone else. We ate and drank, and everyone in attendance made endless toasts to the health of all in attendance that were so outrageously aggrandizing you wanted to crawl under the table from embarrassment. A.A. turned out to have a wonderful appetite, and she warmed up and, without abandoning her regal bearing, suddenly became quite down-to-earth. Overall, she turned out to be more down-to-earth, more elderly, moderately good-natured, and moderately plump than one might imagine from all the legends, but there was no fire, not even warmth, just her keen, cool gaze at those around her now a bit under the influence, their souls bared.

I remember how toward the end of dinner Boris read some of his latest (at the time) poems, and one could only gasp in amazement at his inexhaustible, unfading, broad, ranging talent. That's how people *begin* to write, when they still have everything, when nothing has been spent yet, and there is no reason to hold back; when you are not surrounded by dullards or enviers, and life is still "my sister" and hasn't yet taught you to be cautious or look over your shoulder. But to have all this breadth, this depth, this freedom, and even an unusual lightness when you're over sixty and life is one set of hurdles after another!

Pasternak is always unusual and full of a certain special warmth all his alone, but when he begins to read his poems, people are always taken by surprise, dropping their jaws and throwing up their hands: how could one person be given so much that he can give and give and give of what he has, and become even richer? . . . Livanov listened, wiping away his usual drunken tears of affection; Andriusha sat and watched with affection, but without any amazement, like a well-mannered Catholic schoolboy just visited by the Mother of God—the Virgin exists, he exists, he is good, and there is absolutely nothing amazing in the fact that she appeared to him. Neygauz listened so closely, so deeply, his gray head bent to one side: Pasternak, born of music must be especially close to him, while Anna Akhmatova listened, her keen gaze covered over by her heavy eyelids, and remained, on the surface, totally *impassive*. What must it be like for someone who has spent herself and now lives in her own reflection to listen to that?

When we all began to leave, A.A. took down my phone number and said that she would call and that she wanted to meet, but I somehow did not quite believe that; on the whole that evening I saw and sensed her only from the outside, whereas Pasternak I always felt from within. . . .

Oh, I forgot to mention that that evening I did not like Fedin: polite, affectionate, and cold; something was wrong, but what? He was there for just a short time, then they came for him, brought him proofs to read, and he never returned. Maybe it's the Polishness in his appearance, those bright eyes and narrow lips? He distantly sort of reminded me of the hero of *Poem of the End,* only he had lots of charm, subtlety, grace, while this one was made of ice.

But Akhmatova did call. It was winter or early, early spring 1957. More likely winter, but that's not important. She gave me the address of [Viktor Efimovich—trans.] Ardov's apartment, where she always stayed when she came in from Leningrad, and she invited me to visit her and promised to tell me about Mama.

I went to see her in the evening. It turned out she lived in Zamoskvorechie, not far from the "Writers' House" and the Tretyakov Gallery, near the round church.[41] Either the house was under renovation or it was just crumbling on its own, but in one place there was a gaping hole instead of a staircase, which immediately reminded me of my early childhood and the years of the civil war and of how Moscow had suddenly turned into one big gaping hole with ruts.

I rang. A maid opened the door and in response to my query said, "Madam is resting." I found myself in an apartment that when it was still new had been customized by the owners, who added all sorts of overhead storage, built-in cabinets, and other convenient household hideaways, and then at some point got accustomed to the place, grew tired of it, and let it fall into disrepair. I waited for a while, looked around at the knick-knacks that filled the dining room, and then knocked at A.A.'s door. After a while I heard a sleepy voice, then the door opened, and there stood A.A.

in a lilac nightgown down to her ankles and not yet quite awake. The little room she occupied at the Ardovs' was so small it reminded me of a cabin on a ship, but with high ceilings and a large window: a daybed, a small round table, two chairs, a shelf, and not more than two people could be in the room at the same time. A.A. turned on the light, which made the room cozier, and we sat down at the round table, she still in her nightshirt: calm, indifferent, and regal.

We began to talk. She asked me what I was doing, and I asked her about her son, who had recently returned [from exile—trans.]. She said that he was working in Leningrad and beginning to get accustomed to his new life but that the transition from his old situation to the new was very difficult for him and he was having a hard time adjusting. She said that she was finally happy and calm, now that he had returned.

"He was given papers announcing twenty-two years of repression for nothing, 'a lack of evidence of any crime. . . .'

"And Marina Ivanovna's book?"

I tell her about it.

"And how many pages?"

I answer.

"My book—the one they're supposed to print—is sixty pages, including the translations. . . .

". . . You know, Marina Ivanovna visited me right here in this same room and sat right there where you're sitting now. We had met for the first time before the war. She had told Boris Leonidovich that she wanted to meet with me when I came to Moscow, and when I arrived from Leningrad, I found out from B.L. that M.I. was here and gave him my telephone to give her and asked her to call whenever she was free. But she didn't call, and so I called her, because I had come to Moscow just for a short stay and had to leave soon. M.I. was at home. She was cold and seemed not to want to talk to me. (Later I learned that, for one thing, she did not like talking on telephones—'don't know how,' and that she was sure all phone calls were being listened to, for another.) She said that, unfortunately, she could not invite me to her place because it was very cramped or that there was something in general wrong with it, and asked to come to my place. I had to explain to her in considerable detail where I lived because M.I. was not very good at directions, and she warned me, moreover, that she couldn't ride taxis, buses, or trolleys, but could come only by foot, metro, or tram.

And she came. We had a good meeting. We did not size each other up, or look each other up and down, but just talked. M.I. told me a lot about her return to the USSR, about you and your father, and about everything that had happened. I know that one version of her suicide was that she was mentally ill and did it in a moment of depression. Don't believe it. She was murdered by the times; it killed us just as it murdered others, just as it tried to kill me. We were the healthy ones, the madness was all around us: arrests, executions, suspicion, distrust among one and all for everyone and everything. Our letters were opened and our telephone conversations listened to; any friend could turn out to be an enemy, and anyone you had a conversation with—a stool pigeon; constant surveillance, moreover, open and blatant; how well I knew the pair that used to follow me around, standing in separate doorways on the street, following me everywhere, and never attempting to conceal what they were doing!

"M.I. read me some of her poems that I didn't know. I had an appointment that evening and was supposed to go to the theater to see [Lope de Vega's—trans.] *El maestro de danzar*. The evening came too fast, and we didn't want to part. We went to the theater together, worked out the tickets, and sat next to each other. After the theater, we saw each other off. And agreed to meet the next day. Marina Ivanovna arrived in the morning and we spent the whole day together, sitting in this room, talking, reading and listening to poetry. Someone brought us food, someone brought us tea.[42]

"M.I. gave me this." (A.A. gets up and takes from the tiny shelf near the door a set of dark amber—I think—beads, each one of them different, with something spaced between them.) "These are prayer beads." And she told me their story.

I remember the story poorly now and I'm afraid I might have it mixed up, but the prayer beads, I believe, were Middle Eastern, special, the kind one gets only at the grave of the Prophet. Or, maybe we were talking about something else, because I remember that Mama gave A.A. antique prayer beads and something else, maybe a different set of beads? Or a ring? Or a brooch? In any case, the only thing I remember for sure was that A.A. told me how when she was evacuated to Tashkent she had shown these beads—or that other thing—to a local scholar who had confirmed—no, not confirmed, but replied in answer to her question what it was—that for a Muslim it was a sacred object because such (prayer beads?) could belong only to a person who had been to the grave of the Prophet.

(It was those beads I had noticed back then on January 1, when I had seen A.A. at Pasternak's.) A.A. wears them around her neck all the time and, according to her, never parts with them. On the shelf there lay another small piece of jewelry, also antique and very beautiful, and a ring with a semiprecious stone that had a crack in it. A.A. said that sometimes the things one loves warn you of oncoming sorrow: the stone had cracked on the day, or the eve, of her husband's [Nikolai Gumilyov's—trans.] death.

Then A.A. read me her poem dedicated to Mama in which she mentions Marina Mniszek and the tower, and said that the lines had been written long before Mama's death.[43] She gave me her most recent poem (in fact, it had been written a long time ago), the one with the orchid—or is it a chrysanthemum?—on the floor.[44]

She told me that when Mama was at her place, she had copied out for her several of the poems that A.A. had especially liked and had presented her with the typographer's proofs of her *Poem of the Mountain* and *Poem of the End*. All of it that had been copied or inscribed by her hand was confiscated during just one more search when they arrested A.A.'s husband or, for the umpteenth time, her son.

When I told A.A. about Mandelstam's posthumous rehabilitation, which I had heard about from Ehrenburg the night before, Akhmatova got excited, was transformed, and asked me at long length whether it was true and not just a rumor. Convinced of the authenticity of the news, she went straight to the telephone in the dining room and dialed Mandelstam's wife, who knew nothing about it. Judging by her choice of words, Akhmatova was trying to convince Mandelstam's wife that it was true, while she didn't want to believe her ears, and I had to give her Ehrenburg's telephone number so that he could confirm it firsthand.

We sat and talked, and Ardov's son [Aleksei Batalov—trans.] brought us tea. Then the phone rang: Mandelstam's wife had checked with Ehrenburg and now believed the news.

FROM A LETTER TO ANNA AKHMATOVA

Not too long ago I finally made the acquaintance of [Nadezhda Yakovlevna Mandelstam—trans.], Osip Emilevich's widow; it all came about quite unexpectedly.[45] We wound up in the same car for four hours, and we quietly, politely, and venomously argued the entire way. It was hate "at first sight," as they usually say about lovers. She sat, back arched and fur ruffled, in one corner with her Mandelstam, and I sat in the other, back also arched and fur also ruffled, in the other, with my Tsvetaeva, and the two of us hissed and spat at each other. I think you would have enjoyed it, but at the same time I fear that wouldn't have. . . .

ON LOVING POETRY AND POETS

Mama's poetry appeared in print for the first time in almost twenty years in the Moscow almanac *Poetry Day* September 30, 1956—eleven poems total.[46] Tarasenkov's foreword was banal to the point of awkwardness, but— rest his soul—he tried so hard to help with Mama's book at Goslitizdat, and he had prepared this selection of poems and foreword for publication at *October* with only minimal assistance from Stepan Shchipachov. The poems just lay around for several months at *October*'s editorial offices, and then they were rejected altogether, not so much by the editorial board as by the editor in chief [Fyodor Ivanovich Panfyorov—trans.], once he returned from vacation.

When the *Poetry Day* almanac was being compiled, Masha Tarasenkova [Maria Belkina—trans.] suggested the poems with Tarasenkov's foreword to Zinovy Paperny. Paperny declared the "*October* boys" idiots and included the poems in the almanac, together, unfortunately, with the foreword. But, as I said earlier, let him rest in peace!

After endless appointments, inquiries, and reminders, on October 3, 1956, I received certification from the Military Collegium of the Supreme Court of my father's posthumous rehabilitation. I had known long ago that he was no longer alive, but it was not until I saw the word "posthumous" in black and white that I believed it. If his "case" had been reviewed and his "sentence" delivered before the war began, he might have survived. But his sentence was delivered in July 1941,[47] and that says it all. Apparently, Mama, who perished in August 1941, outlived him by only a little, if you can imagine what kind of life that was.

A long, long time ago she wrote:

Thus we sink into the night,
Cradlemates together.[48]

Oh, how she always knew, how she always knew and sensed everything! Since their deaths I have stopped living and lost all sense of time.
My (internal) clock has stopped, and there is no repairing it. Such things
cannot be fixed. That I run about trying to get Mama's things published,
that I got Papa's case reviewed—all that comes not from the heart but
from common sense (or at least what is left of it). It has to be done, and if
I do not do it, it either will not get done at all or it will not get done soon
or will be done worse. Essentially it is all the same to me whether Mama's
poems come out a century earlier or a century later; it will still be after her
death. And hers was not just any death.

As I do all this, I think least of all about Mama's readers today or, in
Papa's case, of "the triumph of justice." It is just that this is all that I am
able to do in their honor, in their memory. As for those who "like" Mama's
poems I am subconsciously (consciously, rather, since I admit to it!) angry
at all of you: where were you and what did you do to help her when she
was alive, still alive in those horrible years, days, and hours?! . . .

Before you have the right to love poetry, you have to love the poet
herself. Alas, I know that this condition I set, this attitude toward contemporary readers and posthumous admirers is silliness, but *ça ne tient
pas debout* [here Efron uses the phrase in its broader sense, as an apol-
ogy—trans.], there is nothing I can do about it.

Translator's Notes

NOTE ON THE TEXT

1. As Irma Kudrova tells the story, it was her idea to write a letter from Ariadna Efron (without Efron's knowledge) to the editor in chief of *Zvezda*, G. K. Kholopov, proposing submission of her memoirs, on the basis of which Kholopov sent Efron a contract. Without responding or acknowledging receipt of the contract, Efron submitted her manuscript exactly within the deadline and page limitations set in the contract, and no editorial changes were made to the manuscripts Efron submitted. Irma Kudrova, "Put' k Tsvetaevoi," in *Put' komet: Zhizn' Mariny Tsvattaevoi* (Saint Petersburg: Vita Nova, 2002), 764–65.

INTRODUCTION

1. At the time that Efron was working with Anna Saakiants on Marina Tsvetaeva, *Izbrannoe,* intro. Vladimir Orlov (Moscow: Khudozhestvennaia literatura, 1961), she explained to Maria Belkina:

> . . . Don't think that when I speak of "Tsvetaeva control" I'm exaggerating my own importance. The fact is that I am the last living witness to the entirety of Mama's life and the entirety of her work (with the exception of the last three years). I know by heart her attitude toward each thing, and she called me her absolute reader. For that reason alone I insist on a careful selection of her works that considers all factors (including the political). The way Mama is being published abroad is horrid, sensationalistic; someone there is building a little career on it. And this kind of premature "discovery" is what I'd like to avoid, at least in this country.
>
> Keep in mind that I have in manuscript, in notebooks recopied in 1939, etc. all of the lyric verse (that is, everything that was written, whether or not it was published over the years). There are insignifi-

cant lacunae—ten or so poems, perhaps, that somehow disappeared. Therefore, any comparison, any verification, can be made with complete authority only against the materials in my possession, for they—the manuscripts, including those recopied and corrected by Mama in 1939—are free of the distortions of the "lists" and of the typographical errors, censored ellipses, etc. found in the published texts.

This letter, dated March 25, 1961, is housed in the archive of the Literary-Historical Society Vozvrashchenie in Moscow.

2. Details of Efron's agreement with TsGALI (now RGALI) can be found in an interview with Natalya Borisovna Volkova for an online journal (A. Man'kovskii, "'Ia schitaiu, chto vse eto dolzhno byt' v RGALI . . . ,'" *Nashe nasledie, Podshivka zhurnala,* http://www.nasledie-rus.ru/podshivka/6110.php, accessed July 7, 2008), and in N. B. Volkova, "Rol' A. S. Efron v sokhranenii tvorcheskogo naslediia Mariny Tsvetaevoi," *Marina Tsvetaeva: lichnye i tvorcheskie vstrechi, perevody ee sochinenii. Vos'maia tsvetaevskaia mezhdunarodnaia nauchno-tematicheskaia konferentsiia (9–13 October 2000). Sbornik dokladov* (Moscow: Dom-muzei Mariny Tsvetaevoi, 2001), 386–90.

3. As this volume was going to press, a French translation of Efron's "Pages" appeared: Ariadna Efron, *Ma mère,* trans. Simone Goblot (Paris: Editions des Syrtes, 2008).

4. I have documented reception of Efron's memoirs in the non-Russian scholarly community in D. Nemec Ignashev, "Of Politics and Poetry: Ariadna Efron, Redux," *Russian History/Histoire Russe* 36, no. 4 (2009). Among Russian biographers Efron's account was most seriously challenged by Irma Kudrova in her biography of Tsvetaeva, *Put' komet: Zhizn' Mariny Tsvetaevoi* (Saint Petersburg: Vita Nova, 2002), and in her investigation of events leading up to Tsvetaeva's suicide, *Gibel' Mariny Tsvetaevoi* (Moscow: Nezavisimaia gazeta, 1999), the latter available in English: Irma Kudrova, *The Death of a Poet: The Last Days of Marina Tsvetaeva,* trans. Mary Ann Szporluk (London: Duckworth Overlook, 2004). Galina Vanečková's *Letopis' bytija i byta: Marina Cvetajeva v Čechii 1922–1925* (Prague and Moscow: Slavjanskaja biblioteka; Dom-muzej Mariny Cvetajevoj, 2006) is also an invaluable companion to Efron.

5. This "decentering" approach to Russian women's autobiography was first proposed by Sarah Pratt, "Angels in the Stalinist House," in *Engendering Slavic Literatures,* ed. Pamela Chester and Sibelan Forrester, 158–73 (Bloomington: Indiana University Press, 1996).

6. Marina Tsvetaeva, "Ale" ["To Alya"], June 5, 1914, in *Sobranie sochinenii v semi tomakh,* comp. and ed. A. Saakiants and L. Mnukhin (Moscow: Terra, 1997–), vol. 1, bk. 2, 203.

7. Olga Ivinskaya, *A Captive of Time,* trans. Max Hayward (New York: Doubleday, 1978), 130–31.

8. Anna Saakiants, *Tol'ko li o Marine Tsvetaevoi? Vospominaniia* (Moscow: Agraf, 2002), 21.

9. Veronika Losskaia [Véronique Lossky], *Marina Tsvetaeva v zhizni: neizdannye vospominaniia* (Moscow: Kul'tura i traditsiia, 1992), 11.

10. According to Ada Federolf, Efron's partner of twenty-five years, by the early 1960s Efron was "well-known in literary circles, and by the mid-1960s her correspondence was huge. People wrote to her from Moscow, Leningrad, and from abroad. Letters addressed to her simply as 'A. Efron. Tarusa' found their way to our house." Ada Federolf, "Alongside Alya," in Ariadna Efron and Ada Federolf, *Unforced Labors,* comp., ed., and trans. Diane Nemec Ignashev (Moscow: Vozvrashchenie, 2006), 229.

11. M. I. Belkina, *Skreshchenie sudeb* (Moscow: Izografus, 2005), 724.

12. Ariadna Efron, "Moscow, 1955," in Efron and Federolf, *Unforced Labors,* 319. Efron draws the phrase "the ashes of Claes" from Charles De Coster's *Thyl Ulenspiegel:* Thyl takes ashes from the body of his adopted father, Claes, who was burned at the stake as a heretic. Thyl wears the ashes in a small sack around his neck.

13. The French periodicals in which Efron published were *Nash soiuz* (*Our Union*), edited by her father, *Illiustrirovannaia Rossiia* (*Illustrated Russia*), *Russie d'aujourd'hui* (*Russia Today*), and *France—URSS.* Efron refers to her work at *Pour vous* (*For You*) in her "Autobiography," written in 1961 in petition for admission to the Union of Soviet Writers (Ariadna Efron, "Avtobiografiia," in Ariadna Efron and Ada Federol'f, *Miroedikha: Riadom s Alei* [Moscow: Vozvrashchenie, 1996], 7). For additional information on Ariadna Efron's work as a journalist in the 1930s, see Kudrova, *Put' komet,* 524–26.

14. Kudrova, *Put' komet,* 525–26.

15. S[ofiia] N[ikolaevna] L'vova [Klepinina], "'. . . Togda zhili strashnoi zhizn'iu,'" *Bolshevo: Literaturnyi istoriko-kraevedcheskii al'manakh* 2 (1992): 258–59. Sophia Klepinina is the daughter of Nikolai and Nina Klepinin; Ariadna Efron's testimony supplied the evidence necessary for their executions.

16. Writer Boris Zaitsev's daughter Natalya was Alya's close friend; Zaitsev angered the adult Ariadna Efron with this picture of life in Tsvetaeva's apartment in 1919:

> There was no forgetting all this. I'm hauling [them] some firewood on a sled through the Moscow snow: it is only a couple degrees above freezing at Marina's place. The apartment is not small and is laid out so that the middle room—at one time the dining room—is illuminated only by a skylight, with no windows along the sides. Passing

through frozen rooms with freezing snow in the corners, I knock at the familiar door and dump the pile of firewood on the floor. The scene is as usual: in the middle of the room stands a table, the electric lamp above it turned on even during the day, Marina with her gray, nervously blinking eyes sits in her coat at the table, writing. Against the wall, in a bed that never gets made, under a pile of warm rags, is Alya. All that's visible is her head and those huge eyes—gray like her mother's, but slightly bulging, as if too large for their sockets. Her face is somewhat bloated: they eat only irregularly.

Marina thanks me, but she is distracted, absent. She is occupied with her own concerns. That is: in large, almost printed letters she is copying out an essay by Prince [Sergei Mikhailovich] Volkonsky (she was taken with his writing at that time). Nothing else mattered. Stove—stove, firewood—firewood.

"Alya, sit still, you're fidgeting again. . . ."

"Mama, I'm afraid of rats: they went running behind the cabinet again. When you leave, they're going to jump on me."

"Don't be silly, nothing's going to jump on you. . . ."

Alya knows better, but Marina cannot sit with her the whole day. She usually leaves, locking the door: sit and wait in the cold with the rats for your mama.

Sometimes Alya gets brought over to our place: she is friends with my daughter. We feed her and warm her up. Her huge, gray, bulging, water-colored eyes take on a happier look, and she plays and giggles with Natasha. [. . .]

The daughter of a poetess and a gifted little girl in general, Alya at first conducted herself like a little poetess: she had unusual dreams, composed verses ("By the gypsy starlight of love")—she was seven at the time, and she was terrific at imitating Marina.

Sitting in the dining room drinking coffee with my mother one morning, she described how that night in a dream she had seen three intersecting suns with angels above them sprinkling golden flower petals, Marina below in an emerald-studded crown.

"You know," my mother said, "children in our house don't have such poetic dreams. Either you ate too much kasha before going to bed or you're just making this up."

The next day, at coffee again, Alya described her dream from the last night [to my mother]. This time it was just Klim, our helper, hauling manure in a two-wheeled cart.

"That's more like it. . . ."

Translated from Boris Zaitsev, "Iz knigi *Dalekoe*," in *Marina Tsvetaeva v vospomina-niiakh sovremennikov. Rozhdenie poeta,* comp. and ed. L. Mnukhin and L. Turchinskii (Moscow: Agraf, 2002), 105–6.

PAGES OF MEMORIES

1. "Stal'naia vypravka khrebta": Ariadna Efron quotes this phrase from the first line of Tsvetaeva's 1921 untitled poem dedicated to Prince Sergei Mikhailovich Volkonsky, *Sobranie sochinenii,* vol. 2, 24.

2. The house—Tryokhprudny Lane, 8—was Varvara Ilovaiskaya's dowry; following Ivan Tsvetaev's death in 1913 the house went to his children Andrei and Valeria. Following the revolution of 1917 it was dismantled for firewood.

3. Sergei Efron was born one year and three days after Marina, on October 11 [September 29 OS], 1893.

4. Efron's original text stated 1855 as Elizaveta Petrovna Durnovo's birth year; I have corrected it to 1853.

5. Founded by Catherine II as a trade school, the Imperial Technical Higher School evolved into Moscow's present-day Nikolai Bauman Technical University.

6. Formed in 1879, the short-lived "Black Repartition" (*Chorny peredel*), which took its name from the notion of a (rumored) reallotment of Russia's "black" (fertile) lands, emerged from the "Land and Liberty" (*Zemlya i volya*) faction of the "People's Will" (*Narodnaia volya*) movement.

7. The original Russian phrase *vlastvovat' soboi* (rendered here as "to keep a grip on oneself") alludes to Onegin's lessons on self-restraint to the infatuated Tatiana Larina in Aleksandr Pushkin's *Evgeny Onegin,* canto 3:26.

8. Perhaps to place her father's family among Russian nobility credited by Soviet historians with their liberal and later radical politics, Ariadna Efron may here be alluding to the title of Ivan Turgenev's 1859 novel *A Nest of Gentlefolk* (*Dvorianskoe gnezdo*).

9. Ariadna Efron either was not aware or chose not to reveal that in 1905, with funds inherited from her parents, Elizaveta Durnovo and her husband built a three-story brick house at 29 Gagarinsky Lane in Moscow's historically elite area along the Prechistenka, just south of the Kremlin. The house has survived to this day. See Lidiia Aniskovich, *Krylatyi lev, ili . . . Sudite sami* (Moscow: Moskovskii Parnas, 2005), 54–56.

10. In July 1906 Elizaveta Durnovo was arrested for her participation in a "peasant revolutionary" organization aimed at the overthrow of the czar's government. She was held in Moscow's Butyrki Prison until released on bail in March 1907. Soon after, she emigrated to Switzerland and in 1908 to Paris with her youngest son, Konstantin.

11. Yakov Efron died of cancer in June 1909 in Paris. Fourteen-year-old Konstantin committed suicide by hanging himself in the family's Paris apartment in

February 1910; his mother took her own life the same evening. Aniskovich, *Krylatyi lev*, 72–75.

12. According to Tsvetaeva biographer Irma Kudrova, Sergei Efron joined the volunteer White Army in December 1917 and fought with General Lavr Kornilov at Ekaterinodar (Krasnodar) in 1918. Kudrova, *Put' komet*, 172–75.

13. In fact, Ehrenburg found Efron in Istanbul. Kudrova, *Put' komet*, 248.

14. *The Demesne of the Swans* (*Lebedinyi stan*), Tsvetaeva's cycle to honor the anti-Bolshevist resistance, begins on the day of Nicholas II's abdication in March 1917 and concludes in 1921 with the defeat of the White Army. It first appeared in print in 1957 in Munich, in an edition prepared by Gleb Struve and with an introduction by Yuri Ivask. For Ariadna Efron, recently returned from exile in Turukhansk, this publication must have been a serious blow to her own efforts to restore her parents' reputations as Soviet patriots. *The Demesne of the Swans* is available in English translation; see Marina Tsvetaeva, *The Demense of the Swans*, trans. Robin Kemball (Ann Arbor, Mich.: Ardis, 1980); in Russian see Marina Tsvetaeva, *Sobranie sochinenii*, where the poems from this cycle are dispersed chronologically over the first two volumes.

15. Tsvetaeva, "Rassvet na rel'sakh," October 12, 1922, *Sobranie sochinenii*, vol. 2, 159–60.

16. Sobachya (Dog) Square was a small triangular city park at the northern end of Nikolopeskovskaya (Nicholas-of-the-Sands) Street in the Arbat district of downtown Moscow. In 1962 it was razed, together with the houses surrounding it, to make way for the skyscrapers on Novaya Arbatskaya Street.

17. These verses are from Mikhail Lermontov's *Vozdushnyi korabl'* (*The Flying Ship*), an approximate translation (influenced by an earlier rendering by Vasily Zhukovsky) of Joseph Christian von Zedlitz's ballad *Das Geisterschiff.* The poem appealed to Lermontov (and Tsvetaeva, no doubt) for its portrait of Napoleon.

18. The iron maiden of Nuremberg was a torture device built in the eighteenth century in the shape of and bearing the likeness of the Virgin Mary. Large enough to accommodate an adult male, it was studded on the inside with sharp spikes. The concept of the iron maiden is said to have originated during the Inquisition.

19. Aleksei Mikhailovich (1629–76)—second czar of the Romanov dynasty and father of Peter the Great.

20. "General Tuchkov"—Major General Aleksandr Alekseevich Tuchkov (1778–1812), who perished at the Battle of Borodino.

21. The last of Nikolai Gogol's "ghost stories," *Vii* is a staple of the Russian middle-school canon, but it would have been far beyond toddler Alya's comprehension.

22. Ariadna Efron likely refers here to the music from act 1, scene 6 of Pyotr Tchaikovsky's ballet, *The Nutcracker.*

23. Aleksandr Pushkin wrote *The Gypsies* in 1823–24 while exiled in the Crimea and Caucasus Mountain regions. The poem, written under the influence of European romanticism and "Orientalism," later inspired Sergei Rachmaninov's one-act opera *Aleko*.

24. Tsvetaeva, "Kamennoi glyboi seroi" *Sivilla 2* [*Sybil 2*], August 6, 1922, *Sobranie sochinenii*, vol. 2, 137.

25. In 1918 the Soviet government reformed the Cyrillic writing system, simplifying spelling to remove redundancies and better approximate pronunciation. For a seven-year-old to master complex Russian spelling rules before these reforms was, indeed, a feat worth noting.

26. Tsvetaeva, "Stikhi rastut, kak zvezdy i kak rozy . . . ," August 14, 1918, *Sobranie sochinenii*, vol. 1, bk. 2, 104.

27. The Church of the Intercession of the Virgin at Fili (1690–96) was commissioned by Prince Lev Naryshkin in the area west of Moscow's central city. Comparatively small, the church is shaped like a Greek cross, with short round annexes and tiers that resemble layers of an elaborate wedding cake.

28. The Naryshkin (Moscow) baroque of the late seventeenth and early eighteenth centuries is a highly ornamented architectural style that combines Byzantine and European baroque elements; its characteristic red stone with white trim makes it easy to recognize. The style takes its name from the boyar family that funded a number of structures built in this manner; Peter the Great's mother, the second wife of Czar Aleksei Mikhailovich, was descended from this family. In addition to the church at Fili, the Naryshkin baroque style can be seen at Moscow's Novodevichy Convent.

29. "Je désire, que mes cendres reposent sur les bords de la Seine, au milieu de ce peuple français, que j'ai tant aimé."

30. Rostand, Edmond Eugène Alexis (1868–1918), French neoromantic poet and dramatist, best remembered for his play *Cyrano de Bergerac*. Rostand's *L'Aiglon*, a tragedy based on the life of Napoleon Bonaparte's son, the Duke of Reichstadt, whose nickname inspired the title, opened in 1900 with Sarah Bernhardt in the title role.

31. The cycle "Lanes and Alleys" ("Pereulochki") was composed by Tsvetaeva in April 1922 and published for the first time in the collection *Remeslo* [*Craft*] (Berlin: Gelikon, 1922). See Tsvetaeva, *Sobranie sochinenii*, vol. 3, bk. 1, 270–79.

32. With this line Efron paraphrases an event from chapter 12 ("The Prodigal Son Returns Home") of Ilf and Petrov's 1930 comic novel *The Golden Calf* (*Zolotoi telënok*) to layer a rather nasty dig at Chabrov (translated from http://www.klassika .ru/read.html?proza/ilf-petrov/telenok.txt&page=32, accessed July 7, 2008):

> The Catholic priests took possession of Adam Kozlevich's soul at
> the changing station where the "Antelope" stood in fertilizer mush

among two-horsed German freight vans and Moldavian fruit stalls. Father Kushakovsky would drop by the changing station to discuss morality with the Catholic colonists. Noticing the "Antelope," this minister of cult religious practice walked around it and stroked one of the tires. On speaking with Kozlevich, he learned that Adam Kazimirovich belonged to the Roman Catholic Church but had not practiced for nearly twenty years. Uttering, "That's not good, that's not good, Pan Kozlevich," Father Kushakovsky set off on his way, raising the hem of his black cassock with both hands and hopping over frothy puddles of beer. The great con man [Ostap Bender] did not like priests. He had equally low regard for rabbis, Dalai Lamas, Orthodox priests, muezzins, shamans, and other ministers of cult religious practices.

33. James 1:6 (AV): "But let him ask in faith, nothing wavering. For he that wavereth is like a wave of the sea driven with the wind and tossed."

34. Tsvetaeva, *Komed'iant*, 1919, in *Sobranie sochinenii*, vol. 1, bk. 2, 136–48.

35. Tsvetaeva, *Stikhi k Sonechke*, 1919, in *Sobranie sochinenii*, vol. 1, bk. 2, 154–61. "Cruel romance" (*zhestokii romans*) refers to the genre of urban ballads of unhappy, passionate love (and death) that became popular in the last third of the nineteenth century and the early twentieth century.

36. Tsvetaeva, "Cherdachnyi dvorets moi, dvortsovyi cherdak!" October 1919, in *Sobranie sochinenii*, vol. 1, bk. 2, 174–75.

37. Ariadna Efron here quotes the last stanza of Tsvetaeva's nineteenth poem in the *Komed'iant* series, "Druz'ia moi! Rodnoe troedinstvo!" January 13, 1919, in *Sobranie sochinenii*, vol. 1, bk. 2, 145–46.

38. The magical names here are, of course, titles of plays: E. T. A. Hoffmann's *Princess Brambilla* (1821), Eugène Scribe and Ernest Legouvé's *Adrienne Lecouvreur* (1849), Innokenty Annensky's *Thanyras Cytharoede* (1906), Sir William Jones's English-language rendering of the ancient Indian writer Kālidāsa's Sanskrit play *Sacontala*, Maurice Maeterlinck's *La miracle de Saint-Antoine* (1919), Carlo Gozzi's *Turandot* (1762), and Henning Berger's *Syndafloden* (1907).

39. An early anonymous French farce (ca. 1470) about a crafty, ne'er-do-well lawyer who contrives elaborate strings of deals and deceptions. Loaded with social criticism, *Maître Pathelin* was a popular stage piece in revolutionary Russia.

40. The characters described here appear in Maeterlinck's *L'oiseau bleu* (*The Bluebird*), which premiered at Stanislavsky's Moscow Art Theater in 1908. By the time Ariadna Efron saw it, *L'oiseau bleu* had become a staple of the theater's repertoire.

41. Efron here recalls Vakhtangov Third Studio's 1921 staging of Maeterlinck's *La miracle de Saint-Antoine,* with Yuri Zavadsky in the lead role.

42. In order of provenance, Tsvetaeva's writing for theater from this period included: *Jack of Hearts* (*Chervonnyi valet*), *The Snowstorm* (*Metel'*), *Fortune* (*Fortuna*), *The Adventure* (*Prikliuchenie*), *The Stone Angel* (*Kamennyi angel*), and *The Phoenix* (*Feniks*), all of them written in 1918–19. *The Adventure* and *The Phoenix* (originally titled *The End of Casanova* [*Konets Kazanovy*]) were both drawn from the life of Giacomo Casanova (1725–98). Tsvetaeva's dramas are available in Tsvetaeva, *Sobranie sochinenii*, vol. 3, bk. 2, 6–237.

43. In 1922 Tsvetaeva revised *The Phoenix* and retitled it *The End of Casanova* (*Konets Kazanovy*). The same words of Heine (I have so far been unable to identify the original source) occur in Tsvetaeva's *The Story of Sonechka* (*Povest' o Sonechke*), when the narrator compares herself to the more lively Sonechka, the type for whom she wrote roles like "Rosanetta in *Fortuna,* the little girl in *Adventure,* and Francesca in *The End of Casanova.*" In addition to the epigraph from Heine, *The End of Casanova* bears a dedication to Ariadna Efron: "Docheri moei Ariadne—Venetsianskim ee glazam" ("To my daughter Ariadna, to her Venetian eyes").

44. The phrase "companions in that youthful time" ("sputniki iunoi pory") is a paraphrase of Tsvetaeva's 1917 poem "Dear companions, who shared a night's lodgings" ("Milye sputniki, delivshie s nami nochleg"), the first line of the fifth stanza of which reads, "You weren't detained, companions in that wondrous time . . ." ("Ne uderzhali vas, sputniki chudnoi pory . . ."). See Tsvetaeva, *Sobranie sochinenii,* vol. 1, bk. 2, 18–19.

45. The original Russian *vstrechnaia pamiat'* (reciprocal memory) is a pun on the cliché *vechnaia pamiat'* (eternal memory).

46. Ariadna Efron here quotes the second and third stanzas of Tsvetaeva's nineteenth poem in the *Komed'iant* series: "Druz'ia moi! Rodnoe troedinstvo!" ("My dearest friends! A kindred triple union!"). See Tsvetaeva, *Sobranie sochinenii,* vol. 1, bk. 2, 145–46.

47. Efron's fascination with this house merits a bit more detail than usual. Built in the Moscow classical style at the end of the eighteenth century, 52 Povarskaya Street originally belonged to the Dolgorukov family. In the mid-nineteenth century, Count Vladimir Sollogub took possession of the house, and in 1859 ownership transferred to Baron Mikhail Bode-Kolyshev. In the early 1920s the structure was designated Palace of the Arts, center for the Commissariat of Enlightenment headed by Anatoly Lunacharsky (who resided in the house along with his second wife and family) and was the venue for literary soirees attended by Soviet Russia's major writers at the time, including Aleksandr Blok, Sergei Esenin, Vladimir Mayakovsky, and Boris Pasternak. In 1932 stewardship of the house passed to the newly formed Union of Soviet Writers (in its current reincarnation, the Union of Writers of the Russian Federation), which continues to occupy the structure. According to legend, Lev Tolstoy modeled the Rostov family house in *War and Peace* on the building, which to this day is known as the Natasha Rostova House.

48. "Roza" was Natalya Aleksandrovna Rozenel, Lunacharsky's second wife. The thin man resembling Don Quixote was in all likelihood Lunacharsky himself.

49. The "poetess" was Nadezhda Aleksandrovna Pavlóvich (1895–1979). In addition to her memoirs of Aleksandr Blok, Pavlóvich supplied Maria Belkina with details about the fate of Tsvetaeva's archive after her suicide. See Belkina, *Skreshchenie sudeb,* 717–21.

50. Tsvetaeva, "Ale" ["To Alya"], August 24, 1918, *Sobranie sochinenii,* vol. 1, bk. 2, 107–8. On the theme of the icon *Saint George and the Dragon,* see Tsvetaeva, "Moskovskii gerb: geroi pronzaet gada" ["Moscow's emblem: the hero stabs the serpent"], May 9, 1918, *Sobranie sochinenii,* vol. 1, bk. 2, 85. Regarding the name George, see also "Pages from the Past," note 69.

51. Ariadna Efron refers here to the vernacular style of narrative technique (*skaz*) known to Russian readers from Nikolai Leskov's novels and short stories, for example.

52. The Russian text of this feuilleton is "*Chudo s loshad'mi (Dostovernyi sluchai),*" *Sobranie sochinenii,* vol. 5, bk. 1, 220–24.

53. Vasily Zhukovsky's 1825–31 variation on a medieval German legend about a young soldier who braved monsters and other perils of the sea for his majesty's "loving cup" and then perished rather than accept the reward is based on Friedrich Schiller's poem *Der Taucher* (*The Diver;* 1797).

54. Aleksandr Blok's reading at the Palace of Arts took place on May 14, 1920. It was at this reading that Ariadna Efron delivered her mother's poem to Blok.

55. Efron's description of the building on Povarskaya Street that housed the Palace of the Arts echoes in many of its details Tsvetaeva's description in her 1918–19 essay "My Employments" ("Moi sluzhby"). See Tsvetaeva, *Sobranie sochinenii,* vol. 4, bk. 2, 39–63. The "silver idol with lance in hand" refers to a suit of armor, of which several were left in the palace by its former owners and described by Tsvetaeva as "idols" in her essay.

56. Aleksandr Blok, *Vozmezdie* (1910–21). The poem was inspired by Blok's own trip to Warsaw upon the death of his father, a prominent jurist whom the poet barely knew. Aleksandr Blok, *Sobranie sochinenii v vos'mi tomakh,* 8 vols., ed. V. Orlov, A. Surkov, and K. Chukovskii (Moscow: Gosudarstvennoe izdatel'stvo khudozhestvennoi literatury, 1960), vol. 3, 295–344. Many would agree with Efron that this poem is among Blok's "fundamental of fundamentals."

57. The lines Efron paraphrases are from one of Blok's best-known poems, "Sedoe utro" ("A Gray Morning"), in Aleksandr Blok, *Sobranie sochinenii,* vol. 3, 297. The image of the young singer who looks like a young boy echoes Efron's description of her young mother.

58. Trediakovsky, Vasily Kirillovich (1703–60), one of Russia's first major poets and theoretician of Russian language and versification.

59. Ariadna Efron here quotes "The Work Bench" ("Stanok"), July 9, 1933, the third poem in Tsvetaeva's cycle *Stikhi k Pushkinu, Sobranie sochinenii,* vol. 2, 286–87.

60. As indicated by Maria Belkina in her notes to Ariadna Efron (*Marina Tsvetaeva: Vospominaniia docheri. Pis'ma* [Kaliningrad: OGUP Kaliningradskoe knizhnoe izdatel'stvo and GIPP Iantarnyi skaz, 2000], 631 n. 12), the volume referred to here is the 1918 Alkonost (Saint Petersburg) edition of Blok's poem *Dvenadtsat'* (*The Twelve*).

61. Tsvetaeva, *Na krasnom kone,* 1921, *Sobranie sochinenii,* vol. 3, bk. 1, 16–23. The poem first appeared in print in the collection *Psikheia: Romantika* [*Psyche: Romantics*] (Berlin: Grzhebin, 1923).

62. The Balmont celebration at the Palace of Arts occurred on May 27, 1920, to mark the thirtieth anniversary of Balmont's career as a writer. Balmont emigrated from Russia the next month.

63. Liudmila Danilova identifies Iname as Iname Yamagata, one of Nikolai Vysheslavtsev's portrait subjects, a "Japanese poetess who enjoyed popularity among [Russian] Silver Age poets," including Balmont. Liudmila Danilova, "Bol'shaia, tikhaia doroga Nikolaia Vysheslavtseva," *Russkoe iskusstvo* [*Russian Art*], http://www.rusiskusstvo.ru/journal/1-2006/a1097/ (accessed July 7, 2008).

64. Ariadna Efron extracted this detail—along with the inspiration for this section of her memoir—from Tsvetaeva's 1936 essay "Slovo o Bal'monte" ("A Discourse on Balmont"). See Tsvetaeva, *Sobranie sochinenii,* vol. 4, bk. 1, 271–80.

65. The segment "The Writers' Shop" was added by editor Maria Belkina to posthumous book editions of Efron's memoirs and did not appear in the 1973 *Zvezda* publication. The Writers' Shop (*Lavka pisatelei*) came into being in the fall of 1918 and existed for four years, by which time most of its founding members would have left Russia. According to Mikhail Osorgin, the shop sold 250 original books created by twenty-three writers, including five by Tsvetaeva. Marina Tsvetaeva, *Neizdannoe: Svodnye tetradi,* comp. and ed. E. B. Korkina and I. D. Shevelenko (Moscow: Ellis Lak, 1997), 567 n. 63.

66. *Lubok*—popular woodcut folk prints; this genre emerged in mid-seventeenth-century Russia.

67. Physical inactivity and corpulence are characteristic features of Ilya Oblomov, the protagonist of Ivan Goncharov's eponymous 1858 novel.

PAGES FROM THE PAST

1. Tsvetaeva and Ariadna Efron departed Moscow for Berlin on Thursday, May 11, 1922.

2. "Verweile doch, du bist so schön . . ." Goethe, *Faust,* v. 1700.

3. Tsvetaeva inserted this juvenile variation on a stanza from Aleksandr Push-kin's *Songs of the Eastern Slavs* (*Pesni o vostochnykh slavianakh*), Song 16: "The Steed" ("Kon'"), in her essay "The Story of One Dedication" ("Istoriia odnogo pos-viashcheniia"), written in 1931, in Tsvetaeva, *Sobranie sochinenii,* vol. 4, bk. 1, 130–58. Part of the essay is available in English translation in Angela Livingstone, ed., *Art in the Light of Conscience: Eight Essays on Poetry by Marina Tsvetaeva* (Cambridge, Mass.: Harvard University Press, 1992), 64–85.

4. This list indeed survived in Tsvetaeva's notebook: Tsvetaeva, *Neizdannoe: Svodnye tetradi,* 76.

5. Tsvetaeva to Ilya Grigorievich Ehrenburg, March 7, 1922, in Tsvetaeva, *Neiz-dannoe: Svodnye tetradi,* 81–82.

6. Cheka—An acronym (ChK) for the Extraordinary Commission for Com-bating Counterrevolution, Profiteering, and Corruption, established in December 1917 as the principal security force of postrevolutionary Russia and, later, the USSR; the antecedent of the NKVD, KGB, and FSB.

7. Alexanderplatz, Zoo, Friedrichstrasse.

8. Prager Pension, Pragerplatz 4a.

9. Ariadna Efron cites the last line of Tsvetaeva's "Chto zhe mne delat', sleptsu i pasynku . . . ," ("What am I—blind and orphaned—to do"), April 22, 1923, the third poem in her cycle *Poets* (*Poety*). See Tsvetaeva, *Sobranie sochinenii,* vol. 2, 185–86.

10. According to Catherine Ciepiela, those "circumstances in general" included "a complicated set of love affairs involving both [Tsvetaeva and Ehrenburg]. While in Berlin, Tsvetaeva had a short-lived affair with Abram Vishniak, the addressee of her poems about the Eternal Masculine. At the same time, Ehrenburg was involved with Vishniak's wife, Vera." As Ciepiela tells it, "Ehrenburg did not appreciate Tsve-taeva's indignation when she discovered he was trying to get Vishniak to publish a book of Ehrenburg's erotic poems to Vera Vishniak." Catherine Ciepiela, *The Same Solitude: Boris Pasternak and Marina Tsvetaeva* (Ithaca, N.Y.: Cornell University Press, 2006), 85.

11. Ilya Grigorievich Ehrenburg, *Liudi, gody, zhizn'* (1960–65, 1990). Ehrenburg devoted an entire chapter (book 2, chapter 3) of his memoirs to Tsvetaeva. For an English translation of the relevant pages, see Ilya Ehrenburg, *People and Life, 1981–1921,* trans. Anna Bostock and Yvonne Kapp (New York: Knopf, 1962), 252–59. Ehren-burg's claim in those pages that Tsvetaeva had declined offers to publish her *Swans' Encampment* abroad is untrue: in a letter dated December 4, 1924, she offered the collection to Pyotr Bernardovich Struve. Tsvetaeva, *Sobranie sochinenii,* vol. 6, 312.

12. Valery Briusov lived at 30 Pervaya Meshchanskaya Street (today Prospekt Mira), not far from Sukharevskaya Square on Moscow's Sadovoe (Garden) Ring.

13. The hotel Knyazhy dvor (Prince's Court) was located at 14 Volkhonka Street, the present-day site of Moscow's Museum of Private Collections. The Pasternaks lived in the same building.

14. The Madonna described here suggests a variation on the Immaculate Heart, and the "prayer" Ehrenburg writes on his *Madonna with the Golden Heart* paraphrases the Roman Catholic prayer Hail Mary.

15. Sergei Aksakov's 1858 autobiographical novel.

16. Apparently, it was Pasternak who delivered the letter, as he himself recollected in a letter to Tsvetaeva dated March 31, 1928. Comparison of all letters between Tsvetaeva and Pasternak cited by or alluded to by Ariadna Efron in her memoirs was made against those available in *Marina Tsvetaeva. Boris Pasternak. Dushi nachinaiut videt'. Pis'ma 1922–26 godov,* comp. E. B. Korkina and I. D. Shevelenko (Moscow: Vagrius, 2004), 481 (hereafter cited as *Tsvetaeva-Pasternak*).

17. In their correspondence (and, as recorded by Ariadna Efron, in conversation at home), Sergei Efron and Marina Tsvetaeva used the polite form of address (*Vy*) with each other, as did Ariadna with her mother. Also, when original documents Ariadna Efron cited were available, I compared them with the versions she incorporated into her own text. Changes she made to the originals are indicated throughout in square brackets.

18. Tsvetaeva, *Neizdannoe: Svodnye tetradi,* 41.

19. Ibid., 53–54.

20. Tsvetaeva, "Pereulochki," in *Sobranie sochinenii,* vol. 3, bk. 1, 270–79.

21. Tsvetaeva, *Mólodets* (Prague: Plamia, 1924 [1925]). See Tsvetaeva, *Sobranie sochinenii,* vol. 3, bk. 1, 280–340.

22. Tsvetaeva, *Egorushka.* Tsvetaeva abandoned work on this poem, begun in 1921, in 1928.

23. Ariadna Efron borrows the phrase *muzyka revoliutsii* from Aleksandr Blok's *Dvenadtsat'* (*The Twelve,* 1918).

24. Afanasiev, Aleksandr (1826–71)—Russian historian, literary critic, and folklorist whose *Russian Folk Tales* (1855–63) was the first systematic recording of this oral tradition.

25. The phrase *reshilis' sud'by mira* derives from the poem "Anthony" ("Antonii," 1905) by the Russian Symbolist poet Valery Briusov. In her 1925 memoir of Briusov, "Hero of Labor" ("Geroi truda"), Tsvetaeva cites "Anthony" among poems that distinguished Briusov in her youthful poetic imagination.

26. Il'ia Erenburg, *Trinadtsat' trubok* (Moscow: Gelicon, 1923).

27. Tsvetaeva, "Plennyi dukh" (1934), available in English translation in Marina Tsvetaeva, *A Captive Spirit: Selected Prose,* ed. and trans. J. Marin King (Ann Arbor,

Mich.: Ardis, 1980), 52–93; in Russian in Tsvetaeva, *Sobranie sochinenii*, vol. 4, bk. 1, 221–70.

28. Sergei Efron arrived in Berlin five weeks after Tsvetaeva and Ariadna Efron. Kudrova, *Put' komet*, 268.

29. Kudrova estimates Efron spent only a week or two in Berlin before returning to Prague alone. Ibid., 271.

30. The Russian imperial gold reserves are said to have been smuggled through Siberia by agents of the White admiral, Aleksandr Kolchak, and to have found their way from Harbin to the banks of Prague. The fate of the Russian imperial gold reserves remains a mystery to this day.

31. Tsvetaeva, *Neizdannoe: Svodnye tetradi*, 86.

32. Ibid., 90.

33. Tsvetaeva, *Psikheia*. This collection contains twenty childhood poems by Ariadna Efron.

34. Tsvetaeva, *Remeslo* (Berlin: Gelikon, 1923).

35. Tsvetaeva, *Tsar-Dévitsa*, illus. L. E. Chirikova-Shnitnikova (Moscow: Epokha, 1922).

36. Tsvetaeva, "Florentiiskie nochi" (completed 1932), in *Sobranie sochinenii*, vol. 5, bk. 2, 141–61.

37. Tsvetaeva, "Svetovoi liven'" (completed in 1922), in *Sobranie sochinenii*, vol. 5, bk. 2, 231–45. Available in English translation in Livingstone, *Art in the Light of Conscience*, 21–38.

38. Tsvetaeva, *Razluka* (Berlin: Gelikon, 1922).

39. Tsvetaeva, *Stikhi k Bloku* (Berlin: Ogon'ki, 1922).

40. As Belkina points out in her notes to the text, Tsvetaeva translated Mayakovsky's poem "Scum" ("Svolochi") into French, not German. The translation was published in Berlin in the journal *Vesch'* 3 (1922):5. See Belkina, *Marina Tsvetaeva*, 632 n. 5.

41. Tsvetaeva, "Luchina," June 1931, *Sobranie sochinenii*, vol. 2, 280.

42. According to Saakiants, Mayakovsky arrived in Paris on October 15, 1928. Sometime during this visit, Tsvetaeva presented him with an autographed copy of her book *After Russia* (*Posle Rossii*, Paris, 1928), which Mayakovsky did not take with him back to Russia. On November 7, he and Tsvetaeva met at the poetry reading at the Café Voltaire mentioned by Ariadna Efron, and on November 24, the first issue of *Eurasia* (*Evraziia*), edited by Sergei Efron, together with Dmitry Sviatopolk-Mirsky, Pyotr Suvchinsky, and others, came out, containing Tsvetaeva's address to Mayakovsky. In citing the address only in part, Ariadna Efron obliterates nuances not insignificant for our understanding of Tsvetaeva's relationship with Mayakovsky. For that reason I cite the address here in its entirety; the emphasis is mine:

To Mayakovsky

On 28 [*sic*] April 1922, on the eve of my departure from Russia, early in the morning, in absolutely deserted Kuznetsky Most street, I met Mayakovsky.

"So, Mayakovsky, what do you want me to pass on to Europe from you?"

"That the truth is here."

On November 7, late in the evening, on the way out of the Café Voltaire in answer to the question: "What do you have to say about Russia after Mayakovsky's reading?" I answered without hesitation, "That the *power* is there."

(Anna Saakiants, *Zhizn' Tsvetaevoi. Bessmertnaia ptitsa-feniks* [Moscow: Tsentropoligraf, 2000], 546–47.)

As for Tsvetaeva's "excommunication" from Miliukov's editorial board at *Poslednie novosti,* the situation was, of course, complicated by the fact that the newspaper in which her address to Mayakovsky appeared and the entire Eurasia movement then developing in leftist Russian émigré circles in Paris was hardly to the liking of émigré monarchists who regarded Mayakovsky as a Bolshevik thug and Eurasiaism as an attempt to justify the Soviet takeover.

43. No documentation of this meeting in April 1929 has been cited by any of Tsvetaeva's biographers, and Saakiants, for several reasons, doubts the meeting could have occurred. Saakiants, *Zhizn' Tsvetaevoi,* 551–52.

44. Tsvetaeva, "Beregis'" (1922). As Irma Kudrova points out, this poem of "cruel formulae for singular self-sufficiency" in matters of the heart bears no relevance to Tsvetaeva's relationship with Mayakovsky but speaks directly to Tsvetaeva's feelings of being cramped in her relationship with Sergei Efron within months after they had been reunited. Kudrova, *Put'komet,* 286.

45. *Maiakovskomu,* a cycle of seven poems, composed in August 1930, three months after Mayakovsky's suicide in April. See Tsvetaeva, *Sobranie sochinenii v semi tomakh,* vol. 2, 273–80.

46. Tsvetaeva, "Epos i lirika sovremennoi Rossii" (1932). Available in English translation in Livingstone, *Art in the Light of Conscience,* 104–29.

47. In her 1921 "Prevyshe krestov i trub," Tsvetaeva compares Mayakovsky to an "archangel" baptized by fire and smoke. See Tsvetaeva, *Sobranie sochinenii,* vol. 2, 54–55.

48. Influenced by the imagist movement in Anglo-American poetry, imagism (*imazhinism*) in Russia emerged (by manifesto) in 1919 and included among its ranks Vadim Shershenevich (1893–1942) and Sergei Esenin (1895–1925). At the time of Pasternak's first letter to Tsvetaeva, both poets were at the height of their popularity and inspired numerous imitators.

49. In the original letter the Russian phrase translated here from Efron's memoir (*podobnykh Maiakovskomu, Akmatovoi*) in fact reads "such as that name blessed by your dedication" (*podobnykh imeni, oschastlivlennomu Vashim posviashchen'em*), that is, Akhmatova alone, as the addressee of Tsvetaeva's dedication of her collection *Mileposts* (*Vyorsty*). *Tsvetaeva-Pasternak,* 11. The three poems referred to by Pasternak—"Znaiu, umru na zare," "I rasskazhu tebe pro velikii obman," and "Viorsty i viorsty i viorsty i chiorstvyi khleb"—all appeared in Tsvetaeva's 1921 collection of poems *Vyorsty* [*Mileposts*] (Moscow: Kostry, 1921; reprinted with corrections, 1922). They are available in Tsvetaeva, *Sobranie sochinenii*, vol. 1, bk. 2, 259, 91, 18–19, respectively.

50. Pasternak admired Algernon Charles Swinburne (1837–1909) and here alludes to motifs that echo the English poet's in Tsvetaeva's collection *Mileposts* (*Vyorsty*).

51. The original letter here reads "as Jakobsen and Russia move freely within Rilke" ("kak Jakobsen i Rossiia vol'no v Ril'ke"). *Tsvetaeva-Pasternak,* 11.

52. Tsvetaeva to Boris Leonidovich Pasternak, June 29, 1922. Ibid., 13–16.

53. From Aleksandr Pushkin's 1827 poem to Ekaterina Ushakova.

54. The fate of Tsvetaeva's and Pasternak's correspondence merits more detail than space allows here. The majority of Pasternak's letters are housed in the Tsvetaeva fund (1190, op. 3) at the Russian State Archive for Literature and Art (RGALI) in Moscow; twelve more letters from Pasternak to Tsvetaeva are in the possession of Pasternak's heirs. As for Tsvetaeva's letters to Pasternak, multiple drafts are to be found among Tsvetaeva's papers and notebooks, also housed at RGALI. Of actual letters received by Pasternak, only several have survived, the majority lost during the war when Pasternak's friend who worked at the Scriabin museum and carried Tsvetaeva's letters with her on her daily commutes to work forgot them in a commuter train. Archivists Korkina and Shevelenko offer a somewhat different take on Kruchonykh's copies than does Ariadna Efron. According to their version, the letters that happened to be in Kruchonykh's possession were the only ones to survive. Finally, of Tsvetaeva's thirty-nine letters to Pasternak between spring 1928 and spring 1931, only fragments have survived, housed at RGALI. See *Tsvetaeva-Pasternak,* 5–8.

55. The congress, convened in June 1935 under the presidency of André Gide, was attended by more than two hundred delegates from forty countries. The delegation from the USSR included (besides Pasternak) Anatoly Shcherbakov, Mikhail Koltsov (who later hired Ariadna Efron to work at Zhurgaz in 1937), Nikolai Tikhonov, Isaac Babel, and Ilya Ehrenburg.

56. In 1931 Pasternak began an affair with Zinaida Nikolaevna Eremeeva (Neygauz, 1897–1966), who at the time was married to the musician Genrikh Neygauz.

The breakup of both marriages was complicated, at one point driving Pasternak to a suicide attempt.

57. For additional information about Tsvetaeva's interaction with Pasternak following the close of their correspondence, particularly after her return to Russia, English-language readers are directed to Ciepiela, *Same Solitude,* esp. 236–46.

58. Ariadna Efron's unusual choice of words here is explained by Tsvetaeva's use of the Russian word *prorva* as a positive feature, a womblike space that accommodates her thought.

59. Pasternak to Tsvetaeva, November 15, 1922, *Tsvetaeva-Pasternak,* 17–18.

60. Ibid., 21–22.

61. Tsvetaeva to Pasternak, March 9, 1923, *Tsvetaeva-Pasternak,* 50–51.

62. *Beyond the Barriers* is Pasternak's second book of poetry. Boris Pasternak, *Poverkh bar'erov* (Moscow: Tsentrifuga, Gryzunova, 1917).

63. Pasternak to Tsvetaeva, June 14, 1924, *Tsvetaeva-Pasternak,* 93–96.

64. Ariadna Efron takes liberties with the record. The letter cited (with several ellipses and changes not indicated in Ariadna Efron's published memoirs but marked herein in square brackets) was written at the end of March 1923 (see *Tsvetaeva-Pasternak,* 64–65). The fragment from the poem "Terpelivo, kak shcheben' b'iut" was not part of this letter but is taken from the cycle *Conducti* (*Provoda*), written at approximately the same time: the poem is dated March 26, 1923. *Tsvetaeva-Pasternak,* 79. The poem, along with the rest of this cycle, is dedicated to Pasternak. It is available in Russian in Tsvetaeva, *Sobranie sochinenii,* vol. 2, 174–82.

65. Ariadna Efron drew these four fragments from Tsvetaeva's "consolidated" notebooks; Tsvetaeva, *Neizdannoe: Svodnye tetradi,* 130–31. Tsvetaeva incorporated only the first two of these fragments into her letter to Pasternak dated late March 1923. *Tsvetaeva-Pasternak,* 66–67.

66. Nowhere in available published documents have I been able to find evidence that Tsvetaeva commented in any way on the Pasternaks' choice of the name Evgeny. As for Tsvetaeva's choice of the name Georgy for her own son, see "Pages from the Past," note 69.

67. Tsvetaeva to Pasternak, autumn 1924, *Tsvetaeva-Pasternak,* 99–100.

68. Tsvetaeva, *Neizdannoe: Svodnye tetradi,* 338.

69. Judging by the persistence with which Tsvetaeva repeated the news of the birth of Georgy (Mur) in her subsequent letters, she was clearly anxious that Pasternak learn the news from her and that she explain to him her reasons for not naming the child Boris, as she had originally planned. In her memoirs, Ariadna Efron cites the reasons why *not* Boris but hedges on the choice of Georgy, here as explained more fully by Tsvetaeva in passages not cited by Efron from this same February 14, 1925, letter to Pasternak:

... Render the panther [*bars*] harmless. (Barsik would have been—
would it have been—the diminutive form.) Clear and simple: if I were
to call him Boris, I would be saying good-bye forever to the Future:
to you, Boris, and to a son by you. Thus, naming him Georgy, I preserve my rights to Boris, to you, and little Boriushka. This is not madness. I am simply listening closely to myself, you, and the Future.

Georgy is my tribute to duty, allegiance, valor, and the Volunteer
[White Army—trans.] movement. This is also I. I don't deny it. But
not your I. Your I is in Boris. (*Tsvetaeva-Pasternak,* 101)

In a second draft of this letter Tsvetaeva added:

(Boris remains inside me.) After all, you could not name your daughter Marina, right? So that everyone called [her that] and knew? Make
her common property? Render harmless, legitimize?

Boris he was for as long as no one knew. Having said it, I came to
covet the sound. (Ibid., 104)

70. VKhuTEMAS—acronym for Higher Art and Technical Studios, the Moscow state art school of the USSR, as it was known briefly in 1920, again renamed
as an Institute (VKhuTEIN) in 1926, disbanded in 1930, and restored in 1945 as the
Moscow (formerly Stroganov) Higher Art and Technical Studios. Pasternak's first
wife, Evgenia Lurie, was a student at the school.

71. Pasternak to Tsvetaeva, April 12, 1926, *Tsvetaeva-Pasternak,* 179.

72. Ibid., 180.

73. Pasternak to Tsvetaeva, March 25, 1926, *Tsvetaeva-Pasternak,* 148–49.

74. Pasternak to Tsvetaeva, March 27, 1926, *Tsvetaeva-Pasternak,* 155.

75. Pasternak to Tsvetaeva, August 7, 1927, *Tsvetaeva-Pasternak,* 376.

76. The editors of *Svoimi putiami* published only prose by Boris Pasternak,
his "Aerial Ways," ("Vozdushnye puti") in *Svoimi putiami* 6–7 (1925): 11–17. I thank
Lukáš Babka, director of the Slavic Division (Slovanská knihovna) of the National
Library of the Czech Republic for his help with this research.

77. *Russkii sovremennik* 3 (1924).

78. *Moskovskie poety* (Velikii Ustiug: n.p., 1924).

79. I have been unable to locate the source of this fragment. In a letter to Tsvetaeva dated July 30, 1926, Pasternak mentions that "Aseev's student and favorite,
Kirsanov, stained the pores of his fingers with ink while copying [*Poem of the End*—
trans.]. I think he did it in one night. . . . They dream of publishing *Poem* in *LEF.*
I am not asking for your agreement, because I consider this dream unrealizable.
Glavlit will not approve your name, although before *glavlit,* it's true, there is Maya-
kovsky, who everyone is sure will be insanely delighted with the piece." *Tsvetaeva-
Pasternak,* 261.

80. Tsvetaeva to Pasternak, May 31, 1927, *Tsvetaeva-Pasternak,* 347.

81. Tsvetaeva to Pasternak, June 2, 1927, *Tsvetaeva-Pasternak,* 347.

82. I have been unable to locate the source of this excerpt.

83. Pasternak to Tsvetaeva, August 7–8, 1927, *Tsvetaeva-Pasternak,* 378.

84. Merzliakovsky Lane is located in central Moscow just north of the Novyi Arbat parallel to the Boulevard Ring; Volkhonka Street, where the Pushkin Museum of Fine Arts stands, crosses the Boulevard Ring at the next major intersection, about fifteen minutes by foot from the Arbat.

85. Tsvetaeva, *S moria,* May 1926, *Sobranie sochinenii,* vol. 3, bk. 1, 109–13.

86. Tsvetaeva, *Novogodnee,* February 7, 1927, *Sobranie sochinenii,* vol. 3, bk. 1, 132–36.

87. Ariadna Efron reordered these fragments from Pasternak's letter to Tsvetaeva dated October 15, 1927. *Tsvetaeva-Pasternak,* 404–7.

88. Apropos "tired" poems and poets, Tsvetaeva recorded the following conversation with Ariadna, preserved in a fragment excerpted from one of her lost notebooks:

> Today Alya said, looking at the fireplace where my entire correspondence for this summer was burning (you were not burning, Boris; you will burn with me—I won't let them bury me. Remember how Achilles was burned?) [said]:
>
> "It's been so long since you've had any letters from Pasternak . . . and the fellow with the woman's name. . . . Rilke. . . ."
>
> "They're tired, Alya." (*Tsvetaeva-Pasternak,* 624)

89. In fact, a draft of the letter, dated tentatively July 1935, did survive, and Ariadna Efron could not have *not* known of its existence. *Tsvetaeva-Pasternak,* 554–55. Catherine Ciepiela has translated a large portion of Tsvetaeva's last letter to Pasternak in her final chapter on the last years of the poets' relationship; see Ciepiela, *Same Solitude,* 237–46.

90. "The House at Old Pimen" ("Dom u starogo Pimena," 1933), "A Living Word About a Living Man" ("Zhivoe o zhivom," 1933), and "Mother and Music" ("Mat' i muzyka," 1934) are available in English translation in Tsvetaeva, *Captive Spirit;* see *Art in the Light of Conscience* for the fourth essay.

91. Ariadna Efron appended a footnote: "Excerpts from it were published in a selection of Tsvetaeva's letters in the journal *Novyi mir* 4, 1969." Tsvetaeva's letter to Pasternak of July 1935 is available in full in *Tsvetaeva-Pasternak,* 554–56.

92. Only this fragment of the letter has survived. It was published recently in Boris Pasternak, "Novootkrytye pis'ma k Ariadne Efron. Publikatsiia M.A. Rashkovskoi. Soprovoditel'nyi tekst E.B. Pasternaka," *Znamia* 11 (2003), http://magazines .russ.ru/znamia/2003/11/paster.html (accessed December 8, 2008).

93. Tsvetaeva and Ariadna Efron arrived in Prague by train from Berlin August 1, 1922, at the Wilson Station (Wilsonovo nádraží) and stayed not at Svobodárna but at the Hudobinec.

94. Referring to "Mokropsy" as "canine," Ariadna Efron has in mind the similarity of sounds between the name of the Czech town and the Russian words for "dogs" (*psy*) combined with the attribute "damp" (*mokro*); to the Russian ear, "Mokropsy" sounds like "Dampdogs." "Dolní" ("valley" in Czech) to the Russian ear suggests as well an adjectival derivative of the word "fate" (*dolya*).

95. In the original Russian text, Ariadna Efron begins the list of towns where they lived with Horní Mokropsy. In fact, Tsvetaeva and Ariadna moved to Horní Mokropsy at the end of September. Before that they rented a room in Nový Dvůr. See Vanečková, *Letopis' bytija i byta,* 34–35, 40.

96. Another example of "false cognates" between Russian and Czech. The Czech word *rychlík* derives from the root *rychl*—"quick, fast." The Russian word *rykhlyi* means "crumbly, loose," an intriguing attribute for an express train.

97. Tsvetaeva, "Rassvet na rel'sakh," October 12, 1922, *Sobranie sochinenii,* vol. 2, 159–60.

98. Tsvetaeva, "V sirom vozdukhe zagrobnom," October 28, 1922, *Sobranie sochinenii,* vol. 2, 160–61.

99. Tsvetaeva, "Sivilla: vyzhzhena, sivilla: stvol," August 5, 1922, *Sobranie sochinenii,* vol. 2, 136.

100. Tsvetaeva, *Posle Rossii, 1922–25* (Paris: Union, 1928).

101. Tsvetaeva, *Mólodets,* completed December 24, 1922, *Sobranie sochinenii,* vol. 3, bk. 1, 280–340.

102. The cycle Trees (*Derev'ia*) includes nine poems written in 1923–24, *Sobranie sochinenii,* vol. 2, 141–49.

103. For a concise introduction to Tsvetaeva's treatment of the Sibyl theme, see Michael Makin, *Marina Tsvetaeva: Poetics of Appropriation* (Oxford: Clarendon Press, 1993), 218–25.

104. "Beregis'," August 8, 1922, *Sobranie sochinenii,* vol. 2, 139–40.

105. *The Cricket on the Hearth* was performed in Prague that season by the First Studio of the Moscow Art Theater. Konstantin Rodzevich joined Sergei Efron in meeting Tsvetaeva and Ariadna Efron at the train station and spent the day with them. Vanečková, *Letopis' bytija i byta,* 36.

106. Tsvetaeva, "Zavódskie-1," September 22, 1922, *Sobranie sochinenii,* vol. 2, 150–51.

107. Tsvetaeva, "Zavódskie-2," September 26, 1922, *Sobranie sochinenii,* vol. 2, 151–53.

108. Tsvetaeva, "Spasi, Gospodi, dym!" September 30, 1922, *Sobranie sochinenii,* vol. 2, 154–55.

109. The move described here is from Nový Dvůr to Horní Mokropsy (house number 19, now 66). Vanečková, *Letopis' bytija i byta,* 40.

110. In November the family moved within Horní Mokropsy to 3 Grubner Street, now part of Všenory. Ibid.

111. Among innumerable possibilities where the word *défroque* might appear in a story "about a young girl, a young boy, spring," Alfonse Daudet's *Sapho* (1884) seems not unlikely: the word appears in the text of Daudet's novel four times.

112. Here Ariadna Efron quotes Francesca da Rimini in Dante's *Inferno* (canto 5, lines 134–35), cited here from Dante Alighieri, *The Divine Comedy,* trans. H. F. Cary (New York: E.P. Dutton, 1908), The Electronic Literature Foundation (ELF), http://www.divinecomedy.org/divine_comedy.html (accessed December 8, 2008).

113. Nozdrev is a principal character in Nikolai Gogol's picaresque novel *Dead Souls* (1842).

114. François Bonivard (1493–1570)—Geneva patriot, hero of Byron's poem *The Prisoner of Chillon* and Tsvetaeva's childhood hero—is depicted with enormous chains in *La délivrance de Bonivard* (1898) by Franck-Edouard Lossier (1852–1925).

115. Efron and Tsvetaeva moved to Všenory on September 23, 1924. Saint Mikuláš (Nicholas) Day is celebrated December 5.

116. The traditional red-bloused jester of Russian puppet theater, similar to the English Punch.

117. In a notation in her "Biulleten' bolezni" addressed to Aleksandr Bakhrakh dated August 5, Tsvetaeva wrote: "I have no one to talk to about you. Alya, who from age two to nine was my 'echo in the mountains,' now plays with dolls and is profoundly indifferent to me" (Tsvetaeva, *Sobranie sochinenii,* vol. 6, 593). On September 9, after Alya had matriculated at the Bogengardt school, Tsvetaeva wrote to Bakhrakh: "And that's it: ten years of life removed as if by hand. It is almost a catastrophe. This parting is making me younger; ten years' experience has been lifted, and I am once again beginning *my own* life, without responsibility for someone else, and my sense of being unneeded makes me feel empty and light: I weigh even less; I am less." Tsvetaeva, *Sobranie sochinenii,* vol. 6, 605. After Alya had spent her first night in the dormitory, Tsvetaeva wrote to Konstantin Rodzevich: "indulged, loved, admired, and with her hair done up in a new style: she has turned away from me and is not mine." Tsvetaeva to Konstantin Rodzevich, September 8, 1923, translated from Marina Tsvetaeva, *Pis'ma k Konstantinu Rodzevichu,* comp. Elena Korkina (Ulianovo: Ul'ianovskii dom pechati, 2001), 15.

118. Efron and Tsvetaeva moved to Prague at the end of August 1923. On September 7, they traveled with Alya to Moravská Třebová, where they remained until September 17, returning then to Prague, where they settled at Praha-Smíchov, Švedská ul. č. 51/1373. Vanečková, *Letopis' bytija i byta,* 117–23.

119. Tsvetaeva herself described the children's situation after she once passed through a boys' dormitory at the Bogengardt school: "It was eleven P.M. They were already sleeping. There are so many of them in one barracks: about forty. Their ages: from seven to ten. Forty shaved heads: white, dark, dark blond, (there are red-heads too!), forty shaved sleeping heads—with dreams and without dreams—under identical gray blankets, on identical flat pillows. Russian boys without Russia and (what's more painful) little boys without mothers—rise and shine tomorrow, go to lessons, and grow, day after day, and then day-after-tomorrow they may have to go to war." Tsvetaeva to Rodzevich, September 12, 1923, *Pis'ma k Rodzevichu*, 35. Ariadna Efron will use the last phrase, repeated in Tsvetaeva's notebooks, to close her own memoirs, obviously with her own brother's death at the front in 1944 in mind.

120. Tsvetaeva and Efron arrived in Moravská Třebová December 24, 1923, and remained there until January 9, 1924. Vanečková, *Letopis' bytija i byta*, 146–60.

121. The prototype for the conversation (re)constructed here took place December 27–29, 1922. See Vanečková, *Letopis' bytija i byta*, 146–47.

122. Tsvetaeva wrote this stanza as an inscription to her daughter in a copy of her (Tsvetaeva's) second published volume of poetry, *Volshebnyi fonar'* (*The Magic Lantern*). A variation of the inscription also appears in her notebook dated "May 1, 1914." Marina Tsvetaeva, *Neizdannoe. Zapisnye knizhki 1:1913–19*, comp. E. B. Korkina and M. G. Krutikova (Moscow: Ellis Lak, 2000), 86, 480.

123. As Véronique Lossky, among others, has written, Tsvetaeva had a number of sources for her variation on the "Pied Piper," including the medieval legend as retold by the Brothers Grimm, Goethe's *Der Rattenfänger von Hammeln*, and a poem by Heine ("Tsvetaeva and Avant-garde," *Ars interpres* 6–7 [September 2006], http://www.arsint.com/2006/v_l_6.html, accessed July 7, 2008). Tsvetaeva's poem is available in English in Marina Tsvetaeva, *The Ratcatcher: A Lyrical Satire*, trans. Angela Livingstone (Evanston, Ill.: Northwestern University Press, 2000); in Russian, see *Krysolov*, in Tsvetaeva, *Sobranie sochinenii*, vol. 3, bk. 1, 51–108.

124. Tsvetaeva, "Khvala vremeni" ("In Praise of Time"), May 10, 1923; only the poem's title appears in the notebook. Tsvetaeva, *Neizdannoe: Svodnye tetradi*, 172.

125. Tsvetaeva, "Prokrast'sia," May 14, 1923. Ariadna Efron cites a variation of this poem, the origin of which I have been unable to determine.

126. Tsvetaeva, "Landshaft serdtsa" (fragment, May 1923), *Neizdannoe: Svodnye tetradi*, 174.

127. These lines are variations, again of unknown origin, of "Landshaft serdtsa." Ibid.

128. Tsvetaeva, "Zanaves," June 23, 1923, *Sobranie sochinenii*, vol. 2, 204–5.

129. Tsvetaeva, "Vsio tak zhe, tak zhe v morskuiu sin'," July 24, 1923, *Sobranie sochinenii*, vol. 2, 213.

130. Tsvetaeva, "Rel'sy," July 10, 1923, *Sobranie sochinenii,* vol. 2, 208–9.

131. Tsvetaeva, "Chas dushi–1," July 14, 1923, *Sobranie sochinenii,* vol. 2, 210.

132. Tsvetaeva, "Chas dushi–3," August 14, 1923, *Sobranie sochinenii,* vol. 2, 211–12.

133. Tsvetaeva, "Akhill na valu," September 13, 1923, *Sobranie sochinenii,* vol. 2, 225–26.

134. Tsvetaeva, "Minuta," August 12, 1923, *Sobranie sochinenii,* vol. 2, 217–18.

135. Tsvetaeva, "Kak by dym tvoikh ni gorek . . . ," August 30, 1923, *Sobranie sochinenii,* vol. 2, 223.

136. Tsvetaeva, fragment, in *Neizdannoe: Svodnye tetradi,* 216.

137. Tsvetaeva, "Po naberezhnym, gde sedye derev'ia," September 28, 1923, *Sobranie sochinenii,* vol. 2, 229.

138. Tsvetaeva, "Oko," October 23, 1923, *Sobranie sochinenii,* vol. 2, 234.

139. Tsvetaeva, fragment, in *Neizdannoe: Svodnye tetradi,* 269.

140. I have been unable to locate the source of this fragment.

141. Tsvetaeva, "Prazhskii rytsar'," September 27, 1923, *Sobranie sochinenii,* vol. 2, 228.

142. "Marina's notation" reads: "December 12, 1923 (Wednesday)—the end of my life. I want to die in Prague, to be burned alive" (Tsvetaeva, *Neizdannoe: Svodnye tetradi,* 272). Tsvetaeva scholars continue to debate what actually happened to elicit this note and whether the poem that she completed that same day—"You who loved me as a lie" ("[Ty, menia liubivshii fal'sh'iu]")—was addressed to her husband, Sergei Efron, or to her lover, Konstantin Rodzevich. See, for example, Kudrova, *Put' komet,* 323–26. The poem is available in Tsvetaeva, *Sobranie sochinenii,* vol. 2, 235.

143. The prototype for the male protagonist in *Poem of the End* and *Poem of the Mountain* was Konstantin Boleslavovich Rodzevich (see Bibliographic Glossary).

144. For more on Efron's running battle with Tsvetaeva scholars abroad, see Diane Nemec Ignashev, "Of Politics and Poetry: Ariadna Efron, Redux," *Russian History/Histoire Russe* 36, no. 4 (2009): forthcoming.

145. Ariadna Efron cites Bulgakov's memoirs, written in 1924 and recently published as Valentin Bulgakov, "Marina Ivanovna Tsvetaeva (Iz neopublikovannykh zapisok 'Kak prozhita zhizn''')," in *Marina Tsvetaeva v vospominaniiakh sovremennikov. Gody emigratsii,* comp. and ed. L. Mnukhin and L. Turchinsky (Moscow: Agraf, 2002), 148–50.

146. The person Rodzevich chose to deliver the letters was Vladimir Bronislavovich Sosinsky (1903–87), writer and diplomat and a member of the Soviet delegation to the United Nations. Asked by Rodzevich in 1960 to deliver Tsvetaeva's letters to Ariadna Efron, Sosinsky apparently made copies of two of the letters, which subsequently circulated in literary Moscow, much angering Efron. For additional

information about the history of Tsvetaeva's correspondence with Rodzevich, see Saakiants, *Zhizn' Tsvetaevoi*, 381–82. Tsvetaeva's letters to Rodzevich were published in their entirety by Elena Korkina in Tsvetaeva, *Pis'ma k Rodzevichu*.

147. Spoken by Henriette to Casanova in scene four of Tsvetaeva's play *The Adventure* (*Prikliuchenie*), 1918–23.

148. The literary journal *Kovcheg* (*The Ark*) published in 1926 by the Union of Russian Writers in Prague should not be confused with the almanac *Kovcheg* published in Feodosia (Ukraine) by Maksimilian Voloshin in 1920. Tsvetaeva was involved in the publication of both.

149. Genesis 7:2: "Of every pure animal take seven pairs, the male and his female, and a pair of the unpure animals, the male and his female."

150. Sergei Efron, *Detstvo* (Moscow: Ole-Lukoie, 1912).

151. Ephrem (Ephraem, Ephraim) Syrus (ca. 306–73) wrote a variety of hymns, prayers, poems, and homilies in verse, which remained popular long after his death. As a child raised in the Russian Orthodox tradition, Ariadna Efron would have memorized Ephrem's prayer of repentance, which includes the lines, in part quoted in the text: "O Lord and Master of my life, grant not unto me a spirit of idleness, of discouragement, of lust for power, and of vain speaking. But bestow upon me, Thy servant, the spirit of chastity, of meekness, of patience, and of love" (cited from Michael Vezie, The Orthodox Christian Page, http://www.ocf.org/OrthodoxPage/prayers/ephraim.html, accessed December 8, 2008).

152. This expression, said to have its origins in a tale told by Cervantes' Sancho Panza, derives from an anecdote about an artist commissioned to draw a lion for a religious scene. Questioning—perhaps not without foundation—the veracity of his depiction, he added the caption to clarify his intentions.

153. Bulgakov, "Marina Ivanovna Tsvetaeva," 150–51.

154. TsGALI—Central State Archives for Literature and Art, now known as RGALI (Russian State Archives for Art and Literature), in Moscow.

155. The Old Testament golem evolved as a metaphor for unthinking beings who serve as well as harm human beings. The Prague legend involves Rabbi Judah Loew the Maharal, a sixteenth-century rabbi who fashioned a golem out of clay from the Vltava to defend Prague's Josefov ghetto from attack. As the golem grew, it became more violent, killing people and spreading fear. Rabbi Loew was told that attacks on Jews would stop if he destroyed the golem. He put the golem into "hibernation" by erasing the first letter from the Hebrew word *emet* (truth) written on the golem's forehead to produce the Hebrew word *met* (death). According to the legend, the remains of the golem of Prague—stored in the attic of Prague's Altneuschul—can be revived, should the need arise.

156. On the Mala-Strana side of Prague's Karlov most [Charles Bridge], between the bridge's ninth and tenth statues, stands a monument to Bruncvik, whose magic sword is said to be buried under the Charles Bridge to protect it from evil. Anyone familiar with Tsvetaeva's photographs will immediately notice the resemblance between her and Bruncvik, in profile.

157. *Ustav* is a majuscule Cyrillic script developed in the ninth century and characterized by square proportions, strong contrast, vertical stems with small serifs, long ascenders and descenders, and no lowercase. *Half-ustav* script, a kind of shorthand of *ustav* developed in the fourteenth century, is smaller, with long letter extenders, many ligatures, and diacritics.

158. *Volia Rossii* began as a daily newspaper in Prague and evolved into a monthly journal published in Paris, its run lasting from 1922 to 1932. In addition to those named by Ariadna Efron, its editorial board included Vladimir Zenzinov, Aleksandr Kerensky, and Mark Slonim. Besides Tsvetaeva, at various times Balmont, Khodasevich, Remizov, and Zaitsev all worked in the journal's literary section.

159. Tsvetaeva, "Khvala bogatym," September 30, 1922, *Sobranie sochinenii*, vol. 2, 155–56.

160. Among fragments from Ariadna Efron's notes to emerge after publication of her memoirs is the following, which describes in further detail Tsvetaeva's isolation among Russian émigrés:

> Marina seemed to be the same as she was in Moscow: the same bangs, the same silver bracelets, the same eyes that looked past whoever she might be talking with into her own and their distances; the same unswerving habits of morning work, nighttime insomnia, long walks, black coffee; the same mutually exclusive traits—restraint and indomitableness, implacability and gentleness, irascibility and patience, gregariousness and thirst for solitude, fascination with (and fascination for) people coupled with an internal incapacity, inability, to prolong relationships with them.
>
> But within her as human being and within her as poet an irreversible change—still invisible to the untrained eye and inaudible to the inexperienced ear—had occurred: an excommunication from her environment, in which she no longer felt herself participant. Her ability to exist on life's surface—afloat in it, alongside it (even if in opposition)—had switched itself off. An imperviousness to life—a disjunction from it, from what was now alien, belonged to others, and existed only outwardly—had set in: a distrust of her surroundings, a sense of their inauthenticity, in spite of her "success."
>
> A child not of location but of birthplace, Marina—having departed from her country—did not seek and could not have sought any substitution for it in her "surroundings," no matter what they

might be. Émigré society turned immediately into a splintering environment disintegrated into unreliable microcosms of cliques, congregations, and chapters, which for Marina—had she attempted to live with them and within them—would have been suffocating, confining, and devoid of meaning. A deep, hard line of solitariness was making itself visible on the palm of her fate.
Translated from A. Efron, "Odinochestvo Mariny Tsvetaevoi [neopublikovannyi otryvok iz rukopisi 'Stranitsy bylogo']," *Marina Tsvetaeva v vospominaniiakh sovremennikov: Gody emigratsii,* comp. and ed. L. Mnukhin and L. Turchinskii [Moscow: Agraf, 2002], 5–6.

161. Tsvetaeva to V. F. Khodasevich, in Tsvetaeva, *Neizdannoe: Svodnye tetradi,* 267.

162. Tsvetaeva, "Gordost' i robost'," September 23, 1923, *Sobranie sochinenii,* vol. 2, 55.

163. The phrase "inscribed on the tablets" derives from Tsvetaeva's 1920 poem "I wrote on a slate tablet . . ." ("Pisala ia na aspidnoi doske," May 18, 1920). "Inscribed on the tablets" was the name of Marina's husband, Sergei, engraved on the inside of the ring. Ariadna Efron, "A dusha ne tonet . . ." *Pis'ma 1942–75. Vospominaniia,* comp. and annot. Ruf' Val'be (Moscow: Kul'tura, 1996), 395–97. The poem is available in Tsvetaeva, *Sobranie sochinenii,* vol. 1, bk. 2, 224.

164. Here Ariadna Efron puns with the meaning of Aleksei Peshkov's pseudonym, Maksim Gorky. The Russian word *gorky* translates as "bitter."

165. "Pis'ma Mariny Tsvetaevoi," Publikatsiia, podgotovka teksta i vstupitel'naia zametka A.S. Efron. Kommentarii A.A. Saakiants, *Novyi mir* 4 (1969): 200–201.

166. The 1908 novel by Gilbert Keith Chesterton.

167. Tsvetaeva to Pasternak, October 22, 1927, *Tsvetaeva-Pasternak,* 417.

168. Suvchinsky, who had visited Gorky in Sorrento in 1927, was himself in close contact with Gorky—who in turn corresponded on his behalf with Stalin—regarding the fate of the Eurasia movement, to which Sergei Efron belonged and in whose publications Marina Tsvetaeva had published. In 1930 Suvchinsky initiated negotiations with Stalin, by way of Gorky, on ways in which the ten members (including Efron) of the core Eurasia movement might make themselves useful to the cause of the USSR. The Eurasians were looking to Moscow for funding for their publications. (None materialized.) There were also suggestions of how the Eurasians could be helpful to Soviet information-gathering efforts. Suvchinsky's 1930 correspondence with Gorky is referenced online in M. Gor'kii to I. Stalin, February 17, 1930, note 1 in "Perepiska M. Gor'kogo s I. Stalinym," at Eksperimental'naia studiia "Ramina," Babroteka: Biblioteka babra, http://lib.babr.ru/index.php?book=2140 (accessed December 8, 2008).

169. The Efrons lived in Jíloviště (Průjezdní č. 8) from June 1 to July 20, 1924, in Dolní Mokropsy (Černošice, Sluneční č. 642) from July 20 until September 23, 1924, and in Všenory (Květoslava Mašity, č. 324) from September 23, 1924, until October 31, 1925, when Marina and the children left for Paris. Vanečková, *Letopis' bytija i byta,* 302–3.

170. Tsvetaeva by this time was pregnant with her son Georgy, born February 1, 1925.

171. Leonid Andreev, *Samson v okovakh* (1914).

172. In Russian one letter distinguishes "chains" (*okovy*) from "trenches" (*okopy*).

173. Here and throughout, underlined text indicates passages Ariadna Efron excised from the documents she cited. Interpolations Ariadna Efron inserted are indicated in square brackets and italics.

174. Sergei Efron to Elizaveta Efron, April 6, 1924, Mir Mariny Tsvetaevoi, http://www.ipmce.su/~tsvet/WIN/familySE.html (accessed July 7, 2008).

175. Sergei Efron to Elizaveta Efron, fall 1924, Mir Mariny Tsvetaevoi, http://www.ipmce.su/~tsvet/WIN/familySE.html (accessed July 7, 2008).

176. Tsvetaeva, June 9, 1924, *Neizdannoe: Svodnye tetradi,* 296.

177. Tsvetaeva, July 21, 1924, *Neizdannoe: Svodnye tetradi,* 296.

178. Tsvetaeva, *Neizdannoe: Svodnye tetradi,* 312.

179. Ibid., 302–3.

180. Ibid., 295.

181. Ibid., 298.

182. Ibid., 328.

183. Ibid., 302.

184. Ibid., 347.

185. Ibid., 361.

186. Ibid.

187. Ibid.

188. Ibid., 325.

189. In Russian the phrase "thought uttered" recalls Fyodor Tiutchev's poem "Silentium" (1836), a meditation on the impossibility of expressing thought in words: "A thought uttered is a lie" (*Mysl' izrechennaia est' lozh'*).

190. Tsvetaeva, "Pod shal'iu," August 5, 1924, *Sobranie sochinenii,* vol. 2, 239–41.

191. Ibid.

192. Tsvetaeva to Efron, February 27, 1921, in Marina Tsvetaeva, *Neizdannoe. Zapisnye knizhki* vol. 2, 1919–39, comp. E. B. Korkina and M. G. Krutikova (Moscow: Ellis Lak, 2000 [2001]), 259.

193. Tsvetaeva, *Neizdannoe: Svodnye tetradi,* 326.

194. Ibid.

195. As noted by the editors of *Svodnye tetradi,* this is an inaccurate quotation from Friedrich Nietzsche's "Ecce Homo," from the first—verse—section of his book *Die fröliche Wissenschaft.* Tsvetaeva quoted it in its entirety, again with inaccuracies, in her *The Story of Sonechka* (*Povest o Sonechke*), together with her own translation into Russian. Tsvetaeva, *Neizdannoe: Svodnye tetradi,* 590.

196. The seventh nanny, about whom Tsvetaeva wrote several pages later in her notebook, was Anna Mikhailovna Igumnova.

197. Tsvetaeva here refers to the legend of Stepan Razin, according to which the seventeenth-century peasant rebel captured a "Persian princess" and then—under pressure from his men, disgruntled by their leader's "unheroic" displays of emotion—threw her overboard.

198. Tsvetaeva here paraphrases Shakespeare's *Hamlet* (act 1, scene 5, lines 166–67): "There are more things in heaven and earth, Horatio, Than are dreamt of in your philosophy."

199. Flyonushka is a novice nun and the illegitimate daughter of Mother Superior Manefa in Pavel Melnikov-Pechersky's two-part novel of Russian Orthodox Old Believers *In the Forest* (*V lesu,* 1874) and *In the Hills* (*Na gorakh,* 1881). A typical ingénue, Flyonushka distinguishes herself with her exceptional energy as matchmaker and interloper.

200. *The Magic Lantern* (*Volshebnyi fonar'*), Tsvetaeva's second collection of verse, was published in Moscow in 1912.

201. Aleksandra Turzhanskaya and her son Oleg rented a room in the same house as the Efrons in Horní Mokropsy in the summer and fall of 1922.

202. Nikolai Gogol, "Strashnaia mest'" (1829–32).

203. Aleksandr Ostrovsky, *Groza* (1859).

204. Tsvetaeva nicknamed her son "Mur" after Tom-Cat Mur of *Lebens-Ansichten des Katers Murr nebst fragmentarischer Biographie des Kapellmeisters Johannes Kreisler in zufälligen Makulaturblättern herausgegeben von E. T. A. Hoffman* (1819–21).

205. This unlikely set of associations can be explained by way of George Sand's novel *Consuelo* (1843), in which the heroine travels to Bohemia, where at the Château of Rudolstadt she encounters the Comte, who believes that he was Jan Žižka and describes events that took place three hundred years earlier.

206. At this point in her notebook Tsvetaeva incorporates into her own record entries from Alya's notebook (titled "Mur") written in 1928. Ariadna Efron chose to exclude these from her memoirs. See Tsvetaeva, *Neizdannoe: Svodnye tetradi,* 336–45. Tsvetaeva's next note occurs March 10, 1925, more than a month after her son's birth.

207. Tsvetaeva, *Neizdannoe: Svodnye tetradi,* 326–53.

208. Ariadna Efron here skips ten pages of her mother's second consolidated notebook. See Tsvetaeva, *Neizdannoe: Svodnye tetradi,* 345–53.

209. Ibid., 353.

FROM *TALES TOLD IN TARUSA*

Tales Told in Tarusa is translated from Ariadna Efron and Ada Federol'f, *Miroedikha: Riadom s Alei* (Moscow: Vozvrashchenie, 1996), 95–106. These stories first appeared in Ariadna Efron, "Ustnye rasskazy," ed. E. B. Korkina, *Zvezda* 7 (1988): 41–55.

1. Stolitsa, Lyubov Nikitichna (née Ershova, 1884–1934)—Russian poet whose lyrics were set to music by composers such as Aleksandr Grechaninov and Reinholdt Glière. Her novel in verse, *Elena Deeva,* appeared in print in 1916. Stolitsa died in emigration in Bulgaria.

FRAGMENTS

1. Translated from Ariadna Efron, "Popytka zapisei o Mame," in *"A dusha ne tonet . . . ,"* 395–97 (hereafter cited as "Popytka").

2. Ibid., 397.

3. Ibid., 399.

4. Ibid., 399–400.

5. Ariadna Efron was, in fact, twenty-four years old when she returned to the USSR in March 1937.

6. In the 1930s Zhurgaz was, in today's terms, a mega media holding company. It was founded and overseen by Mikhail Koltsov until his arrest in 1940. In addition to the foreign-language organ that came to be known as *Moscow News*—at the French offices of which, *Revue de Moscou,* Ariadna Efron found employment between 1937 and 1939—Zhurgaz encompassed nearly forty periodicals, including *Literaturnaia gazeta, Sovetskoe kino,* and *Za rubezhom,* and its editors also oversaw publication of the *Zhizn' zamechatel'nikh liudei* series and *Literaturnoe nasledstvo.*

7. Ariadna Efron, "Popytka," 399–400.

8. Ibid., 400–405.

9. House 6 in Borisoglebsky Lane has survived and since 1990 has housed the Marina Tsvetaeva House-Museum and Cultural Center.

10. Tsvetaeva, "Dva dereva khotiat drug k drugu . . . ," 1919, *Sobranie sochinenii,* vol. 1, bk. 2, 169–70.

11. Greuze, Jean-Baptiste (1725–1805). Presumably, Ariadna Efron has in mind Greuze's well-known painting *Jeune fille pleurant son oiseau mort* (*Young Girl Crying over Her Dead Bird,* 1765).

12. See "Pages of Memories," note 20.

13. A miniature reproduction of the Iron Maiden of Nuremberg. See "Pages of Memories," note 18.

14. Of the two paintings cited by Ariadna Efron, *Pan* (1899) depicts an aged, weary satyr, while *The Swan Princess* presents the artist's wife, Nadezhda Zabela, costumed for her role as the heroine of Rimsky-Korsakov's 1899–1900 opera based Aleksandr Pushkin's *The Tale of Czar Saltan*.

15. See "Pages from the Past," page 87.

16. The center of the Russian Orthodox Church, the Trinity Lavra of Saint Sergius (Troitse-Sergieva Lavra), is located in the town of Sergiev Posad (literally "Sergii's settlement" after Saint Sergii Radonezhsky; in Soviet times known as "Zagorsk"), a small administrative center approximately fifty miles north of Moscow.

17. Ariadna Efron, "Popytka," 406–8.

18. The two books illustrated by Doré to which Ariadna Efron refers are *Volshebnyia skazki Perro,* trans. Ivan Sergeevich Turgenev and illustr. Gustave Doré (Saint Petersburg: M.O. Vol'fa, 1867), which is the Russian translation of Charles Perrault, *Les contes de Perrault* (Paris: J. Hetzel, 1864), and *Bibliia, ili, Sviashchennyia knigi vetkhago i novago zaveta: russkii perevod,* illustr. Gustave Doré (Saint Petersburg: Knigoprodavtsa-tipografa Mavrikiia Osipovicha Vol'fa, 1876–78), which is the Russian translation of *La Sainte Bible: Traduction nouvelle selon la Vulgate,* trans. M. M.-J. Bourasse and P. Janvier, illus. Gustave Doré (Tours: Alfred Mame et fils, 1866). Contradicting Ariadna Efron's memory, Doré's engraving of the Ogre's sleeping daughters depicts them already without their crowns. As for the edition of Gogol's works, Efron appears to be describing the three-volume 1901 edition by Nikolai Tikhonravov published by A. F. Marks.

19. Ariadna Efron, "Popytka," 410.

20. Ibid.

21. Ibid., 408–9.

22. Ibid., 409.

23. Ibid., 410–11.

24. Ibid., 411–12.

25. Ibid., 412–14.

26. *Russkie vedomosti*—a politically conservative prerevolutionary Moscow newspaper.

27. Ariadna Efron, "Popytka," 415–16.

28. Ibid., 415.

29. Ibid., 414.

30. In this draft version of events described in her published memoirs Efron confuses the two cups. Two coffee cups matching the descriptions in Efron's memoirs, said to have belonged to Marina Tsvetaeva, have survived and are housed in the collection of the Tsvetaeva Memorial Museum in Moscow. The cup bearing a woman's image, Josephine's, was obviously repaired, glued together from many broken pieces.

31. From a letter from Ariadna Sergeevna Efron to Pavel Antokolsky, June 21, 1966, "Sviatoe remeslo poeta. Pis'ma i vospominaniia A. Efron o materi—Marine Tsvetaevoi," comp. and comm. L. A. Mnukhin, *Literaturnoe obozrenie* 12 (1981): 93.

32. The Cathedral of Christ the Savior, constructed to commemorate Russia's victory over Napoleon in 1812, was consecrated in 1883 and dynamited by the Soviet government in 1931 to make room for a projected Palace of Soviets that never materialized. The cathedral was reconstructed in the 1990s and consecrated in August 2000.

33. Ariadna Efron, "Popytka," 416.

34. Ariadna Efron, "Iz zapisei i pisem," *Marina Tsvetaeva,* 331–33. According to compiler Maria Belkina, Ariadna Efron sent this and the next fragment to Ilya Ehrenburg in a letter dated October 1, 1966. Belkina, *Marina Tsvetaeva,* 638 n. 22.

35. Ariadna Efron, "Iz zapisei i pisem," *Marina Tsvetaeva,* 333–36.

36. Ariadna Efron to M[aria] S[ergeevna] Bulgakova, February 18, 1968, translated from "Sviatoe remeslo poeta," 89–103.

37. Ariadna Efron, "Iz zapisei i pisem," *Marina Tsvetaeva,* 342.

38. Ibid., 343–54.

39. Akhmatova's "Stories about Pushkin," on which she was working at the time, was published only after her death, in 1967. Efron probably had in mind the series *Literaturnoe nasledstvo* (*Literary Heritage*) when she wrote *Literary Archive* (*Literaturnyi arkhiv*).

40. Ariadna Efron is being coy here; she not only remembered "Andriusha" Voznesensky's surname, her unpublished notes contain a brilliant parody of one of his most famous poems, "I am Goya."

41. Viktor Efimovich Ardov (1900–1976) and his family resided at 17 Bolshaya Ordynka, opposite the Church of the Theotokos, Joy of All Who Sorrow, designed by architects O. Bove and V. Bazhenov in 1790.

42. The meeting between Tsvetaeva and Akhmatova as recounted by Akhmatova and reported by Ariadna Efron took place in June 1941 and has been described somewhat differently by others. According to Viktor Ardov, the owner of the apartment where they met, Tsvetaeva called Akhmatova after he had informed her that she might. He also reported that they met only once, not twice, and that Tsvetaeva left the apartment on her own. He makes no mention of the two having gone to the theater together that evening. (Viktor Ardov, "Vstrechi Anny Akhmatovoi s Marinoi Tsvetaevoi," in *Marina Tsvetaeva v vospominaniiakh sovremennikov: Vozvrashchenie na rodinu,* comp. and ed. L. Mnukhin and L. Turchinskii [Moscow: Agraf, 2002],

148–53.) Belkina corroborates Ardov's version that Akhmatova and Tsvetaeva did not attend the theater together, and she adds that they spent the next day at the home of art historian Nikolai Khardzhiev (1903–96) (Belkina, *Marina Tsvetaeva,* 638 n. 31). It also appears that Lope de Vega's *El maestro de danzar* (1594), translated by Tatiana Shchepkina-Kupernik, was first staged at the Theater of the Red Army only in 1946.

43. According to Mnukhin, this poem, "The Answer Came Too Late" ("Pozdnii otvet"), which begins with the line *"Nevidimka, dvoinik, peresmeshnik . . . ,"* was written March 16, 1940, and did not appear in print until after Akhmatova's death, in *Literaturnaia Gruziia* 7 (1979): 86. See "Sviatoe remeslo poeta," 103.

44. According to Mnukhin, Ariadna Efron cites lines from the second part of Akhmatova's *Poem without a Hero* (ibid.).

45. Ariadna Efron to Anna Akhmatova, May 29, 1959, *"A dusha ne tonet . . . ,"* 154.

46. "On Loving Poetry and Poets" is from Ariadna Efron, Ada Federol'f, *Miroedikha. Riadom s Alei* (Moscow: Vozvrashchenie, 1996), 162–64. Among the poems published in *Den' poezii* (Moscow: Moskovskii rabochii, 1956) were: "I wrote on a slate tablet" ("Pisala ia na aspidnoi doske"), May 18, 1920; "Yesterday you still looked into my eyes" ("Vchera eshche v glaza gliadel . . . "), June 14, 1920; "To Mayakovsky" ("Maiakovskomu"), September 18, 1921; "Poet and Czar" ("Poet i tsar' "), July 1931; "Newspaper Readers" ("Chitateli gazet"), November 1–15, 1935; and *Verses for Czechia* (*Stikhi k Chekhii*), 1939.

47. Sergei Efron was executed on October 16, 1941. Irma Kudrova, *Gibel' Mariny Tsvetaevoi* (Moscow: Nezavisimaia gazeta, 1999), 91.

48. Tsvetaeva, "Kak po tem donskim boiam . . . ," December 13, 1921, *Sobranie sochinenii,* vol. 2, 75–76.

Biographical Glossary

Abrikosov, Vladimir Vladimirovich (1880–1966). Oxford-trained Russian Byzantine Rite Catholic priest ordained to serve the Catholic community in Moscow, he was deported from the USSR in 1922. In emigration he participated in the Russian exarchy until its dissolution in 1926, after which he served as parish priest in Paris, maintaining ties with other exarchists (e.g., Pyotr Volkonsky and Sergei Obolensky).

Akhmatova, Anna Andreevna (née Gorenko, 1889–1966). Russian poet and translator with whom Tsvetaeva is often compared. Tsvetaeva once said that she was a poet and Akhmatova a poetess; Akhmatova is said to have called Tsvetaeva "a poet better than I." Akhmatova and Tsvetaeva met only once, in Moscow, in 1940. On return to Moscow from exile in Turukhansk in 1956, Ariadna Efron visited Akhmatova, whom she admired.

Alekseev, Vladimir Vasilievich ("Volodya," 1892–1920). An actor, Tsvetaeva met him through Vakhtangov's Third Studio, and he figures centrally in her *Story of Sonechka* (*Povest' o Sonechke*). Alekseev perished while on theatrical tour in the south of Russia.

Altschuler, Grigory Isaakovich (1895–1983). The son of Chekhov's and Tolstoy's physician, he was a medical student in Prague when summoned to assist the delivery of Tsvetaeva's son, Georgy, February 1, 1925. Altschuler was married to Vera Aleksandrovna Pelopidas (1895–1943), and the couple's daughter, Katya, was a childhood friend of Ariadna Efron.

Andreev, Leonid Nikolaevich (1871–1919). A prolific writer who was discovered by Maksim Gorky, his work spanned Russian symbolism and realism. Andreev did not accept the Bolshevik revolution and died in poverty in Finland. By his first marriage to Anna Wielhorska, Andreev had two sons, whom Efron knew as adults: Daniil, who remained in Russia and became a writer in his own right and served ten years in prison (1947–57), and Vadim, also a writer, who moved to France. His second wife was Anna Ilinichna Andreeva.

Andreev, Vadim Leonidovich (1902–76). The son of writer Leonid Nikolaevich Andreev by his first marriage to Anna Wielhorska, a veteran of the White Army and, later, of the French Resistance, and a writer, Andreev and his wife Ariadna Kolbasina-Andreeva (parents of Olga Andreeva-Carlisle) traveled to the USSR several times in the 1960s and 1970s and visited Ariadna Efron in Tarusa.

Andreeva, Anna Ilinichna (née Denisovich, 1883–1948, Karnitskaya in first marriage). The widow (second wife) of writer Leonid Nikolaevich Andreev, she was Tsvetaeva's close friend in Všenory and later in France. Her children by Andreev were Vera, Savva, and Valentin.

Annenkov, Yuri Pavlovich (1889–1974). Russian portraitist, set designer, and graphic artist (whose work bears obvious influences of futurism and cubism). Before emigrating to Paris in 1924, he established his reputation in Russia with a series of portraits of artists and intellectuals and with illustrations to the first edition of Blok's poem *The Twelve* (*Dvenadtsat'*, 1918). His memoirs were banned in the USSR, and he himself was persona non grata. Ariadna Efron admired his work.

Antokolsky, Pavel Grigorievich (1896–1978). Poet and actor in Evgeny Vakhtangov's theater, where Tsvetaeva made his acquaintance in 1917, he introduced her to fellow actor Yuri Zavadsky. Tsvetaeva and Antokolsky dedicated poems to each other, and he is included among the central characters in her *Story of Sonechka* (*Povest' o Sonechke*). On return from exile in Turukhansk Ariadna Efron corresponded with Antokolsky; she disagreed with his portrait of Tsvetaeva in his memoirs *Contemporaries* (*Sovremenniki*, 1971).

Ardov, Viktor Efimovich (1900–76). Satirical writer and playwright, who together with his wife, actress Nina Antonovna Olshevskaya (1907–91), and her son Aleksei Batalov (1928–), often hosted Anna Akhmatova at their Moscow apartment (17 Bolshaya Ordynka), the site of her meeting with Tsvetaeva in 1940 and with Ariadna Efron in winter or early spring 1956–57.

Aseev, Nikolai Nikolaevich (1889–1963). Soviet poet and critic, close associate of Vladimir Mayakovsky and member of the Left Front of Arts (LEF) movement. At the time of Tsvetaeva's suicide Aseev was in Chistopol, and in one of her two suicide notes she entrusts sixteen-year-old Georgy Efron to his care. On release from forced labor in 1947, Ariadna Efron wrote several letters to Aseev requesting details about her mother's life after her evacuation from Moscow, her brother's fate after their mother's death, the suicide itself, and the state of her mother's archive. The extent of Aseev's culpability in Tsvetaeva's demise (of which Ariadna Efron was convinced) and his negligence (and/or inability to care for Georgy) require further investigation.

Bakhrakh (Bacherac), Aleksandr Vasilievich (1902–85). Literary critic with whom Tsvetaeva was briefly infatuated and corresponded frequently in 1923–24, following his positive review of her collection *Craft (Remeslo)*. After moving to Paris, Bakhrakh served several decades as Ivan Bunin's literary secretary, then headed the literary section at Radio Liberty (Svoboda).

Balmont, Konstantin Dmitrievich (1867–1942). Prolific Russian symbolist poet and translator, part dandy and part showman, whose political views forced him into self-imposed exile twice before the revolution (1900–3, 1905–15). Categorically rejecting Bolshevik power, Balmont emigrated permanently to Paris by way of Germany in 1920 together with his third wife, Elena Konstantinovna Tsvetkovskaya (1880–1944), and their daughter, Mirra (1907–70). Tsvetaeva met Balmont in 1918, and, as Ariadna Efron describes in her memoirs, the families remained close.

Bashkirtseva, Maria Konstantinovna (1860–84). Artist and memoirist whose notebooks, written in French and published in Russian and English translation shortly after her death, were read by the young Tsvetaeva, who later claimed that they influenced her own passion for journal-writing.

Bauman, Nikolai Ernestovich (1873–1905). A Bolshevik revolutionary, he was beaten to death by a Black Hundreds mob that attacked a Russian Social-Democratic Workers Party demonstration near the Moscow Imperial Technological Institute, which now bears his name. He is said to have married his wife, Kapitolina Medvedeva (no dates available), at Lenin's behest to acquire her family's money for Bolshevik Party purposes.

Belkina, Maria Iosifovna (d. 2008). Essayist, memoirist, wife of Anatoly Tarasenkov, she met Tsvetaeva shortly after the latter returned from France, and Ariadna Efron—in 1955–56 when Efron approached Tarasenkov for help restoring her mother's archive. Belkina compiled a largely anecdotal but useful biography of Tsvetaeva and her children, *A Juncture of Fates (Skreshchenie sudeb,* first published in 1988).

Bely, Andrei (Bugaev, Boris Nikolaevich; 1880–1934). Son of a Moscow University mathematician, he preferred poetry and philosophy to mathematics. Bely's writing was profoundly influenced by Vladimir Soloviev and later the theosophist Rudolf Steiner. Among the most distinguished of Russian symbolists (both early and late periods), a prolific writer of prose and poetry, and a significant contributor to Russian verse theory, Bely was closely associated with Aleksandr Blok, whose wife—Liubov Mendeleeva—he regarded as the earthly incarnation of the divine feminine. As Ariadna Efron records, Tsvetaeva admired Bely and his work, and the friendship the two poets developed in Berlin in 1922 would continue after Bely returned to Moscow and Tsvetaeva moved to Paris. Bely's estranged wife at the time he met Tsvetaeva in Berlin was Anna Alekseevna

("Asya") Turgeneva (1890–1966). Tsvetaeva dedicated to Bely a number of poems and her 1934 essay "A Captive Spirit" ("Plennyi dukh").

Berdiaev, Nikolai Aleksandrovich (1874–1948). Among Russia's most influential twentieth-century religious thinkers, he taught at Moscow University (1918–22) and collaborated with the Writers' Shop before being expelled from the USSR in 1922. He moved first to Berlin, where he established temporary headquarters for his academy of philosophy, and then in 1925 settled in Paris, where he continued to write and founded YMCA press. Berdiaev and his wife Lidia, with whom Tsvetaeva had been acquainted since 1915, were the Efrons' neighbors in Clamart. Berdiaev suffered from a *tic douloureux* (trigeminal neuralgia).

Bernhardt, Sarah (1844–1923). Tsvetaeva greatly admired the French tragedienne and saw her perform in Rostand's *L'Aiglon* in Paris in 1909. Bernhardt performed in Russia in 1881, 1898, and 1908.

Bilibin, Ivan Yakovlevich (1876–1942). Russian artist, theatrical set and costume designer, book illustrator, and a member of the World of Art circle, he created a distinctive style based on Northern Russian folk designs. Bilibin was a student of Ilya Repin and was profoundly influenced by the work of Viktor Vasnetsov. Like the Efrons, he repatriated to the USSR in 1935; he died in Leningrad during the nine-hundred-day siege.

Blok, Aleksandr Aleksandrovich (1880–1921). The son of a University of Warsaw jurist and the grandson of the rector of Saint Petersburg University, Aleksandr Beketov, Blok began writing while still a child. Like Bely's, Blok's career spanned both phases of Russian symbolism. His attitude toward the Bolshevik revolution was complicated (as is apparent from his long poem *The Twelve* [*Dvenadtsat'*]), and his alienation from society deepened over the last three years of his life. Tsvetaeva admired Blok and his work, and she dedicated a number of poems to him. The story of how in 1919 she sent her six-year-old daughter to deliver her poems to him is among the most famous of Russian literary legends. Blok's marriage to Liubov Dmitrievna Mendeleeva (1882–1939) was fraught with complexities (not the least of which were caused by Bely). The circumstances of his death in Petrograd are still debated.

Bogengardt, Vsevolod Aleksandrovich (1892–1961). Sergei Efron's civil war comrade, he and his wife Olga Nikolaevna (1893–1967) ran a boarding school for Russian orphans in the Czech town of Moravská Třebová, which Ariadna Efron attended during the 1923–24 school year. The Efrons and Bogengardts renewed their friendship after moving to France, where Bogengardt supported their many foster children by driving cabs.

Bokov, Viktor Fyodorovich (1914–). Peasant-born poet whose verse was noticed by Boris Pasternak. In 1942, a year after the scene described by Ariadna Efron,

Bokov, then in the army, was arrested for anti-Soviet agitation and served five years in hard labor camps.

Brei, Aleksandr Aleksandrovich (d. 1931). An actor (of English heritage) trained at the Studio of the Moscow Art Theater, he was acclaimed in émigré circles for his artistic readings.

Briusov, Valery Yakovlevich (1873–1924). Of merchant origins, educated at the same lyceum as Andrei Bely, and trained in mathematics at Moscow University, he was a prolific symbolist (decadent) poet and literary critic who later collaborated with the Bolsheviks and laid the institutional foundations for Soviet literature. Briusov was among the first critics to note Tsvetaeva's work, which he compared with that of another then emerging poet, Ilya Ehrenburg. Praising Tsvetaeva for introducing the "mundane" into poetry, he at once cautioned her against "the household" and "sweet nothings." Tsvetaeva returned his backhanded praise over a decade later in her first critical essay—"A Hero of Labor" ("Geroi truda," 1925).

Bulgakov, Valentin Fyodorovich (1886–1966). Lev Tolstoy's last secretary and a practitioner of Tolstoy's theories, Bulgakov was deported from the USSR in 1922. He met Tsvetaeva and Sergei Efron while serving as chair of the Union of Russian Writers and Artists in Czechoslovakia, and in 1925 he and Tsvetaeva collaborated on the editorial board of that organization's journal, *The Ark* (*Kovcheg*). In 1934 Bulgakov helped found the Russian Historical Cultural Museum in Zbraslav, and he also collaborated with the Russian Historical Archive Abroad (Russkii zagranichnyi istoricheskii arkhiv [RZIA]). In 1948, having spent two years in a Nazi concentration camp (1943–45), he returned to the USSR, where he headed the Tolstoy museum at Yasnaya Polyana and oversaw the cataloging of Tolstoy's archive and the creation and maintenance of both Tolstoy museums in Moscow.

Bulgakova, Maria Sergeevna ("Muna," 1898–1979, later Stepuzhinskaya). Daughter of philosopher Sergei Nikolaevich Bulgakov (1871–1944), she settled with her family first in Prague, where her father taught at the Law Faculty of Charles University, and later, in 1925, moved to Paris. In 1925 she married Konstantin Rodzevich. The marriage was short-lived and childless.

Bunin, Ivan Alekseevich (1870–1953). Russian writer and translator, recipient of the Nobel Prize in Literature (1933), in 1917 Bunin emigrated from Russia to Paris, where he remained for the rest of his life. An authority in the Paris émigré community and staunchly opposed to Soviet power, Bunin was sought out by Tsvetaeva on a number of occasions for advice; he is said to have warned Ariadna Efron not to return to Moscow in 1937.

Chabrov, Aleksei Aleksandrovich (Podgaetsky, ca. 1888–ca. 1936). Musician and actor at Tairov's "Free Theater" and a close friend of the Scriabin family, he and Tsvetaeva became friends shortly before she emigrated. Chabrov left Russia in 1923; in 1927 he converted to Roman Catholicism, later to be ordained as a Catholic priest. His last known parish assignment was in Corsica. Tsvetaeva dedicated her cycle "Lanes and Alleys" ("Pereulochki") to him.

Chaliapin, Fyodor Ivanovich (1873–1938). Kazan-born, peasant-bred, operatic bass with an extraordinarily flexible, powerful voice and mesmerizing stage presence, Chaliapin began singing in a church choir. His professional career took him from Tbilisi to the Imperial Theater in Petersburg, then, by way of Moscow's Bolshoi Theater and two private companies (Zimin and Mamontov), to La Scala (1901), New York (1907), Paris (1913), and London (1913). Chaliapin supported two families—one in Moscow, the second in Petersburg. When he followed his close friend Sergei Rachmaninoff into emigration in 1922 (ostensibly on tour, but never to return), he was accompanied by his Petersburg family. In 1928 the Soviet government deprived him of the title of People's Artist of the Soviet Union and of the right to return to Russia. In 1932, when Ariadna Efron encountered him in Paris, he had just completed filming *Don Quixote* with George Pabst in Nice.

Charskaya, Lidia Alekseevna Churilova (née Voronova, ca. 1875–1937). Fin de siècle writer of romantic fiction for adolescents and young women, Charskaya enjoyed a scandalous reputation for her free interpolation of Russian history as well as for the piquancy of the situations in which she placed her fictional heroines.

Chernova-Kolbasina, Olga Eliseevna. See Kolbasina-Chernova, Olga Eliseevna.

Chicherin, Georgy Vasilievich (1872–1936). "Father of Soviet foreign policy" between 1918 and his retirement in 1928. In April 1922, when Tsvetaeva and Ariadna Efron encountered him, Chicherin's secretary Boris Korotkov was en route to a conference of European nations in Genoa on the reconstruction of the European economy.

Chirikov, Evgeny Nikolaevich (1864–1932). Kazan-born novelist, playwright, publicist, memoirist, and social activist in the 1880s, he did not accept the Bolshevik revolution (he called Maksim Gorky "the Smerdiakov of the Russian revolution") and left Russia with his family in 1920. In Czechoslovakia Chirikov was active in émigré cultural circles and at publications where Tsvetaeva placed her work. He married Valentina Grigorieva; the couple's children included Novella (Retivova, by marriage), Lyudmila, Valentina, and Evgeny.

Chirikova, Lyudmila Evgenievna (later Shnitnikova, 1896–1990). Artist and friend of Tsvetaeva who designed the cover for the Berlin edition of *The Czar-Maiden* (*Tsar'-devitsa*); daughter of Evgeny Nikolaevich Chirikov and Valentina Grigorieva.

Chirikova, Valentina Georgievna (née Grigorieva, 1875–1966). An actress (stage name Iolshina), the wife of Evgeny Nikolaevich Chirikov and mother of Novella,

Lyudmila, Valentina, and Evgeny Chirikov, she was one of Georgy Efron's Všenory nannies.

Dovgello, Serafima Pavlovna. See Remizov, Aleksei Mikhailovich.

Duncan, Isadora (1877–1927). American dancer and choreographer, in 1921 she arrived in Russia, where, in addition to setting up a school of dance, she met and married Sergei Esenin. The train trip Ariadna Efron shared must be Duncan's disastrous, scandalous journey on tour with Esenin on their way to the United States in 1922.

Durnovo, Elizaveta Petrovna (1853–1910). Ariadna Efron's paternal grandmother, wife of Yakov Konstantinovich Efron, she descended from the Russian nobility and the merchant class. Following the advice of neighbor Pyotr Kropotkin, she entered radical political circles in the early 1880s and later joined the Social Revolutionary Party (SR). After her first arrest in 1881, she fled to Switzerland, then France, where she married Yakov Efron. Returning to Moscow in 1888, Durnovo continued her involvement in radical politics. In 1906, following a second arrest, she emigrated to Paris with her youngest son, Konstantin. On discovering her son's suicide, she took her own life the same evening.

Dzhivelegov, Aleksei Karpovich (1875–1952). Literary and theater scholar who published widely on subjects as diverse as Leonardo da Vinci, Dante Alighieri, and peasant movements in Western Europe and Russia. From 1930 until his death Dzhivelegov taught at the State Lunacharsky Institute of Theater Art (Russian Academy of Theatrical Arts) in Moscow. He was among the organizers of the Writers' Shop.

Efron, Aleksei Yakovlevich ("Alyosha," 1890–92). The sixth of Yakov Efron's and Elizaveta Durnovo's children, he died in infancy from meningitis.

Efron, Anna Yakovlevna ("Nyutya," later Trupchinskaya, 1883–1971). The eldest of Yakov Efron's and Elizaveta Durnovo's daughters, she followed her mother in radical politics and settled in Leningrad. She had two daughters—Anna Aleksandrovna (1909–82) and Elizaveta Aleksandrovna (1910–) Trupchinskaya—both of whom were interrogated but not arrested in connection with Sergei Efron's case and both of whom survived the siege of Leningrad.

Efron, Elizaveta Yakovlevna ("Aunt Lilya," 1885–1976). The third of Efron's and Durnovo's nine children, she spent several summers at the Voloshins' Koktebel artists' colony, to which she brought her younger brother, Sergei Efron, in 1911. Like her sister Vera, she worked in the theater: briefly in the provinces (establishing a short-lived amateur company in the Pskov oblast in 1919), then joining the Vakhtangov Theater and assisting Yuri Zavadsky at his Studio-Theater (1924–31) before retiring (for health reasons) to private practice as a drama coach in the early 1930s. (Dmitry Nikolaevich Zhuravlyov [1900–91] was her most distinguished student.) Together with her sister Vera, in 1918–19 she cared for Ariadna's sister, Irina, and in 1920 she asked Marina Tsvetaeva to place both her daughters with them rather than send them to the children's refuge in Kuntsovo. From 1929 until her death, Lilya shared her small room ("cubbyhole," as Ariadna Efron called it) in a Moscow communal apartment in Merzliakovsky Lane with Zinaida Mitrofanovna Shirkevich (1888–1977), to whom Ariadna Efron also referred as her "aunt."

Efron, Georgy Sergeevich ("Mur," 1925–44). Tsvetaeva's third child and only son, whom she originally intended to name "Boris" after Pasternak. Although as a teenager Ariadna Efron resented the long hours she spent babysitting Georgy, her relationship with him appears to have been loving, and when they were reunited in Moscow in 1939 she drew him into her friendship with Samuil Gurevich. Spoiled by his mother and a social misfit, Georgy had few friends (Dmitry Sezeman, son of Nina Klepinina by her first marriage, was closest to him in Moscow). Following Tsvetaeva's suicide Georgy made his way to Moscow, then Tashkent; in January 1943 he was drafted into the Soviet Army. A grave marker bearing his name is located in the village of Druika near Polotsk, where he is said to have died in battle July 7, 1944. His (fascinating and disturbing) diaries were published in 2005.

Efron, Gleb Yakovlevich (1889–97). The fifth of Efron's and Durnovo's nine children, his death deepened his mother's deepening depression.

Efron, Yakov Konstantinovich (1854–1909). Ariadna Efron's paternal grandfather, the son of a rabbi, he began his education at Moscow's Petrovsky Agricultural Institute, where he joined the "Black Repartition" (*Chornyi peredel*) faction of the "Land and Will" (*Zemlya i volya*) movement. In 1879 he was expelled after being arrested as a suspect in the murder of a fellow student, police informer Nikolai Reinshtein. In 1882 he married Elizaveta Durnovo in Marseilles, returning to Russia following an amnesty in 1888, after which he supported the children and his wife's political endeavors by working as an insurance agent. He died in Paris of cancer.

Efron, Irina Sergeevna (1917–20). Tsvetaeva's second child, Irina is reported to have shown early signs of delayed development—the likely result of poor prenatal care and diet, and Tsvetaeva clearly favored her precocious older daughter to this child, often leaving her alone at home while she and Alya went out. Irina died of neglect and malnutrition in a children's refuge in Kuntsovo (Moscow), two months after Tsvetaeva had removed Alya from the same institution. In her published memoirs Ariadna Efron skirts questions about her sister's death and her mother's culpability, and this aspect of their lives together requires further investigation.

Efron, Konstantin Yakovlevich (1895–1910). The youngest of Yakov Efron's and Elizaveta Durnovo's nine children, he appears to have shared his mother's (and brother Sergei's) susceptibility to depression. For reasons still unclear, he committed suicide February 2, 1910, after returning home one afternoon from classes at Paris's Lycée Montaigne. His mother, after discovering his body, took her own life that same evening.

Efron, Pyotr Yakovlevich ("Petya," 1881–1914). The eldest of the Efron-Durnovo children, he shared his mother's revolutionary politics, participating in the Moscow uprising of 1907, after which he fled abroad. An actor by profession, in 1913 he returned to Russia, where he soon succumbed to tuberculosis. He was married to dancer Vera Mikhailovna Ravich; the couple's one child—Elizaveta Petrovna Efron—died in early childhood (1909).

Efron, Sergei Yakovlevich ("Seryozha," 1893–1941). Eighth of the nine Efron-Durnovo children, he met his future wife in 1911 at Voloshin's Koktebel (Crimea) artists' colony. In 1912 he and Tsvetaeva married; shortly thereafter she funded publication of his autobiographical fiction (*Childhood* [*Detstvo*]). In 1915 Sergei Efron volunteered as a nurse in the Russian army. Following the 1917 revolution, he joined the White Army, serving on the southern front until 1921, when he made his way to Berlin by way of Gallipoli and Istanbul. In 1922, through the agency of Ilya Ehrenburg, he was reunited with Tsvetaeva and Ariadna in Berlin, after which the family moved to Prague, where Sergei was close friends with Konstantin Rodzevich and the Reitlinger sisters. In Prague he enrolled in doctoral studies at Charles University (he completed his high school exams only with Marina's help in Koktebel, and he never completed his doctoral degree requirements) under Professor Nikodim Pavlovich Kondakov (1844–1925). After moving to Paris in 1925, he tried his hand at writing and filmmaking, his efforts culminating in a handful of walk-on roles. In Paris he continued his ties with the "leftist" branch of the Eurasianist movement, while at the same time homesickness, nostalgia, and family unhappiness fed his sympathy for the Soviet cause. After restoring his Soviet citizenship in 1931, Sergei Efron collaborated with the NKVD, for which he recruited other émigrés (including fellow Eurasianists Nikolai Klepinin and his wife Antonina Klepinina, and Emilia Litauer, all three of whom would be tried and sentenced along with him in 1941) and his own daughter. Suspected by French authorities of complicity in the October 1937 murder of Soviet informer Ignace Reis (Ignaty Poretsky), Sergei Efron fled Paris, following Ariadna back to the USSR. Sequestered by the NKVD at a dacha in the Moscow suburb of Bolshevo, where he lived under the assumed name of Andreev, he was arrested on October 10, 1939 (the eve of his forty-sixth birthday), in the presence of his wife (two days after her birthday) and son. After spending two years in a series of NKVD prisons, during which period he underwent repeated psychological crises, he was executed by military tribunal on October 16, 1941, the sentence based on evidence against him provided in part by his own daughter, who had been subjected to psychological and physical torture.

Efron, Tatyana Yakovlevna ("Tanya," 1891–92). The seventh of Yakov Efron's and Elizaveta Durnovo's nine children, she died in infancy from meningitis.

Efron, Vera Yakovlevna (1888–1945). Fourth of the Efron-Durnovo children and the youngest of the Efron sisters. Together with sister Lilya, she attempted to care for her nieces during the hardship years of 1918–19. Also like her sister, Vera was involved in theater, initially as an actress at Aleksandr Tairov's Chamber (Kamerny) Theater (1915–17) and later in amateur companies. In 1930 she joined Moscow's Lenin Library. Her husband, Mikhail Yakovlevich Feldshtein, was arrested and executed in 1939; her son, Konstantin Mikhailovich ("Kot," 1921–) still resides in Moscow. Vera Yakovlevna died of pneumonia in evacuation from wartime Moscow.

Ehrenburg, Ilya Grigorievich (1891–1967). Journalist, novelist, poet, and memoirist, whose early poetry Valery Briusov compared to Tsvetaeva's, he first appeared in the Tsvetaeva-Efron household in 1917–18 with a message for Tsvetaeva from Koktebel poet Maksimilian Voloshin. Four years later he facilitated Tsvetaeva's reunion with Sergei Efron in Berlin. Ehrenburg's short novel *The Thaw* (*Ottepel'*, 1954) provided the name for the period of political and social relaxation that followed Stalin's death; in his memoirs *People, Years, Lives* (*Liudi, gody, zhizni*), he wrote at length about Tsvetaeva. He was married to artist Lyubov Kozintseva. Ariadna Efron remained in contact with him until his death.

Eremeeva, Zinaida Nikolaevna (1897–1966). Pianist; second wife of Boris Pasternak; mother of Stanislav Neygauz by her first husband, Genrikh Neygauz, and of Leonid Borisovich Pasternak (1937–76). Eremeeva joined Pasternak in 1931 and remained with him to his death. Her relationship with Ariadna Efron was strained by the latter's friendship with Olga Ivinskaya.

Esenin, Sergei Aleksandrovich (1895–1925). Peasant-born poet who migrated to Moscow as a teenager and was briefly aligned with the "Imaginist" movement, his highly melodic lyrics filled with romantic (nostalgic) images of the Russian countryside remain among the best known of twentieth-century Russian poetry. Esenin's legacy stems in part from his rowdy alcoholism and nomadic life style. He was married briefly to Zinaida Raikh (1894–1939) and in 1921–23 to Isadora Duncan (1877–1927). In 1925 his body was found in Leningrad's Angleterre Hotel. The circumstances of his death (suicide or murder) are still debated.

Federolf, Ada Aleksandrovna (Shkodina in last marriage, 1900–96). Descended of Russified Scandinavians, an English teacher by profession, Federolf was married to an Englishman and briefly lived in England, which later served as the basis for her arrest under suspicion of espionage and eight years in hard labor camps in Kolyma (1938–47). On release from her first arrest, she settled in Ryazan, where she was arrested again in 1948. In the Ryazan prison in February 1949, she met Ariadna Efron, with whom she would spend the next twenty-five years of her life. For details of their life together see *Unforced Labors.* Together with Elena Korkina, Federolf collected and transferred Ariadna Efron's and Tsvetaeva's papers to TsGALI following Efron's death.

Fedin, Konstantin Aleksandrovich (1892–1977). A promising young prose writer and member of the "Serapion Brothers" in the 1920s, Fedin rose through the ranks of the Soviet literary bureaucracy in the 1930s. From 1959 to 1971 he was First Secretary of the Union of Soviet Writers and served as a deputy to the Supreme Soviet of the USSR.

Furmanov, Emili Aleksandrovich (n.d.). Odessa poet and journalist.

Gollidei, Sophia Evgenievna ("Sonechka," 1896–1934). Daughter of Russified English father and Italian mother (both talented pianists trained by Anton Rubinshtein), she was educated at the Petersburg Mariinsky Gymnasium and in 1916 invited by Konstantin Stanislavsky to join the Moscow Art Theater. She met Tsvetaeva in 1918 at Evgeny Vakhtangov's Third Studio. In addition to *The Story of Sonechka* (*Povest' o Sonechke,* 1937), written by Tsvetaeva after she learned of Gollidei's death (from cancer) from Ariadna Efron, Tsvetaeva also devoted a cycle of poems to her (*Stikhi dlia Sonechki,* 1919) and created roles for her in her plays of 1918–21.

Goncharova, Natalya Sergeevna (1881–1962). Russian artist, grandniece of the wife of Aleksandr Pushkin, she trained with Konstantin Korovin in Moscow and in 1900 joined with future husband and colleague Mikhail Larionov (1881–1964) in the "Jack of Diamonds" art movement and a stream of others that ensued. In 1914 she designed Diaghilev's production of Rimsky-Korsakov's *The Golden Cockerel* (*Zolotoi petushok*) and then settled with Larionov in Paris permanently, where she continued to paint and to teach at the Louvre's École des Beaux Arts. At Tsvetaeva's request, Goncharova facilitated Ariadna Efron's matriculation at the École, where she studied with Goncharova and Vasily Shukhaev.

Gorky, Maksim (Peshkov, Aleksei Maksimovich; 1868–1936). Influential writer from the Nizhnii Novgorod region who achieved notoriety for his descriptions of Russia's working poor, for which, despite his ambiguous attitude toward Bolshevik politics, he was heralded as "the father of socialist realism." In the mid-1920s Tsvetaeva corresponded with him about her sister, and Anastasia Tsvetaeva visited Gorky in Italy, where he lived in self-imposed exile, 1921–29.

Griftsov, Boris Aleksandrovich (1885–1950). Literary historian and theoretician who specialized in Romance languages and French literature (of which he produced numerous skilled translations), he coauthored the first Russian-Italian dictionary (1934) and was among the founders of the Writers' Shop.

Grinyova. See Kuznetsova, Maria Ivanovna.

Gurevich, Samuil Davydovich ("Mulya," "Mulka," 1904–52). Born in New York City of Russian Jewish émigrés who returned to Russia following the revolution of 1917, Gurevich was hired by Mikhail Koltsov at Zhurgaz, where he edited *Abroad* (*Za rubezhom*), later moving on to TASS. Married to psychiatrist Aleksandra Levinson, the daughter of Kremlin doctors, Gurevich was romantically involved with Ariadna Efron in 1938–39, after which she would refer to him as her "husband." Arrested in 1950 and executed in 1952, Gurevich (who outlived almost all of his friends and most of his employers) appears to have been an informer planted by the NKVD to monitor goings-on at the Efron dacha in Bolshevo. In his diaries from 1939–44, Ariadna Efron's brother Georgy credits Gurevich with assisting Tsvetaeva after the arrests of Ariadna and Sergei Efron. See Kudrova, *Death of a Poet,* for additional details.

Helicon. See Vishniak, Abram Grigorievich.

Igumnova, Anna Mikhailovna (née Gertsenshtein, later Levitskaia, ca. 1888–ca. 1986). Daughter of a Russian economist murdered by a Black Hundreds mob in 1906, she was one of Georgy Efron's seven nannies in Všenory.

Ilovaiskaya, Varvara Dmitrievna (1858–90). Daughter of historian Dmitry Ilovaisky, trained as an opera singer, she was the first wife of Ivan Vladimirovich Tsvetaev and mother of Tsvetaeva's half siblings Valeria and Andrei. Ilovaiskaya's death at age thirty-two (nine days after the birth of Andrei), her vocal talents, and the story of her love for a married man whom she forsook—at her father's insistence—to marry Tsvetaev, have fueled a stream of legends about her.

Ilovaisky, Dmitry Ivanovich ("Grandfather," 1832–1920). Moscow University Russian historian, he challenged Western ("Normanist") theories of the origins of the Russian state. His ideas were severely criticized in his time—in part thanks to his ultraconservative, anti-Western political leanings—and suppressed in the Soviet period. Since the late 1980s Ilovaisky's work has been republished. Tsvetaeva recorded her own memories and family legends about Ilovaisky's eccentricities in her essay "The House at Old Pimen" ("Dom u starogo Pimena," 1933).

Ivanov, Viacheslav Ivanovich (1866–1949). Russian symbolist writer, philosopher, translator, and literary scholar, his apartment in Saint Petersburg (known as "the tower" [*bashnya*]) was a gathering place for turn-of-the-century intellectuals and artists. Ivanov's complex poetry reflects his scholarly erudition and would, indeed, have been a challenge for seven-year-old Ariadna Efron.

Ivinskaya, Olga Vsevolodovna (1912–95). Trained in Russian literature, Ivinskaya met Boris Pasternak at the editorial offices of *New World* (*Novyi mir*) in 1946, after which she became his personal secretary and, from 1947, intimate partner. Ivinskaya, said to be the prototype for Larisa Antipova in *Doctor Zhivago,* was the mother of Efron memoirist Irina Emelianova and Dmitry (Mitya) Vinogradov. Together with her daughter Irina, she served a short sentence in a labor camp near Irkutsk for accepting payment from Pasternak's Italian publishers for *Doctor Zhivago.* In her (highly subjective) memoirs of life with Pasternak, *A Captive Spirit,* she describes Ariadna Efron and her relationship with Pasternak.

Izvolskaya, Elena Aleksandrovna (Hélène Isvolsky, 1897–1974). Daughter of the last Russian ambassador to France before the revolution of 1917, poet and translator, she was one of the few émigrés in Paris Tsvetaeva would call "friend." In the early 1950s in New York she published two memoirs of Tsvetaeva.

Khazina, Nadezhda Yakovlevna. See Mandelstam, Nadezhda Yakovlevna.

Khodasevich, Vladislav Felitsianovich (1886–1939). Russian poet of Polish descent who emigrated from Russia in 1922, settling in Paris in the mid-1920s. In addition to writing fine poetry (Vladimir Nabokov considered him the greatest modern poet), Khodasevich was respected in Paris émigré circles as a critic and mentor of Russian poets abroad. Khodasevich's relationship with Marina Ivanovna evolved slowly, from enmity in the mid-1920s to mutual appreciation and even closeness in the 1930s.

Kirienko-Voloshina, Elena Ottobaldovna ("Pra," 1850–1923). Artist, mother of Maksimilian Voloshin, she hosted artists and intellectuals in their home in Koktebel (Crimea). At the Voloshin dacha Tsvetaeva met Sergei Efron. "Pra" was Ariadna Efron's godmother.

Kirsanov, Semyon Isaakovich (1906/07–72). Odessa-born Soviet poet discovered by Vladimir Mayakovsky, who published his work in *LEF,* the journal of the Left Front of Arts. A talented poet, Kirsanov (unfortunately) is remembered solely for his humoristic verse.

Klepinin, Nikolai Andreevich (1900–41). After emigrating from Russia in 1920, a member of the Russian Christian Student Movement, in Czechoslovakia Klepinin edited the journal *Eurasia,* through which he came into contact with Tsvetaeva and Sergei Efron (who later in Paris recruited him and his wife for the NKVD). In 1937 he collaborated with Berdiaev's YMCA-Press, before leaving France (just before Sergei Efron) under suspicion for the Ignace Reis (Poretsky) murder. On the night of November 6–7, 1939, he was arrested at the Bolshevo dacha that he and his family shared with the Efrons, and he was executed by decision of a military tribunal in August 1941.

Klepinina, Nina (Antonina) Nikolaevna (née Nasonova, 1894–1941). Daughter of a distinguished academic, a graduate of the Smolny Institute for Noble Women and trained as an art historian, mother (by first marriage) of Aleksei and Dmitry

Sezeman (Georgy Efron's closest friend), she was the wife of Eurasianist Nikolai Klepinin and mother of Sophia Nikolaevna Klepinina-Lvov (1929–2000). Like her husband, she is said to have been recruited by Sergei Efron for the NKVD while in Paris. Returning to the USSR in 1938 and residing next door to the Efron family at the safe house in Bolshovo, she was arrested with her husband on November 6–7, 1939, and executed in August 1941.

Kogan, Pyotr Semyonovich (1872–1932). Moscow University–trained literary historian and critic, he taught Western European literature and literary theory at Petrograd/Leningrad State University. For a while Tsvetaeva believed Kogan's son by wife Nadezhda Nolle-Kogan, Aleksandr, to be the son of Aleksandr Blok.

Kolbasina-Chernova, Olga Eliseevna (1886–1964). Writer and memoirist, daughter of writer Elisei Yakovlevich Kolbasin and (until 1923) the second wife of Vladimir Chernov, a minister in Aleksandr Kerensky's provisional government. Tsvetaeva met her and her daughters (Natalya ["Natasha"] Viktorovna Chernova-Reznikova, 1903–92; Olga ["Olya"] Viktorovna Chernova-Andreeva, 1903–79; and Ariadna Viktorovna Chernova-Sosinskaya, 1908–74) in Prague in 1923 and continued to correspond with them after they left for Paris in 1924. After arriving in Paris, in 1925–26 Tsvetaeva and her two children lived briefly with the Chernovs. Kolbasina-Chernova's son-in-law (Ariadna's husband), diplomat Vladimir Bronislavovich Sosinsky (1903–87), was responsible for carrying Tsvetaeva's letters to Konstantin Rodzevich to Ariadna Efron—as well as for leaking the more erotic of them to the public.

Koltsov, Mikhail Efimovich (Fridliand, 1898–1942). Writer and journalist known for his feuilletons published in *Pravda* in the 1930s, he was editor in chief at the giant united Soviet publishing house Zhurgaz when Ariadna Efron and Gurevich worked there. He was arrested in 1939 and died in a labor camp in 1942.

Koonen, Alisa Georgievna (1889–1974). A leading Soviet actress trained by Konstantin Stanislavsky at the Moscow Art Theater and greatly influenced by Isadora Duncan, she joined her future husband, Aleksandr Tairov, at his newly founded Kamerny Theater in 1914, where until the theater closed in 1949 she occupied center stage. Her most notable roles included Salomé, Phèdre, and Adrienne Lecouvrier.

Korkina, Elena Baurdzhanovna. Literary archivist, textologist, leading specialist on the life and works of Marina Tsvetaeva, senior researcher at the Russian Archives for Literature and Art (RGALI), curator of the Tsvetaeva fund, and current editor of the series *Marina Tsvetaeva: Unpublished Works* (*Marina Tsvetaeva: Neizdannoe*) in progress at Ellis Lak/Vagrius publishers, she is the daughter of musician and pedagogue Klavdia Georgievna Korkina and Kazakh writer and Soviet military hero Momysh-Uly Baurdzhan (1911–82). In her memoirs

Ada Federolf tells the (likely embellished) story of how Korkina found Ariadna Efron at the Tarusa dacha and eventually replaced Anna Saakiants as Efron's secretary.

Koussevitsky, Sergei (1874–1951). Double-bass virtuouso, composer, and conductor, Koussevitsky established his reputation in Europe nearly a decade before the Russian Revolution, but he returned to Russia briefly in the period immediately following to conduct in Petrograd. Efron would have encountered him at the Scriabin's during his trips to Moscow in this period.

Kozintseva, Liubov Mikhailovna (1900–71). Painter (a student of Aleksandra Ekster) and sister of Soviet film director Georgy Kozintsev, she married Ilya Ehrenburg in 1919 in Kiev and remained his close companion throughout their lives together.

Kropotkin, Pyotr Alekseevich (1842–1921). Known as "the anarchist prince," this political theoretician who was descended from the Riurik dynasty and influenced by Bakunin spent the larger part of his political career in exile in Western Europe and returned permanently to Russia on the eve of the February revolution of 1917. The Christmas party Ariadna Efron describes in her memoirs must have occurred in January 1917, shortly after Kropotkin returned to Russia from exile, when Sergei Efron was in Moscow.

Kruchyonykh, Aleksei Eliseevich (1886–1968). Poet-futurist, close associate of Nikolai Aseev, an addictive bibliophile and an acquaintance of Boris Pasternak, he collected manuscripts, including several of Tsvetaeva's, obtained, likely, from Georgy Efron, who following his mother's suicide was in desperate need of money. When Ariadna Efron later discovered that Kruchyonykh had sold her mother's papers to private collectors for exorbitant sums she could never have offered him, she broke off all relations and refused to acknowledge him in public.

Kubka, František (1894–1969). Czech writer, critic, and translator who knew Tsvetaeva and Sergei Efron while the two were in Czechoslovakia. Kubka translated several of Tsvetaeva's poems into Czech and devoted several pages of his memoirs to her.

Kudashova, Maria Pavlovna (née Cuvilier, "Maya," 1895–1986). Daughter of a French governess, in 1913, while still an eighth-grade gymnasium student, she composed poetry in French and joined Voloshin's circle, where she met Tsvetaeva, Sergei Efron, and his sisters. In 1916 she married Prince Sergei Kudashov, who died at the front in 1919–20. In the mid-1920s she moved to France, and in 1934 she married writer Romain Rolland.

Kuzmin, Mikhail Alekseevich (1872–1936). A student of Rimsky-Korsakov, Kuzmin first developed as a poet under the influence of symbolist writers at Viacheslav Ivanov's "tower" and at the journals *World of Art* and *Apollo*. His 1910 essay "On Beautiful Clarity" contributed to later formulation of Russian Acmeism by Osip Mandelstam, who was influenced by Kuzmin. Although he did not belong to the futurist movement, futurist sensibilities are apparent in his work.

Kuznetsova, Maria Ivanovna (stage name: Grinyova, 1895–1966). An actress at the Vakhtangov theater, Kuznetsova married Anastasia Tsvetaeva's first husband, Boris Trukhachov.

Lebedeva, Margarita Nikolaevna (née Spengler, 1885–1958). A doctor by training, she was married to French Foreign Legion veteran and SR leader Vladimir Ivanovich Lebedev (1854–1956), who was one of the editors of the Eurasianist journal *Will of Russia* (*Volia Rossii*), editor of *Russian Archive* (*Russkii arkhiv,* Belgrade), and—after emigrating to the United States in 1936—served on the editorial staff at New York's Russian-émigré newspaper *The New Russian Word* (*Novoe russkoe slovo*). Tsvetaeva maintained her friendship with the Lebedevs in Paris, and she left a significant portion of her archive with them (subsequently destroyed during the war). Their daughter, Irina Vladimirovna, was Ariadna Efron's close childhood friend.

Livanov, Boris Nikolaevich (1904–72). Film and stage actor at the Moscow Art Theater, a student of Konstantin Stanislavsky, he was greatly admired by Boris Pasternak, with whom he was friends from 1934 until the poet's death. The first Soviet cinematographic Sherlock Holmes, he was married to Evgenia Kazimirovna Livanova (1907–78).

Lunacharsky, Anatoly Vasilievich (1875–1933). Art and political theoretician and critic, after 1917 he served as Commissar of Enlightenment and until his death exercised considerable influence over cultural life in the USSR. Between 1917 and Tsvetaeva's departure for Germany, she appealed to Lunacharsky for assistance resolving professional and personal crises, her own as well as those of friends, such as Maksimilian Voloshin (during the famine in the Crimea) and Aleksandr Scriabin's widow, Tatiana Schloezer.

Mandelstam, Nadezhda Yakovlevna (née Khazina, 1899–1980). Memoirist, widow of poet Osip Emilievich Mandelstam (1891–1938), she was Ariadna Efron's neighbor in Tarusa. In her three-volume memoir, two volumes of which are available in English as *Hope Against Hope* and *Hope Abandoned,* she noted her husband's acquaintance with Tsvetaeva and described Ariadna Efron as a child.

Mandelstam, Osip Emilevich (1891–1938). Poet and "Acmeist" theoretician and colleague of Anna Akhmatova and Nikolai Gumilyov, he figured among Tsvetaeva's poetic and romantic "diversions" in 1916. Arrested twice, the second time in 1938, Mandelstam perished in a Siberian transit camp shortly thereafter.

Mayakovsky, Vladimir Vladimirovich (1893–1930). Marxist, futurist, politically outspoken graphic artist, poet, and performer whose innovative writing Tsvetaeva admired. Disillusioned by the bureaucratization of Soviet literature and his own marginalization, Mayakovsky committed suicide in Moscow. (The circumstances of his death, like Esenin's, are now under debate.) Tsvetaeva dedicated several poems to him, as well as her essay "Epos and Lyric in Contemporary Russia," on the work of Mayakovsky and Pasternak. Her enthusiasm for his work evoked hostility in Russian-émigré circles.

Medvedeva, Kapitolina. See Bauman, Nikolai Ernestovich.

Meyerhold, Vsevolod Emilievich (1874–1940). Actor and theater director, he trained with Vladimir Nemirovich-Danchenko at Moscow Conservatory courses that formed the basis for the Moscow Art Theater, founded by Nemirovich-Danchenko and Konstantin Stanislavsky. In 1902 he broke with Stanislavsky to found his own troupe, with which he staged over 170 plays in the eight years of its existence. After the revolution, Meyerhold increasingly associated with leftist artists, collaborating with Vladimir Mayakovsky. At his Moscow Theater of the Revolution (now known as the Mayakovsky Theater), with Lunacharsky's support, Meyerhold began to develop his own theory of acting, "biomechanics." Arrested in 1939, he was executed in 1940. He was married to Zinaida Raikh, who was brutally murdered shortly after his arrest.

Meyn, Maria Aleksandrovna (1868–1906). An accomplished pianist, Ivan Tsvetaev's second wife (and secretary) and mother of Marina and Anastasia, she died of tuberculosis when her daughters were teenagers. Marina's relationship with her mother has been the subject of much scholarly discussion, prompted, in large part, by her 1935 essay "Mother and Music" ("Mat' i muzyka"). In addition to raising their children, Maria Meyn served as Tsvetaev's secretary and principal assistant on his museum project.

Miliotti, Vasily Dmitrievich (1875–1943). Son of marine painter Dmitry Miliotti, he was a painter, restorer, and collector of icons. His residence and studio were located in the Sollogub house, then the Palace of the Arts on Povarskaya Street.

Miliukov, Pavel Nikolaevich (1859–1943). Moscow University–trained historian (student of Vladimir Kliuchevsky), founder of the Cadet Party (in 1905), and influential member of the prerevolutionary Duma, he served as minister of foreign affairs for the provisional government, later emigrating to Germany, Czechoslovakia, and finally France. From 1921 through 1940 he was editor in chief of Paris's Russian-émigré newspaper *Latest News* (*Poslednie novosti*), on whose editorial board Tsvetaeva served until 1928.

Muratov, Pavel Pavlovich (1881–1951). Historian and specialist in Italian art who published on a variety of subjects—Cézanne, Byzantine art, and early Russian painting and architecture—he was expelled from Russia in 1922 and spent his exile in Italy and France. He was among the organizers of the Writers' Shop.

Nakhman, Magda Maksimilianovna (1885–1953[?], Nachman-Achariya). Artist friend and onetime roommate and colleague of Elizaveta Efron (with whom in 1919 she traveled to the village of Dolysy, Vitebskaya guberniya, and organized an amateur theater), Nakhman painted portraits of both Tsvetaeva and Sergei Efron at Voloshin's Koktebel dacha. She later met Indian activist M. P. T. Achariya, with whom she first emigrated to Berlin, then to Bombay (now Mumbai), where she died. Her portrait of Vladimir Nabokov also is well known.

Neygauz, Genrikh Gustavovich (1888–1964). Pianist, professor at the Moscow Conservatory, he was a friend of Pasternak and the first husband of Pasternak's second wife, Zinaida Nikolaevna Eremeeva.

Neygauz, Stanislav Genrikhovich (1927–80). Pianist, son of Genrikh Neygauz and Zinaida Eremeeva.

Nikolsky, Yuri Sergeevich (1895–1962). Composer, conductor, a member of Evgeny Vakhtangov's and Vsevolod Meyerhold's studios, he was one of the first Soviet composers to write for radio and film, and many of his songs (especially for children) are considered classics.

Nolle-Kogan, Nadezhda Aleksandrovna (1888–1966). Wife of literary historian Pyotr Kogan and a close acquaintance of Aleksandr Blok, she met Tsvetaeva in 1921. Tsvetaeva for a time believed that Nolle-Kogan's son Aleksandr ("Sasha") had been fathered by Blok.

Osorgin, Mikhail Andreevich (Ilin, 1878–1943). Journalist, revolutionary, he emigrated to Italy after 1905 and returned to Russia in 1916, where, until 1922, he edited several newspapers, headed the Union of Journalists, and helped found the Writers' Shop. Expelled from Russia in 1922, Osorgin died in Chabry, France, during the Nazi occupation.

Panfyorov, Fyodor Ivanovich (1896–1960). Proletarian writer mentored by Maksim Gorky, by the mid-1930s he rose to the top ranks of the Soviet literary bureaucracy. He was also a member of the Supreme Soviet of the USSR and from 1931 until his death served as editor in chief of the literary journal *October,* notorious for its antiliberal politics.

Panina, Varvara Vasilievna (1872–1911). Turn-of-the-century chanteuse with an unusual contralto voice whose repertoire spanned the classics of the Russian romance (Alabiev, Varlamov) to fashionable works by fin de siècle composers.

Paperny, Zinovy Samuilovich (1919–96). Literary critic and historian who published at *New World* (*Novyi mir*) in the 1960s and 1970s, where he defended a number of literary causes, including Pasternak's *Doctor Zhivago.*

Parnok, Sophia Yakovlevna ("Sonya," 1885–1933). Poet, translator, literary critic, with whom Tsvetaeva was romantically involved in 1914–16, their affair inspiring Tsvetaeva's "Girlfriend" ("Podruga") cycle and Parnok's responses. Parnok was also instrumental in introducing Tsvetaeva to literary associates and publishers in Petersburg. Tsvetaeva revisited her experience with Parnok (from a diametrically opposed perspective) in her 1932–34 piece "Lettre à l'Amazone" ("Letter to the Amazon"), which is addressed to Parnok and Nathalie Barney.

Pasternak, Boris Leonidovich ("Borya," 1890–1960). Son of painter Leonid Pasternak and pianist Roza Kaufman, poet, translator, and novelist, he was awarded the Nobel Prize in 1958 for *Doctor Zhivago* (declined under pressure from Nikita Khrushchev). Pasternak knew of Tsvetaeva in Moscow before she emigrated, but their most significant interactions took place almost entirely by correspondence, particularly between 1923 and 1926 (including Rainer Maria Rilke in 1926). As a delegate to the First International Congress of Writers for the Defense of Culture, Pasternak met Tsvetaeva in Paris in 1935, but she unexpectedly left town, abandoning him (at the time in the midst of a depression) to the care of her daughter. Pasternak and Tsvetaeva met again after she returned to Moscow in 1939, and there is speculation that he experienced guilt for not having interceded on her behalf at this most difficult point in her life. After returning to the USSR, Ariadna Efron met several times with Pasternak before her arrest in 1939; after her arrest he continued to correspond and assist her (as well as Tsvetaeva's sister, Anastasia) throughout her prison term and exile. Following Ariadna Efron's return to Moscow, Pasternak helped her establish contacts with her mother's contemporaries (e.g., Anna Akhmatova) and in the Soviet publishing world (e.g., through translator-critic-editor Nikolai Nikolaevich Viliam-Vilmont [1901–86], whose sister was married to Pasternak's brother, Aleksandr). When Pasternak was attacked for publishing *Doctor Zhivago* abroad, Ariadna Efron participated in the team of friends who wrote his letter declining the Nobel Prize. On a first-name basis with each other since 1935, the two remained close through his illness; Efron is said to have been too distraught to attend Pasternak's funeral; she might also have wanted to avoid one of the most famous demonstrations of Soviet dissidence. Pasternak was married twice, the first time to artist Evgenia Vladimirovna Lurie (1898–1965), with whom he had a son, Evgeny Borisovich Pasternak (1923–), and the second time to Zinaida Nikolaevna Eremeeva, with whom he had a second son, Leonid Borisovich (1938–76).

Pavlóvich, Nadezhda Aleksandrovna (1895–1979). Poet and translator, she served as secretary of the Petrograd Union of Poets when Aleksandr Blok headed it briefly. She left valuable memoirs of Blok and supplied Maria Belkina with details about Tsvetaeva's archive.

Peshkova, Ekaterina Pavlovna (née Volzhina, "Katya," 1866–1965). Born of a noble family in the Poltava region, she was the first wife of Maksim Gorky, mother of his children Maksim and Ekaterina. She participated actively in organizing the writer's archive after his death.

Podgaetsky-Chabrov. See Chabrov, Aleksei Aleksandrovich.

Reitlinger, Ekaterina Nikolaevna Kist (1901–89) and Yulia Nikolaevna (Sister Ioanna, 1898–1988). Daughters of a czarist functionary and a Smolny convent graduate (who herself was a student of Pestalozzi-influenced Russian pedagogue Konstantin Ushinsky and raised her daughters in this tradition), the Reitlinger sisters left Russia by way of the Crimea in 1921 for Warsaw, traveling later to Prague and settling in Paris. They were both close to Tsvetaeva and Sergei Efron (Ekaterina may have been romantically involved with him in 1923–24). In 1921 Yulia became the spiritual daughter (Sister Ioanna) of Father Sergei Bulgakov, dedicating her life to religious painting and in 1956 returning to Russia, where she later became a follower of Father Aleksandr Men.

Remizov, Aleksei Mikhailovich (1877–1957). Descended from a merchant family, exiled (briefly) to the Russian Far North when arrested by mistake in 1905, Remizov was among the most unique stylists in modern Russian literature, and he had a lifelong fascination with Old Russian culture and writing. He was married to paleographer-medievalist Serafima Pavlovna Dovgello (1876–1943). The couple moved to Germany in 1921 and took up permanent residence in Paris in 1923.

Retivova, Novella Evgenievna. See Chirikov, Evgeny Nikolaevich.

Rilke, Rainer Maria (1875–1926). Prague-born Austrian poet who visited and was captivated by Russia (where he met the child Pasternak and was painted by the poet's father, Leonid). Tsvetaeva admired his work. Pasternak introduced her to him by correspondence, and in the last year of Rilke's life the three conducted a trilateral correspondence.

Rodzevich, Konstantin Boleslavovich (Louis Cordé, Luis Cordes, 1895–1988). Russian émigré, soldier of fortune, artist, member of the Russian communities in Prague in 1923 and Paris after 1925, briefly married to Maria Bulgakova, he was Marina Tsvetaeva's romantic passion in 1923–25, a recipient of her letters, and the prototype for the male protagonist of her *Poem of the Mountain* (*Poema gory*) and *Poem of the End* (*Poema kontsa*). Before the Tsvetaeva archive was opened in 2000, Tsvetaeva's letters to Rodzevich evoked considerable speculation, and in 1963, when several letters were leaked by the courier entrusted to return them from France (Vladimir Sosinsky), the gossip that arose in large part spurred Efron to sequester her mother's archive. Rodzevich and his wife visited Ariadna Efron and Ada Federolf in Tarusa in June 1967.

Rozenel, Natalya Aleksandrovna (née Sats, 1900–62). An actress at Moscow's Maly Theater and of the Soviet screen, she was Anatoly Lunacharsky's second wife (married 1922).

Rukavishnikov, Ivan Sergeevich (1877–1930). Descended from Nizhniy Novgorod Old Believer millionaires and an extraordinarily prolific poet and translator (of Ukrainian poetry), he organized the Palace of the Arts in the Sollogub house on Povarskaya Street, to which Ariadna Efron repeatedly refers in her memoirs. He later taught versification at the Briusov Literary Institute. In addition to "Miracle with Horses" (Chudo s loshadmi), Rukovishnikov figures in Tsvetaeva's essay "A Captive Spirit" ("Plennyi dukh"). He was married to Nina Isaakovna Zusman, appointed by Lunacharsky (said to be her lover) in 1919 as circus commissar, but later removed owing to her merchant background.

Saakiants, Anna Aleksandrovna (1932–2002). A lawyer's daughter, trained at Moscow University's Philological Faculty in Russian literature, she worked in the Russian literature section at Goslitizdat and was assigned to assist Ariadna Efron in preparing Tsvetaeva's work for publication. Saakiants worked on and off with Efron until the late 1960s, when she was replaced by Elena Korkina. In addition to writing on Bunin, Chekhov, Akhmatova, and Solzhenitsyn, she authored numerous articles on Tsvetaeva and compiled the most comprehensive (albeit poorly documented) biography of the writer to date. She also left memoirs of her collaboration with Efron in *Thank You!* (*Spasibo Vam!* 1998) and *Only About Marina Tsvetaeva?* (*Tol'ko li o Marine Tsvetaevoi?* 2002).

Schloezer, Tatyana Fyodorovna (1883–1922). Belgian national and the niece of Moscow Conservatory professor Pavel Schloezer, she was the second, common-law wife (widow) of composer Aleksandr Nikolaevich Scriabin (1872–1915) and mother of three of his children (Ariadna, Marina, and Yulian). Schloezer met Tsvetaeva in Moscow in 1920 and remained close friends with her until death. Tsvetaeva dedicated her 1921 poem "Insomnia! My friend . . . !" ("Bessonitsa! Drug moi! . . .") to Schloezer.

Scriabin, Aleksandr Nikolaevich (1872–1915). Pianist and composer, his compositions exemplify mutual influences across music, literature, and philosophy during the silver age of Russian culture at the turn of the nineteenth century. (Influenced by the ideas of Sergei Solovyov, whose work he knew through Prince Sergei Mikhailovich Volkonsky, Scriabin's music in turn profoundly influenced young Pasternak.) Married to Vera Ivanovna Isakovich, with whom he performed, in 1904 Scriabin became involved with Tatiana Schloezer, with whom he had three children.

Scriabina. See Schloezer, Tatyana Fyodorovna.

Serov, Georgy Valentinovich ("Yura," 1894—1929). Son of the renowned Russian painter Valentin Serov, he was an actor at Vakhtangov's studio, emigrating in 1922 to Paris, where he worked on stage and in the cinema (with film director Viacheslav Turzhansky). He was the first Russian actor to play Sherlock Holmes.

Shaliapin. See Chaliapin, Fyodor Ivanovich.

Shchipachov, Stepan Petrovich (1899–1980). Poet, remembered for his 1951 work commemorating Pavlik Morozov; editor of the poetry section at *October* at its peak in the 1960s and 1970s as the bastion of literary and political conservatism and chief opposition to the liberal *New World* (*Novyi mir*).

Shik, Elena Vladimirovna ("Lilya," n.d.). Actress, Vakhtangov Studios.

Shirkevich, Zinaida Mitrofanovna ("Zina," 1895–1977). Daughter of a village priest, she was the lifelong friend of Elizaveta ("Lilya") Efron, whom she met in 1919 in the village of Dolysy (now Pskov oblast), where Shirkevich worked as a librarian and Efron had come (with artist Magda Nakhman) to establish an amateur theater. In 1929 Shirkevich joined Efron in Moscow, remaining with her for the rest of her life, officially registered in Efron's communal room in Merzlyakovsky Lane as "housekeeper."

Shukhaev, Vasily Ivanovich (1887–1973). Stage designer, painter, book illustrator, trained (under Korovin) at the Moscow Stroganov Technical Arts College (known in the 1920s as VKhuTEMAS) and the Saint Petersburg Academy of Arts. A member of the World of Art group, he collaborated with Aleksandr Yakovlev (1887–1938) on set designs for Meyerhold's *Columbine's Scarf* (*Sharf Kolombiny,* 1911). In 1920 Shukhaev emigrated to France, where he set up his studio and gave private lessons (Ariadna Efron was among his students). In 1934 he returned to the Soviet Union, working briefly in the theater until his arrest in 1937, followed by eight years of hard labor in Kolyma, after which he resumed his career, first doing sets for the Magadan Theatre. In 1947 the artist and his wife moved to Georgia; in 1948 he was arrested again for a few months. His first personal exhibit in the USSR occurred only in 1962. In addition to his set designs and book illustrations, he is remembered for his portraits of distinguished Soviet intellectuals.

Sologub, Fyodor Kuzmich (Teternikov, 1863–1927). A writer whose work spanned both the Russian decadent and Russian symbolist movements, he is best remembered for his novel *The Petty Demon* (*Melkii bes,* 1902). Sologub's work, like Marina Tsvetaeva's, was rarely published in the Soviet period.

Stolitsa, Lyubov Nikitichna (née Ershova, 1884–1934). Russian poet whose lyrics were set to music by composers such as Aleksandr Grechaninov and Reinholdt Glière. Stolitsa's novel in verse, *Elena Deeva,* appeared in print in 1916. Stolitsa died an émigré in Bulgaria. Her name, translated literally, means "Love Capital."

Struve, Pyotr Bernardovich (1877–1944). Russian philosopher, historian, publicist, and political activist, he began as a Marxist, then joined the Cadet Party (1905–15), and in 1917 headed the economic section of the Ministry of Foreign Affairs of Kerensky's provisional government. He opposed the Bolsheviks, was active in

Vrangel's government, then fled Russia to Sofia (1921), Prague (1921–23), Berlin (1923–26), and Paris (1927–44). In Czechoslovakia (December 4, 1924) Tsvetaeva wrote to Struve regarding publication of her "counterrevolutionary" poems *The Demesne of the Swans* (*Lebediny stan*) in the journal *Russkaia mysl'* (1922). Those same poems were later (1957) published in Germany (without Ariadna Efron's permission) by Struve's son, Gleb (1898–1985), Professor of Slavic Languages and Literatures at the University of California at Berkeley.

Suvchinsky, Pyotr Petrovich (1892–1985). Son of a Polish-Russian oil magnate, Petersburg University–trained Russian musicologist who studied piano and voice, collaborator with Igor Stravinsky, Nikolai Rimsky-Korsakov, Aleksandr Blok, and Sergei Prokofiev, he left Russia in 1920. In Czechoslovakia and Paris Suvchinsky was prominent among Eurasianists, working with Sergei Efron and Tsvetaeva at the journal *Mileposts* (*Vyorsty*, 1926–28). He married Vera Aleksandrovna Guchkova (later Traill, 1901–87).

Sviatopolk-Mirsky, Dmitry Petrovich (1890–1939). Prince, Petersburg University–trained philologist who while still a student associated with poets and literary theorists as diverse as Vladimir Zhirmunsky, Mikhail Kuzmin, Nikolai Gumilev, Anna Akhmatova, and Osip Mandelstam, he was a regular at Viacheslav Ivanov's Tower. After emigrating in 1922, Mirsky taught Russian literature at the School of Slavonic Studies, King's College, University College of London, where he invited Tsvetaeva to visit. Over the next decade he lectured (brilliantly) on Russian literature and penned a steady stream of short articles and introductions to various translations, which culminated in his two-volume *A History of Russian Literature* (1927). In 1927, together with fellow Eurasianist Pyotr Suvchinsky, he visited Maksim Gorky in Sorrento; in 1931, influenced by Suvchinsky's wife (Vera Guchkova Traill) he joined the British Communist Party. In 1932 he returned to Russia, where he wrote literary history and theory, until his arrest in 1937. He died in Kolyma.

Tairov [Kornblit], Aleksandr Yakovlevich (1855–1950). Trained as a lawyer in Kiev, in 1906 he joined Vera Kommissarzhevskaya's theater under director Vsevolod Meyerhold. In Moscow in 1914 Tairov opened his own Chamber (Kamerny) Theater, where, following Meyerhold, he developed theater as spectacle. His most notable productions featured his wife, actress Alisa Georgievna Koonen: Annensky's *Thamirys Kytharodos,* Wilde's *Salomé,* Racine's *Phèdre,* Brecht's *Threepenny Opera,* and several works by Eugene O'Neill. Artists Natalya Goncharova and Mikhail Larionov, Aleksandra Ekster, and the brothers Sternberg designed sets for Tairov's early productions.

Tarasenkov, Anatoly Kuzmich (1909–56). Literary critic, bibliographer, and bibliophile, he amassed a unique collection of first and signed editions of Russian literature, including works by Tsvetaeva (e.g., a copy of her *Tsar-devitsa* [*Czar-Maiden*] autographed for her daughter). Before evacuating to Yelabuga in 1941, Tsvetaeva left part of her archive with him. On returning from Turukhansk in 1955, Ariadna Efron approached him for assistance collecting and publishing her mother's work in the USSR. With Emmanuil Kazakevich he coedited *Literaturnaia Moskva* (*Literary Moscow,* 1955), in which Tsvetaeva's work first appeared in the USSR. In 1974 his wife, Maria Belkina, entrusted a portion of his collection to the Rare Book Collection of the Lenin (now Russian State) Library.

Tarasenkova, Masha. See Belkina, Maria Iosifovna.

Tesková, Anna Antonovna (1872–1954). Czech writer, translator, teacher, and principal organizer of the Czech-Russian Union (Česko-ruská Jednota), she had spent part of her childhood in Saint Petersburg, where she learned Russian and acquired a lifelong love of Russian culture. She and Tsvetaeva became acquainted shortly after the latter arrived in Czechoslovakia and remained friends until the poet's death. Tsvetaeva's letters to Tesková remain a significant source of information on the poet's life and work.

Trukhachov, Andrei Borisovich (1912–93). Ariadna Efron's cousin, son of Anastasia Tsvetaeva and her first husband, Boris Trukhachov.

Trukhachova, Maria Ivanovna. See Kuznetsova, Maria Ivanovna.

Trupchinskaya, Anna Yakovlevna. See Efron, Anna Yakovlevna.

Tsvetaev, Andrei Ivanovich (1890–1933). Marina Ivanovna's older half brother, Ivan Vladimirovich's son by his first wife, Varvara Dmitrievna Ilovaiskaya, Andrei died before Marina returned to the USSR; his widow, Evgenia Mikhailovna Tsvetaeva ("Baba Zhenya"), with whom Ariadna Efron was on friendly terms, inherited Valeria Tsvetaeva's dacha in Tarusa.

Tsvetaev, Ivan Vladimirovich (1847–1913). Moscow University classicist and art historian, founder of Moscow's Pushkin Museum of Fine Arts, his children include: Valeria and Andrei Tsvetaeva (by his first wife, Varvara Dmitrievna Ilovaiskaya) and Marina and Anastasia Tsvetaeva (by his second wife, Maria Aleksandrovna Meyn). In her autobiographical essays Tsvetaeva underscored Tsvetaev's dedication to his life project, noting that "the museum" inhibited considerably his interactions with his family.

Tsvetaeva, Anastasia Ivanovna ("Asya," 1894–1993). Writer, memoirist, daughter of Ivan Vladimirovich Tsvetaev and Maria Aleksandrovna Meyn, Tsvetaeva's younger sister, married briefly to Boris Trukhachov, mother of Andrei Borisovich Trukhachov. A quirky intellectual with a wide range of acquaintances, among them writer Maksim Gorky, Tsvetaeva was arrested three times—in 1931, 1937, and 1949—and spent over twenty years in exile. Her memoirs provide a controversial but rich source of information on her sister. Ariadna Efron's relationship with her aunt was complicated.

Tsvetaeva, Valeria Ivanovna (1882–1966). Ivan Tsvetaev's oldest daughter, from his first marriage to Varvara Ilovaiskaya, she participated in Isadora Duncan's studio in Moscow in 1921 and then founded her own studio of "natural dance," which she later moved to Tarusa, where she became a central member of the town's cultural life. Married to Moscow University classicist Sergei Shevliagin, Valeria quarreled with her half sisters Marina and Anastasia over inheritance rights to the Tsvetaev home in Tryokhprudny Lane, and Ariadna Efron inherited Marina's smoldering dislike for her. In 1956, when Efron returned to Moscow, Valeria Ivanovna offered her a parcel of land next to her own, where Efron and her partner Ada Aleksandrovna Federolf built their own home.

Turzhanskaya, Aleksandra Zakharovna (née Dmitrieva, 1916–74). An actress, briefly married to film-director Viacheslav Turzhansky, mother of "that boy," Oleg Turzhansky, she was one of Georgy Efron's nannies in Všenory. She later moved to Paris, where she remained among Tsvetaeva's trusted confidantes.

Turzhansky, Oleg Viacheslavovich ("Lelik," 1916–80). Son of Aleksandra Zakharovna Turzhanskaya and film-director Viacheslav Turzhansky, "that boy" and Ariadna Efron would remain close friends through her time in Paris.

Usievich, Elena Feliksovna (1893–1968). The daughter of revolutionary Feliks Kon, in 1917 she returned from emigration together with Vladimir Lenin. A proponent of "pure Leninism in literary theory" and theoretician of socialist realism, she published her first major collection of critical articles in 1936. Efron likely mentions her by name to underscore her parents' (father's) links with figures in the Soviet artistic and political elite.

Vakhtangov, Evgeny Bagrationovich (1883–1922). Descended of a Russian-Armenian family from Vladikavkaz, he began his theater activity in 1906 while still a student at Moscow University, later training with Konstantin Stanislavsky's collaborator Leopold Sulerzhitsky (1872–1916) and joining the Moscow Art Theater in 1911, where in that theater's First Studio he experimented in "theater without theater." He later established his own Third Studio on the Arbat, where Tsvetaeva's sisters-in-law worked and where Marina met actors Yuri Zavadsky, Pavel Antokolsky, Sonya Gollidei, and others, and for which she wrote her plays in verse in 1919.

Vialtseva, Anastasia Dmitrievna (1871–1913). Turn-of-the-century mezzo-soprano who began her theater career at age thirteen in the chorus lines of provincial theaters, gradually working her way to the role of Carmen at Petersburg's Mariinsky Theater. She combined a stunning appearance with a voice of deep chest tones and a talent for gypsy romances.

Vishniak, Abram Grigorievich ("Helicon," 1893–1944). Moscow University-trained philologist married to New York–born Vera Arkina (their son Evgeny—Zhenya—was born in 1917), Vishniak emigrated to Berlin in 1921, taking with him the Helicon publishing company he had established in Moscow. In Berlin Vishniak published two of Tsvetaeva's poetry collections—*Separation* (*Razluka*, 1922) and *Craft* (*Remeslo*, 1923). During her short stay in Berlin she was romantically involved with him briefly, and their relationship figures in her cycle "The Youth" ("Otrok," 1922), which she dedicated to him, as well as in her "Florentine Nights" ("Florentiiskie nochi," 1933). He and his wife perished in Nazi concentration camps.

Volkonsky, Sergei Mikhailovich (1860–1937). Grandson of Decembrist Sergei Volkonsky, art historian and director of the Imperial Theaters (1899–1902), he was instrumental in introducing Dalcroze method to Russian ballet training and wrote extensively on Russian aesthetics. (In 1893 he was commissioned by the Russian Ministry of Enlightenment to deliver a series of lectures on Russian culture at the World's Columbian Exposition in Chicago.) Tsvetaeva made his acquaintance in postrevolutionary Moscow, admired his work, and corresponded with him while the two were émigrés (he in Germany, Austria, France, and Belgium) until his death.

Volkova, Natalya Borisovna (1927–). Director of the Russian Archive for Literature and Art (RGALI, formerly TsGALI) from 1963 to 2003 with whom Ariadna Efron concluded an agreement that her mother's archive not be opened until 2000.

Voloshin, Maksimilian Aleksandrovich (Kirienko, 1877–1932). Poet, translator, critic, and artist, his artists' refuge at Koktebel in the Crimea hosted, among others, the Efrons and the Tsvetaev sisters, and it was there that Sergei Efron and Marina Tsvetaeva met in May 1911. Voloshin remained a close friend to both Marina and Sergei; it was Voloshin to whom Sergei divulged details of difficulties in their marriage in 1923–24.

Voloshina, Elena Ottobaldovna. See Kirienko-Voloshina, Elena Ottobaldovna.

Voznesensky, Andrei Andreevich ("Andriusha," 1933–). Poet and understudy of Boris Pasternak, he established his reputation in the mid-1950s. His poetry is marked by formal experimentation reminiscent of the beginning of the century. One of Ariadna Efron's notebooks contains a clever parody of Voznesenky's poem "I am Goya" ["Ya—Goya"].

Vrubel, Mikhail Aleksandrovich (1856–1910). Russian turn-of-the-century painter best remembered for his renderings of neoromantic troubled "demons," which combined elements of Byzantine iconography with a gloomy impressionism. His principal model was his wife, opera singer Nadezhda Ivanovna Zabela-Vrubel (1868–1913).

Vysheslavtsev, Nikolai Nikolaevich (1890–1952). Graphic artist trained under Ilya Mashkov at the Moscow Stroganov School (VKhuTEMAS), in Italy, and in Paris, and from 1918 a resident of the Palace of Arts on Povarskaya, Vysheslavtsev modeled his work on DaVinci's and left a remarkable set of portraits of Russian cultural figures, including Andrei Bely, Pavel Florensky, Vladislav Khodasevich, Vladimir Solovyov, Fyodor Sologub, and pianist Anna Goldenveizer. Tsvetaeva met him through Dmitry Miliotti in 1920 shortly after the death of her daughter Irina, and during her brief but intense infatuation with him (in part inspired by the fact that he had never known his mother), she dedicated twenty-seven poems to him.

Zaitsev, Boris Konstantinovich (1881–1972). Trained as a chemist, at age seventeen he sent his first stories to Chekhov, Andreev, Korolenko, and Bunin. An active member of the Moscow literary community before the revolution, he afterward helped found the Writers' Shop and in 1921 served as first president of the All-Russian Union of Writers (Vserossiiskii soiuz pisatelei). Granted a visa to go abroad for health reasons in 1922, he settled in Paris in 1924. As Ariadna Efron describes, Zaitsev helped Tsvetaeva through the physical trials of postrevolutionary life in Moscow, and Efron was close friends with Zaitsev's wife (Vera Oreshnikova) and daughter (Natalya Borisovna Zaitseva-Sollogub, 1912–), who in 1937 was the first in Paris to receive her letters from Moscow. (She spent her last summer in Russia, 1921, with the Zaitsevs in the village of Pritykino in the Tulskaya guberniya.) Despite the families' closeness in Moscow, the two writers were distant in Paris, and Zaitsev left scathing memoirs of Tsvetaeva as a mother. Ariadna Efron responded with an ambiguous portrait of Zaitsev, according to which Tsvetaeva's relationship with him was one of "amicable enmity in Russia and lost even the facade of amicability abroad."

Zasulich, Vera Ivanovna (1849–1919). A Marxist, revolutionary terrorist, and writer, Zasulich moved in the same underground circles as Elizaveta Durnovo. In Switzerland at the time, Zasulich may have assisted Durnovo when the latter fled Russia for Geneva in 1880.

Zavadsky, Sergei Vladislavovich (1871–1935). Distinguished Russian jurist and literary critic, he emigrated to Czechoslovakia in 1922, where he was active in the Union of Russian Writers Abroad and edited the Eurasianist almanac *The Ark* (*Kovcheg*).

Zavadsky, Yuri Aleksandrovich ("Yura," 1894–1977). Actor and student of Evgeny Vakhtangov, Zavadsky established his own theatrical studio in 1924, where Elizaveta Efron worked as an assistant. While still with Vakhtangov, Zavadsky was introduced to Tsvetaeva by his intimate friend Pavel Antokolsky and Sophia Gollidei. Tsvetaeva dedicated to him her cycle *The Comedian* (*Komediant*) and several poems (1918–19), and he appears in her *Story of Sonechka* (*Povest' o Sonechke*, 1937). From 1941 until his death, Zavadsky headed Moscow's Mossovet Theater.

Additional Reading

I undertook this project in part out of frustration with inaccuracies and inconsistencies in the presentation of Ariadna Efron's memoirs in English-language sources about Tsvetaeva. Readers familiar with Tsvetaeva criticism will recognize that the sources listed below vary greatly in scholarly quality and reliability; newcomers to Tsvetaeva studies are cautioned always to consult multiple sources. The list below draws primarily on biographical sources and on critical analysis with strong biographical elements relevant to questions raised by Efron's memoirs of her mother.

Baltsvinik, Mikhail, and Irma Kudrova. *Tsvetaeva: A Pictorial Biography.* 3rd ed. Translated by J. Marin King. Ann Arbor, Mich.: Ardis, 1989.

Bazin, Paulina. "Shifting Perceptions of a Female Artist: Marina Tsvetayeva as Soviet Romantic Heroine or Western Bohemian Individualist." In *Performance for a Lifetime: A Festschrift Honoring Dorothy Harrell Brown: Essays on Women, Religion, and the Renaissance,* edited by Barbara C. Ewell and Mary A. McCay, with introduction by Georgiann L. Potts, 42–60. New Orleans, La.: Loyola University, New Orleans, 1997.

Bethea, David M. *Joseph Brodsky and the Creation of Exile.* Princeton, N.J.: Princeton University Press, 1994.

Boym, Svetlana. *Death in Quotation Marks: Cultural Myths of the Modern Poet.* Harvard Studies in Comparative Literature. Cambridge, Mass.: Harvard University Press, 1991.

Burgin, Diana Lewis. *Sophia Parnok: The Life and Work of Russia's Sappho.* New York: New York University Press, 1994.

Chester, Pamela. "Painted Mirrors: Landscape and Self-Representation in Russian Women's Verbal and Visual Art." In *Russian Literature, Modernism and the*

Visual Arts, edited by Catriona Kelly and Stephen Lovell, 278–305. Cambridge Studies in Russian Literature. Cambridge: Cambridge University Press, 2000.

———. "Strawberries and Chocolate: Tsvetaeva, Mandelstam, and the Plight of the Hungry Poet." In *Food in Russian History and Culture,* edited by Musya Glants and Joyce Toomre, 146–61. Indiana-Michigan Series in Russian and East European Studies. Bloomington: Indiana University Press, 1997.

Ciepiela, Catherine. *The Same Solitude: Boris Pasternak and Marina Tsvetaeva.* Ithaca, N.Y.: Cornell University Press, 2006.

Dinega, Alyssa W. *A Russian Psyche: The Poetic Mind of Marina Tsvetaeva.* Madison: University of Wisconsin Press, 2001.

Efron, Ariadna, and Ada Federolf. *Unforced Labors: The Memoirs of Ada Federolf and Selected Prose by Ariadna Efron.* Compiled, edited, and translated by Diane Nemec Ignashev. Moscow: Vozvrashchenie, 2006.

Ehrenburg, Ilya. *People and Life, 1981–21.* Translated by Anna Bostock and Yvonne Kapp. New York: Knopf, 1962.

Feiler, Lily. *Marina Tsvetaeva: The Double Beat of Heaven and Hell.* Durham, N.C.: Duke University Press, 1994.

Feinstein, Elaine. *A Captive Lion: The Life of Marina Tsvetayeva.* New York: Dutton, 1987.

———, trans. *Marina Tsvetaeva. Selected Poems.* Cambridge: Chadwick-Healey, 2000.

Gevorkian, Tat'iana. "A Poet with History or a Poet without History? Reading Marina Tsvetaeva's Collated Notebooks." *Russian Studies in Literature: A Journal of Translations* 37, no. 2 (2001): 26–48.

Grelz, Karin. *Beyond the Noise of Time: Readings of Marina Tsvetaeva's Memories of Childhood.* Stockholm Studies in Russian Literature 35. Stockholm: Almqvist och Wiksell International, 2004.

Hasty, Olga Peters. "Cvetaeva's Sibylline Lyrics." *Russian, Croatian and Serbian, Czech and Slovak, Polish Literature* 19 (May 1986): 323–40.

———. "Reading Suicide: Tsvetaeva on Esenin and Maiakovskii." *Slavic Review* 50, no. 4 (1991): 836–46.

Ivinskaya, Olga. *A Captive of Time.* Translated by Max Hayward. New York: Doubleday, 1978.

Karlinsky, Simon. *Marina Cvetaeva: Her Life and Art.* Berkeley and Los Angeles: University of California Press, 1966.

———. *Marina Tsvetaeva. The Woman, Her World, and Her Poetry.* Cambridge: Cambridge University Press, 1985.

Kelly, Catriona, comp. and ed. *An Anthology of Russian Women's Writing, 1777–1992.* Oxford: Oxford University Press, 1994.

———. *A History of Russian Women's Writing, 1820–1992.* Oxford: Clarendon Press; New York: Oxford University Press, 1994.

Kemball, Robin. "Marina Tsvetaeva in English: Notes of a Verse Translator." In *Essays in the Art and Theory of Translation,* edited by Lenore Grenoble and John M. Kopper, 301–22. Lampeter, Wales: Mellen, 1997.

Kirilcuk, Alexander. "Moving Mountains: The Spiritual Topography of Prague in Marina Tsvetaeva's 'Poema kontsa.'" *Russian Review* 65, no. 2 (2006): 194–207.

Knapp, Liza. "Tsvetaeva and the Two Natal'ia Goncharovas: Dual Life." In *Cultural Mythologies of Russian Modernism: From the Golden Age to the Silver Age,* edited by Boris Gasparov, Robert P. Hughes, and Irina Paperno, 88–108. California Slavic Studies 15. Berkeley and Los Angeles: University of California Press, 1992.

Kolchevska, Natasha. "Mothers and Daughters: Variations on Family Themes in Tsvetaeva's *The House at Old Pimen.*" In *Engendering Slavic Literatures,* edited by Pamela Chester and Sibelan Forrester, 135–57. Bloomington: Indiana University Press, 1996.

Kudrova, Irma. *The Death of a Poet: The Last Days of Marina Tsvetaeva.* Translated by Mary Ann Szporluk. London: Duckworth Overlook, 2004.

Livingstone, Angela, ed. and trans. *Art in the Light of Conscience: Eight Essays on Poetry by Marina Tsvetaeva.* Cambridge, Mass.: Harvard University Press, 1992.

Loewen, Donald. *The Most Dangerous Art: Poetry, Politics, and Autobiography after the Russian Revolution.* Lanham, Md.: Lexington Books, 2008.

Lossky, Véronique. "Tsvetaeva and Avant-garde." *Ars interpres* 6–7 (September 2006), http://www.arsint.com/2006/v_l_6.html.

Maddock, Mary, ed. and trans. *Three Russian Women Poets: Anna Akhmatova, Marina Tsvetayeva, Bella Akhmadulina.* Trumansburg, N.Y.: Crossing Press, 1983.

Makin, Michael. *Marina Tsvetaeva: Poetics of Appropriation.* Oxford: Clarendon Press, 1993.

Mandelstam, Nadezhda. *Hope Abandoned.* Translated by Max Hayward. New York: Atheneum, 1974.

———. *Hope Against Hope: A Memoir.* Translated by Max Hayward, with introduction by Clarence Brown. New York: Atheneum, 1970.

Mirsky, D. S. "Marina Tsvetaeva." *TriQuarterly* 28 (1973): 88–93.

Nemec Ignashev, Diane. "MarginAlya: Rereading the Memoirs of Ariadna Efron." In *Poetics, Self, Place: Essays in Honor of Anna Lisa Crone,* edited by Nicole Boudreau, Sarah Krive, and Catherine O'Neil, 648–72. Bloomington, Ind.: Slavica Press, 2007.

———. "Of Poetry and Politics: Ariadna Efron, Redux." *Russian History/Histoire Russe* 36, no. 4 (2009): forthcoming.

————. "(Re)constructing Alia: The Autobiographical Fiction of Ariadna Efron." In *Out of the Shadows: Neglected Works in Soviet Prose; Selected Essays,* edited by Nicholas Luker, 79–108. Nottingham, Eng.: Astra Press, 2003.

Pasternak, Boris Leonidovich, Marina Tsvetaeva, and Rainer Maria Rilke. *Letters, Summer 1926: Boris Pasternak, Marina Tsvetayeva, Rainer Maria Rilke,* edited by E. B. Pasternak, E. V. Pasternak, and K. Azadovskii, translated by Margaret Wettlin, Walter W. Arndt, and Jamey Gambrell. New York: New York Review Books, 2001.

Pierpont, Claudia Roth. "The Rage of Aphrodite: Marina Tsvetaeva." In *Passionate Minds: Women Rewriting the World,* 175–98. New York: Knopf, 2000.

Razumovsky, Maria, and Aleksey Gibson. *Marina Tsvetayeva: A Critical Biography.* Newcastle upon Tyne, U.K.: Bloodaxe Books, 1994.

Schweitzer, Viktoria. *Tsvetaeva.* Edited by Angela Livingstone. Translated by Robert Chandler and H. T. Willetts. Poetry translated by Peter Norman. New York: Farrar, Straus and Giroux, 1993.

Schweitzer, Viktoria, Jane Taubman, Peter Scotto, and Tatyana Babyonyshev, eds. *Marina Tsvetaeva: One Hundred Years; Papers from the Tsvetaeva Centenary Symposium, Amherst College, Amherst, Massachusetts, 1992.* Modern Russian Literature and Culture, Studies and Texts 32. Oakland, Calif.: Berkeley Slavic Specialties, 1994.

Slonim, Marc. "Notes on Tsvetaeva." *Russian Review* 31 (1972): 117–25.

Smith, Alexandra. "The Tsvetaeva Theme in Akhmatova's Late Poetry." *Australian Slavonic and East European Studies* 10, no. 2 (1996): 139–56.

Smith, G[erald] S[tanton]. *Mirsky: A Russian-English Life, 1890–1939.* Oxford: Oxford University Press, 2000.

Stock, Ute. *The Ethics of the Poet: Marina Tsvetaeva's Art in the Light of Conscience.* Leeds, U.K.: Maney Publishing for MHRA, 2005.

Taubman, Jane A. *A Life Through Poetry: Marina Tsvetaeva's Lyric Diary.* Columbus, Ohio: Slavica, 1989.

————. "Marina Tsvetaeva." In *Russian Women Writers,* vol. 2, edited by Christine D. Tomei, 835–44. New York: Garland, 1999.

Tavis, Anna. "Lives and Myths of Marina Tsvetaeva." *Slavic Review* 47, no. 3 (1988): 518–21.

Tsvetaevna, Marina. *A Captive Spirit: Selected Prose.* Edited and translated by J. Marin King. Ann Arbor: Ardis Publishers, 1980.

————. *The Demesne of the Swans/Lebedinyi stan.* Translated by Robin Kemball. Ann Arbor, Mich.: Ardis, 1980.

————. *Earthly Signs: Moscow Diaries, 1917–22.* Edited and translated by Jamey Gambrell. New Haven, Conn.: Yale University Press, 2002.

———. *Milestones: A Bilingual Edition.* Translated by Robin Kemball. Evanston, Ill.: Northwestern University Press, 2002.

———. *The Ratcatcher: A Lyrical Satire.* Translated by Angela Livingstone. Evanston, Ill.: Northwestern University Press, 2000.

Venclova, Tomas. "Marina Ivanovna Tsvetaeva." In *Russian Writers of the Silver Age, 1890–1925,* collected by I. G. Vishnevetsky, edited by Judith E. Kalb and J. Alexander Ogden, 387–405. Detroit, Mich.: Thomson Gale, 2004.

Weeks, Laura. "'I Named Her Ariadna . . .': The Demeter-Persephone Myth in Tsvetaeva's 'Tsvetaeva's Poems for her Daughter.'" *Slavic Review* 4 (1990): 568–84.

Zilotina, Tatiana. "The Son Figure in Marina Tsvetaeva's Writings in the Light of Heinz Kohut's Self-Psychology." *West Virginia University Philological Papers* 49 (2002): 63–70.

Index

Above the Barriers (*Poverkh barr'erov*) (Pasternak), 112, 253n62

Abrikosov, Father Vladimir, 178, 269

Adrienne Lecouvreur (Legouvé and Scribe), 37, 244n38

Aerial Waves (*Vozdushnye puti*) (Pasternak), 120–21, 254n76

Afansiev, Aleksandr, 90, 249n23; *Russian Folk Tales*, 249n23

Akhmatova, Anna (Gorenko), 55–56, 87, 105, 108, 228–34, 252n49, 267n39, 267–68n42, 268nn43–44, 269, 270, 284, 287, 291; "The Answer Came Too Late" ("Pozdnii otvet"), 234, 268n43; and Efron, Ariadna, 234–35, 268n45; *Poem without a Hero* (*Poema bez geroia*), 234, 268n44; "Stories About Pushkin" ("Slovo o Pushkine"), 267n39; and Tsvetaeva, 55–56, 87–88, 108, 232–34, 267–68n42, 268n43, 269, 287

Aksakov, Sergei, *The Childhood Years of Grandson Bagrov* (*Detstvo Bagrova vnuka*), 85, 249n15

Aleko (Rachmaninov), 243n23

Alekseev, Vladimir, 36, 219, 269

Aleksei Mikhailovich, Czar, 23, 242n19, 243n28

Alfonso XIII, King, 191

All-Russian Union of Writers (*Vserossiiskii soiuz pisatelei*), 295

Altschuler, Grigory, 171, 172, 201, 269

Altschuler, Isaak, 171, 269

Andersen, Hans Christian, *The Little Girl Who Trod on the Loaf*, 29

Andreev, Daniil, 269

Andreev, Leonid, 164–65, 174; *Samson in Chains* (*Samson v tsepiakh*), 165, 263n171, 269

Andreev, Savva, 164, 270

Andreev, Vadim, 270

Andreev, Valentin, 164, 270

Andreeva, Anna, 164–65, 171, 172–74, 270

Andreeva, Vera, 164, 270

Andreeva-Carlisle, Olga, 270

Aniskovich, Lidiia, 241n9, 242n11

Annenkov, Yuri, 56, 229, 247n60, 270; illustrations to Blok's *The Twelve* (*Dvenadtsat'*), 56, 247n60; portrait of Akhmatova, 229

Annensky, Inokenty, 244n38, 291; *Thanyras Cytharoede* (*Thamirys Kytharodos*), 244n38, 291

"The Answer Came Too Late" ("Pozdnii otvet") (Akhmatova), 234, 268n43

Anthony (*Antonii*) (Briusov), 249n25

Antokolsky, Pavel, 31, 33, 35, 36, 39, 53, 56, 167, 270; Ariadna Efron's letter to, 221–22, 267n31; *Puss in Boots* (*Kot v sapogakh*), 31–33. *See also* Tsvetaeva, Marina: Verse, cycles: *The Player* (*Komed'iant*)

Ardov, Viktor, 231–32, 234, 267n41, 267–68n42, 270
The Ark (*Kovcheg,* almanac), 152, 153–55, 260nn148–49, 273, 295; publication of Tsvetaeva's *Poem of the End* (*Poema kontsa*), 153–54; Tsvetaeva names the almanac, 152, 260n149
Arkina, Vera, 224–25, 248n10, 293–94
Aseev, Nikolai, 107, 110, 121, 254n79, 270

Babel, Isaac, 252n55
Babka, Lukás, 254n76
Bach, Johann Sebastian, 147
Bakhrakh (Bacherac), Aleksandr, 271. *See also under* Tsvetaeva, Marina
Bakunin, Mikhail, 283
Balmont, Elena Tsvetkovskaya, 39, 42, 57, 62–64, 271
Balmont, Konstantin, 39–43, 57–64, 247nn62–64, 261n158, 271. *See also under* Tsvetaeva, Marina
Balmont, Mirra, 39, 57, 59, 271
Bashkirtseva, Maria, 23, 271
Batalov, Aleksei, 234, 270
Bauman, Nikolai, 17, 271, 285; Nikolai Bauman Technical University, 241n5
Bazhenov, Vasily, 231, 267n41
Beauharnais, Joséphine de, 23, 220–21, 266–67n30
The Beautiful Mill-Girl (*Die schöne Müllerin*) (Schubert), 44
Belkina, Maria (Tarasenkova), ix, xix, 235, 237n1, 239n11, 246n49, 247n60, 247n65, 250n40, 267n34, 268n42, 271; *A Juncture of Fates* (*Skreshchenie sudeb*), 271. *See also* Efron, Ariadna
Bely (Bugaev), Andrei (Boris), 91, 93–94, 110, 225, 271–72, 273, 295; letter to Tsvetaeva, 93–94
Berdiaev, Nikolai, 65, 67, 272, 281
Berger, Henning, 37, 244n38; *Syndafloden,* 37, 244n38
Bernhardt, Sarah, 23, 33, 243n30, 272
Bilibin, Ivan, 90, 272
"Black Repartition" (*Chornyi peredel*), 15, 241n6, 276

Blok, Aleksandr, 52–57, 59, 83, 100, 108, 123, 161, 206–7, 245n47, 246n49, 246n54, 246n57, 247n60, 249n23, 270, 271, 272, 282, 286, 287; *A Gray Morning* (*Sedoe utro*), 54, 246n57; *The Puppet Show* (*Balagan*), 56; *Retribution* (*Vozmezdie*), 53, 246n56; *The Stranger* (*Neznakomka*), 54; Tsvetaeva's letter to, 54–55, 161, 246n54; *The Twelve* (*Dvenadtsat'*), 54, 56–57, 247n60, 249n23, 270, 272
The Blue Bird (*L'oiseau bleu*) (Maeterlinck), 37, 244nn40–41
Bode-Kolyshev, Baron Mikhail, 245n47
Bogengardt, Olga, 144, 146, 163, 257n117, 258n119, 272
Bogengardt, Vsevolod, 144, 146, 163, 257n117, 258n119, 272
Bokov, Viktor, 126, 272–73
Bonaparte, Napoleon, 23, 33, 35, 190, 220–21, 242n17, 243nn29–30, 267n32
Bonaparte, Napoleon, II, 33, 35; as depicted in Rostand's *L'Aiglon,* 33, 243n30
Bonivard, François, 71, 257n114
Bove, Osip, 231, 267n41
Brei, Aleksandr, 165, 273
Briusov, Valery, 84, 248n12, 249n25, 273, 278; *Anthony* (*Antonii*), 249n25; Ehrenburg's portrait of, 84, 273; Tsvetaeva's "Hero of Labor" ("Geroi truda"), 249n25, 273
Bruncvik ("Prague Knight"), 150, 156, 259n141, 260n156
Bulgakov, Sergei, 273, 288
Bulgakov, Valentin, 151, 152–56, 259n145, 260n153, 273; and *The Ark* (*Kovcheg*), 153, 273; and Lev Tolstoy, 151, 152, 273; memoirs of Tsvetaeva, 154, 259n145, 260n153; and Russian Historical-Cultural Museum in Zbraslav, 154–56, 273
Bulgakova, Maria (Muna), 173, 267n36, 273, 288; Ariadna Efron's letter to, 267n36
Bunin, Ivan, 271, 273, 289, 295

By Our Own Paths (Svoimi putiami), 121, 167, 254n76
Byron, Lord George Gordon, 53, 105; *Prisoner of Chillon*, 257n114

Casanova, Giacomo, 245n42. *See also under* Tsvetaeva, Marina: Dramas
Cervantes, Miguel de (*Don Quixote*), 40, 41, 98, 229
Česko-ruská Jednota. See Czech-Russian Union
Chabrov (Pogaetsky), Aleksei, 34, 74, 76–79, 243–44n32, 273–74, 288. *See also under* Tsvetaeva, Marina: Verse, cycles: *Lanes and Alleys* (*Pereulochki*)
Chaliapin, Fyodor, 174, 189–90, 274; as Don Quixote, 190, 274
Chamber (*Kamerny*) Theater, 34, 278, 282, 291
Charskaya, Lidia, 146, 274
Chekhov, Anton, 269, 289, 295
Chekhov, Mikhail, 134, 256n105, 273
Chernova-Andreeva, Olga, 226, 274, 282
Chernova-Kolbasina, Olga. *See* Kolbasina-Chernova, Olga
Chernova-Reznikova, Natalya, 226, 282
Chernova-Sosinskaya, Ariadna, 282
Chester, Pamela, 238n5
Chesterton, Gilbert Keith, *The Man Who Was Thursday*, 162, 262n166
Chicherin, Georgy, 80, 274
Childhood (Detstvo) (Efron), 153, 260n150
Childhood (Detstvo) (Gorky), 138
The Childhood Years of Grandson Bagrov (Detstvo Bagrova vnuka) (Aksakov), 85, 249n15
Chirikov, Evgeny, 90, 164, 165–66, 274
Chirikova, Lyudmila Shnitikova, 90, 98–99, 143, 166, 274; illustrations to Tsvetaeva's *Czar-Maiden*, 250n35, 274
Chirikova, Novella (Retivova), 274, 288
Chirikova, Valentina (Iloshina), 166, 172–73, 274–75
Chopin, Frédéric, 90
Chukovskaya, Lidia, xvii
Chukovsky, Kornei, 246n56

Ciepiela, Catherine, 248n10, 253n57, 255n89
Committee for the Welfare of Russian Writers and Journalists Residing in Czechoslovakia (*Komitet po uluchsheniiu byta russkikh pisatelei i zhurnalistov, prozhivaiushchikh v Chekhoslovakii*), 96, 152, 153, 260n148, 273, 298
Consuelo (Sand), 179, 205n64
Coster, Charles de: *Thyl Ulenspiegel*, xx, 239n12
Cricket on the Hearth (Dickens), 134, 253n105
Cyrano de Bergerac (Rostand), 34, 243n30
Czech-Russian Union (*Česko-ruská Jednota*), 160, 292

Danilova, Liudmila, 247n63
Dante Alighieri, 69; *The Divine Comedy*, 139, 257n112, 275
Daudet, Alfonse, 257n111; *Sapho*, 135, 257n111
David Copperfield (Dickens), 171
Dead Souls (Mërtvye dushi) (Gogol), 140, 257n113
de Beauharnais, Joséphine. *See* Beauharnais, Joséphine de
de Coster, Charles. *See* Coster, Charles de
Den' poezii (almanac). See *Poetry Day*
Der Rattenfänger von Hammeln (The Piedpiper of Hamelin) (Goethe), 147, 258n123
Der Struwwelpeter (Hoffmann, H.), 23
de Vega, Lope. *See* Vega, Lope de
Dickens, Charles, 134, 138, 256n105; *Cricket on the Hearth*, 134, 256n105; *David Copperfield*, 171; *Dombey and Son*, 138; *Little Dorritt*, 138
The Diver (Der Taucher) (Schiller), 246n53
Doctor Zhivago (Doktor Zhivago) (Pasternak), 228–29
Dolgorukov family, 245n47
Dombey and Son (Dickens), 138
Donkey Skin (Peau-d'âne) (Perrault), 211
Don Quixote: (Cervantes), 98, 229; (Pabst), 190, 274

Doré, Gustave, illustrations, 8, 23, 210, 266n18

Dovgello, Serafima Pavlovna, 157–58, 275, 288

Duke of Reichstadt. See Bonaparte, Napoleon, II

Duncan, Isadora, 79, 275, 278, 282, 293

Dunya (Tsvetaeva's milkwoman), 47–52

Dürer, Albrecht, book illustrations, 8

Durnovo, Elizaveta, 15–18, 213, 241n4, 241nn9–10, 242n11, 275, 276, 277, 278, 296

Dzhivelegov, Aleksei, 65, 67, 275

Eckermann, Johann Peter, v, xii

Efron, Aleksei, 16, 275

Efron, Anna Trupchinskaya ("Nyutya"), 16, 17, 33, 275, 283, 293

Efron, Ariadna: and Akhmatova, 228–34; and Blok, 54–55, 83; and Bulgakov, Valentin, 155; and Mandelstam (Khazina), 234–35

—Correspondence: Akhmatova, 234–35; Antokolsky, 267n31

—Published writing: "A dusha ne tonet. . . ." Pis'ma 1942–1975: Vospominaniia ("But the soul never drowns. . . ." Letters 1941–1975: Memoirs), ix; "Avtobiografiia" ("Autobiography"), 239n13; "Iz zapisnykh knizhek" ("From Notebooks"), x; Marina Tsvetaeva: Vospominaniia docheri; Pis'ma (Marina Tsvetaeva: Her Daughter's Memoirs; Letters), ix; Miroedikha: Riadom s Alei (Miroedikha: Alongside Alya), ix, x, 265; "O Kazakeviche" (fragment) ("Moscow, 1955"), x; O Marine Tsvetaevoi: Vospominaniia docheri, ix; "Odinochestvo Mariny Tsvetaevoi" ("The Loneliness of Marina Tsvetaeva"), 261–62n160; "Popytka zapisi o mame" ("Attempt at Writing about Mama"), ix, 265n1, 265n7, 266nn19–25, 266n27–29, 267n33; "Stranitsy bylogo" ("Pages from the Past"), x; "Stranitsy

vospominanii" ("Pages of Memoirs"), ix, x, 247n65; Stranitsy vospominanii (Pages of Memoirs), ix; Unforced Labors, 239n10, 239n12, 279; "Ustnye rasskazy" ("Oral Tales"; "Tales Told in Tarusa"), ix

Efron, Elizaveta (Lilya), 16, 33, 166–67, 183, 205, 263nn174–75, 275–76, 278, 283, 290, 293; Sergei Efron's letters to, 166, 263nn174–75

Efron, Georgy (Mur), 102, 115, 116, 170–78, 179, 185–86, 226, 253n66, 253–54n69, 263n170, 264n204, 264n206, 269, 270, 275, 276, 280, 282, 283, 293

Efron, Gleb, 16, 276

Efron, Irina, 36, 50, 51, 170, 221–22, 267n31, 276, 295; "Two hands lightly lowered" ("Dve ruki, legko opushchennye"), 222

Efron, Konstantin, 17, 241nn10–11, 275, 277

Efron, Pyotr, 16, 17, 34, 204, 277

Efron, Sergei (Seryozha), xx, xxi, 15–20, 26, 33–34, 35, 36, 73, 74, 75, 79, 85–87, 92, 94–97, 104, 116, 120, 127, 129–30, 133, 134, 136–41, 143–47, 152, 153, 161, 166–68, 170, 171–72, 175, 179, 183–84, 185, 198, 204, 205–7, 209–10, 211, 212, 213–14, 216, 219, 225–27, 235–36, 239n13, 241n3, 242nn12–14, 249n17, 250nn28–29, 250n42, 251n44, 256n105, 259n142, 260n150, 262n163, 262n168, 263nn174–75, 263n192, 268nn47–48, 272, 273, 275, 277–78, 280, 281, 282, 283, 286, 288, 291, 294; acting career, 33–34; Childhood (Detstvo), 153, 260n150; and Ehrenburg, 19, 85–87, 95, 170, 223–24, 242n13, 277, 278; and Eurasianists, 250n42, 262n168, 277–78, 281, 291; and NKVD, xx, xxi, 17, 20, 239n13, 262n168, 277–78, 280, 281, 282; and Reitlinger, Ekaterina, 175, 288; and Rodzevich, 152, 256n105, 277–78; and Turzhanskaya, 175; and Voloshin, 18, 168, 286, 294; and White Guard, 19–20, 242n12, 272, 277–78. See also Tsvetaeva, Marina: Verse,

cycles: *The Demesne of the Swans*
(*Lebedinnyi stan*); Tsvetaeva, Marina:
Verse, poems: "My attic-loft castle, my
castlelike loft" ("Cherdachnyi dvorets
moi, dvortsovyi cherdak"), "Two is
too many even for a morning's joy"
("No tesna vdvoëm"), "You who loved
me as a lie" ("Ty, menia liubivshii
fal'sh'iu")
—correspondence: Efron, Elizaveta, 166–
67, 263nn174–75; Tsvetaeva, Marina,
85–87, 170, 249n17, 263n192; death,
235, 268n47; postscript to Alya, 87;
rehabilitation, 235–36, 242n14
Efron, Tatiana (Tanya), 16, 178
Efron, Vera, 17, 33, 168, 183, 207, 275, 276,
278, 283, 293
Efron, Yakov, 15–18, 241n9, 241n11, 275–79
Ehrenburg, Ilya Grigorievich, 19, 75, 77,
81–87, 90, 91, 92, 95, 96, 100, 104–5,
121, 155, 170, 188, 223–24, 225, 227–28,
234, 242n14, 248n5, 248nn10–11,
249n14, 249n26, 252n55, 267n34, 273,
277, 278, 283; and Efron, Sergei, 19,
85–87, 95, 170, 223–24, 242n13, 277,
278; and Pasternak, 104–5, 121; *People,
Years, Lives* (*Liudi, gody, zhizn'*), 83,
248n11; *The Thaw* (*Ottepel'*), 278;
Thirteen Pipes (*Trinadtsat' trubok*), 92,
96, 249n26
Elena Deeva (Stolitsa), 265n1, 290
El maestro de danzar (Vega), 233, 268n42
Ephrem of Syria, Saint, 153, 260n151
Eremeeva, Zinaida, 228, 230, 252–53n56,
278, 286, 287
Esenin, Sergei, 41, 42, 79, 94, 245n47,
251n48, 275, 278, 285
Eurasianists (*evraziitsy*), 250n42, 262n168,
277–78, 281, 291
Evgeny Onegin (Pushkin), 16, 241n7

Fairbanks, Douglas, 187–89
Faust (Goethe), 74, 147, 248n2
Federolf, Ada (Shkodina), 239n10, 239n12,
278–79, 283, 288, 293
Fedin, Konstantin, 230–31, 279

First International Congress of Writers
for the Defense of Culture, 108, 124,
252n55
First Studio (Moscow Art Theater), 134,
256n105, 273
Florensky, Pavel, 295
The Flying Ship (*Vozdushnyi korabl'*)
(Lermontov), 242n17
Forrester, Sibelan, 238n5
For You (*Pour vous*), 239n13
France—URSS, 239n13
Free (*Svobodnyi*) Theater, 273, 282. *See also*
Tairov, Aleksandr
Furmanov, Emili, 121, 279

The Gay Science (*Die fröliche Wissenschaft*)
(Nietzsche), 173, 264n195
George, Saint, 41, 57, 246n50
The Ghostship (*Das Geisterschiff*)
(Zedlitz), 242n17
Gide, André, 252n55
Ginzburg, Evgenia, xvii
Glière, Reinholdt, 265n1, 290
Glinka, Mikhail, *La Séparation*, 206
Goblot, Simone, 238n3
Goethe, Johann Wolfgang, v, xii, 74, 89,
111, 143, 147, 248n2, 258n123; *Der
Rattenfänger von Hammeln* (*Piedpiper
of Hameln*), 147, 258n123; *Faust*, 74,
147, 248n2; *Hermann und Dorothea*,
147; *Wilhelm Meister*, 147
Gogol, Nikolai, 24, 127, 137–38, 210–11,
242n21, 257n113, 264n202, 266n18;
Dead Souls (*Mërtvye dushi*), 140,
257n113; *Inspector General* (*Revizor*),
137; *Terrible Revenge* (*Strashnaia
mest'*), 177, 264n202; *Vii*, 24, 210–11,
242n21
The Golden Calf (*Zolotoi telënok*) (Ilf and
Petrov), 34, 243n32
The Golden Cockerel (*Zolotoi petushok*)
(Rimsky-Korsakov), 279
"The Golem of Prague," 156, 260n155
Gollidei, Sophia ("Sonya," "Sonechka"),
36, 39, 221, 279, 293, 295; *Story of
Sonechka* (*Povest' o Sonechke*), 39;

Verses for Sonechka (*Stikhi dlia Sonechki*), 36
Goncharov, Ivan: *Oblomov,* 69, 247n67
Goncharova, Natalya, 279, 291
Gorky, Maksim (Peshkov, Aleksei), 122, 124, 138, 160–63, 262nn164–65, 262n168, 269, 274, 279, 286, 287–88, 291, 292; *Childhood* (*Detstvo*), 138; and Pasternak, 122–24; and Suvchinsky, 162–63, 262n168; and Tsvetaeva, Anastasia, 122, 161, 292; visit to Prague, 160–63. *See also under* Tsvetaeva, Marina: Correspondence
Gozzi, Carlo, 244n38; *Turandot,* 37, 244n38
Granskaya, Efrosinya Mikhailovna, 52
A Gray Morning (*Sedoe utro*) (Blok), 54, 246n57
Grechaninov, Aleksandr, 265n1, 290
Greuze, Jean-Baptiste: *Young Girl Crying over Her Dead Bird* (*Jeune fille pleurant son oiseau mort*), 203, 265n11
Griftsov, Boris, 67, 68, 279–80
Grimm, Jakob and Wilhelm: *The Piedpiper of Hamelin,* 258n123
Grinyova, Maria. *See* Kuznetsova, Maria
Gumilyov, Lev, 234
Gumilyov, Nikolai, 234, 284
Gurevich, Samuil ("Mulya"), 276, 280, 282
The Gypsies (*Tsygane*) (Pushkin), 24, 243n23

Hamlet (Shakespeare), 176, 264n198
Heine, Heinrich, 39, 245n43, 258n123
Helicon. *See* Vishniak, Abram
Hermann und Dorothea (Goethe), 147
Hoffmann, E. T. A., 244n38, 264n204; *Life and Opinions of Tomcat Murr* (*Lebens-Ansichten des Katers Murr . . .*), 264n204; *Princess Brambilla,* 37, 244n38
Hoffmann, Heinrich: *Der Struwwelpeter,* 23

Igumnova, Anna, 173, 264n196, 280
Ilf, Ilya (Fainzilberg), 243n32; *The Golden Calf* (*Zolotoi telënok*), 34, 243n32

Illustrated Russia (*Illiustrirovannaia Rossiia*), 239n13
Ilovaiskaya, Varvara, 11, 12–13, 241n2, 280, 292, 293
Ilovaisky, Dmitry, 12, 280
Imagism (*Imaginism*), 105, 251n48
Iname. *See* Yamagata, Iname
Inspector General (*Revizor*) (Gogol), 137
In the Forest (*V lesu*) (Melnikov-Pechersky), 176, 264n199
In the Mountains (*Na gorakh*) (Melnikov-Pechersky), 176, 264n199
Ivanov, Viacheslav, 57, 58, 280, 283–84, 291
Ivask, Yuri, 242n14
Ivinskaya, Olga, xix, 239n7, 278, 280–81
Izvolskaya, Elena, 190–91, 281

Jack the Poodle, 21, 209, 214
Jakobsen, Jens Peter, 252n51
Jones, Sir William, 244n38; *Sacontala,* 37, 244n38

Kālidāsa: *Sacontala,* 37, 244n38
Kamerny Theater. *See* Chamber (Kamerny) Theater
Kašparek, 142, 257n116
Kaufman, Roza, 287
Kazakevich, Emannuil, 292
Kemball, Robin, 242n14
Kerensky, Aleksandr, 282, 290; and *Volia Russii* (*Russia's Will*), 261n158
Khardzhiev, Nikolai, 268n42
Khazina, Nadezhda. *See* Mandelstam, Nadezhda
Khodasevich, Vladislav, 67, 69, 160–61, 261n158, 262n161, 281, 295
Kholopov, Georgy, 237n1
King, J. Marin, 249n27, 255n90
Kirienko, Maksimilian. *See* Voloshin, Maksimilian
Kirienko-Voloshina, Elena ("Pra"), 83, 199, 200–201, 204, 275, 277, 281, 286
Kirsanov, Semyon, 121, 254n79, 281
Klepinin, Nikolai, 239n15, 277, 281
Klepinina, Antonina (Nina), 239n15, 276, 277, 281–82

Klepinina, Sophia (L'vova), xxi, 239n15, 282

Kogan, Aleksandr ("Sasha"), 206, 282, 286

Kogan, Pyotr, 52, 207, 282, 286

Kolbasina-Andreeva, Ariadna, 270

Kolbasina-Chernova, Olga, 282

Kolchak, Admiral Aleksandr, 250n30

Koltsov, Mikhail (Fridliand), 252n55, 265n6, 280, 282

Koonen, Alisa, 34, 282

Korkina, Elena, ix, xi, xii, 195, 247n65, 249n16, 252n54, 257n117, 258n122, 260n146, 263n192, 265, 279, 282–83, 289

Kornilov, General Lavr, 242n12

Korotkin, Boris, 80, 274

Koussevitsky, Sergei, 61, 283

Kovcheg (almanac). See *The Ark*

Kozintsev, Georgy, 283

Kozintseva, Lyubov, 90, 92–93, 95, 96, 223–24, 224–25, 227–29, 278, 283

Kropotkin, Pyotr, 15, 213–14, 275, 283

Kruchonykh, Aleksei, 107, 252n54

Krutikova, Maria, xi, 258n122, 263n192

Kubka, František, 160–61, 283

Kudashova, Maria ("Maya"), 76, 124, 283

Kudrova, Irma, 237n1, 238n4, 239nn13–14, 242nn12–13, 250nn28–29, 251n44, 259n142, 268n47, 280

Kusaka (Tsvetaeva's cat), 204–5

Kuzmin, Mikhail, 110, 283–84, 291

Kuznetsova, Maria ("Marusya"), 76, 77, 284, 292

La délivrance de Bonivard (Lossier), 257n114

L'Aiglon (Rostand), 33, 243n30, 272

"Land and Liberty" (*Zemlya i volya*), 241n6, 276

La Séparation (Glinka), 206

Lebedev, Vladimir, 158–60, 284

Lebedeva, Margarita, 158–60, 284

LEF (Left Front of Arts), 254n79, 270

Legouvé, Ernest, 244n38; *Adrienne Lecouvreur*, 37, 244n38

Lenin, Vladimir (Ulianov), 75, 271, 293

"Lenin Library" (Russian State Library), 67, 278, 292

Lermontov, Mikhail, 23, 105, 242n17; *Flying Ship* (*Vozdushnyi korabl'*), 242n17

Leskov, Nikolai, 45, 246n51

Lieutenant Schmidt (*Leitenant Shmidt*) (Pasternak), 127

The Life and Opinions of Tomcat Murr (*Lebens-Ansichten des Katers Murr . . .*) (Hoffman, E. T. A.), 264n204

Litauer, Emilia, 277

Literary-Historical Society *Vozvrashchenie*, 238n1

Literary Moscow (*Literaturnaia Moskva*, almanac), 292

Little Dorritt (Dickens), 138

The Little Girl Who Trod on the Loaf (Andersen), 29

Livanov, Boris, 229–30, 284

Livanova, Evgenia, 229–30, 284

Livingstone, Angela, 248n3, 250n37, 251n46, 258n123

Loew, Rabbi Judah, Maharal of Prague, 260n155

Lossier, Franck-Edouard: *La délivrance de Bonivard*, 257n114

Lossky, Véronique, xix, 239n9, 258n123

The Loving Cup (*Kubok*) (Zhukhovsky), 46, 139, 246n53

Lunacharsky, Anatoly, 40, 41, 43, 65, 184, 245n47, 246n48, 284, 285, 288, 289; State Lunacharsky Institute of Theater Arts, 275

Lurie, Evgenia, 115, 117, 254n70, 287

L'vova, Sofiia. See Klepinina, Sofiia

Maeterlinck, Maurice, 244nn38–40; *The Blue Bird* (*L'oiseau bleu*), 37, 244n40, 244n41; *Miracle of St. Anthony* (*La miracle de Saint-Antoine*), 37, 244n38

Maître Pathelin, 37, 244n39

Makin, Michael, 256n103

Mandelstam, Nadezhda (Khazina), xvii, 234, 234–35, 284

Mandelstam, Osip, 206, 234, 235, 284, 291

Man'kovskii, Aleksei, 238n2
Masaryk, Tomáš, 96
Mayakovsky, Vladimir, 55, 89, 100, 105,
    108, 110, 245n47, 250n40, 250–51n42,
    251nn43–47, 252n49, 268n46, 270, 281,
    284–85; "Scum" ("Svolochi"), 100,
    250n40. *See also under* Tsvetaeva,
    Marina
Medvedeva, Kapitolina, 17, 271, 285
Melnikov-Pechersky, Pavel, 264n199; *In
    the Forest (V lesu)*, 176, 264n199; *In the
    Mountains (Na gorakh)*, 176, 264n199
Men, Father Aleksandr, 288
Mendeleeva, Liubov, 272
Meyerhold, Vsevolod, 37, 167, 285, 286,
    290, 291
Meyn, Maria, 8, 11–14, 24, 30, 73, 81, 202–3,
    210, 285, 292. *See also* Tsvetaeva,
    Marina: Prose: "Mother and Music"
    ("Mat' i muzyka")
Michelangelo Buonarroti, 118
Miliotti, Dmitry, 285
Miliotti, Vasily, 52, 53, 54, 58, 285, 295;
    escorts Alya to Blok, 58
Miliukov, Pavel, 285; *Latest News
    (Poslednie novosti)*, 101, 251n42, 285
*The Miracle of St. Anthony (La miracle
    de Saint-Antoine)* (Maeterlinck), 37,
    244n38
Mniszek, Marina, 39, 234, 268n43
Mnukhin, Lev, 238n6, 241n16, 259n145,
    262n160, 267n31, 267n42, 268nn43–44
Modigliani, Amedeo, 188
Moscow State Stroganov Technical Arts
    University, 117, 254n70, 290, 294
Muratov, Pavel, 67, 285
My Sister—Life (Sestra moia—zhizn')
    (Pasternak), 230

Nakhman (Achariya), Magda, 73, 205,
    286, 290
Naryshkin, Prince Lev, 31, 243n27
Naryshkina, Czarina Natalya, 243n28
Nash soiuz. See *Our Union*
Nemec Ignashev, Diane, 238n4, 239n10,
    259n144

A Nest of Gentlefolk (Dvorianskoe gnezdo)
    (Turgenev), 16, 241n8
New World (Novyi mir, journal), 280, 286,
    290
Neygauz, Genrikh, 230, 231, 252–53n56,
    278, 286
Neygauz, Stanislav, 230, 231, 278, 286
Nicholas I, Czar, 15
Nicholas II, Czar, 242n14
Nietzsche, Friedrich, 264n195; *The Gay
    Science (Die fröliche Wissenschaft)*,
    173, 264n195
Nikolsky, Yuri, 36, 286
Nolle-Kogan, Nadezhda, 207, 282, 286
Novyi mir (journal). See *New World*
The Nutcracker (Shchelkunshchik)
    (Tchaikovsky), 24, 242n22

Oblomov (Goncharov), 69, 247n67
Obolensky, Sergei, 269, 289
October (Oktiabr'), 235, 286, 290
Olshevskaya, Nina, 270
Oreshnikova, Vera, 68–69, 295
Orlov, Vladimir, 237n1, 246n56
Osorgin, Mikhail, 64–68, 83, 247n65, 286
Ostrovsky, Aleksandr, 264n203; *The
    Thunderstorm (Groza)*, 177, 264n203
Our Union (Nash soiuz), 239n13

Panfyorov, Fyodor, 235, 286
Panina, Varvara, 24–25, 286
Paperny, Zinovy, 235, 286
Parnok, Sophia (Sonya), 214–15, 286–87
Pasternak, Aleksandr, 287
Pasternak, Boris, xix, 55, 61, 100, 103–27,
    130, 160, 162, 172, 175, 177, 179, 228–31,
    232, 234, 245n47, 249n13, 249n16,
    251n48, 252nn49–55, 252–53n56,
    253n57, 253n59, 253nn62–64,
    253nn66–67, 253–54n69, 254nn70–76,
    254n79, 255nn80–81, 255n83, 255n87,
    255nn88–89, 255nn91–92, 287, 288;
    and Aseev, 107, 121, 283, 287; and
    Efron, Georgy ("Boris"), 172, 177,
    179, 253n66, 253–54n67; and Gorky,
    124; and Kuzmin, 110; and Tsvetaeva,

Anastasia, 123. *See also under*
Tsvetaeva, Marina
—Collections: *Above the Barriers (Poverkh
bar'erov)*, 111, 112, 253n62; *My Sister—
Life (Sestra moia—zhizn')*, 230
—Correspondence: Efron, Ariadna,
xix, 126–27, 255n92, 287; Tsvetaeva,
61, 103–27, 162, 252n49, 252nn51–52,
252n54, 253nn59–60, 253n63, 254nn71–
75, 254n79, 255n83, 255n87, 255n89, 287
—Prose: "Aerial Waves" ("Vozdushnye
puti"), 120–21, 254n76; *Doctor Zhivago
(Doktor Zhivago)*, 228–29, 287
—Verse, narratives: *1905*, 127; *Lieutenant
Schmidt (Leitenant Shmidt)*, 127
—Verse, poems: "I love you blackened
by ashes" ("Liubliu tebia chornoi ot
sazhi"), 112
Pasternak, Evgenia Lurie. *See* Lurie,
Evgenia
Pasternak, Evgeny, 115, 116–17, 255n92, 287
Pasternak, Leonid Borisovich, 278, 287
Pasternak, Leonid Osipovich, 287, 288
Pasternak, Roza. *See* Kaufman, Roza
Pasternak, Zinaida. *See* Eremeeva, Zinaida
Pavlóvich, Nadezhda, 41, 246n49
People, Years, Lives (Liudi, gody, zhizn')
(Ehrenburg), 83, 248n11
"People's Will" (*Narodnaya volya*), 16,
241n6
Perrault, Charles, 23, 210–11, 266n18;
Donkey Skin (Peau-d'âne), 211; *Prince
Ricky of the Tuft (Riquet à la houppe)*,
211; *Tom Thumb (Le Petit Poucet)*, 184,
210–11, 266n18
Peshkov, Aleksei. *See* Gorky, Maksim
Peshkova, Ekaterina, 123, 287–88
Peter I, Czar, 165, 242n19, 243n28
Petrov, Adrian, 145
Petrov, Evgeny (Kataev): *Golden Calf
(Zolotoi telënok)*, 34, 243n32
*Piedpiper of Hamelin (Der Rattenfänger
von Hammeln)* (Goethe), 147, 248n2;
and Brothers Grimm, 258n123. *See
also under* Tsvetaeva, Marina: Verse,
narratives: *The Ratcatcher (Krysolov)*

Poem without a Hero (Poema bez geroia)
(Akhmatova), 234, 268n44
Poetry Day (Den' poezii, almanac), 235,
268n46
Poretsky, Ignaty. *See* Reis, Ignace
Pour vous (journal). See *For You*
Povarskaya Street, House 52 ("Natasha
Rostova House," "Palace of the Arts"),
39–40, 43–45, 245–46n47
Pratt, Sarah, 238n5
Prince and the Pauper (Twain), 156
*Prince Ricky of the Tuft (Riquet à la
houppe)* (Perrault), 211
Princess Brambilla (Hoffman, E. T. A.), 37,
244n38
The Puppet Show (Balagan) (Blok), 56
Pushkin, Aleksandr, 52, 55, 59, 69, 106, 145,
202, 229, 241n7, 243n23, 248n3, 252n53,
266n14; *Evgeny Onegin*, 16, 241n7; *The
Gypsies (Tsygane)*, 24, 243n23; *Songs of
the Eastern Slavs (Pesni o vostochnykh
slavianakh)*, 248n3; *Tale of Czar Saltan
(Skazka o tsare Saltane)*, 266n14; "You
have been pampered by nature" ("Vy
izbalovany prirodoi"), 106, 252n53
Pushkin Museum of Fine Arts, 11, 14,
255n84, 292. *See also* Tsvetaev, Ivan
Puss in Boots (Kot v sapogakh)
(Antokolsky), 31–33

Rachmaninov, Sergei, 243n23; *Aleko*,
243n23
Raikh, Zinaida, 278, 285
Rashkovskaya, Maria, 255n92
Razin, Stepan, 173, 264n97
Reinshtein, Nikolai, 15, 276
Reis, Ignace (Poretsky, Ignaty), 277, 281
Reitlinger, Ekaterina ("Katya"), 173, 175,
277, 288
Reitlinger, Yulia (Sister Ioanna), 173, 175,
277, 288; and Efron, Sergei, 175, 288
Remizov, Aleksei, 157–58, 261n158, 275, 288
Remizova, Serafima. *See* Dovgello,
Serafima Pavlovna
Retivova, Novella. *See* Chirikova, Novella
Retribution (Vozmezdie) (Blok), 53, 246n56

Revue de Moscou (*Moscow News*), xx, 201,
    252, 265n6, 282
RGALI, Russian State Archives for
    Literature and Art (*Rossiiskii
    gosudarstvennyi arkhiv literatury i
    iskusstva*). *See* TsGALI
Rilke, Rainer Maria, 55, 61, 105, 126, 130,
    252n51, 255n88, 287, 288. *See also
    under* Tsvetaeva, Marina
Rimsky-Korsakov, Nikolai, 266n14, 279,
    283, 291; *Golden Cockerel* (*Zolotoi
    petushok*), 279; *The Tale of Czar
    Saltan* (*Skazka o tsare Saltane*),
    266n14
Rodzevich, Konstantin, 134, 150–52, 173,
    175, 231, 256n105, 257n117, 258n119,
    259nn142–43, 259–60n146, 273, 277,
    282, 288
Rolland, Romain, 76, 124, 283
Rostand, Edmond, 33–34, 89, 243n30,
    272; *Cyrano de Bergerac*, 34, 243n30;
    L'Aiglon, 33, 243n30, 272
Rozenel, Natalya, 40–41, 43, 246n48, 288
Rukavishnikov, Ivan, 45, 59, 289
Rukavishnikova, Nina. *See* Zusman, Nina
Russian Chronicles (newspaper), 218,
    266n26
Russian Folk Tales (Afanasiev), 249n23
Russian Historical Archive Abroad, 273
Russian Historical-Cultural Museum
    (Zbraslav), 154–55, 273
Russia's Will (journal), 158, 261n158, 284
Russia Today (journal), 239n13
Russie d'aujourd'hui. *See* Russia Today
Russkie vedomosti. *See* Russian Chronicles
RZIA (*Russkii zagranichnyi istoricheskii
    arkhiv*). *See* Russian Historical
    Archive Abroad

Saakiants, Anna, xix, 237n1, 238n6, 239n8,
    250–51n42, 251n43, 260n146, 262n165,
    283, 289
Sacontala (Jones), 37, 244n38
Samson in Chains (*Samson v tsepiakh*)
    (Andreev), 165, 263n171, 269
Sancho Panza, 40, 41, 98

Sand, George (Aurore Dupin), 37, 179,
    205n64; *Consuelo*, 179, 205n64
Sapho (Daudet), 135, 257n111
Schiller, Friedrich, 46, 246n53; *The Diver*
    (*Der Taucher*), 246n53
Schloezer, Tatiana, 61–62, 76, 105, 184, 273,
    283, 284, 289
Schnitzler, Arthur: *Veil of Pierrette*, 34
Schubert, Franz: *The Beautiful Mill-Girl*
    (*Die schöne Müllerin*), 44
Scriabin, Aleksandr, 44, 61, 62, 77, 184,
    252n54, 273, 283, 284, 289
Scriabin, Yulian, 289
Scriabina, Ariadna, 61, 289
Scriabina, Marina (Mara), 61, 76, 184, 289
Scriabina, Tatiana. *See* Schloezer, Tatiana
Scribe, Eugène, 244n38; *Adrienne
    Lecouvreur*, 37, 244n38
"Scum" ("Svolochi") (Mayakovsky), 100,
    250n40
Sergievskaya, Maria, xix
Sergius of Radonezh, Saint, 206
Serov, Georgy (Yuri), 36, 289
Serov, Valentin, 289
Sezeman, Dmitry, 276, 281–82
Shakespeare, William, 176; *Hamlet*, 176,
    264n198
Shcherbakov, Anatoly, 252n55
Shchipachov, Stepan, 235, 290
Shershenevich, Vadim, 251n48
Shevelenko, Irina, xi, xii, 247n65, 249n16,
    252n54
Shevliagin, Sergei, 293
Shik, Elena, 36, 290
Shirkevich, Zinaida, 276, 290
Shkodina, Ada. *See* Federolf, Ada
Shukhaev, Vasily, 187, 279, 290
Silentium (Tiutchev), 170, 263n189
Slonim, Mark, 261n158
*Soiuz russkikh pisatelei i khudozhnikov
    za rubezhom*. *See* Committee for
    the Welfare of Russian Writers
    and Journalists Residing in
    Czechoslovakia
Soiuz sovetskikh pisatelei. *See* Union of
    Soviet Writers

Soiuz zhurnalistov. See Union of
  Journalists
Sollogub, Count Vladimir, 39, 40, 43, 57,
  59, 245–46n7, 285, 289
Sollogub, Countess, 39, 40, 42, 43, 57, 59,
  285
Sollogub, Fyodor (Teternikov), 59, 290, 295
*Songs of the Eastern Slavs (Pesni o
  vostochnykh slavianakh)* (Pushkin),
  248n3
Sosinsky, Vladimir, 152, 259n146, 282, 288
Stalin, Iosif, xix, xx, 195, 238n5, 262n168,
  278
Stanislavsky, Konstantin, 37, 244n40, 279,
  282, 284, 285, 293
Stolitsa, Lyubov, 185, 265n1, 290; *Elena
  Deeva,* 265n1, 290
"Stories about Pushkin" ("Slovo o
  Pushkine") (Akhmatova), 267n39
The Stranger (Neznakomka) (Blok), 54
Stroganov Higher Art and Technical
  School. *See* Moscow State Stroganov
  Technical Arts University
Struve, Gleb, 242n14, 259n44, 291
Struve, Pyotr, 248n11, 290–91
Studio-Theater, 275, 295. *See also*
  Zavadsky, Yuri
Surkov, Anatoly, 246n56
Suvchinsky, Pyotr, 162–63, 250n42,
  262n168, 291
Sviatopolk-Mirsky, Prince Dmitry,
  250n42, 291
Svoimi putiami. See By Our Own Paths
Swinburne, Algernon, 251n50
Syndafloden (Berger), 37, 244n38
Szporluk, Mary Ann, 238n4

Tairov, Aleksandr, 34, 37, 273, 278, 282, 291
*The Tale of Czar Saltan (Skazka o tsare
  Saltane)* (Pushkin), 266n14; (Rimsky-
  Korsakov), 266n14
Tarasenkov, Anatoly, 235, 271, 291–92
Tarasenkova, Maria. *See* Belkina, Maria
Tchaikovsky, Pyotr, 242n22; *The
  Nutcracker (Shchelkunshchik),* 24,
  242n22

The Terrible Revenge (Strashnaia mest')
  (Gogol), 177, 264n202
Tesková, Anna, 160, 178, 292
*Thanyras Cytharoede (Thamirys
  Kytharodos)* (Annensky), 244n38, 291
The Thaw (Ottepel') (Ehrenburg), 278
Thing (journal), 100, 250n40
Third Studio (Moscow Art Theater),
  31–32, 35–39, 167, 269, 270, 275, 279,
  284, 286, 289, 290, 293, 295. *See also*
  Vakhtangov, Evgeny
Thirteen Pipes (Trinadtsat' trubok)
  (Ehrenburg), 92, 96, 249n26
The Thunderstorm (Groza) (Ostrovsky),
  177, 264n203
Thyl Ulenspiegel (Coster, de), xx, 239n12
Tikhonov, Nikolai, 252n55
Tiutchev, Fyodor, 263n189; *Silentium,* 170,
  263n189
Tolstoy, Lev, 43, 118, 136, 151, 152, 153, 171,
  183, 246n47, 269, 273; *War and Peace,*
  43, 136, 183, 246n47
Tom Thumb (Le Petit Poucet) (Perrault),
  184, 210–11, 266n18
Trediakovsky, Vasily, 55, 131, 247n58
Trukhachov, Andrei, 76, 199–200, 204, 292
Trukhachov, Boris, 76, 292
Trukhachova, Irina, 76, 77
Trukhachova, Maria. *See* Kuznetsova,
  Maria ("Marusya")
Trupchinskaya, Anna Aleksandrovna, 275
Trupchinskaya, Anna Yakovlevna, 275, 292
Trupchinskaya, Elizaveta, 275
TsGALI, Central State Archives for
  Literature and Art (*Tsentral'nyi
  gosudarstvennyi arkhiv literatury i
  iskusstva*), xvii, 156, 195, 238n2, 252n54,
  260n154, 279, 282, 294
Tsvetaev, Andrei, 11–14, 241n2, 280, 292
Tsvetaev, Ivan, 5, 8, 10–14, 23, 73, 203,
  241n2, 292
Tsvetaeva, Anastasia, 12–15, 74, 76, 88,
  122–23, 143, 161, 199, 201, 279, 292, 293;
  and Gorky, 122, 161, 279, 292, 294
Tsvetaeva, Marina: **and Akhmatova,**
  55–56, 87–88, 108, 230–34,

267–68n42, 268n43, 269, 287; dedication of *Mileposts* (*Vyorsty*) to, 252n49; dedication of *On a Red Steed* (*Na krasnom kone*) to, 56; **and Antokolsky,** 35–36, 39, 270; **and Bakhrakh,** 257n117, 271; **and Balmont,** 39–43, 57–64, 247n64, 271; **and Bely,** 93–94, 271–72; **and Bernhardt,** 33; **and Blok,** 52–57, 59, 100, 161, 206, 282, 286; influence on *On a Red Steed* (*Na krasnom kone*), 56–57; *Poems to Blok* (*Stikhi k Bloku*), 100, 250n39; **and Briusov,** 151, 273; "Hero of Labor" ("Geroi truda"), 249n25, 273; **and Bulgakov, Valentin,** 151, 152–54, 259n145, 260n153, 273; **and Chabrov,** 34–35, 77, 274; *Lanes and Alleys* (*Pereulochki*), 34; **and Chirikova, Lyudmila,** 90, 98–99, 143, 166, 250n35, 274; **and Ehrenburg,** 19, 75, 77, 81–87, 90, 91, 92, 95, 96, 100, 104, 121, 155, 170, 188, 223–24, 225, 227–28, 234, 242n14, 248n10, 249n14, 252n55, 267n34, 273, 277, 278, 283; **and Gollidei,** 36, 39, 221, 279, 293, 295; **and Gorky,** 122, 124, 138, 160–63, 262nn164–65, 262n168, 269, 274, 279, 286, 287–88, 291, 292; **and Ilovaiskaya, Varvara,** 11, 12–13, 241n2, 280, 292, 293; **and Khodasevich,** 69, 160–61, 281; **and the Lebedev family,** 158–60, 284; **and Lunacharsky,** 40, 41, 43, 65, 184, 245n47, 246n48, 284, 285, 288, 289; **and Mayakovsky,** 55, 89, 108, 110, 251n44, 251n47, 252n49, 270, 281, 284–85, 285; [address to], 250–51n42; "Epos and Lyric of Contemporary Russia" ["Epos i lirika sovremennoi Rossii"] 108, 251n46; *To Mayakovsky* (*Maiakovskomu*), 251n45; "To Mayakovsky," 268n46; translation of "Scum" ("Svolochi"); **and Meyn, Maria,** 11–14, 210, 285, 292; "Mother and Music" ("Mat' i muzyka"), 285; **and Parnok,** 214–15, 285–87; **and Pasternak,** 61, 100, 103–27, 130, 162,

172, 175, 179, 228–31, 232, 234, 245n47, 249n16, 252n49, 252nn51–52, 252n54, 253n57, 253nn59–60, 253nn62–68, 253–54n69, 254nn71–75, 254n79, 255nn80–83, 255nn87–89, 255nn91–92; **and Pushkin,** 24, 52, 53, 59; *Poems to Pushkin* (*Stikhi k Pushkinu*), 247n59; **and Rilke,** 55, 61, 126, 130, 252n51, 255n88, 288; **and Rodzevich,** 150–52, 173, 256n104, 259nn142–43, 288; **and Vishniak, Abram (Helicon),** 90, 91–92, 224–25, 248n10, 293–94; **and Zaitsev,** 68–69, 239–40n16, 295

—Collections: *After Russia* (*Posle Rossii*), 131, 250n42, 256n100; *Craft* (*Remeslo*), 34, 88, 100, 243n31, 250n34, 271, 294; *Czar-Maiden* (*Tsar'-Dévitsa*), 82, 100, 250n35, 274, 292; *Magic Lantern* (*Volshebnyi fonar'*), 176, 258n122, 264n200; *Mileposts* (*Vyorsty*), 105, 252n49, 291; *Poems to Blok* (*Stikhi k Bloku*), 100, 250n39; *Psyche* (*Psikheia*), 100, 247n61, 250n33; *Separation* (*Razluka*), 100, 250n38, 294

—Correspondence: Akhmatova, 87–88; Bakhrakh, 257n117; Bely, 93–94; Blok, 54–55, 161, 246n54; Efron, Sergei, 170, 263n192; Ehrenburg, 77, 104, 248n5; Gorky, 161–63, 262n165; Khodasevich, 262n161; Mayakovsky, 89; Pasternak, 61, 103–27, 162, 249n16, 252n52, 252n54, 253n57, 253n61, 253nn64–67, 253–54n69, 255nn80–82, 255nn88–89, 255n91, 262n167, 287, 288; Rilke, 255n88, 288; Rodzevich, 257n117, 258n119, 259–60n146, 282, 288

—Dedications: "To my daughter Ariadna, to her Venetian eyes" ("Docheri moei Ariadna—Venetskianskim ee glazam"), 245n43; "We were— remember in the future" ("Byli my— pomni ob etom"), 146, 258n122

—Dramas: *Adventure* (*Prikliuchenie*), 38, 245n42; *David,* 88; *End of Casanova* (*Konets Kazanovy*), 152, 245nn42–43, 260n147; *Fortune* (*Fortuna*), 38,

254n42; *Jack of Hearts* (*Chervonnyi valet*), 38, 245n42; *Phaedra* (*Fedra*), 156, 168; *Phoenix* (*Feniks*), 38, 39, 245nn42–43; *Snowstorm* (*Metel'*), 38, 245n92; *Stone Angel* (*Kamennyi angel*), 38, 245n42; *Theseus* (*Ariadna*), 149, 150, 156, 168, 170, 263n177, 263n178
—Fragments: "Everything is more important . . ." ("Vsë vazhnee, vsë nuzhnee . . ."), 169, 263n180; "I writhed in captivity . . ." ("Kak bilas' v svoëm plenu . . ."), 169, 263n188; "The lane's last scarlet light" ("Allei poslledniaia alost'"), 149, 259n136; "Not having the right to give presents . . ." ("Ne umet' uzhe prava darit'. . ."), 169, 263n184; "Phantoms are evoked by longing . . ." ("Prizraki vyzyvaiutsia nashei toskoi . . ."), 169, 263n186; "The soul cannot be filled . . ." ("Dusha ne mozhet byt' zapolnena . . ."), 169, 263n185; "The streets bear no blame for the horrors of our soul" ("Ulitsy ne vinovaty v uzhasakh nashei dushi"), 150, 259n139; "Tears not shed don't count" ("Slëzy: neprolivaiushchiesia, v schët ne idushchie"), 169, 263n187; "A torn shawl on a thin shoulder" ("Rvanoi planok na khudom pleche"), 169, 263n183; "To know how to die . . ." ("Nado umeret' . . ."), 169, 263n181; "This life's closeness and closedness" ("Etoi zhizni—mestnost' i tesnost'"), 169, 263n182
—Prose: address to Mayakovsky, 101, 250–51n42; "Art in the Light of Conscience" ("Iskusstvo pri svete sovesti"), 125, 255n90; "A Captive Spirit" ("Plennyi dukh"), 94, 249–50n27, 272, 289; "A Discourse on Balmont" ("Slovo o Balmonte"), 62, 246n64; "Downpour of Light" ("Svetovoi liven'"), 100, 108, 250n37; "Epos and Lyric of Contemporary Russia" ("Epos i lirika sovremennoi Rossii"), 103, 108, 251n46, 285;

"Florentine Nights" ("Florentiiskie nochi"), 100, 250n36, 293–94; "A Hero of Labor" ("Geroi truda"), 249n25, 273; "The House at Old Pimen" ("Dom u starogo Pimena," 1933), 125, 255n90, 280; "A Living Word About a Living Man" ("Zhivoe o zhivom"), 125, 255n90; "A Miracle with Horses: A True Story" ("Le miracle des chevaux. Fait authentique"), 45, 246n52, 289; "Mother and Music" ("Mat' i muzyka"), 125, 255n90, 285; "My Employments" ("Moi sluzhby"), 53, 246n55; "On the New Russian Children's Book" ("O novoi russkoi detskoi knigi"), 158; "Sickness Report" ("Biulleten' bolezni"), 257n117; "Story of a Certain Dedication" ("Istoriia odnogo posviashcheniia"), 248n3; *Story of Sonechka* (*Povest' o Sonechke*), 39, 264n195, 269, 270, 279, 295
—Translations: Mayakovsky, "Scum" ("Svolochi"), 100, 250n40
—Verse, cycles: *Conducti* (*Provoda*), 113, 253n64; *The Demesne of the Swans* (*Lebedinyi stan*), 19–20, 242n14, 291; *Poems to Blok* (*Stikhi k Bloku*), 100, 250n39; *Poems to Czechia* (*Stikhi k Chekhii*), 268n146; *Factory Testaments* (*Zavódskie*), 134, 256nn106–7; *Girlfriend* (*Podruga*), 214–15, 285–86; *Hour of the Soul* (*Chas dushi*), 148, 259nn131–32; *Lanes and Alleys* (*Pereulochki*), 34, 88, 243n31, 249n20, 274; *Mayakovsky* (*Maiakovskomu*), 103, 251n45, 268n46; *The Player* (*Komed'iant*), 35, 36, 244n34, 244nn36–37, 245n46, 295; *Poems to Pushkin* (*Stikhi k Pushkinu*), 55, 247n59; *Sibyl* (*Sivilla*), 25, 131–32, 256n103; *To Berlin* (*Berlinu*), 100; *Trees* (*Derev'ia*), 132, 134, 256n102; *Verses for Sonechka* (*Stikhi dlia Sonechki*), 35, 36, 244n35, 279
—Verse, narratives: *Czar-Maiden* (*Tsar'-Devitsa*), 82, 100, 250n35, 274;

Egorushka, 88, 249n22; *On a Red Steed* (*Na krasnom kone*), 56, 90, 132, 247n61, 312; *Poem of the End* (*Poema kontsa*), 118, 121, 150–52, 153, 156, 158, 168, 231, 234, 259n143, 263n176, 288; *Poem of the Mountain* (*Poema gory*), 150–52, 156, 158, 234, 254n79, 259n143, 288; *The Ratcatcher* (*Krysolov*), 116, 121, 147, 156, 258n123; *The Swain* (*Mólodets*), 88, 132, 139, 249n21, 256n101

—Verse, poems: "Achilles on the Ramparts" ("Akhill na valu"), 149, 259n133; "Acrid though your chimneys' smoke be" ("Kak by dym tvoikh ni gorek"), 149, 259n135; "Along embankments, where trees are gray" ("Po naberezhnym, gde sedye derev'ia"), 149, 259n137; "As always, as ever, towards the sea so blue" ("Vsë takzhe, takzhe, v morskuiu sin'"), 148, 258n129; "As through those battles on the Don" ("Kak po tem donskim boiam"), 268n146; "The Curtain" ("Zanaves"), 148, 258n128; "Daybreak on the rails" ("Rassvet na rel'sakh"), 20, 130, 242n15, 255n97; "Dear companions, who shared with us a night's lodgings" ("Milye sputniki, delivshie s nami nochleg"), 39, 245n44; "The Eye" ("Oko"), 150, 259n138; "Fly afar, my stallion prancing" ("Ty leti, moi kon' retivyi,"), 74, 248n3; "From the Sea" ("S moria"), 123, 255n85; "God save—the smoke" ("Spasi, gospodi, dym"), 134–35, 256n108; "A gray boulder . . ." *Sybil* 2 ("Kamennoi glyboi seroi," *Sivilla* 2), 25, 243n24; "High above crosses and chimneys . . ." ("Prevyshe krestov i trub"), 103, 251n47; "I know I shall die at sunrise or sunset" ("Znaiu, umru na zare"), 105, 252n49; "I shall tell you a tale of enormous deceit" ("Ia rasskazhu tebe pro velikii obman"), 105, 252n49; "I wrote on a slate tablet"

("Pisala ia na aspidnoi doske"), 161, 262n163, 268n146; "In orphaned air beyond the grave" ("V sirom vozdukhe zagrobnom"), 131, 256n98; "In Praise of the Rich" ("Pokhvala bogatym"), 134, 159, 261n159; "In Praise of Time" ("Khvala vremeni"), 147, 258n124; "Insomnia! My friend!" ("Bessonitsa! Drug moi . . . !"), 289; "Landscape of the Heart" ("Landshaft serdtsa"), 148, 258nn126–27; "Milestones, milestones, milestones, and dry hard bread!" ("Viorsty i viorsty i viorsty i chorstvyi khleb"), 105, 252n49; "A Minute" ("Minuta"), 149, 259n134; "My attic-loft castle, my castlelike loft" ("Cherdachnyi dvorets moi, dvortsovyi cherdak"), 36–37, 244n36; "My friends! My own, my trinity of brothers!" ("Druz'ia moi! Rodnoe troedinstvo!"), 37, 39, 244n37, 245n46; "My Russia! Oh, my Russia, why do you burn so bright?" ("Luchina"), 101, 250n41; "Newspaper Readers" ("Chitateli gazet"), 268n146; "New Year's Poem" ("Novogodnee"), 123, 255n86; "Poems appear like stars above" ("Stikhi rastut kak zvëzdy"), 30–31, 243n26; "Poet and Czar" ("Poet i tsar"), 268n146; "Prague, a poem writ in stone," 150, 259n140; "Prague Knight" ("Prazhskii rytsar'"), 150, 259n141; "Pride and Timidity" ("Gordost' i robost'"), 161, 262n162; "Rails" ("Rel'sy"), 148, 259n130; "Rain sings a lullaby to pain" ("Dozhd' ubaiukivaet bol'"), 100; "Sibyl has burned; the Sibyl a tree trunk" ("Sivilla: vyzhzhena, sivilla: stvol"), 131, 256n99; "So suasively," ("Do ubeditelnosti, do ubistvennosti"), 100, 250n32; "Steal Away" ("Prokrast'sia"), 147, 258n125; "To Alya," ("Ale," 1914), xviii–xix, 238n6; "To Alya" ("Ale," 1918), 41, 246n50; "To a player" ("Komediantu"), 35, 244n34; "To

Mayakovsky," ("Maiakovskomu"), 268n146; "To S. M. Volkonsky" ("S. M. Volkonskomu"), 5, 241n1; "Two hands lightly lowered" ("Dve ruki, legko opushchennye"), 222; "Two is too many even for a morning's joy" ("No tesna vdvoëm"), 103, 133, 251n44, 256n104; "Two trees yearn for each other" ("Dva dereva khotiat drug k drugu"), 202, 265n10; "Under that shawl" ("Pod shal'iu"), 170, 263nn190–91; "Under the cobblestones, under the wheels" ("Pod bulyzhnikami, pod kolësami"), 100, 250n31; "What am I—blind and orphaned—to do" ("Chto zhe mne delat', sleptsu i pasynku"), 82, 248n9; "With the patience of crushing gravel" ("Terpelivo, kak shcheben' b'iut"), 113, 253n64; "The Work Bench" ("Stanok"), 55, 247n59; "Yesterday you still looked into my eyes" ("Vchera eshche v glaza gliadel"), 268n146; "The Youth" ("Otrok"), 248n10, 294; "You who loved me as a lie" ("Ty, menia liubivshii fal'sh'iu"), 259n142

Tsvetaeva, Valeria, 11–14, 241n2, 280, 292, 293

Tsvetaeva House-Museum and Cultural Center, 265n9, 267n30

Tuchkov, Major General Aleksandr, 23, 74, 203, 242n20

Turandot (Gozzi), 37, 244n38

Turchinsky, Lev, 241n16, 259n145, 262n160, 267n42

Turgenev, Ivan, 241n8, 266n18; *A Nest of Gentlefolk* (*Dvorianskoe gnezdo*), 16, 241n8

Turgeneva, Anna ("Asya"), 93, 272

Turzhanskaya, Aleksandra, 173, 175–77, 264n201, 293; and Efron, Sergei, 175

Turzhansky, Oleg ("Lelik," "that boy"), 173, 175, 264n201, 293

Turzhansky, Viacheslav, 289, 293

Twain, Mark (Samuel Clemens), 156; *The Prince and the Pauper*, 156

Twelve (*Dvenadtsat'*) (Blok), 54, 56–57, 247n60, 249n23, 270

Union of Journalists (*Soiuz zhurnalistov*), 286

Union of Poets, Petrograd (*Petrogradskii soiuz poetov*), 287

Union of Russian Writers and Artists Abroad. *See* Committee for the Welfare of Russian Writers and Journalists Residing in Czechoslovakia

Union of Soviet Writers, 239n13, 245n47, 279

Ushakova, Ekaterina, 252n53; "You have been pampered by nature" ("Vy izbalovany prirodoi") (Pushkin), 106, 252n53

Usievich, Elena Feliksovna, 201, 293

Vakhtangov, Evgeny, 31, 34, 35, 37, 167, 244n41, 269, 270, 275, 279, 284, 286, 289, 290, 293, 295. *See also* Third Studio (Moscow Art Theater)

Val'be, Ruf', ix, 262n163

Vanečková, Galina, 238n4, 256n95, 256n105, 257nn109–10, 257n118, 258nn120–21, 263n169

Vega, Lope de: *El maestro de danzar*, 233, 268n42

The Veil of Pierrette (Schnitzler), 34

Veshch'. *See Thing* (journal)

Vialtseva, Anastasia, 24–25, 293

Vii (Gogol), 24, 210–11, 242n21

Viliam, Irina, 287

Viliam-Vilmont, Nikolai, 287

Vishniak, Abram ("Helicon"), 90, 91–92, 224–25, 248n10, 293–94; and Tsvetaeva's "The Youth" ("Otrok") and "Florentine Nights" ("Florentiiskie nochi"), 248n10, 293–94

Vishniak, Evgeny (Zhenya), 92, 224–25, 248n10

Vishniak, Vera. *See* Arkina, Vera

VKhuTEIN (*Vysshii khudozhestvennyi tekhnicheskii institute*). *See* Moscow

State Stroganov Technical Arts University
VKhuTEMAS (*Vysshie khudozhestvennye tekhnicheskie masterskie*). *See* Moscow State Stroganov Technical Arts University
Volia Rossii (journal). *See Russia's Will*
Volkonsky, Pyotr, 269
Volkonsky, Sergei, 240, 289, 294; Tsvetaeva's "To S. M. Volkonsky" ("S. M. Volkonskomu"), 5, 240n16, 241n1
Volkova, Natalya, 238n2, 294
Voloshin, Maksimilian (Kirienko, "Max"), 18, 75, 76, 83, 87, 125, 143, 167–68, 199, 204, 213, 260n148, 275, 277, 278, 281, 283, 284, 286, 294
Voloshina, Elena. *See* Kirienko-Voloshina, Elena
von Zedlitz, Joseph Christian. *See* Zedlitz, Joseph Christian von
Voznesensky, Andrei, 230, 267n40, 294; "Goya," 267n40
Vozvrashchenie. *See* Literary-Historical Society *Vozvrashchenie*
Vrubel, Mikhail, 205, 266n14, 294; *Pan* (*Pan*), 205, 266n14; *Swan-Princess* (*Tsarevna-Lebed*), 205, 266n14
Vysheslavtsev, Nikolai, 53, 247n63, 294–95

War and Peace (Tolstoy), 43, 136, 183, 246n47
Wilhelm Meister (Goethe), 147

Writers' Shop (*Lavka pisatelei*), 64–69, 106, 247n65, 272, 275, 280, 285, 286, 295

Yamagata, Iname, 58, 247n63
"You have been pampered by nature" ("Vy izbalovany prirodoi") (Pushkin), 106, 252n53
Young Girl Crying over Her Dead Bird (*Jeune fille pleurant son oiseau mort*) (Greuze), 203, 265n11

Zabela-Vrubel, Nadezhda, 266n14, 294
Zaitsev, Boris, 67, 68–69, 239–41n16, 261n158, 295
Zaitseva, Vera. *See* Oreshnikova, Vera
Zaitseva-Sollogub, Natalya ("Natasha"), 69, 239–40n16, 295
Zavadsky, Sergei, 162, 295
Zavadsky, Yuri, 31, 33, 36, 39, 244n41, 270, 275, 293, 295. *See also under* Tsvetaeva, Marina: Verse, cycles: *The Player* (*Komed'iant*)
Zedlitz, Joseph Christian von, 242n17; *Ghostship* (*Das Geisterschiff*), 242n17
Zenzinov, Vladimir, 261n158
Zhukovsky, Vasily, 23, 46, 139, 242n17, 246n53; *The Loving Cup* (*Kubok*), 46, 139, 246n53
Zhurgaz, xx, 201, 252n55, 265n6, 280, 282
Žižka, Jan, 179, 264n205
Zusman, Nina, 45, 289
Zvezda (journal), xvii, 237n1, 247n65, 265